Bradley County
Tennessee

MINUTES OF THE CIRCUIT COURT

BOOK "B"

1838–1841

WPA RECORDS

Heritage Books
2025

HERITAGE BOOKS

AN IMPRINT OF HERITAGE BOOKS, INC.

Books, CDs, and more—Worldwide

For our listing of thousands of titles see our website
at
www.HeritageBooks.com

A Facsimile Reprint
Published 2025 by
HERITAGE BOOKS, INC.
Publishing Division
5810 Ruatan Street
Berwyn Heights, MD 20740

Prepared by
The Tennessee Historical Records Survey
Division of Community Service Programs
Work Projects Administration
1941

International Standard Book Number
Paperbound: 978-0-7884-8776-7

Know all men by these presents that we Elijah C. Rice
and John Rice, are jointly and severally held and firmly
bound unto John L. McCarty ---- in the penal sum of Twohundred and fifty dollars, to be paid on condition that the
said Elijah C. Rice will with effect prosecute a suit by
action of covenent Broken which he this day commended
against the said John L. McCarty --- in the Circuit of Bradley County, or in case of failure of such prosecution pay
and sattisfy all costs and damages as may be awarded against
them by our said Court witnesses

Our hands and seals this 28th day of March 1838

Tst   (Elijah C. Rice
         (
         (John Rice

Henry Price,
State of Tennessee,

To the Sheriff of Bradley County Greeting --

You are hereby commanded to Summon John L. McCarty, Ex-
exutor of the last Will and Testament of John Walker Deceased
if to be found in your county to appear before our Circuit
Court to be held for the County of Bradley, at the Courthouse in Cleveland on the Second Monday of May next, to answer Elijah C. Rice of a plea of Covenent Broken to his
damage Five Thousand dollars, herein fail not and have you
them there.

This writ Witness ---

Henry Price, Clerk of our said Court
at office in Cleveland, the Second Monday of January 1838.
And of American Independence the 62nd

(P-2)   Henry Price, Clerk

Endorsement Cap - Ad Resp -- Elijah Rice vs John L. Mc-
Carty --- Isd - March 28th 1838.

To May Term --- I acknowledge the servis of the within
writ Witness my hand and seal This 29th March 1829

John L. McCarty, Executor
of John Walker, Deceased

Declaration --

State of Tennessee   )   Circuit Court
)
Bradley County   )   August Term 1838

Elijah C. Rice, by his attorney complains of John L. Mc-
Carty, Executor of the last Will and Testament of John Walker, Deceased, who was summond by the Sheriff of a plea of
Covenant Broken &c for that the said defendant by his attorney in fact Duly & fully authorized and Impowerd for this
purpose. Thomas I. Campbell, by the discription of Thomas
I. Campbell, on the 10th day of June 1839, at to wit
in the County of Bradley, aforesaid by his Covenant in writing of that date duly Executed - and none to this Court here
--- in Consideration that said Elijah C. Rice would substan-
tuate a place in a condition to be obtained from the commissioners of the United States to the Cherokee Nation in favor
of the estate of the said John Walker, deceased, founded
upon a last Ferry and Island in the Nation and other depre-
dations appended thereto he said defendant by his Attorney
in fact as aforesaid did therein Many other things ---- and
agree with the said plaintiff to Execute to him such instrument of writing as should ---- him the said plaintiff to
draw from and recover of the commissions of the United
States, to Execute the late Cherokee Treaty or such other
person or persons as it might be necessary to effect the
same one half (P-3) of said Claim first deducting 10 per
cents on the hole amount.

Now the said plaintiff in fact says and avows that he
did to wit: on the day and year aforesaid at the County
afore said substantiate the said Claim & plan the same in
a condition to be obtained from the commissioners aforesaid in money and form as he was bound to do,*hath not yet
Executed to the said plaintiff such Instrument of Writing
as should authorise him the said plantiff to draw from and
recover of the commissions of the United States, to execute the late Cherokee Treaty or such other person or persons as it might be necessary to effect the same the one
half of said claim, as aforesaid, but hath hereto and still
doth refuse so to do, and so the said plaintiff his covenant
aforesaid hath not kept but hath broken the same to the
damage of the said plaintiff, of Five Thousand dollars and
therefore he brings Suit and pledges &c

                    T. Vernon Vandyke,

                    Attorney for Plaintiff
*but the said defendant although often requested so to do

Elijah C. Rice)
)
vs)
) Bradley County Circuit
) Court August Term 1838
John L. McCarty, Extr.) The defendant by his
of John Walker, Deceased) Attorney, comes into
) Court and ----- of the
Covenant send on in the
cause and it is read to him in the words and figures fol-
lowing To wit; Whereas John L. McCarty, Executor of John
Walker, Deceased on the 5th day of June 1837, employed
Thomas I. Campbell, and Alexander D. Keys, his attorneys
at law to asertain the condition of a claim against the
Cherokee Nation, in favor of said Estate the evedence concerning which was in possession and knowledge of Elijah C.
Rice, alone and therein authorised his said Attorneys or
either of them to do such things in the investigation thereof as in their (P-4) Judgment desertion might be necessary
to effect a substanceation of the same now I, Thomas I. Campbell, one of the said Attornys having seen and confessed
with the said Elijah C. Rice, tuching the claim aforesaid
The same being founded upon a last Ferry and Island in the
Nation and the other appertenances appended there to and
upon such confirmed do agree and bind the said John L. Mc-
Carty to Execute to the said Elijah C. Rice, such instrument
of writing as shall authorize the said Elijah C. Rice to d
draw from and receive of the sum imposed of the United
States to Execute the date, Cherokee Treaty or such other
person or persons as it may be necessary to Effect the same
one half of said Claim upon the said Elijah C. Rice, substan-
tiated the said claim and placing the same in a condition
to be obtained from the commissions aforesaid, with out other
or futher expense to the said John L. McCarty, then 10 per
cent upon the hole amount of said Claim which the said Elijah C. Rice, agrees to the said John L. McCarty, shall
retain thereon before the devetion of the said fund as aforesaid between the said John L. McCarty and the said Elijah
C. Rice to defraying such Expences as may have been incurred by the said John L. McCarty in and consuming -----
the words one half of said Claim Interlined before signed.

Witness my hand and Seal June 10th at Rosses Landing.

Thomas I. Campbell
(Seal)

Witness ---

Allen Kennedy,

All of which being read and signed by said defendants and

he comes and (P-5) appoints the --- and --- when &c and
say the plaintiff his said action against him ought not
to have and mention because he says, said alterations and
the matters and things therein contained in maner and form
as there set forth are not good and sufficient in law to--
said plaintiff to have and mentains his said actions against
his defendant nor is he bound by the laws of the land to
make any other or futher answer to said declaration then
by demurre and this the said defendant is ready to verify
wherefore he prays Judgment &c. Bind the said defendant
according to the forms of the ---- in such cases made and
provided here states and shows to the Court the following
cases of Demurrer to said --- 1st the amount of damages are
not stated 2nd the instrument is void to this defendant
and argers as the ground of this suit is not the contract
of Defendant Nor can an action of Covenent against him be
supported thereon. 3rd said declration unfounded uncertain
and Insufficient

                    Jarnagin & Bradford

                    Attorneys for Defendant

and founder in Demurer,   )
Vandyke, and J. F. Gillespie,   )
for Plaintiff   )

    Statement of Onslone G. Murrel, relative to a conversa-
tion between J. L. McCarty,Esq. himself and others sum
twelve or fifteen Months ago. John L. McCarty, Esq. Executor of John Walker, Deceased, called on me and requested
that I would meet him and some of his friends at the law
office of T. I. Campbell, Esq. for the purpose of hearing
from him a statement of sum matters connetted with the estate of John Walker, In and then to give my advice as to
the corece he ought to pursue if my reclection (P-6)
serves me correctly he made the following statement to
those present William Lowry, T. I. Campbell, T. N.Vandyke,
A. D. Keys, Esq. and myself That the Estate of J. Walker,
had a claim on sum Ferry on Tennessee River and the evidence necessary to establish the clame of Walker could not
be had unless he would agree to give one half the assessed
valuation of said ferry, That Elijah C. Rice was the only
person the evidence could be had from, and that he refused
to produce the necessary Testemony unless J. L. McCarty,
would agree and secure to him one half the ---- value of
the Ferry, he further stated that unless the Testimony of
Rice was procured the Estate of Walker would certainly
loose the hole amount of the Claim after making the above
statement he ast those present how he should act, for the
best intrest of the heirs of Walker, and whether he should
agree to the terms preposed by Rice those present were unanimous
in their opinion that he ought make the contract with Rice and

we did advise him to give Rice one half of the afore said value for produceing testimony sufficient to secure Walkers claim, McCarty acting upon the advice given him authorised Mr. Campbell & Mr. Keyes to visit with Rice, and make the best bargain they could with him.

Onslow G. Murrell

Athens, the 25th August, 1838.

Elijah C. Rice	)	
	)	
vs	)	
	)	
John I. McCarty	)	Came the parties by their
Administrator of	)	attoneys and the Demurrer
John Walker, Deceased	)	to the plaintiffs declara-
		tion having been read (P-7)
		and understood by the

Court and because it appears to the Court that the Plaintiff's declaration is not sufficient in law to sustain his action, it is therefore considered by the Court that the Demurrer be sustained and that the defendant go hence with out delay and recover of the plaintiff his cost by him about his defence in this behalf expended for which an execution may issue.

Bill of cost
on the above suit --

State Tax - - - - - - - - - - -		2.25
Issuing writ 75 bond 20¢		----
Docketing Cause 50¢		----
Judgment on Demurrer	37½	----
Issuing 4 subpoenas	50	----
2 Witness Probits:	12½	----
Final Judgements	75	----
Bill of Cost	25	----
Copy of Cost	25	----
Recording Proceedings	162½	5.33
Sheriff Beavers, serving) ----		----
2 subpoenas)		50

Hiram K. Turk 2 days at 1.00   ----

Travelling 22 miles   2.88

J. W. McMillan 3 days at 75¢   2.25

                                                     13.21

State,   )
)
    vs   )
)   To the Sheriff of
John Mahaffy &   )   Bradley County, Greeting
Plesant Brandon   )
William Sears   )   Where as heretofore, to Wit; On the
                             day of January 1838 - at to wit;
                             in the County of Bradley, John Ma-
haffy, Pleasant Brannon, and William Sears entered into ---
before the Honorable Judge, of the Circuit Court wherein
they acknowledged themselves Jointly and saverlely indebted
to the State of Tennessee in the sum of One Thousand dollars to be levied on their goods and chattles lands and
tenements to the use of the State of Tennessee ---- to be
void on conditions that the said John Mahaffey, make his
personal appearance a_t the Court House in the town of
Cleveland, on the first Tuesday after the 2nd Monday in
January, 1838. And then answer a charge of for petit larceny and at this day to wit at Circuit Court held for the
County of Bradley, at the Court house in Cleveland, on the
first Tuesday after the second Monday in of January 1838
Came on the State by their Attorney General and the said
John Mahaffey, being Solomly called to come into Court and
answer said charge came not and the said Pleasant Brandon a
and William Sears, being solamley called to come into Court
and bring with them the boddy of the said John Mahaffy, in
discharge of their said ---- came not, but made default
where upon it is considered by the Court that the said defendants had jointly and severaly forfited to the State of
Tennessee the sum of One thousand dollars unless they show
sufficient cause to the contrary at the next term of this
Court and you are therefore hereby commanded to make known
to the said John Mahaffey and William Sears, to be and appear before the Judge of our next Circuit Court to be held
for the County of Bradley in the Town of Cleveland, on the
first Wednesday after the 2nd Monday of August 1838, to
show cause if any - then can be why the States Examination
ought (P-9) not to have Jointly and saveraly Issued against
them.

    Pleasant Brandon having been notifyed for the sum of
One Thousand dollars, according to the ---- Effect of their
said ---- herein fail not and have you then & there this
writ - Witness - Henry Price Clerk of the Circuit Court at

office in Cleveland the 2nd Monday of May 1838.

Henry Price

Clerk

Endorsement on Alias - - - -

The State   )
)
    vs   )
)
John Mahaffee &   )   Isd. August 18th 1838 -
William Sears   )
                          Came to hand the 21st of August
                          1838. Made known to William Sears
this the 22nd day of August, 1838. The said Mahaffee, not to
to be found in my County, but is a resident of Rhea County
or I am informed and believe James Lauderdale, by John Brown

Depts plea State of Tennessee   )   Circuit Court
)
        Bradley County   )   August Term 1838

The State   )   ------ upon recognizance, Pleasant Bran-
)   ham and William Sears, the said defend-
    vs   )   ant Pleasant Branham, by leve of the
)   Court, first said and obtained for that
)   purpose by Attorney, causes and defend-
John Mahaffee)   ants the wrong and --- when &c. and says
                          that there is not any record of the sup-
posed recognizance and necessary in the said Serafaues mentioned remaining in the said Circuit Court of Bradley County
Tennessee, in manner and form as the said plaintiff The State
of Tennessee, hath avered in the surafacias mentioned and
alleged and others he is ready to verify wherefore he prays
judgement if the said plaintiff ought to have and maintain
his aforsaid action there of against him. (P-10)

Trewhitt, Atty. for Defendant and the said defendant
for futher plea in their behalf, says that the State has
others aforesaid against him ought not have and maintain
against him because he says that after the making and entering*default in the said Seriafacias mentioned To wit upon the
1st day of January 1838 at to wit, in the County of Bradley
aforesaid this defendant in discharge of his said recognizance surrendered up the boddy of John Mahaffee, his principal into the custady of A. A. Clingan, high Sheriff of Bradley County Tennessee, And the said defendant avers that the
*into the recognizance in the Seriafacias mentioned and be-
for the calling out entering

said Alexander A. Clingan high sheriff aforesaid, and as
Sheriff afore said did then and there accept of and recieve
into the Custody the Body of the said John Mahaffee, in discharge of this defendants liability upon said recognizance
in said Seriafacias mentioned and this he is reddy to verify wherefore he prays the judgement of the Court if the
said State his action by Seriafacias aforesaid ought to him
---- against him

Trewhitt, Atty for
Defendant

And the said defendant for futher plea in this behalf says
that the State his Seriafacias aforesaid against this defendant ought not to have & maintain because he says that
the recognizance mentioned in the plaintiffs Surafacias
was not entered into before any legal authorized judge of
the Circuit Court for the State of Tennessee, and this the
defendant is reddy to verify wherefore he prays the judgement of the court if the plaintiff the State his action by
Surafacias ought to have and maintain against him.

Trewhitt, Atty for
Defendant.

(P-11)

Endorsment on plea the State Surafacias vs
Pleasant Branham, filed 29th August 1838,
and the 3rd day of the Term.

_____

James Butrum)
)
    vs   )
)
Sylvanas Couch)

Warrent

State of Tennessee)
)
Bradley County   )   To any lawful officer to execute and
                       and return you are thereby commanded
to Summons James Butram to appear before me or some other
Justice of the Peace, for said County to answer the complaint of Sylvanus Couch of a plea of Tresspassing on the

case with force and arms, for cutting into the Plaintiffs close and ---- and knocking down the Plaintiffs corn, seeds and grass to his grate damage, Fifty dollars, herein fail not, given under my hand and Seal this the 6th day of August 1838

Solomon Summy,

Justice of the Peace

Endorsement Damage Warrent S. Couch vs J. Butram
V. V. Coe Executed and returned before S. Summey
and James Sheddle, on the 10th instant for trial
by

John S. Oneil, Const

Judgment or Warrent.

At my house August the 14th day 1838 the parties being present, the warrent being read and the Testimony of both parties being heard and understood, It considered by me that the defendant go hence without delay and receive of the plaintiff the costs in this behalf accrued for which Execution may issue and from which judgement the plaintiff prays an appeal to the next Circuit Court to be held for the County of Bradley at the Court house in Cleveland on the 4th Monday of this instant and tenders this Riley A. Horn, and (P-12) T. J. Williams for his Securitys which is granted,

Solomon Summey,

A Justice of the Peace.

Sylvanas Couch)
)
vs)
)
James Butrum)   On motion of the Defendant This day
the defendant by his Attorney, and
it appearing to the satisfaction
of the Court from afidavit that the surety in this cause
is insufficient. It is therefore ordered by the Court that
on or before the second day of the next of this Court the
plaintiff give Counter surety or justefy the present or his
suit will be Dismissed.

December Term 1838

Sylvanus Couch)
)
vs)

James Butrum   )   This day came the defendant by his at-
                         torney, and the plaintiff having failed
                         to give counter surety or justify pres-
                         ent according to the Rule at the last
Term It is therefore considered by the Court that the plaintiffs appeal be dismissed and that the defendant recover of
the plaintiff his costs by him about his defence in his behalf Expended for which Execution may issue.

Arnett Shields   )
)
    vs   )
)
John C. Kennedy   )

                    State of Tennessee)
)
                    Bradley County   )

    The Sheriff or any constable for said County. Greeting,
you are hereby commanded to summons John C. Kennedy to appear before me or some other (P-13) Justice of the peace
for said County to answer Arnett Shields, of a plea of
wrongfully Refuseing to --- to him the said Arnett Shields,
a certain Horse beast of him the said Arnett Shields, or
pay the --- for the same according to promise to the damage of the said plaintiff forty dollars, herein fail not,
and make due returns as the law directs.

    given under my hand and seal this 29th day of August
1838.

                         Jesse Poe (seal)

                         Justice of the Peace

Summond for the Plaintiff   )
)
Robert Carter, and   )
Scion Carter   )

                    Indorsement damage Warrent

Arnett Shields   )
)
    vs   )   Came to hand the 29th August, 1838

John C. Kennedy   )   Executed the 30th of August returned
                               for trial the 8th of September, 1838.

before Jesse Poe, David Ragen, Const, Judgment,

Arnett Shields   )
)
  vs   )   In this cause after having the Test-
)   emony as well on behalf of the de-
John Kennedy   )   fendant as the plaintiff It is con-
                        sidered by me that the Plaintiff re-
cover of the defendant the sum of Seventeen dollars damage
and the sum of Two dollars twenty five cents cost given under my hand and seal this 21st day of September, 1838.

                         Jesse Poe, Justice of the Peace

    Appeal from the foregoing Judgment the defendant prays
an appeal to the next Term of the Circuit Court, to be held
for the County of Bradley, which to him is granted he having entered into bond with John Hardwick, Security

    Conditioned as the law directs, given under my hand this
24th day of September 1838.

                        Jesse Poe, J. P.

(P-14)
  Bond   State of Tennessee   )
)
        Bradley County   )

    Know all men by these presents that We, John Kennedy,
and John Hardwick, are held and firmly bound in the penel
sum of Thirty four dollars, to be paid on condition that
the said John C. Kennedy doth prosecute with effect an appeal by having prayed to the next Circuit Court of the said
County and to him granted from a Judgment this day obtained
by the said Arnett Shields, against the said John C. Kennedy
before Jesse Poe, one of the Justices of the peace in and for
said County for the sum of Seventeen dollars debt, and the
further sum of Two dollars and Twenty five cents, costs, as
Witness our hands and seals this the 24th day of Sept. 1838.

                        John C. Kennedy (seal)

                        John Hardwick (seal)

In the Circuit Court,

Arnett Shields   )
)
     vs   )   On motion of the Plaintiff by his
)   attorney   a rule is granted him to
John C. Kennedy   )   show cause why the Judgement of the
                          justice of the peace should be con-
firmed.

Judgment --

Arnett Shields   )
)
     vs   )   This day the Plaintiff comes with
)   his attorney and brings with him into
John C. Kennedy   )   open Court the papers and proseddings
                          had before the Justice of the Peace
in this cause, and because it appears from the Examination
of the papers in said cause that Plaintiff on the 2nd day
of September, 1838 (P-15) Received a Judgment against the
defendant for the Sum of Seventeen dollars, damage and the
sum of Two dollars and Twenty five*cost and the defendant
prays an ------ an appeal from said judgment to the next
Term of the Circuit Court, to the County of Bradley to wit
December Term 1838, and failed to bring up his said appeal
to saidTerm being the 2nd Term after the defendant abated
his said appeal brought into Court the said papers and by
his Attorney, moves the Court for the Judgment of the Justice of the peace to be affirmed.

     It is therefore considered by the Court that the Plan-
tiff recover of the defendant the sum of Seventeen dollars
for his damage aforesaid and the sum of fifty nine cents.
It being the amount of intrest upon said Judgment at the
rate of six per annum from the date of said judgment to this
time togather with all costs as well, as the costs before
the justice & the costs of this Court for which Examination
may issue &c.

April Term 1839

Arnett Shields   )
)
     vs   )   On motion of the defendant by his
)   attorney a rule is granted him to
John C. Kennedy   )   show cause if any he has or can
                          show why the judgment heretofore
entered in this cause should be set aside. This they came
on for argument the Rule of the Defendant to set a side the
Plaintiffs Judgment which being fully argued and considered
of the Court said motion is discharged.

     Know all men by these presents that we Lewis Sheppard
*cents

and Levi Trewhitt, are jointly and severally held and firmly
bound unto James Edmondson and Jesse Mayfield, in the penal
sum of Two hundred and fifty dollars, to be void on conditions that the said Lewis Shepard, will with Effect prosecute a suit by action of --- which he this day commenced
against the saidJames Edwards & Jesse Mayfield in the Circuit Court of Bradley County or in case of failure of such
prosecution pay and sattisfy all costs and damages as may
be awarded against him by our said Court.

Witness our hands and seals this 27th day of August 1838.

Lewis Sheppard (Seal)

Levi Trewhitt (Seal)

Writ   State of Tennessee,

To the Sheriff of Bradley County, Greeting.

You are hereby commanded to take the Bodys of James Edmondson and Jesse Mayfield, if to be found in your County
and then safley keep so that you have them before the Judge
our Circuit Court to be held for the County of Bradley, at
the Court House in Cleveland, on the 4th Monday of December,
next - To answer Lewis Sheppard, of a plea that they render
unto him the Sum of Four hundred dollars, which they owe
and from him unjustly actions to his damage Two hundred dollars. Herein fail not -- and have you them there, this Writ
Witness,

Henry Price, Clerk of
our said Court at office
in Cleveland, the 4th Monday of August, 1838.

Henry Price, Clerk

Endorsment No. 40.

Lewis Sheppherd   )
)
    vs   )
)
)
James Edmondson   )
Jesse Mayfield   )

(P-17) Issued the 27th of August 1838, debt $400 ---

Came to hand the same day Issued and Executed on the within Defendants and their Bonds taken for their appearance
at December Court this 27th August 1838.

James Lauderdale, Sheriff.

Appearance Bond

  State of Tennessee   )
)
  Bradley County   ) We, James Edmondson
                and Jesse Mayfield &
                William Hammond, James

Berry, acknowledge our selves indebted to James Lauderdale,
Shff, of said County in the sum of Twelve hundred Dollars
To be void on conditions that to James Edmondson & Jesse
Mayfield who has been arrested by me James Lauderdale, Shff.
by virtue of a Capias ---- to answer the complaint of Lewis
Sheppherd, of a plea of Trespassing on the case to his damage Twelve hundred dollars shall make their personal appearance before the Judge of the Circuit Court to be held for
said County at the Court House in the Town of Cleveland, on
the 4th Monday of December, next --- and iff condemed the
action will sattisfy the -- of the Court or render themselves to Prison given under our hands and Seals this 27th
August 1838.

          James Edmondson (Seal)

          Jesse Mayfield (Seal)

          William Hammond (Seal)

          James Berry (Seal)

Endorsement I, James Lauderdale, Sheriff of Bradley County,
        Do hereby assigne within conditions or obli-
        gations To Lewis Shepphard, the Bond herein
        named for his use according to an act of the
        general assembly in such case made and pro-
        vided.

    This the 19th November, 1838,

        James Lauderdale,

         Sherriff

(P-18)
Declaration ---

    State of Tennessee   ) Circuit Court
)
    Bradley County   ) December Term 1838

  Lewis Sheppherd, by his attorney, complains of James Edmondson, and Jesse Mayfield, in custada of the shff, &c, of
a plea that they rewarded to him the sum of Four hundred dollars which they owe to and unjustly detains from him.

  For that whereas heretofore to wit; In the County of
Bradley aforesaid the said defendants together with one

certain John B. Maston, who is not sued in this action for
value received made corrected and signed with their own
proper names and delivered to the said plaintiff their promissory note and which is now shown to the court here, the
date where is the same day and year last aforesaid wherein
and whereby they promised one month after date (meaning one
month after the date last aforesaid) to pay to the said Plaintiff or his barer four hundred dollars for value Received
yet the said defendants although often requested so to do,
have not as yet paid the said sum of Four hundred dollars,
above demanded or any part thereof to the said Plaintiff,
They, the defendants have hereunto wholly refused and still
refuse so to do, to the damage of the said Plaintiff Two
hundred dollars, and therefore he bringing his suit and pledges
toProsecute.

Trewhitt, Att. for

Plaintiff

Endorsement

    Lewis Sheppard

        vs

    James Edmondson and
    Jesse Mayfield

        Note inclosed filed 25th December, 1838.
        2nd day of the Term.

(P-19)   Plea, and the Defendants by their Attorney comes
into Court and defends the wrong and ----- when and C and
for plea say the Plaintiff, his action aforesaid against
them ought not to have and maintain because they say they
do not owe the debt, in the Plaintiffs declaration mentioned and of this they put themselves upon the County.

Campbell & Vandyke,

Attys for Defendants

And the Plaintiff
Likewise Trewhitt,
      For Plaintiff --

Record --

    Lewis Shepperd   )
)
)
        vs   )   Debt

James Edmondson   )   This day came the Parties by their
Jesse Mayfield   )   Attorneys and thereupon came the
                                  following Jury - to wit;

      Robert A. Farmer, Daniel A. Stafford,
      John F. Larrison, Thomas Taylor,
      Herman Bedwell, George W. Cate,
      John Carter, Robert H. Ellison,
      William Parks, John W. Kennedy,
      Joseph Igou, and Elias Price, which being Duly summond
Elected tried and sworn the truth to speak upon the issue
named by the parties upon their oath aforesaid do say that
thedefendants do owe the debt of four hundred dollars in
the plaintiffs declaration mentioned and agrese the Plaintiffs damage by reason of the -- thereof, to thirty six dollars. It is therefore considered by the Court that the
Plaintiff recover of the Defendants his debt and damages
afore said together with the costs in this behalf Expended
for which Execution may Issue &c.

(P-20)
     Presentment ---

         State of Tennessee   )   Circuit Court
)
         Bradley County   )   April Term
                                    Eighteen hundred Thirty-
                                    nine
     The grand Jurrors in behalf The State of Tennessee, El-
ected empanled sworn and charged to enquire for the body of
the County of Bradley, aforesaid upon their oaths present
that a certain Winsten C. Rose, late of said County --- on
the 5th day of March in the year of our Lord one Thousand
and Eight hundred and Thirty nine, with force and arms in
the county of Bradley, aforesaid unlawfully did vend and
sell by Retail in quantities less than one quart a certain
kind of spirits liquors called whiskey, and other kind of
spirits and liquors to one Joseph Mee, and to Divers other
persons and the Jurors aforesaid upon this oath aforesaid
do futher present and say that the said Winsten C. Rose on
the fifth day of March Eighteen hundred and Thirty nine and
on divers other days with force and useing in the County of
Bradley, aforesaid unlawfully did vend and sell by Retail
spiritous liquors called whiskey and other kinds of spiritous
liquors to one Joseph Mee, and to divers other persons and
so the persons aforesaid upon their oath aforesaid do say
that the said Winsten C. Rose was there and then guilty of
keeping a Tipling house contrary to the form of the statues
in such case made and provided and against the peace and

dignity of the State.

Endorsment State vs W. C. Rose, found on the information
of Joseph Mee (P-21) Jurors names --- William Grant, Ezekiel Spriggs, Elias Hutcherson, James A. Fletcher, Ben Mc-
Carty, Alfred Davis, John Anderson, Lewis Price, Joseph
Seabourn, Thomas W. Back, Alex Perry, Record April Term
1839.

State   )
)
  vs   )   The grand Jury appeared in open
Winsten C. Rose)   Court and Returned a Presentment
)   against W. C. Rose for keeping a
Tipling house, signed by all of said grand Jury.

     Judgment --

          State   )
)
          vs Tipling   )   Came the attorney General
)   who presents for the State
          Winsten C. Rose)   as well as the defendant in
                               his own proper person who
being charged upon the presentment for keeping a Tipling
house for plea say that because he is guilty he will not contend but submits to the judgment of the Court. It is therefore considered by the court that the defendant for such his
offence pay a fine of one dollar to the State of Tennessee
and that he pay the costs of this Presentment and Remane in
Custody till fine and costs are paid or surety given therefore and thereupon the defendant paid into Court here the
sum of Twelve dollars the amount of the fine and costs aforesaid.

(P-22)
State

     vs

Thomas J. Davis, Jr.
Phillip Davis, Sr. Phillip Davis, Jr.
and John Wilburn.

          State of Tennessee,

               To the Sheriff of Blunt County, Greeting -

Whereas heretofore to wit; on the 30th day of August 1838

At and to wit; in the County of Bradley, and State aforesaid
a said Thomas J. Davis, Jr. and Phillip Davis, Sr. & Phillip
Davis, Jr. and John Wilburn, Entered into recognizance before the Honerable Judge and acknowledged them selves indebted
to the State of Tennessee in the sum of Two Thousand dollars
that is to say Thomas J. Davis, in the sum of One Thousand
dollars and Phillip Davis, Sr. and Phillip Davis Jr. & John
Wilburn, all jointly in the sum of one Thousand dollars, to
be levyed on their goods and chattles lands and tenements
to the use of the State, but to be void on condition that
the Thomas J. Davis, made his personal appearance before the
Judge of the Circuit*to be held for the County of Bradley at
the Court House in Cleveland on the first Wednesday after the
4th Monday in December 1838, There to answer a charge of the
State ----- against him for Horse Stealing and not depart
the Court without leve.

Whereupon came the State by the Attorney General and the
said Thomas J. Davis, being --- called to come into Court
and answer said charge, came not but made default and the
said Phillip Davis, Sr. and (P-23) Phillip, Jr. and John
Wilburn, being solemly called to come into Court and bring
with them the body of Thomas J. Davis, to answer said charge
came not but made default.

It is therefore considered by the Court that the said
Phillip Davis, Sr. and Phillip Davis, Jr. and John Wilburn
has forfeited to the State of Tennessee, the sum of one Thousand dollars unless they show good and sufficient cause at
the next Term of this Court and you are therefore hereby
commanded to make known to the said Phillip Davis, Sr. &
Phillip Davis, Jr. and John Wilburn, to make there personal
appearance before the Judge of the Circuit Court at a Court
to be held for the County of Bradley at the Courthouse in
Cleveland on the first Wednesday after the 4th Monday of
April next to show cause if any there can be why the States
Execution ought not to inforce against them jointly for the
sum of one Thousand dollars according to the tenner and effect of their said recognizance here in fail not and have
you them this writ;

Witness ---

Henry Price, Clerk of our said Court at office in Cleveland, This the 4th Monday of December, 1838.

                    Henry Price,

                    Clerk

Endorsment made known to Phillip Davis, Sr. on the 26th
*Court

March 1839. By reading this writ to him

Will Wallis, Sheriff

of Blunt County

Made known to Phillip Davis, Jr. and John Wilburn, on the 9th day of April 1839.

John McClanahan, Dept.

Sheriff of Blunt County
(P-24)   Spatial Deposition
    I, William Wallis, Sheriff of Blunt County do hereby lawfully depitise and appoint John McClanahan, my lawful depty Sheriff to Execute this writ of Serafaecas in as ample manner I could do.

    given under my hand and seal this the 6th day of April 1839.

William Wallis

Sheriff of Blunt County

```
      State                    )
                               )
    vs. Serafacias             )
                               )
Phillip Davis, Sr.            )   Came the Attorney General who
Phillip Davis, Jr. &          )   prosecutes for the State, and
John Wilburn                  )   also came into Court Phillip
                                  Davis, Sr., Phillip Davis, Jr.
```
and John Wilburn, and brought with the body of Thomas J. Davis into open Court and surrendered him into the custaday of the Sheriff of Bradley County who is ordered by the Court to be taken in charge of him and on motion the forfeiture heretofore taken against them is set aside by leve of the Caust and the said Phillip Davis, Sr. Phillip Davis, Jr. and John Wilburn, confess judgment for all costs that have accrued on this behalf.

    It is therefore considered by the Court that the State of Tennessee recover of the said Phillip Davis, Sr. Phillip Davis, Jr. and John Wilburn jointly the costs as aforesaid confessed by them and that Execution Issue &c.

Circuit Court
April Term 1839

State   )
)
  vs   Tipling   )   Came the Attorney General and the
)   grand Jury, came into open Court
George Wesmoreland   )   and returned a bill of Indictment
                               against the Defendant for Tipling
Endorsed thereon a True bill by William Grant, their foreman
(P-25) Which bill of Indictment is in the words and figures
following to wit:

State of Tennessee   )
)
Bradley County   )   Circuit Court April Term 1839

    The grand Jurors in behalf of the State of Tennessee el-
ected impaneled sworn and charged to inquire for the body of
the County of Bradley aforesaid upon their oath present that
a certain ---- Jacob Robbs, late of said County ---- on the
tenth day of March in the year of our Lord one Thousand Eight
hundred and Thirty nine and on divers other days and times
with force and arms in the County of Bradley aforesaid unlawfully did vend and sell by Retail in less quanities than
one quart a certain kind of spiritous Liquors called whiskey
to one Rutherford Rose and to divers other persons and the
Jurors afore said upon their oath aforesaid do futher present that the said Jacob Robbs on the Tenth of March Eighteen
hundred and Thirty nine and on divers other days with force
and arms in the County of Bradley, aforesaid, unlawfully did
vend and sell by Retail Certain kind of Spiritious liquors
called whiskey and other kind of spiritious liquors to Rutherford Rose and to divers other persons and the persons aforesaid upon their oath afore said do say that the said Jacob
Robbs was then & there guilty of keeping a Tipling house contrary to the form of the Statute in such case made and provided and against the peace and degrety of the State.

                         Samuel Frazier, Attorney
                         General for the 3rd District

endorsement Indictment

The State vs Jacob Robbs

     William H. Strane, prosecutor

     Rutherford Rose, Fredrick A. Cans,

     Sworn in open Court and sent to the Grand Jury 25th
     April 1839.

                    Henry Price,

                    Clerk

(P-26)   Endorsed   Wm. Grant, Foreman of the Grand Jury.

The State   )
)
    vs   )   Came the Attorney General who prosecutes
)   for the State as well as the Defendant
Jacob Robbs   )   in his own proper person who being charged
                      upon the bill of Indictment for Tipling
who says because he is guilty he will not contend but submits
to the Judgment of the Court.

It is therefore considered by the Court that for that
his offence he pays a fine of one dollar and that he remain
in Custada of the Sheriff until fines and cost be paid or
security be given therefore and thereupon came John Elliott
into open Court and acknowledged himself surety for the
Defendant for the fine and cost aforesaid. It is therefore
considered by the Court that State of Tennessee recover of
the said defendant and John Elliot, his suerety the fine
and cost aforesaid for which Execution may Issue.

A bond which is in the Words and Figures following to wit;

Know all men by this presents that we William Wooden,
and Charles Cate, are Jointly and severaly held and firmly
bound unto John Borden in the Penal sum of Two hundred and
fifty dollars to be void on condition that the said William
Wooden will with effect prosecute a suit by action ---- on
the case which he this day commenced against the said John
Borden in the Circuit Court for Bradley County, or in case
of failure of such prosecution pay and sattisfy all costs
and damages as may be awarded against him, by our said Court.

Witness our hands and Seals this the 26th day of April
1837.
                              his
                    William X Wooden (Seal)
                              mark
(P-27)   Charles Cate (Seal)

Writ which is in the words and Figures following to Wit;

State of Tennessee

    To the Sheriff of Bradley, Greeting --

You are hereby commanded to Summon John Borden, If to be found in your County to appear before our Circuit Court to be held for the County of Bradley at the Court house in Cleveland on the 2nd Monday of May next to answer William Wooden, of a plea of ---- on the case to his damage Two hundred dollars here in fail not, and have you then & there this Writ

Witness Henry Price, Clerk of our said Court at office in Cleveland, the 2nd Monday of January, 1837, and of American Independence 61

Henry Price,

Clerk

Endorsment Writ of Trespass

William Wooden)
)
vs)   Issued April 24th 1837
)
John Borden)   Came to hand 24th April 1837 - Executed the 26th of April 1837.

A. A. Clingan, Sheriff

Declaration

State of Tennessee, Bradley County

Circuit Court

May Term 1837

William Wooden, by Attorney, Complains of John Borden, who was summond by the Sheriff to answer &c, of a Plea of Trespassing on the case &c, To that whereas the said Plaintiff on the First day of February 1837 - At to wit, in the County of Bradley, afore said a certain bay mare, of the defendant, and the said defendant well knowing the same bay mare to be Infirm unsound infested with a certain Lingering case or desoscer by them and their offenling the said bay Mare to be sound free from any Desease or disorder whatsoever then and there deceitfully sold the said bay mare to the said William Wooden, for the (P-28) Sum of Eighty five dollars, which said bay Mare at the time of the sale thereof was from that time until the time of her death, continued infirm unsound and infected with the said desease or disorder.

To wit, at the County aforesaid and so the said Defend-

ant falsely fraudulently answered the said plaintiff saying
that he is informed and hath sustained damage to the amount
of Two hundred dollars, and therefore he brings his suit
and hath pledged to prosecute and C.

                    Campbell & Vandyke,

                    Attorneys for Plaintiff

Plea -- And the Defendant by his attorney Comes and defends
the wrong and Injury when and where and for plea says said
Plaintiff, his said action against him ought not to have
and maintain because he says he is not guilty in maner and
form as said plaintiff has complained against him, and this
defendant prays may be enquired of by the County

                    John F. Gillespie

                    Attorney for Defendant

And the Plaintiff also   )
Campbell & Vandyke   )
        Attorneys ---   )
)
William Wooden   )   January Term 1838
)
        vs   )   on affidavit of the defendant
)   ordered that this cause be
John Borden   )   continued until next Term of
                                  the Court May Term 1838

        This day came the partys by their attorneys and this
cause is continued on affidavit of the defendant until the
next Term of this Court and it is further ordered by the
Court that a commission be awarded the defendant to take
the depositions of Samuel Craig, of the County to be read
---- in this (P-29) cause, by giving the plaintiff Three
days notice of the time and place of taking the same.

        - - - Circuit Court, April Term 1839. - - -

        Came the parties by their attorneys and thereupon came
a Jury of good and lawful men to wit; Charles Dodd, Robert
Hood, Absalom Coleman, John Towns, Thomas Taylor, Joseph
Billingsley, John McNair, Russell Lawson, John Hughes, Isaac Glanden, Solomon Fouts, & William Carr, who being elected tried and sworn to well and truly try the issue joined
between the parties & by consent of the parties by their
Attorneys the Jury aforesaid from rendering their verdict,
is respited until tomorrow morning.

                    Tuesday 26th of April 1839

Came the parties by their attorneys and thereupon came into Court & the Jury who was on yesterday evening rested from rendering their verdict in this cause until this morning and the said Jury on their oath say they find the issue for the plaintiff and assess his damages by reason of the promises -- to forty dollars & Thirty Two cents. It is therefore considered by the Court that the plaintiff recover of ~~the Court that the plaintiff recover of~~ the defendant of Forty dollars& thirty Two cents the amount so as aforesaid assessed by the Jury & his costs about his suit in this behalf expended, and that he have his execution Thursday April Term 1839.

On motion of the defendents attorney a Rule is granted him to show cause if any he has or can show why a New Trial should be granted in this cause.(P-30)

William Wooden)
)
   vs   )   The parties by their attorneys appear
)   and on argument of council and the
John Borden   )   consideration of the Court the Rule
                heretofore entered in this cause for
a new Trial be granted, is discharged, it is therefore considered by the Court that the plaintiff recover of the defendant the Costs, in this behalf expended and have his Execution.

———————————

Justice Wilson returned into Court the following papers to wit;

State of Tennessee   )   To any lawful officer to execute
)   and Return whare as Information
Bradley County   )   has been --- to me James W. Wil-
                       son, an acting Justice of the
peace for said County by Isaac Smith of said County, that one William Childers of said County did trade traffic for and by one Bales, a slave for life the property of John Town, one bridle bit and head stall, on the 5th of September 1836- in the night time for the promise of Thirty cents lawful money the said slave then and there being under the Control of John Towns, without a permit in writting seting forth the articals to be sold these are therefore to command you to summon the said William Childers, to appear before me or some other Justice of the Peace, for said County to answer the said Isaac Smith of a plea of Debt of Twenty five dollars, due by penalty for the above purchase - herein fail not.

given under my hand and seal this 21st June 1837

James Wilson (seal)

Justice of the Peace

Summons for
The Plaintiff Benjamin Murrey, The Plaintiff requires Bale

Endorsment - Isaac Smith vs William Childress.

Came to hand the same day Issued Returned for Trial the
5th of July 1837 before   James W. Wilson, Esq.
                              Wm. Grogen, Const.

Judgment this day was the within warrant returned for
Trial, the parties being present and the evidence being understood as well, in behalf of the defendant as the plaintiff,
it is therefore considered by me that the plaintiff recover
of the defendant Twenty Five dollars and all costs accrueing
thereunto given under my hand and Seal

This 4th July 1837.

James Wilson, Justice of the
Peace ---

Penal Debt $25.00

Cost   --- 1.25   Appeal for the defendant

The defendant therefore prays an appeal to the next
Court Circuit, to be held for the County of Bradley, which
is granted him he having given bond and Security as the law
directs in such cases made and provided.

James W. Wilson

A Justice of the Peace

State of Tennessee   )
)
Bradley County   )   Know all men that we, William
                           Childers, and Lemuel Childers,
are held and firmly bound unto Isaac Smith, his heirs administrators & assigns in the sum of fifty dollars well & truly
to be paid to the said Isaac Smith, but to be void if the
said William Childers shall prosecute with effect an appeal
by him taken th's day from a Judgment rendered against him
for the sum of Twenty Five dollars, principal & interest &
the futher sum of one dollar & Twenty five cents for costs
accrued thereon in favor of the said Isaac Smith (P-32) be-

fore James Wilson, one of the Justices of the peace for said
County to the next -- Circuit Court to be holden for Bradley
County, commencing on the second Monday in September next
at Cleveland as -- the prays for the appeal, but if the said
William Childress, fail therein there to stay the said Judgment with said damages and cost shall be adjudged against
him in said Court.

Given under our hands and Seals this the 7th day of
July 1837.

his
William X Childress (Seal)
mark
his
Lemuel X Childress (Seal)
mark

No. 1st   Appeal   Came the defendant by Attorneys and
upon motion is ordered by the Court that the plaintiff give
Security on or before the second day of next Term for the
prosecution of his suit or the same will be dismissed.

Warrant No 2nd.

State of Tennessee   )   To any lawful officer to execute
)   and return whereas information
Bradley County   )   has been given by Isaac Smith to
                                 me, James W. Wilson, an acting
Justice of the peace for said County that one William Childress, late of said County, did on the 1st day of October
one Thousand eight hundred & Thirty Six, knowingly permit
a slave by the name of Balaus, a slave for life, the property of one John Towns, to collect and assemble at his dwelling house in said County the said Balaus, then & there not
having a pass in writing setting forth his buisness and
time of absence.

These are, therefore, to command you to summons the said
William Childress, to appear before me or some other justice of the peace for said County to answer the said Isaac(P-33)
Smith, who as well --- for the County aforesaid as for him
self of a plea of debt of Ten dollars due by penalty for the
above premises. Here in fail not.

Given under my hand and seal this 27th of June, 1837.

James W. Wilson (Seal)
Justice of the peace.

Summons for the plaintiff, A. W. Hagler, Hester Satterfield,
Endorsment -- Isaac Smith vs William Childress

Came to hand 4th July returned for 15th July 1837, before J. W. Wilson, Esq.

Wm. Grogan, Const.

This day was the within warrant returned for Trial & the parties present the evidence being understood as well in behalf of the defendant as the Plaintiff it is therefore considered by me that the plantiff recover Ten dollars one half to the County and all costs according thereunto.

Given under my hand and Seal this 5th July, 1837.

James W. Willson

Debt in form $5.00 County $5.00 appeal for defendant, Do Justice 25¢ com. cost 75¢ Appeal bond 50¢

The defendent prays an appeal in this cause to the next Term of the Circuit Court, which is granted him, he having given bond and security as the law requires in such cases made and provided

James W. Willson, Justice of the Peace

State of Tennessee) Know all men that we, William
) Childress & Lemuel Childress, are
Bradley County) held and firmly bound unto Isaac
Smith, his heirs executors, administrators & assigns in the sum of Twenty five dollars, well & truley to be paid to the said Isaac Smith, but to be void if the (P-34) said William Childress, shall prosecute with effect an appeal by him taken this day from a judgment rendered against him for the sum of Ten dollars principal and intrest and the further sum of one dollar and Twenty five cents for costs accrued thereon in favor of the said Isaac Smith before James W. Wilson, one of the Justices of the peace for said County to the next Circuit Court to be holden for Bradley County commencing on the second Monday of September next as in the prayr for the appeal, but if the said William Childress fail therein thereto paying the said judgment with such damages and costs as shall be adjudged against him in the said Court.

Given under our hands and seals, This 7th day of July 1837.

his
William X Childress
mark
his
Lemuel X Childress
mark

Judgment No 2

Isaac Smith   )
)
   vs   )   Came the parties by their Attorneys
)   and thereupon came a Jury of good
William Childress   )   and lawful men, To wit; John Dunn,
Abraham McKisock, John M. Matthews,
Wm. Mee, Mark Black, Robert H. Ellison, Elison Dearmon, George
W. Sallee, Samuel Lane, Noah Fisher, Wm. Thornburgh, & John
Thornburg, who being elected tried and sworn well & truly to
the matters in dispute between the parties, upon their oath
do say that the defendant is not guilty in manner & form as
charged in the warrant.

It is therefore considered by the Court that the defendent go hence with out day and that he recover of the
plaintiff his cost about his defence in this behalf expended for which Execution may Issue

Warrant No 3

State of Tennessee   )
)
Bradley County   )   To any lawful officer to execute
and return whare as Information
has been made by Isaac Smith to me James W. Willson, an acting (P-35) Justice of the Peace for said County that one
William Childress late of said County did on the first Sunday in August1836, knowingly permit a slave by the name of
Balaus, a slave for life, the property of one John Towns to
collect and assemble at his dwelling house in said County the
Ealaus, there and then not having pass in writing his business and time of absence these are therefore to command you
to Summons the said William Childress to appear before me
or some other Justice of the Peace for said County to answer
the said Isaac Smith who --- as well for the County aforesaid
as him self of a plea of debt of Ten dollars duely penelty
for the above premesses here in fail not, given under my
hand and seal this 27th June 1837

                     James W. Willson, (Seal)

                     Justice of the Peace

Summons for the plantiff
Jesse Vann & William Satterfield

Warrant ---

Endorsement   )
Isaac Smith   )   Came to hand 4th July returned for Trial

	)	5th July 1837, before James W. Will-
vs	)	son, Esqr.
William Childress	)	

Wm. Grogan, Const.

This day was the within warrent returned for Trial, the parties present and evedince being understood as well on behalf of the defendent as the plaintiff it is therefore considered by me that the plantiff recover of the defendent Ten dollars, one half to the County and costs accrueing thereunto given under my hand & seal This 5th July

1837. Debt, $	5.00	)	James W. Willson
Do	5.00	)	Justice of the Peace
Court cost	1.00	)	
Jur	.25	)	The defendant prays an
			appeal
Witness	.50		
Appeal Bond	.50		

(P-36)

The defendent prays an appeal to the next Circuit Court to be held for the County of Bradley, which is granted him, he having given bond and security as the law directs in such cases made & provided.

James W. Willison

A Justice of the Peace

State of Tennessee	)	Know all men that we William
	)	Childress & Lemuel Childress,
Bradley County	)	are held and firmly bound unto
		Isaac Smith, his heirs executors

Adminstrators & assigns in the sum of Twenty dollars well & truly to be paid to the said Isaac Smith, but to be void if the said William Childress, shall prosecute with effect an appeal by him taken this day from a judgement rendered against him for the sum of Ten dollars principal and intrest and the futher sum of One dollar & seventy five cents for costs accrued thereon in favor of the said Isaac Smith before James W. Willson, one of the Justices of the Peace for said County for the next Circuit Court to be holden for Bradley County, commencing on the Second Monday of September next, as in the prayr for the appeal but if the said William Childress, fail therein then to pay said judgment with such damages and cost.

Given under our hands and Seals This the 7th day of July 1837.

his
William X Childress
mark
his
Lemuel X Childress
mark

Monday Sept Term 1837

Isaac Smith) No. 3. Came the defendant by at-
) torney and upon motion it is or-
  vs   ) dered by the Court that the Plan-
) tiff give security on or before
William Childress) the second day of the next Term
) for the prosecution of his said
suit, or the same will be dismissed.

Isaac Smith) January 9th 1838
)
  vs   ) No. 3. This day came Allen Blevins
) and undertook for the Plantiff and
William Childress) says if he is cast in Suit and
) does not satisfy and pay all costs
that he will do it for him, and this suit was continued from
Court to Court.

Monday April 22nd 1839.

Judgment No. 3.

Isaac Smith)
)
  vs   ) Came the parties by their attorneys
) and the Plantiff says he will no
William Childress) further prosecute his suit in this
) behalf against the defendent. It
is therefore considered by the Court that the defendant go
hence without day and recover of the plantiff his cost about
his defence in this behalf expended, and that he have his
execution.

State of Tennessee) To any lawful officer To Execute
) and return whereas information
Bradley County) has been given by Isaac Smith to
) me, James W. Willson an acting
Justice of the peace for said County, that William Childress
late of said County, did on the fifteenth of Sept. One Thousand eight hundred & Thirty Six, in the night time, knowingly permit a slave by the name of Balous, a slave for life
the property of one John Towns, to collect and assemble at
his dwelling house in said County, the said Balous, then &
there not having a pass in writing setting forth his business
& time of absence. These are therefore to command you to
summons the said William Childress to appear before me or some
other Justice of the Peace for said County to answer the said
Isaac Smith who says as well for the County aforesaid as for
himself in a plea of debt of Ten dollars due by penalty for
the above premises. Herein fail not -- Given under my hand
and Seal 27th June 1837.

```
Summond for        )    James W. Willson
the Plantiff       )    Justice of the Peace
Benjamin Maury     )
```

Warrant No 4.   Endorsement

```
Isaac Smith        .    )    Came to hand 4th July returned for
                        )    Trial 5th July 1837 before James
   vs                   )    W. Willson,
                        )
William Childress       )             W. Grogan, Const
   Esqr.                )
```

This day was the within warrant returned for Trial the parties present the evidence being understood as on behalf of the defendent as the plantiff, it is therefore considered by me that the Plantiff recover of the defendant Ten dollars one half to the County, and all costs accrueing thereunto.

> Given under my hand and Seal
>   This 5th July 1837.

> > James W. Willson,
> > Justice of the Peace

Debt - $5.00

 Do   5.00

Cost of Con. 75

Jur's Cost   25

Witness cost 25   Appeal for defendant -----

Appeal Bond 50

The defendent prays an appeal in this cause to the next Term of the Circuit Court to be held for Bradley County, which is granted him, he having given bond and security as the law directs in such cases made and provided.

> > James W. Willson
> > A Justice of the Peace

Appeal Bond
No 4.

```
State of Tennessee     )
                       )
Bradley County         )    Know all men that we William
                            Childress, & Lemuel Childress
are held and firmly bound unto Isaac Smith, his heirs exe-
```

cutors Adminstrators and assigns in the sum of Twenty dollars, well and truly to be paid to the said Isaac Smith, but to be void if the said William Childress shall prosecute with effect an appeal by him taken this day from a Judgment rendered against him for the (P-39) Sum of Ten dollars principal & intrest and the futher sum of one dollar & twenty five cents for costs accrued thereon in favor of the said Isaac Smith before James W. Willson, one of the Justices of the peace for said County to the next Circuit Court to be holden for Bradley County commenceing the second Monday in September next at Cleveland as in the prayrs for the appeal but if the said William Childress fail therein then to pay said Judgment with such damages and cost as shall be adjudged against him in said Court. This 7th day of July 1837. Given under our hands and seal.

his
William X Childress (Seal)
mark
his
Lemuel X Childress (Seal)
mark

Isaac Smith	)	No. 4.
vs	)	Came the defendent by attorney and upon motion it is ordered by the Court that the Plaintiff give security on or before the second
William Childress	)	

day of next Term for the prosecution of his said suit or the same will be dismissed.

No. 4.

Isaac Smith	)	
vs	)	This day came Allen Blevins and undertook for the plaintiff and says if he is cast in this suit and does not satisfy and pay all
William Childress	)	

costs that he will do it for him.

(P-40)
Warrants No. 5 ---

State of Tennessee	)	To any lawful officer to execute and return.
Bradley County	)	

Whereas information has been given by Isaac Smith to one James W. Willson, an acting justice of the Peace for said County on the 10th of Oct. 1836 did loan a drum to a slave by the name of Bayles the property of John Towns, with out a pass from the Master or Mistress of said slave or from his overseer expressing the time when & the business upon which the said Slave was permitted to go abroad.

These are therefore to command you to summon the said
William Childress to appear before me or some other Justice
of the Peace for said County to answer the said Isaac Smith
of a plea of debt of Fifteen dollars, due the Master for the
offence due by penalty for the above premises. Herein fail
not.

Given under my hand and Seal this 5th of --- 1837.

James W. Willson
Justice of the Peace

John Towns   )
)   Endoresment
Warrant No. 5.   )

Isaac Smith   )   Came to hand on the 5th of July
)   executed on the same day of July
    vs   )   1837.
)   Returned before James W. Willson,
William Childress   )   Esq. July 7th, 1837.

W. Grogan, Const.

This day was the within warrant returned, the parties p
present the evidence being understood as well for the defendant as for the Plaintiff, it is therefore considered by me
that the Plantiff off the defendant fifteen dollars & all
costs accruing thereunto.

Given under my hand and Seal. This 7th July 1837

James W. Willson,
Justice of the Peace.

Debt $15.00

Cost Con   75

Justice   25   for which the defendent Prays

Witness   25   an appeal.

Appeal   50

(P-41)
     The defendent prays an appeal to the next Circuit Court,
for Bradley County which is granted him, he having given
bond and Security as the law directs in such cases made and
provided.

Appeal Bond No. 5.   James W. Willson
                             Justice of the Peace

State of Tennessee   )   Know all men that we, William
)   Childress and Lemuel Childress
Bradley County   )   are held and firmly bound unto
   Isaac Smith his heirs executors
Adminstrators and assigns in the sum of Thirty dollars, well
& truly to be paid to the said Isaac Smith but to be void if
the said William Childress shall prosecute with effect an
appeal taken by him this day from a Judgment rendered against
him for the sum of fifteen dollars principal and intrest and
the futher sum of one dollar & Twenty five cents for costs
accrued thereon in favor of the said Isaac Smith before James
W. Willson, one of the Justices of the peace for said County
to the next Circuit Court to be holden for Bradley County
Commencing on the second Monday of September next as in the
prayr for appeal, but if the said William Childress fail therein then to pay the said Judgment with such damages & cost as
shall be adjudged against him in said Court.

    Given under our hands & Seals
    This the 7th day of July 1837
           his
       William X Childress
         mark
         his
       Lemuel X Childress
         mark

No. 5.
Isaac Smith   )
)
vs   )   Came the defendent by attorney
)   and upon motion it is ordered
William Childress   )   by the Court that the Plantiff
   give security on or before the
second day of the next term of this Court or his suit will
be dismissed.
(P-42)
Isaac Smith   )
)
vs   )   This day came Allen Blevins and un-
)   dertook for the Plantiff and says
William Childress   )   if he is cast in this cause and
   does not satisfy and pay all costs
he will do it for him.

Judgment No. 5.   May 19th, 1838

Isaac Smith   )
)
vs   )   Came the parties by their Attorneys
)   and the rule comeing on to be ar-
William Childress   )   gued heretofore entered in this

cause to quash the proceedings had before the justice of the peace, and after argument of Counsel & Motion deliberation by the Court had them on; It is therefore considered by the Court that the proceedings from the Justice be quashed and that the defendent recover of the plantiff all costs accrued in this cause for which execution may issue.

Warrant No. 6.

State of Tennessee   )   To any lawful officer to execute
)   and return whereas information
Bradley County   )   has been given by Isaac Smith
                          to me James W. Willson an acting
Justice of the Peace for said County that William Childress late of said County did on the tenth day of September, One Thousand eight hundred & Thirty Six knowingly permit a slave by the name of Beckey with Two other slaves for life the property of one David Westfield to collect and assemble at his dwelling house in said County the said Beckey & her associates then & there not having a pass in writting setting forth her & their business and time of absence. These are therefore to Command you to Summon the said William Childress to appear before me or some other Justice of the peace for said County to answer the said Isaac Smith, who ---as well for the County aforesaid as for himself of a plea of debt, of Ten dollars, due (P-43) by penalty for the above premises Herein fail not,

Given under my hand and Seal, This 29th day of June 1837.

Summons for   )   James W. Willson (Seal)
the Plantiff   )   Justice of the Peace
Benjamin Murry   )

Warrant No. 6.   Endorsement

Isaac Smith   )   Came to hand the 4th July 1837
   vs   )   Executed on William Childress,
William Childress)   this 5th July, 1837, returned
                        for Trial on the 5th July, be-
fore James W. Willson, Esqr. summond one Witness.

W. Grogan, Const

This day was the within warrant returned for trial, parties present the evidence being understood as well for the defendent as for the plantiff, it is therefore considered by me that the Plantiff recover off the defendant Ten dollars, One half to the County.

Given under my hand and seal this 5th July 1837.

James W. Wilson (Seal)
Justice of the Peace

```
Debt            $5.00

 Do             5.00

Con Cost          75

Jur               25

Wit. Cost         25       Appeal for the defemdent

Appeal Bd -       50       The defendant prays an appeal in this
                           Cause to the Term of the Circuit Court
which is granted him he having given bond & security as the
law directs.
```

James W. Willson
A Justice of the Peace

Appeal Bond No. 6

State of Tennessee   )   Know all men that we William Chil-
)   dress & Lemuel Childress are held
Bradley County   )   and firmly bound unto Isaac Smith
                                 his heirs executors, adminstrators
& assigns in the sum of Twenty dollars well & truly to be
paid to the said Isaac Smith but to be void if the said William Childress shall prosecute with effect an appeal by him
taken this day from a Judgment rendered against him for the
sum of Ten Dollars, principal & intrest, and the futher sum
of one dollar and twenty five cents costs accrued thereon
in favor of the said Isaac Smith before me, James W. Willson
one of the Justices of the peace for said County to the (P-44)
next Circuit Court to be holden for Bradley County, commencing on the second Monday in September next at Cleveland as in
the prayr of the appeal but if the said William Childress fail
therein then to pay the said judgment with such damages & costs
as be adjudged against him in said Court.

        Given under my hand and Seals this 7th day of July, 1837.
                                    his
                           William X Childress
                                   mark
                                    his
                           Lemuel X Childress
                                   mark

No. 6.

Isaac Smith   )
)
    vs   )   Came the defendent by attorney
)   and upon motion it was ordered
William Childress   )   by the Court that the Plaintiff

give security on or before the second day of next Term for
the prosecution of his said suit or the same will be dismissed.

No. 6.

Isaac Smith	)	Came the defendent by attorney and
	)	upon motion it was ordered by the
vs	)	Court that the Plaintiff give se-
	)	curity on or before the second day
	)	of next Term for the prosecution
William Childress	)	of his said suit or the same will

be dismissed.

No. 6.

Isaac Smith	)	This day came Allen Blevins and
	)	undertook for the plantiff and
vs	)	says if he is cast in this suit
	)	and does not satisfy and pay all
William Childress	)	costs he will do it for him.

Monday 22nd April 1839.

This suit was continued on from Court to Court.

Judgment No. 6. Came the parties by their attorneys, and
the plantiff says he will no futher prosecute his suit in
this behalf against the defendent.

It is therefore considered by the Court that the defendent go hence without day & recover of the plaintiff his costs
about his defence in this behalf expended, and that he have
his execution.

Warrant No. 7.

State of Tennessee	)	To any lawful officer to execute
	)	and return whereas information
Bradley County	)	has been given by Isaac Smith
		to me James W. Willson, an act-

ing Justice of the peace for said County that William Childress, late of said County did on the seventeenth day of
April one Thousand eight hundred & Thirty six, knowingly
permit a slave by the (P-45) name of Pegga, a slave for
life the property of one James Pettitt, to collect & as-
embled at his dwelling house in said County, the said Pegga,
then & there not having a pass in writing setting forth her
business and time of absence, These are therefore to command you to summon the said William Childress to appear
before me or some other Justice of the Peace for said County to answer the said Isaac Smith who sues as well for the
County aforesaid as for himself of a plea of debt of Ten dollars due by penalty for the above premisies. Herein fail not.

Given under my hand and seal This 29th June 1837.

James W. Willson (Seal)
Justice of the Peace

Summons for the
Plaintiff
Menerva Van   Warrant No. 7.

Isaac Smith   )   Endorsed.   Came to hand on the 4th
)   July, returned for Trial the 5th
    vs   )   July, 1837, before James W. Willson
)   Esqr.
William Childress)
                            W. Grogan, Const.

    This day was the within Warrant returned for Trial, the
parties present, and the evidence being understood as well for
the defendant as the Plantiff, it is therefore considered
by me that the Plantiff recover off the defendent Ten dollars
one half to the County.

    Given under my hand and seal this 5th July 1837.

James W. Willsom
Justice of the Peace

Debt $5.00   )   The defendent prays an appeal.
  Do   5.00   )
Con Cost   75   )   The defendent prays an appeal to
Jur   25   )   the next Circuit Court, to be held
Witness   25   )   for the County of Bradley, which
Appeal bond   50   )   is granted him he having bond and
                          security as the law directs, in such
cases made andprovided.

James W. Willson
A justice of the Peace

(P-46) Appeal Bond No. 7.

State of Tennessee   )
)
Bradley County   )   Know all men that we William Chil-
                           dress and Lemuel Childress, are held
and firmly bound unto Isaac Smith his heirs executors, adminstrators & assigns in the sum of Twenty dollars, Well and
truly to be paid to the said Isaac Smith but to be void if the
said William Childress shall prosecute with effect an appeal
by him taken This day from a judgment rendered against him for
the sum of Ten dollars, principal, and intrest and the futher
sum of One dollar & Twenty five cents for costs accrued there

on in favor of the said Isaac Smith before J. W. Willson one
of the Justices of the Peace for said County to the next Circuit Court to be holden for Bradley County commencing on the
second Monday of September, next at Cleveland as in the prayr
for the appeal but if the said William Childress fail therein then to pay the said judgment with such damages & cost
as shall be adjudged against him in said Court.

Given under our hand and seals This 7th of July 1837.

his
William X Childress (Seal)
mark
his
Lemuel X Childress (Seal)
mark

No. 7.
Isaac Smith)
)
)
vs)   Came the defendent by Attorney,
)   and upon motion it is ordered by
William Childress)   the Court that the Plantiff give
                             security on or before the second
day of next Term for the prosecution of his said suit, or
the same will be dismissed.

No. 7.
Isaac Smith)
)
)
vs)   This day came Allen Blevins and
)   undertook for the Plantiff and
William Childress)   says if he is cast in this suit
                             and does not satisfy and pay all
costs he will do it for him.

Monday 22nd April, 1839.

This suit was continued from Court to Court.

(P-47) Judgment No. 7.

Came the Parties by their Attorneys and the Plantiff
says he will no futher prosecute his suit in this behalf
against the defendent, It is therefore considered by the
Court that the defendent go hence without day & recover
of the plaintiff his costs about his defence in this behalf expended, and that he have his execution.

Warrant No. 8
State of Tennessee)   To any legal officer to execute
)   and return.
Bradley County)   Whereas information has been

given by Isaac Smith to me James W. Willson, an acting justice of the Peace for said County that William Childress late of said County did on the second day of September , one Thousand eight hundred & Thirty Six, Knowingly permit a slave by the name of Nice, a slave for life the property of one James Pettitt, to collect at his dwelling house, in said County the said Nice then and there not having a pass in writing setting forth her business and time of absence.

These are therefore to command you to summons the said William Childress to appear before me or some other Justice of the peace for said County to answer the said Isaac Smith who sues as well for the County aforesaid as for himself of a plea of debt of Ten dollars due by penalty for the above premises Herein fail not.

Given under my hand & Seal this 29th June, 1837.

James W. Willson (Seal)
Justice of the Peace

Summons for the
Plaintiff
Menerva Van,
Elizabeth Saterfield

Warrant -- Isaac Smith

vs

William Childress

Endorsement   Came to hand -- 4th July returned for Trial
                   5th July, 1837 Before

                        James W. Willson, Esqr.

                        W. Grogan,Const.

This day was the within warrant returned for Trial the parties present and the evidence being understood as well on behalf of the defendent as the plantiff it therefore considered by me that the Plantiff recover off the defendent Ten dollars ond half to the County and all costs accrueing thereon.

Given under my hand and Seal this 5th July 1837.

                        James W. Willson
                        Justice of the Peace.

The defendent Prays an appeal.

(P-48)
Debt $5.00

```
Do        $5.00
Con        5.00
Justice      25
Witness      50
Appeal Bond  50
```
The defendent prays an appeal in this cause to the next Circuit Court of Bradley County which is granted him he having given bond and security as the law directs in such cases made and provided.

James W. Willson,
A Justice of the Peace

Appeal Bond No. 8.

State of Tennessee   )   Know all men that we William
)   Childress & Lemuel Childress are
Bradley County   )   held and firmly bound unto Isaac
                             Smith his heirs executors admin-
strators & assigns in the sum of Twenty dollars, well and Truly to be paid unto the said Isaac Smith, but to be void if the said William Childress shall prosecute with effect an appeal by him taken this day from a Judgment rendered against him for the sum of Ten dollars principal and intrest and the futher sum of one dollar and Twenty five cents for costs accrued thereon in favor of the said Isaac Smith before J. W. Willson, one of the Justices of the Peace for said County To the next Circuit Court to be holden for Bradley County. Commenceing on the second Monday of September next at Cleveland as in the prayr for the appeal, but if the said William Childress fail therein then to pay the said judgment with such damages & costs as shall be adjudged against by said Court.

Given under our hands and seals this 7th July 1837.
                              his
                    William XChildress (Seal)
                             mark
                              his
                    Lemuel X Childress (Seal)
                             mark

No. 8. Appeal --
Isaac Smith   )   Came the defendent by Attorney and
)   upon motion it is ordered by the
    vs   )   Court that the plantiff give se-
)   curity on or before the second day
William Childress   )   of the next Term of this Court for
                             the prosecution of his said suit
or the same will be dismissed.

(P-49) No. 8.

Isaac Smith   )   This day came Allen Blevins and undertook

vs   )   for the Plantiff and says if he is
)   cast in this suit and does not sat-
William Childress   )   isfy and pay all costs, he will do
)   it for him.

Monday 22nd April, 1839

    This suit was continued from Court to Court.

                        Judgment No. 8.

Isaac Smith   )   Came the parties by their Attorneys
)   and the Plantiff says he will no
    vs   )   futher prosecute his suit in this
)   behalf against the defendent. It is
William Childress   )   therefore considered by the Court
                            that the defendent go hence without
day and recover of the Plantiff his costs about his suit in
this behalf expended, and that he have his execution.

Warrent No. 9.

State of Tennessee   )   To any lawful officer to execute
)   and return whereas information
Bradley County   )   has been given to me.

                        James W. Willson, an acting
Justice of the Peace for said County by Isaac Smith of said
County that one Anna Childress, wife of William Childress,
of said County did trade and traffic for & buy of one Nicey,
a slave for life the property of one James Pettitt, a comb
the said slave there & then being under the Control of the
said James Pettitt, without a permit in writing setting forth
the articles to be sold. These are therefore to command you
to summon the said Anna Childress to appear before me or Some
other Justice of the Peace for said County to answer the said
Isaac Smith of a debt of Twenty five dollars due by Penalty
for the above premises.

    Herein fail not. Given under my hand and seal This 29th
June 1837.

                        James W. Willson (Seal)
                        Justice of the Peace

Summons for the Plantiff
Elizabeth Saturfield
Menerva Van

The plantiff requires bail.

Warrant --

Isaac Smith)
)
vs)
)
William Childress)

Endorsement, Came to hand the 4th
of July 1837, executed on the 8th
July 1837.

W. Grogan, Const.

(P-50)
Returned for Trial ----

This day was the within warrant returned for Trial the
parties present and the evidence being understood as well
for the defendent as for the plantiff it is therefore considered by me that the Plantiff recover off the defendent
Twenty five dollars and all costs accruing thereunto.

Given under my hand and seal This the 5th July, 1837.

James W. Willson,
Justice of the Peace

Debt	$25.00	)	The defendant prays & appeal
Con Cost.	1.00	)	
Jur	25		
Witness	50		
Appeal	50		

The defendent prays an appeal to the next Circuit Court
for the County of Bradley which is granted him he having
given bond and security as the law directs in such cases
made and provided.

James W. Willson
A Justice of the Peace

Appeal No. 9.
State of Tennessee)
)
Bradley County)

Know all men that we William Childress and Lemuel Childress, are
hereto and firmly bound unto
Isaac Smith, his heirs executors
adminstrators and assigns in the sum of Fifty dollars well
& Truly to be paid to the said Isaac Smith but to be void if
the said William Childress, shall prosecute with effect an
appeal by him taken this day from judgment rendered against
him for the sum of Twenty five dollars principle & intrest
and the futher sum of one dollar & Seventy five cents for
cost accrued thereon in favor of the said Isaac Smith before
me James W. Willson, one of the Justices of the Peace for
said County To the next Circuit Court to be holden for Brad-
ly County, commencing on the second Monday in September next
as in the prayr for the appeal, but if the said William Chil-

dress paid therein to pay the said judgment with such damages
and cost as shall be (P-51) adjudged against him in said Court

    Given under our hands & Seals This 7th day of July 1837.
                              his
                  William X Childress
                        mark
                        his
                  Lemuel X Childress
                        mark

No. 9.
Isaac Smith   )
)
  vs   )   Came the defendant by attorney
)   and upon motion it is ordered by
William Childress   )   the Court that the Plantiff give
                        security on or before the second
day of the next Term of this Court for the prosecution of
his said suit or the same will be dismissed.

Mo. 9.
Isaac Smith   )
)
  vs   )   This day came Allen Blevins and
)   undertook for the Plantiff and says
William Childress   )   if he is cast in this suit and does
                        not satisfy & pay all costs that he
                        will do it for him.

Judgment No. 9.
    Came the parties by their attoneys and the Plantiff says
he will no futher prosecute his suit in this Behalf against
the defendent.

    It is therefore considered by the Court that the defend-
ant go hence with out day & recover of the plantiff his costs
about his defence in this behalf expended, and that he have h
his execution.

Warrant No. 10.
State of Tennessee   )   To any lawful officer to execute
)   and return whereas information
)   has been given by Isaac Smith to
Bradley County   )   me James W. Willson, an acting
Justice of the Peace for said County that William Childress
late of said County did on the First Sunday in April One
Thousand eight hundred and Thirty seven knowingly permit a
slave by the name of Beckey with one other slave for life
the property of David Westfield, to collect and assemble at
his dwelling house in said County The said Beckey (P-52)
or her associates then and there not having a pass in writing

setting forth her & there business and time of absence;
These are therefore to command you to summon the said William
Childress, to appear before me or some other Justice of the
Peace for said County to answer the said Isaac Smith who sues
as well for the County aforesaid as for himself in a plea of
debt of Ten dollars, due by penalty for the above premises.
Herein fail not. Given under my hand and seal, This 29th
June 1837.

James W. Willson
Justice of the Peace

Summon for Plantiff   )
Benjamin Murry   )

        Warrant ---
Isaac Smith vs William Childress

Endorsement. Came to hand the 4th July 1837. Executed on
the 5th of July 1837, returned for Trial before

James W. Willson, Esqr. summoned one Witness.

W. Grogan, Const.

This day was the within warrant returned for Trial the
parties present and the evidence being understood as well
for the defendent as for the plaintiff, it is therefore considered by me that the Plantiff recover off the defendent
Ten dollars one half to the County, and all costs accrueing
thereunto.

Given under my hand & Seal This 5th July, 1837.

James W. Willson,
Justice of the Peace

Debt $5.00   )
 Do   5.00   )   The defendent prays and appeal.
Con Cost   75   )
Justice   25   )   The defendent prays and appeals
Wit,   25   )   to the next Circuit Court for the
Appeal Bond   50   )   County of Bradley which is granted
                           him he having given Bond and se-
curity as the law directs in such cases made and provided.

James W. Willson,
A Justice of the Peace

(P-53)   --- Appeal ---
State of Tennessee   )
)
Bradley County   )   Know all men that we William Chil-

dress and Lemuel Childress are held and firmly bound unto
Isaac Smith his heirs executors adminstrators & assigns in
the sum of Twenty dollars, well and Truly to be paid to the
said Isaac Smith but to be void if the said William Childress shall prosecute with effect an appeal by him taken
this day from a judgment rendered against him for the sum
of Ten dollars principle and intrest and the further sum of
one dollar & Twentyfive cents costs accrued thereon in favor
of the said Isaac Smith before James W. Willson, one of the
Justices of the Peace for said County To the next Circuit
Court To be holden for Bradley County, commencing on the second Monday in September next at Cleveland as the prayr for
the appeal but if the said William Childress fail therein
then to pay the said Judgment with such damages and costs as
shall be adjudged against him in said Court.

Given under our hands & seals, This 7th day of July 1837.

                            his
                William XChildress (Seal)
                        mark
                            his
                Lemuel X Childress (Seal)
                        mark

Isaac Smith   )
)
    vs   )   Came the defendent by attorney
)   and upon motionit is ordered by
William Childress   )   the Court that the plantiff give
                            security on or before the second
day of the next term for the prosecution of his said suit or
it will be dismissed.

Isaac Smith   )
)
    vs   )   This day came Allen Blevins and
)   undertook for the Plantiff and
William Childress   )   says if he is cast in this suit
                            and does not satisfy and pay all
costs he will do it for him.

Came the parties by their attorneys and the plantiff
says he will no futher prosecute his suit in this behalf
against the defendant. It is therefore considered by the
Court that the defendent go hence without day and recover
of the plaintiff his costs about his defence in this behalf
expended and that he have his execution.

(P-54)
State of Tennessee   )   To any lawful officer to execute
)   and return whereas information
Bradley County   )   has been given by Isaac Smith to
me James W. Willson an acting Justice of the Peace for said

County That one William Childress late of said County did
on the first day of September One Thousand eight hundred
& Thirty six, knowingly permit a slave by the name of Daniel with one other slave by the name of Nelson slaves for
life The property of one David Westfield to collect and
assemble at his dwelling house in said County, The said
Daniel and his associate not having a pass in writing setting forth their business & time of absence; These are
therefore to command you to summons the said William Childress to appear before me or some other Justice of the Peace
for said County to answer the said Isaac Smith who sues as
well for the County aforesaid as for himself of a plea of debt
of Ten dollars due by penalty for the above premises. Herein
fail not.

Given under my hand and seal This 27th June 1837.

James W. Willson
Justice of the Peace

Summons for the Plaintiff   )
Benjamin Murry   )

Warrant   Isaac Smith, against William Childress

Came to hand the 4th July returned for Trial the 5th
July 1837, before James W. Willson, Esqr.

W. Grogan, Const.

This day was the within Warrant for Trial the parties
present and the evidence being understood as well on part of
the defendent as the plantiff it is therefore considered by
me that the plantiff recover off the defendent Ten dollars
one half for the County and all costs accrueing thereon.

Given under my hand and seal, This fifth July 1837.

James W. Willson (Seal)
Justice of the Peace.

Debt. $5.00
 Do   5.00
Con Cost   75
Jur   25
Witness   25
Appeal Bond   50

Appeal for the defendent

The defendent prays an appeal in this cause to the Circuit
Court which is granted him , he having given bond and security

as the law directs.

James W. Willson
A Justice of the Peace

State of Tennessee)
)
Bradley County)

Know all men that we Wm. Childress*
are held and firmly bound unto
Isaac Smith his heirs executors &
assigns in the sum of Twenty dollars
well & truly to be paid to the said Isaac Smith but to be void
if the said William Childress shall prosecute with effect an
appeal by him this day taken from a Judgment rendered against
him for the sum of Ten dollars principal & intrest and the
futher sum of one dollar & Twenty five cents for costs accrued
thereon in favor of the said Isaac Smith before James W. Willson one of the justices of the Peace for said County to the
next Circuit Court to be holden for Bradley County on the
second Monday of Sept. next as in the prayr for the appeal but
if the said William Childress fail therein then to pay the said
Judgment with such damages and costs as shall be adjudged
against him by the Court. *and Lemuel Childress

Given under our hands & seals This 7th July 1837.
his
William X Childress
mark
his
Lemuel X Childress
mark

Came the defendent by Attorney and upon motion it is
ordered by the Court that the plantiff give security on or
before the second day of the next Term for the prosecution
of his said suit or the same will be dismissed.

This day came Allen Blevins who undertook for the plantiff and says if he is cast in this suit and does not pay
and satisfy all costs he will do it for him.

(P-56)
Isaac Smith)
)
vs)
)
William Childress)

Came the parties by their attorneys
and the plantiff says he will no
futher prosecute his suit in this
behalf against the defendant. It
is therefore ordered by the Court
that the defendant go hence with-
out day & recover of the plantiff his costs about his defence
in this behalf expended and that he have his execution.

Suit, Know all men by these presents We, William Childress, Sampson H. Prowell and jointly and severly held and firmly bound unto Isaac Smith in the penal sum of Twohundred & fifty dollars to be void on condition that the said William Childress will with effect prosecute a suit by action of Trespass on the case which he this day commenced against the Isaac Smith, in the Circuit Court for Bradley County or in case of failure of such prosecution pay and satisfy all costs and damages as may be awarded against him by our said Court.

Witness our hands & seals, this 16th day of December 1837.
                              his
                    William X Childress (seal)
                              mark

                    S. H. Prowell   (seal)

                    John P. Angelly   (seal)

State of Tennessee,

     To the Sheriff of Bradley County, Greeting:

     You are hereby commanded to summon Isaac Smith if to be found in your County to appear before our Circuit Court to be holden for Bradley County at the Court house in Cleveland on the 2nd Monday of January next to answer William Childress of a plea of Tresspass on the case to his damages one thousand dollars. Here in fail not. And have you then & there this writ:

Witness Henry Price, Clerk of our said Court at office in Cleveland the 2nd Monday of September, 1837, and American Independence 62nd.

                         Henry Price, Clerk
(P-57)
Summons   William Childress vs Isaac Smith

Issued 16th December 1837. Case damage $1000.

Endorsement Came to hand 16th December, 1837. Came to hand to late I had not time to execute the within This 6th of December 1837.

                    Alexander A. Clingan, Sheriff

Summons

State of Tennessee
     To the Sheriff of Bradley County Greeting: You are hereby

commanded as you have heretofore been to summon Isaac Smith
if to be found in your County to appear before our Circuit
Court to be held for County of Bradley at the Court house
in Cleveland on the 2nd Monday May, next, To answer William
Childress, of a plea of Tresspass on the case to his damage
one Thousand dollars. Herein fail not. And have you there
this Writ: Witness Henry Price, Clerk of our said Court at
office in Cleveland, the 2nd Monday of January 1838. And of
American Independence the 62nd.

                    Henry Price, Clk.

--- Summons, William Childress vs Isaac Smith Issued January
19th 1838. Came to hand 22nd of January 1838. The within
is executed on the defendant Isaac Smith this first of Feb.
1838.

                    A. A. Clingan, Sheriff

Declaration --

State of Tennessee   )   Circuit Court May Term, 1837.
)
Bradley County   )   William Childress, by Attorney
                            complaining of Isaac Smith sum-
mond by the Sheriff and of a plea of Tresspass on the case
For whereas the defendant now is a true honest just & faith-
ful citizen of the County aforesaid and as such hath always
behaved and conducted himself and hath not even been guilty
or until the time of the Committing of several grieveances
by the said defendant as herein after mentioned been suspected to have been guilty of felony or any other such crime
by means whereof the said plantiff before the committing of
the several grievances by the said defendant as herein after
mentioned deservedly (P-58)obtained and required a good opin-
on and cridit of all his neighbors, and other good and worthy
citizens of the County and State aforesaid. Yet the said
defendant well knowing the premises, contriving & maliciously
intending to injure said plantiff in his and aforesaid good
man pure & credit and to bring him unto Publick scandal, infamy and disgrace and to cause him the said Plantiff to be
imprisoned for a long space of time and thereby to impover-
ish appress and wholy ruin him heretofore. To wit: Upon the
5th day of July 1837 at to in the County aforesaid Went and appeared before one James W. Willson, then and there being one
of the justice of the Peace in and for the County and State
aforesaid and assigned to keep the Peace of the State in and
for the County of Bradley aforesaid and also authorized em-
powerd & required by law to inquire into and have Testimony
and determine felony and crime committed in said County and
then & there before the said James W. Willson, so being such
justice as afore said to wit: On the 5th day of July 1837,

At to wit in the County aforesaid falsley maliciously and
without any reasonable or probable execuse whatsoever charge
the said Plantiff with having feloniously stolen a bag*from
the possession of James A. Fletcher, and upon such charge
in the said defendant falsely and maliciously and without
any reasonable or probable - whatsoever caused and procured
the said James W. Willson, so being such justice as aforesaid to make and grant his certain Warrant under his hand
and Seal for the taking the said Plantiff and bringing him
the said Plantiff before him, the said James W. Willson, or
some other justice of the Peace for said County of Bradley
to answer the premises and to be dealt with as the law directs and the said defendant under and by virtue of the said
warrant afterwards To wit: On the day (P-59) and year last
aforesaid in the County aforesaid Wrongfully and unjustly
and without any reasonable or probable cause whatsoever caused
and procured the said Plantiff to be arrested by his body and
to be imprisoned and kept and detained in prison for a long
space of time To wit: for the space of forty eight hours,
thence next following, and until he the said defendant afterwards to wit: on the 6th day of July 1837, at to wit: in
the County aforesaid falsley and maliciously and without any
reasonable or Probable Cause whatsoever caused and procured,
The said plantiff to be carried and conveyed in custody, before the said James W. Willson, so being such justice as
aforesaid and to be examined before the said justice vouch-
ing and concerning the said supposed crime which said Justice
having heard and considered all that the defendant could say
or alleged against the said Plantiff, touching and concerning the said supposed offence then and there to wit:, On the
day and year last aforesaid at to wit: in the County aforesaid adjudged that the said Plantiff was not guilty of the
said supposed offence and then and there accusedthe said
plantiff to be discharged out of Custody fully acquitted and
discharged out of Custody fully acquitted and discharged of
the said supposed offence and the said defendant hath not
futher prosecuted his said complaint and hath deserted and
abondoned the same and the said Complainant and prosecution
 is wholly ended and determined, and whereas also the said
defendant futher contriving and maliciously & wickedly intending as aforesaid heretofore to wit: On the day and year
last aforesaid at to wit, in the County aforesaid falsely and
maliciously and with out any reasonable or probable cause
whatsoever charged the said Plantiff with having committed
felony and upon such last mentioned charge he the said defendant then and there to wit: On the same day and year last
aforesaid at to wit: (P-60) in the County aforesaid falsely
and maliciously caused and procured the said plantiff to be
arrestedby his body and to be imprisoned and to be kept and
detained in prison for a long space of time to wit, for the
space of Twenty four hours, there next following, and at the
*of corn

exporition of said time he the said plantiff was duly discharged and acquitted of the said last mentioned offence.
To wit: ~~On the day and year last aforesaid at to wit:~~ On
the day and year last aforesaid at to wit, in the County aforesaid by means of which said several premises he the said Plaintiff hath been and is greatly injured in his said Credit and
reputation and brought into public scandal infamy and disgrace
with and amongst all his neighbours and other good and worthy
citizens of the State and County aforesaid and divers of these
neighbors and citizens to whom his innocence in the premises
was unknown have on the occasion of the premises suspected
and believed and still do suspect and believe that the said
plantiff hath been and is guilty of felony and also the said
Plantiff hath by ---- of the premises suffered great anxiety
and pain in body and mind and hath been forced & obliged to
lay out and expend divers large sums of money in the whole
amount to a large sum of Money, to wit: the sum of Five hundred dollars, in and about defending him self in the premises and the manifestation of his innocence in this behalf and
hath been greatly hindered and prevented by reason of the
premises from Transacting his lawful and necessary affairs
and business. To wit: for the space of one month, and also
byreason and means of the premises he the said plantiff, hath
been and is otherwise greatly injured in his credit and cir-
cumstances to wit: On the day and year last aforesaid at to
wit:
          In the County aforesaid (P-61) Wherefore the said Plan-
tiff saith that he is injured and hath sustained damages to
the value of one Thousand dollars, and therefore he brings
his suit and pledges to Prosecute.

                         Trewhitt, Atty for
                              Plaintiff.

William Childress   )
)
       vs   )   The defendant by attorney, comes
)   into court and defends the wrong
Isaac Smith   )   and injury when & C, and for plea
                                saith the plantiff, his action
aforesaid ought not to have and maintain against him because
he says he is not guilty in Manner & form as the Plantiff
in declaiming thereof aginst him hath alleged & of this he
puts himself upon the County.

                         C. K. Gillespie
                              Atty. for Dft.

And Plaintiff doth the like,
     Jarnagan & Bradford &
     Trewhitt, Attr's for Plaintiff.

Tuesday January 9th, 1838.

William Childress   )
)
    vs   )   Ordered by the Court that an alias
)   summon issue in this cause.
Isaac Smith   )

 Came the Plantiff by his Attorney and the declaration in
this Cause having been filed the said defendant Isaac Smith
being solemuly called to come into Court and plead to the
plantiff declaration failed to do so and made default.

 It is therefore considered by the Court that the plantiff
recover of the defendant his damages in his declaration mentioned hereafter to be ascertained by a Jury.

William Childress   )
)
    vs   )   This day came the parties by their
)   attorneys and the Plantiff attorney
Isaac Smith   )   set aside the judgment entered by
                          default at the last Term of this
Court upon the defendants (P62) Attorney, agreeing to plead
the plea of not guilty only & going to trial at the present
Term and thereupon the defendants Attorney agreed upon record that he would plead the plea of not guilty only that
he would go to trial at the present Term.

William Childress   )
)
    vs   )   Tuesday August 28th, 1838.
)
Isaac Smith   )   Upon sufficient cause disclosed
                          to the Court in the affidavit of
the plantiff a subpeona -- is allowed him directed to Sampson H. Prowell, Esqr. Justice of the Peace of Bradley County
require him to bring into Court the papers and proceedings
on file in his office wherein the State was Plantiff and the
said Plantiff defendant.

Saturday August 31st 1838.

William Childress   )
)
    vs   )   Came the parties by their Attornies
)   and from sufficient reasons shown
Isaac Smith   )   by this affidavit of the defendant
                          it is ordered by the Court that a
commission be awarded the defendant to take the deposition
of William Grogan, to be read ---- in the above cause upon
giving the apposite party Three days notice of the time and

place of taking the same.

Tuesday April Term 1839

William Childress   )
)
    vs   )   Came the parties by their attornies
)   and on affidavit of the defendant
Isaac Smith   )   this cause is continued till next
                                  Term. (P-63)

Tuesday 27th August 1839.

William Childress   )
)
    vs   )   The parties by attorneys appear
)   & also comes a Jury of good and
Isaac Smith   )   lawful men To wit: Thomas W. Back,
                                  Mark Black, George M. Haynes,
James Hawkins, Robert Hood, David Anderson, James Webb, Isaac
Swan, Samuel Dugan, William Weatherly, James Britton & Alexander Pursley, who being elected tried and sworn to well and
truly try the issue joind between the parties on their oath
say they find the issue in favor of the Plantiff and assess
his damages by reason of the premises to Two hundred dollars,

It is therefore considered by the Court that the plantiff
recover of the defendant thedamages by the Jury so assessed
and his cost about his suit in this behalf expended and have
his execution &c.

State of Tennessee   )
)
Bradley County   )   To some lawful officer to execute
                                 and return.

You are hereby commanded to summons Jesse Wimpy, to ap-
pear before me or some other Justice of the Peace for said
County to answer the complaint of John Rains, of a plea of
Tresspass assault and battery, for beating and wounding the
plaintiff to his damage fifty dollars or under warrant.
Herein fail not.

Given under my hand and seal 10th day of March 1837.

                    William Forester,
                    Justice of the Peace

Summons for the Plaintiff

Elizabeth Wooden)

Charles Cate   ) Damage Warrant

W. D. Benton   )

Samuel Lain   ) John Rains against Jesse Wimpy, Ex-

Jesse Wimpy   ecuted 13th March and returned for

trial on Saturday 18th before William Forester & Shaderick

M. Taylor, Justice of the Peace

Wm. I. Larrison

Const.

(P-64) ---- Judgment ----

Warrant returned for trial at twelve oclock, by Wm. I. Larrison the plantiff & Elizabeth Wooden, Charles Cate & Wm. D.
Benton, appeared and examined on oath, she first stating she
saw it the wonds inflicted by Jess Wimpy, on John Rains, in
the inside of Rains enclouser, on the 7th of March 1837. Cate
& Benton stated they would not have the wounds for 50 dollars
nor one hundred dollars.

Judgment rendered for $45. dollars damage & all cost on the
18th of March, 1837.

William Forester

Petition ----

John Rains) State of Tennessee)

)

 vs   ) To Jesse Poe, & Isaac Huffaker, two of the

) acting Justices of the peace for Bradley

Jesse Wimpy) County The petition of Jesse Wimpy, hum-

       bly represents and shows that an execution

was lately issued by William Forester, Esqr. Justice of the
Peace for said County in favor of John Rains about the sum
of forty seven dollars for damages and costs against your pe-
titioner your petitioner was deprived of the benefit of a
Trial before said Justice as he was not notified before what
Justice to appear or at what particular place to appear.

 It is true the Constable, who held the warrant notified
your petitioner that he had a warrant against your Petitioner
in favor of said Rains when your Petitioner was not able to
go to the Trial in consequence of a wound he had received
from said Rains your petitioner informed the Constable that
of his situation and in ability to attend, said Constable
asked your petitioner if he would be able to attend on the
next Saturday. Petitioner replied that he thought that per-

haps he might, but said Constable did not notify petitioner
to attend at any particular place or before any particular
Justice of the Peace. (P-65) Petitioner had no idea or ex-
pectation of said warrant being returned before said Justice
Forester, as said Justice was on unfriendly terms with your
petitioner, and in consequence thereof had said that he did
not think he ought to try a case against your petitioner.
Your petitioner expected said Constable to have given your
petitioner an other notice before he would return said warrant notifying your petitioner before whom, when & where to
appear and answer said Rains, Complaint suit so it was may
it please your worships said Constable went and returned
said warrant before said Justice Forester for trial without notifying your petitioner, that he was going so to do,
said justice rendered a judgment against your petition without your petitioner having any knowledge of the cause being
returned before him for Trial and your petitioner did not
know of said Judgment being against petitioner until it was
too late to appear from said judgment and consequently your
petitioner was deprived of the benefit of trial & appeal
your petitioner futher states that said judgment is unjust
in this that if said Rains received any injury from your petitioner.

It was done by your petitioner in self defence, defending him self from assault and battery of the said Rains.
Your petitioner therefore prays that writ of Certiorari &
supercedias be issued by the Clerk of the Circuit Court for
said County to remove said cause from before said justice
into the next Term of the Circuit Court for said County, that
the same be tried upon the merits that justice be done the
parties.

Petitioner states that this the first application for
writs aforesaid and the premises considered and the writs
granted your petitioner as in duty bound will for ever pray

March 28th, 1837   Jesse Wimpy

(P-66)
State of Tennessee   )
) This day personally appeared be-
Bradley County   ) fore us Jesse Poe and Isaac Huf-
                         faker, Two acting justices of the
Peace for said County Jesse Wimpy, the forgoing Petitioner
and made oath that the facts stated in the foregoing petition as of his own knowledge are true and those that are not
stated of his own knowledge he believes to be true.

                    Jesse Wimpy
Sworn and subscribed before us this the 25th day of March
1837.

Jesse Poe
  Justice of the Peace

Isaac Huffaker
  Justice of the Peace

State of Tennessee,

        To the Clerk of the Circuit Court for Bradley
County let writs of certiorari & supersedias issue according to the prayer of the foregoing petition upon the petitioners giving bond and security according to act of the
General Assembly or otherwise Complying with the law.

    Given under our hands and seals,
    This the 25th day of March 1837.

                        Jesse Poe (Seal)
                          Justice of the Peace

                        Isaac Huffaker (Seal)
                          Justice of the Peace

    Certiorari Bond

    Know all men by these Presents that we Jesse Wimpy and
Samuel G. Blackwell, of Bradley County, and State of Tennessee
our heirs executors and adminstrators, are held and firmly
bound unto John Rains heirs executors*or assigns in the sum
of ninety five dollars to be void on conditions that the said
Jesse Wimpy shall prosecute with effect a writ of certiorari
by him this day obtained to remove the proceedings of a suit
wherein John Rains, Plantiff and Jesse Wimpy (P-67) defendant from before William Forester, Justice into our Circuit
Court for the County of Bradley, or in case of failure therein perform whatever Judgment shall be awarded and rendered
by said Court in said Cause, or in case said Certiorari shall
be dismissed by said Court, for informality or want of sufficient substance or for any other cause pay and satisfy such
judgment as the Justice Forester shall have given against him.

Witness our hands & seals this 25th day of March 1837.

                        Jesse Wimpy (Seal)

                        S. J. Blackwell (Seal)

Certiorari, State of Tennessee

To William Forester, Justice of the Peace for the County of
Bradley, Greeting:-

    Whereas John Rains complained of and lately before you
*adminstrators

recorded a Judgment against Jesse Wimpy and for certain reasons being disirous that the record of that suit should be certified to us do hereby Command you to enclose all papers relative to said suit under your hand and seal distinctly and plainly together with this writ and Transmit the same to a Court to be held by the Judge of the Circuit Court of law for the County of Bradley at the Court house in Cleveland on the 2nd Monday in May, next, in order that our said Court may do therein what of right and according to law what ought to be done.

Witness Henry Price, Clerk of our said Court at office in Cleveland, the 2nd Monday of January, A. D. 1837, and of American Independence, the

Henry Price

Clerk

In pursuence of the within writ, I do hereby enclose to said Court all the papers in said Cause except the Judgt. which is in my record Book and that Judgment I have transcribed and hereby enclose and return perfect transcript of the same as it remain of record in my office.

Given under my hand and seal
This 1st day of January 1837.

William Forester

(P-68)   Monday Sept. 11, 1837.

John Rains   )   This day came the defendent by his attorney
)   and upon his motion a rule is granted him
    vs   )   requiring Plantiff to give security for
)   costs on or before the 2nd day of next
Jesse Wimpy   )   Term or his suit is dismissed, and thereupon came William Wooden & Hiram Rains, and undertook for the
plantiff in this cause and says in case the plantiff in this
cause is cast in this suit and does not pay and satisfy all
costs that they will do it for him.

Tuesday, January 29th, 1838.

---- Damage Suit ----

John Rains   )   By consent this cause is continued by
)   consent.
    vs   )
)   Friday August 31st, 1838
Jesse Wimpy   )

John Rains)
)
vs)   Came the parties by their attorneys and
)   from reason appearing to the satisfac-
Jesse Wimpy)   tion of the Court from the affidavit of
)   the plantiff, this cause is continued
until the next Term of this Court.

December 24th 1838.

John Rains)
)
vs)   Came the Plantiff by his attorney, and
)   from reasons appearing to the satisfac-
Jesse Wimpy)   tion of the Court from the affidavit of
)   the Plantiff, this cause is continued
untill the next term of this Court, and it is futher ordered
by the Court that a commission be awarded the Complainant to
take the deposition of Elizabeth Wooden to read ---- upon
the trial of this cause upon giving the defendant 5 days notice of the time and place of taking the same.

(P-69)   Monday 22nd April, 1839

John Rains)
)
vs)   The parties by their attornies appear
)   and also comes a Jury of good and law-
Jesse Wimpy)   ful men to wit: Charles Dodd, Robert
)   Hood, Absalom Coleman, John Towns, Thomas Taylor, Joseph Billingsley, John McMinn, Russell,Lawson,
John Hays, Isaac Glanden, Solomon Fouts & William Kerr, who
are elected tried & sworn to well and truly try the matters
in dispute between the parties and the plantiff says he will
no futher prosecute his suit in this behalf against the defendant therefore it is considered by the Court that the defendent go hence without day and recover his cost about his
defence in this behalf expended and that he have his execution.

Suit --- Know all men by these presents, That we Thomas Mc-
Callie and James Berry are jointly and severally held and
firmly bound unto Edward Austin in the Penal sum of Two hundred and fifty dollars. To be void on condition that the
said Thomas McCallie will with effect prosecute a suit by
action of covenant broken which he this day commenced against
the said Edward Austin in the Circuit Court for Bradley County or in case of failure of such prosecution pay and satisfy
all costs and damages as may be awarded against by our said

Const. Witness our hands and seals, this 25th day of August 1839.

Thomas McCallie (Seal)
By James Berry, his agent.

James Berry (Seal)

Teste
Henry Price

(P-70)   State of Tennessee,
To the Sheriff of Bradley County, Greeting: You are hereby commanded to summon Edward Austin, if to be found in your County to appear before our Circuit Court to be holden for the County of Bradley at the Court house in Cleveland on the 2nd Monday of September, next, to answer Thomas McCallie of a plea of covenant broken to his damage five hundred dollars Herein fail not, and have you them there, this writ, Witness Henry Price, Clerk of our said Court, at office in Cleveland The 2nd Monday of May 1837, and of American Independence the 61.

Henry Price, Clerk

State of Tennessee	)	Circuit Court,
	)	September Term 1837.
Bradley County	)	

Thomas McCallie, by his attorney, complains of Edward Austin, summond to answer of a plea of covenant broken for that thereas the said defendant on the 8th day of December 1836, at the County of Bradley aforesaid, executed and delivered to the said plantiff his certain Covenant in writing signed with his name and sealed with his seal, the date whereof is the same day and year last aforesaid, and to the Court have now shown wherein and whereby the said defendant for and in Consideration of the sum of Four hundred dollars to him in hand paid by the said Plantiff, transfered to the said Plantiff a lot in the Town of Cleveland, on the Public Square being the same lot which the defendant bought of Andrew Taylor with a house to be finished chunked and daubed and floor laid and chimney built. The said defendant guaranteeing the title of said lot against any person the State excepted and the said plantiff in fact says that on the first day of July 1837 at the (P-71) County of Bradley aforesaid, and before the issuance of the original writ in this cause he requested the said defendant to finish the house on said lot and to cover chunk daub and floor the same and to build a Chimney thereto. And then and there gave to the said defendant reasonable time within which to perform the said work and labour before the institution of this suit to wit: The space of Thirty days and the said plantiff in fact futher says that the said de-

fendant on the 8th day of December, 1836. Nor at any time
since had not Title to a lot in the Town of Cleveland on the
public square, as in and by his aforesaid Covenant guaranteed to have. Yet the said defendant although often required hath not kept and performed his aforesaid Covenant
so as aforesaid made with the said plantiff according to the
tenor and effect true intent and meaning thereof but hath
broken the same - and to keep and perform the said covenant
with the said plantiff according to the tenor and effect,
true and intent and meaning there of the said defendant
hath hitherto wholy failed and refused and still does fail
and refuse in this, To wit, that the said defendant failed
and refused to finish the house in said Covenant mentioned
and to cover chinck, daub and floor the same and to build a
chimney thereunto upon request nor had the said - defendant
a lot in the town of Cleveland on the Public square, as in
said Covenant mentioned - to the damage of the Plaintiff, five
hundred dollars, and therefore he sues &c

Campbell & Vandyke
Attorneys for Plaintiff

(P-72) And the said defendant by attorney comes and defends
the wrong and injury when &c. and ---- of the said Covenant
in the said declaration mentioned which is read to him in the
following words and figures to wit: for and in consideration
of one hundred dollars, to me in hand paid I transfere to
Thomas CmCallie a lot in the town of Cleveland, on the public
square, the lot I bought of Andrew Taylor, with a house to be
finished and covered chincked and daubed and floor laid and
chimney, I guarantee the title from every Person, the State
excepted, in Witness my hand and seal this 6th December 1836.

Edward Austin (Seal)

Witness --
John A. Hook

All of which being read and heard the said defendant
says that the Plaintiff his said action ought not to have
and maintain because he says that he has well & truly kept
and performed the Covenant in the plantiffs declaration mentioned by guaranteeing to the said plantiff Title to a lot
in the Town of Cleveland, upon the Public square the lot
said defendant bought of Andrew Taylor, with a house built
finished and covered chincked and daubed & floor laid & ----
from every Person the State excepted, and thereas the said
defendant puts himself upon the County and the Plaintiff also.

Campbell & Vandyke   )   Trewhitt,
                           Atty. for Defendant.

(P-73)   Second Plea

Thomas McCallie   )
)
   vs   )   And the said defendant for futher Plea
)   in this behalf says that the said Plan-
Edward Austin   )   tiff his action aforesaid ought not to
                      have and maintain his said action there-
of against him because he says that after the making executing
signing sealing and delivering the said Covenant by the said
defendant in the plantiff declaration mentioned and before is-
sueing out the original summon by the said plantiff against the
said defendant in this behalf to wit: on the -- day of 1837,
to wit: in the County aforesaid the said plantiff by his certain writing of release signed with his own proper name which
written release so made and signed & delivered by the said to
the said defendant is now causually brought suit of the power
of the defendant to produce to --- the date whereof is the day
and year aforesaid did release and refrain to except of the s
said defendant all the premises & undertakings in the said
covenant in the said plantiffs declaration mentioned touching
the hours to be finished and covered chincked and daubed and
floor laid & Chimney in the said Plantiffs decleration mentioned.
And the said defendant in fact futher says and avers that he
has well and truly guaranteed unto the said Plaintiff the Title to a lot in the town of Cleveland, on the public square the
lot he bought of Andrew Taylor, from every person except the
State. The said defendant further avers and says that the
said Plantiff in pursueance of said guarantee entered into the
possession of said lot unmolested and in no wise hindered or
delayed or in any other way disturbed from the use enjoyment
or profits of the same and this he is ready to verify wherefore he prays judgment if the said Plantiff his action aforesaid ought to have or maintain.

Demured to   )

                         Trewhitt, Attorney
                           for Plaintiff.

(P-74) And the said defendant for futher Plea in this behalf
says that the Plaintiff his action ought not to have and maintain because he says that the said plantiff did not demand or
request of a lot in the Town of Cleveland, the Public square,
the lot said defendant lot of Henderson Taylor with a house
to be finished and covered chincked and daubed and floor laid
and Chimney and the quarantee of Title from every Person the
State excepted and this he is ready to verify wherefor he
prays judgment &c.

                         Trewhitt, Attorney
                           for Plaintiff

     Demured to -----

State of Tennessee   )
)   Circuit Court

Bradley County   )   September Term 1837.

Thomas McCallie   )

)

   vs   )   The defendant makes oath that the
)   within release in his second plea

Edward Austin   )   plead is now causually lost and
                              out of his Power to prove to the

Court here.

                    (Edward Austin

     Sworn to & subscribed
     in open Court this the
     14th day of September
     1837

              Henry Price, Clk.

Thomas McCallie   )

)

   vs   )   And the plantiff by his attorney
)   comes and defends and for replica-

Edward Austin   )   tion to the 2nd and 3rd pleas of the
                          said defendant says he ought nottto
be barred nor prevented from maintaining his action afore
said against him the said defendant because he says that the
matters in said pleas contained in manner and form as the
same are stated and set forth are not sufficient in law to
bar and preclude the said plantiff from having or maintaining his aforesaid action against the said defendant and
(P-75) that the said plantiff is not bound by the law of the
land to answer the same and this he is ready to verify, whereupon for want of sufficiency in said second and Third pleas,
in this behalf, the said plantiff prays Judgment &c. and for
special cause of demurrer in law to the said second plea according to the form of the Statute the said plantiff shows
to the Court the following to wit:

    1st said plea does not aver that said release was under
seal. 2nd said plea does not show at what time said release
was executed but has left the same in blank. 3rd said plea
is double and the latter aver - ment thereon amount to the
general issue, for these & other causes to be assigned &c,
The said plantiff demurs as aforesaid.

              Campbell & Vandyke.

And the said defendant by attorney comes and says that his

64

said pleas by 2ndly & 3rdly, pleaded the matter & things therein contained in Manner & form as stated and set forth are sufficient in law to bar and preclude the said plantiff from having & maintaining his said action thereof against him and this he is ready to verify wherefore he prays Judgment &c.

Trewhitt, Atto. for Defendant

Covenant --

For and in consideration of one hundred dollars to me in hand paid, I transfer to Thomas McCallie a lot in the town of Cleveland on the public square, the lot I bought of Andrew Taylor with a house to be finished & covered, chunked and daubed and floor laid & Chimney, I guarantee the Title from every person except the State, in Witness my hand & seal. This 8th December, 1836.

Witness - John A. Hook   )   Edward Austin (Seal)

May Term 1837

(P-76)
Thomas McCallie   )
)
    vs   )   This day came the parties by their
)   attorneys and the plantiff by his
Edward Austin   )   attorney suffred a new suit. There-
                            fore it is considered by the Court
that the defendant go hence and recover of the plantiff the costs in this behalf expended for which execution may issue &c.

May Term 1838.

Thomas McCallie   )
)
    vs   )   Came the parties by their attorneys
Edward Austin   )   and came on the plantiff demurrer
to the second & third pleas of the defendant and after arrangement of the counsil and due deliberation of the Court It is considered by the court that the said demurrer be sustained.

August 31st, 1838,

Covenant.

Thomas McCallie   )
)
    vs   )   Came the parties by their attorneys
)   and by consent & with the consent of
Edward Austin   )

the Court this cause is continued untill the next term of
this Court.

April Term 1839

Thomas McCallie)
)
vs) Came the parties by their attorneys
) and also came a Jury of good and law-
Edward Austin) ful men, To wit: Charles Dodd, Robert Hood, Absalom Coleman, John Towns
Thomas Taylor, Joseph Billingsley, John McMinn & William Kerr,
who being elected tried and sworn to well & truly try the
issue joined between the parties upon their oath say that the
defendant hath not well & truly kept & performed his covenant
as the plantiff in declaring hath alleged and by reason of
the premises assessed the plantiff damage to Thirty six dollars & seventy cents.

It is therefore considered by the Court that the plantiff Recover of the (P-77) defendant the sum of Thirty six
dollars and seventy cents, the amount so as aforesaid assessed
by the Jury and his costs about his suit in this behalf expended and that he have execution &c.

December Term 1839.

Thomas McCallie)
)
vs) The plantiff and defendant, by prop-
) er person appear and on motion of
Edward Austin) Thomas J. Campbell, esqr. Attorney
and Joseph R. Mee, John Austin, Jesse
Mee & Alexander A. Clingan, together with the defendant confess judgment for the damages and cost in this cause. It is
therefore considered by the Court that the plantiff recover
of the said defendant and his securities the said -- Joseph
R. Mee, John Austin, Jesse Mee, and Alexander A. Clingan, the
sum of Thirty six dollars & seventy cents the amount and damages aforesaid, for which a judgment has been heretofore rendered in the Court, together with the further sum of One dollar and forty six cents intrest due on said judgment and all
costs that has accrued in this cause and the plantiff agrees
to stay the execution for the space of six months and it appearing to the Court that the said defendant has been arrested on a case in this cause and has given bond and security
to keep the prison bounds. It is therefore considered by the
Court that he go hence and be discharged therefrom.

The State   )   Gaming   ---
)
   vs   )   The grand Jury for the State appeared
)   in open Court and returned present-
Joseph Powell   )   ment against the defendant signed by
                      the whole Grand Jury which is in the
words & figures following --
To wit: State of Tennessee, Bradley County, Circuit Court
May Term eighteen hundred and thirty eight.

The grand jurors in behalf of the (P-78) State of Tennessee elected impanneled sworn and charged to enquire for
the County of Bradley aforesaid, upon their oath present
that a certain Joseph Powell late of said County (Physician)
on the first day of April in the year of our Lord one thousand eight hundred and Thirty eight, with force and arms in
the County of Bradley, aforesaid, unlawfully and play at a
certain game of hazard with cards for one dollar, good and
lawful money of the State of Tennessee and of the United
States, being then and there bet and hazarded at and upon
said game of hazard so plaid with cards as aforesaid contrary to the form of the statutes in such case made & provided and against the peace and dignity of the State.

Presentment --

The State vs Joseph Powell, found on the Testimony of John
D. Traynor, Endorsement -- Daniel Buckner, foreman of the
grand jury, Richard Dean, Amos Potts , Henry R. Swisher,
E. E. Cooper, Wm. Henry, John Mathews, John B. Cate, Wm. D.
Kelley, Joseph Davenport, Charles Cate, A. H. Teener, S. H.
Prowell

      Capias   )   State of Tennessee

              To the Sheriff of Bradley County Greeting:

You are hereby commanded to take the body of Joseph Powell
if to be found in your County; and him safely keep, so that
you have him before the Judge of our Circuit Court at a Court
to be held for Bradley County at the Court house in Cleveland on the 4th Monday of December next, Third day of said
Term. Then and there to answer a charge the State exhibited
against him by presentment for unlawful gaming And have you
then and there this wit: Witness Henry Price, Clerk of
our said Court at office, in Cleveland the 4th Monday of
August, A. D. 1838.

                Henry Price, Clerk.

(P-79)   Sheriff's Return

    Came to hand and executed by arresting the within defendant

and appearance bond taken this 2nd Oct. 1838.

                    James Lauderdale, Sheriff

Appearance Bond   -----

State of Tennessee, Bradley County

     I, James Lauderdale, sheriff in and for the County afore-
said, having on the 2nd day of October, 1838, arrested the
body of Joseph Powell, by virtue of a capias issued from the
Circuit Court of said County, commanding me to take the body
of said Joseph Powell to answer a charge of the State exhibited against him by presentment for unlawful gaming: Therefore the said Joseph Powell, defendant, together with Andrew
Forester, and Isaac Day, security before me James Lauderdale
sheriff as aforesaid, acknowledged themselves jointly and
severaly indebted to the State of Tennessee in the sum of
Two hundred & fifty dollars each to be levied of their goods
& Chattles, lands and Tenements respectively; but to be void
on conditions the said Joseph Powell, shall make his personal appearance before the Judge of the Circuit Court, at a
Court to be held for the County aforesaid at the Court house
in Cleveland on the first Wednesday after the 4th Monday of
December, next, to answer the charge of the State exhibited
against him as aforesaid. And then and there abide by perform and satisfy the Judgment of said Court thereon to be
rendered. And not depart the Court without leave.

                    J. Powell (Seal)

                    Isaac Day (Seal)

                    A . B. Foster (Seal)

The State   )
)
     vs   )   Gaming
)
Joseph Powell   )   Came the attorney General who prose-
                        cutes for the State and by consent
and with the assent of the Court, This cause is continued
untill the next term as on affidavit of the defendant, whereupon came Thomas Foster and (P-30) Isaac Day, into open Court
and acknowledged themselves indebted to the State of Tennessee, in the sum of Five hundred dollars to be levied of their
respective goods and chattles lands & Tenements but to be
void on condition that the said defendant Joseph Powell shall
make his personal appearance at the next Term of the Circuit
Court held for Bradley County at the Court house in Cleveland on the fourth Monday of April, next and on Wednesday of
the same Term.

Then and there to answer a charge of the State Exhibited against him for unlawful gameing and not depart the Court without leave.

Wednesday 24th April, 1839

State   )
)
 vs   ) The attorney general who prosecutes
) for the State comes and also came the
Joseph Powell) defendant by his attorney, John F.
         Gillespie, who submits to the Judgment
of the Court.

   It is therefore considered by the Court that the defendant for the offence charged in the presentment pay to the State of Tennessee, a fine of Ten dollars and pay the costs of this prosecution, and thereupon Andrew B. Foster, and Isaac Day Acknowledged them selves the sureties of the said Joseph Powell for the fine and costs aforesaid.

   It is therefore further considered by the Court that the State of Tennessee recover of the said Joseph Powell, Andrew B. Foster, and Isaac Day, his securities jointly the fine and costs aforesaid, and the execution issue.

State of Tennessee)
)
Bradley County   ) To any lawful officer to execute
           and return; you are hereby com-
manded to summon Andrew Russell, to appear before me or some other justice of the Peace for said County to answer the complaint of Josiah S. Price, (P-81) in a plea of debt due by open account under warrant. Herein fail not.

   Given under my hand and seal

   This 25th day of December 1837.

        William Forester (Seal)
        Justice of the Peace

Witness for Defendant) Came to hand 25 -- executed and
Abagail Grant   ) returned for trial 26 before
N. W. Hays   ) Isaac Day, Esqr. A. ^{T} Rodgers,
John Grant   ) Const. The within warrant was
Levi Carter   ) returned before me on 26th Dec-
) ember, 1837, and put off on oath
Debt $16.00)

Cost	1.50	)
Witness	1.00	)
Is. Day	25	)

of the Defendant untill -- of same and
I found judgment in favor of the plantiff for sixteen dollars & costs which
is two dollars & seventy five cents.

This 30th December, 1838.

Isaac Day

(P-82)   Appeal Bond.

Know all men by these presents that we Andrew Russell &
Levi Trewhitt, are held and firmly bound unto Josiah Price
in the penal sum of Thirty seven dollars for the payment of
which we bind ourselves Jointly severally and firmly by these
presents signed with our names and sealed with our seals and
dated 1st day of January 1838. The condition of the above
obligation is such whereas that the said Josiah S. Price on
the 30th of December, 1837, recovred against the said Andrew
Russell, for the sum of sixteen dollars debt and two dollars
and fifty cents costs before Isaac Day Esqr. justice of the
peace from which judgment the said Andrew Russell has prayed
an appeal from before the said justice to the next Term of
the Circuit Court to be held for the County of Bradley.

Now if the said Andrew Russell shall and truly prosecute
with effect said appeal or in case he is cast to pay & satisfy whatever judgment shall be awarded by said Court, then the
above obligation shall be null & void, otherwise to remain
in full force and effect,

Andrew Russell   (Seal)

Levi Trewhitt   (Seal)

Isaac Day
    Justice of the Peace

State of Tennessee   )

To the honorable Charles Keith, Esqr. one of the
Circuit Judges of law in and for the State of Tennessee

The petition of Andrew Russell, a citizen of the County,*
by his attorney Levi Trewhitt, your petitioner humbly states
and shows to your honor that a certain Josiah Price, lately
sued the said Andrew Russell, and cited him to Trial (P-83)
before Isaac Day, Esqr. justice of the Peace for the County
Aforesaid who on the 30th day of December, 1837, rendered a
judgment against Russell for the sum of sixteen dollars debt
and two dollars & seventy five cents costs, from which said *
Russell prayed an appeal to the Circuit Court to be held for
the County of Bradley on the 2nd Monday of January 1838. which
*of Bradley and State of Tennessee aforesaid, *judgment said

is now at this time in session, said Russell, on the 1st day
of January 1838, executed the appeal bond with sufficient
security for said appeal which said bond said justice accepted and promised to regularly grant said appeal and to
file said appeal in Court on the first day of said Term now
in session which he failed sot to do but was applied on the
second day to wit: Yesterday for said papers and was then
informed by said Justice that he had delivered them to Mr.
Beard, Attorney for the appealee of his examination which
he supposed was then filed in the Clerks office your petitioner never got to examine said papers untill this morning
when he discovered there was no entry of the prayr & grant-
ing said appeal in said papers, your petitioner then went
to said justice who there under his hand and seal granted
said appeal in formal manner which your petitioner filed
with said papers, but when the record of this Morning was
read he found there the appealee or his attorney had taken
said papers into Court & had them docketed and struck from
the docket and the Clerk ordered to hand said papers to said
justice but your petitioner upon exhibiting said formal grant
of said appeal by the justice took a rule of Court to reinstate
the cause upon docket which rule your petitioner believes will
have to be discharged because the Justice signed, said formal
prayer and grant for said appeal after the time allowed him
by law to do the same in your petitioner states and shows to
your honor that not withstanding said rule to reinstate said
cause on docket said papers has been delivered to the justice
who now has them in possession and your petitioner has no
doubt & believes that an execution has or will be immediate-
ly issued against said Russell, your petitioner states and s
shows to your honor that he is informed & believes that said
Russell, is sick and unable to get to Court to see to his
cause, your petitioner states & shows that he is unable to
swear as to the merrits of said Russell's defence to said
action futher than he is advised and believes said advice to
be true, To wit: That Mrs. Grant sent her son to said Price
and got two barrels of flour for her own use and not for said
Russell, that said Russell, acted as agent of said Grant, who
is now absent to in the "General Assembly" when said son of
Grant got the flour for his Mother, who had sent him, said
Price asked him for the money when the son of Grant replied
that Russell would settle for the same, said Russell offered
to settle the account as the Agent of Grant provided said
Price would discount the debt he Price owed to Grant but not
otherwise as the flour was not got by Russell nor by his order but the order of Mrs. Grant & by her son; said Price
brought suit against said Russell upon the above statement
of facts and obtained judgment from which he prayed an appeal
and executed an appeal bond as aforesaid your petitioner prays
writs of certiorari & supercedias to remove said Cause into
the next term of the Circuit Court to be held for Bradley
County and states that this is the first application for writs
aforesaid the premises considered and the writs granted as in

duty bound.

Your Petitioner will ever pray

Andrew Russell
By his attorney
Levi Trewhitt

State of Tennessee   )
)
Bradley County   )   This day personally appeared
                      before me Charles F. Keith, Esqr,
one of the Circuit judges of the Courts of law in and for the
State of Tennessee --

Levi Trewhitt the foregoing petitioner and made oath
that the facts stated in the foregoing petition as of his
own knowledge are true & those that are not stated of his
own knowledge he believeing to be true subscribed and sworn
to, Levi Trewhitt, before me this 10th day of
January 1838.

Charles F. Keith, Judge &c.

State of Tennessee   )   To the Clerk of the Circuit Court
)   of Bradley County in the Third Cir-
Bradley County   )   cuit in the state aforesaid let
                      writs of certiorari & superceidias
issue agreeable to the prayr of the foregoing petition on the
petitioner giveing bond and security as directed by law.

Given under my hand this 10th day of January, 1838.

Charles F. Keith, Judge of the
3rd Judicial Circuit in the
State of Tennessee.

Josiah S. Price   )
)
    vs   )   Certiorari Bond.
)
Andrew Russell   )   Know all men by these presents that
                   we Andrew Russell & Levi Trewhitt
of Bradley County and State of Tennessee, our heirs executors
administrators or assigns in the sum of Thirty seven dollars
& fifty - To be void on condition that the said Andrew Russell shall prosecute with effect a writ of Certiorari, by
him this day obtained to remove the proceedings of a suit
wherein Josiah Price plantiff and Andrew Russell defendant
from before Isaac Day Esqr. Justice of the peace into our
Circuit Court for the County of Bradley, or in case of failure (P86) therein preform whatever judgment shall be awarded

and rendered by said Court in said Cause; or in case said certiorari shall be dismissed by said Court for informality or want of substance or for any other cause pay and satisfy such judgment as the justic Isaac Day shall have given against him.

Witness our hands & seals -- this 10th day of January 1838.

Andrew Russell (Seal)
By Attorney Levi Trewhitt

Levi Trewhitt (Seal)

State of Tennessee, to all Sheriffs and Constables of the County of Bradley, Greeting: You are hereby commanded that from all other proceedings upon a judgment for the sum of Sixteen dollars debt & 2.75 cents cost obtained by Josiah Price against Andrew Russell before Isaac Day one of the justices of the peace in and for Bradley County you desist and altogether --- as the same by our writ of certiorari is removed to our Circuit Court for the County of Bradley and you are hereby also commanded to notify the said Josiah Price to appear before the Judge of our said Circuit Court at a Court to be held for the County aforesaid at the Court house in Cleveland on the 2nd Monday of May next, Then and there to prosecute the said suit and have you them there this writ Witness - Henry Price, Clerk of our said Court, at office in Cleveland, the 2nd Monday of January 1838, and of American Independence the 62.

Henry Price, Clerk.

Executed & returned to the Circuit ---

A. T. Rodgers, Const.

State of Tennessee, To Isaac Day justice of the Peace for the County of Bradley, Greeting: Whereas Josiah Price, lately before you, Isaac Day, complained of and recovered a judgment against Andrew Russell, and we for certain reasons being desirous that the record of that suit should be certified to us do hereby (P-87) command you to enclose all the papers relative to said suit under your hand and seal distinctly and plainly together with this writ and Transmit the same to a Court to be held by the Judge of the Circuit Court of law for the County of Bradley at the Court house in Cleveland on the second Monday in May next in order that our said Court may do therein what of right and according to law ought to be done. Witness Henry Price, Clerk, of our said Court at office in Cleveland, the second Monday of January 1838, and of American Independence 62

Henry Price, Clerk.

I hereby enclose all the papers and proceedings in said cause according to the mandate of the within writ,

Given under my hand the 11th day of January 1838.

Isaac Day
Justice of the Peace

Tuesday January the 9th 1838.

Josiah Price	)	
	)	
vs	)	For reasons appearing to the Court:
	)	Ordered that this cause be stricken
Andrew Russell	)	from the Docket.

Wednesday, January 11th, 1838.

Josiah S. Price	)	
	)	
	)	
vs	)	This day came the defendant by his
	)	Attorney and upon his motion a rule
Andrew Russell	)	is granted to show cause why this
*		cause should be reinstated upon docket.

(P-88)   Tuesday the 23rd day of April 1839.

Josiah S. Price	)	
	)	
	)	
vs	)	Came the parties by their attorneys
	)	and also came a jury of good and law-
Andrew Russell	)	ful men, To wit: David Anderson, Rob-
		ert A. Farmer, Isaac Smith, William

Thornburgh, Preston Parker, George M. Hayns, James Donohoo, John Pharris, William Blair, John Hannah, William Coker & Samuel Samples, who being elected tried and sworn to well and truly try the matters in dispute between the parties on their oath say the find for the defendant. It is therefore consid- ered by the Court that the defendant go hence without day and recover of the plantiff his costs about his suit in this behalf expended and that he have his executiom.

Know all men by these presents that we David Harland, & S. Jarnagin are jointly and severally held and firmly bound unto John Hardwick & Charles Hardwick, in the Penal sum of Two hundred and fifty dollars to be void on condition that the said David Helderbrand will with effect prosecute a suit *Josiah Price vs Andrew Russell, this day came the defendant by his attorney and withdrew his rule to reinstate the cause upon docket

by action of debt which he this day commenced against the
said John Hardwick and Charles Hardwick in the Circuit Court
for Bradley County or in case of failure of such prosecution
pay and satisfy all costs and damages as may be awarded
against him by our said Court witness our hands and seals
this the 9th day of April, 1838.

Teste --

Henry Price   David Helderbrand (Seal)

                               S. Jarnagin (Seal)

State of Tennessee, To the Sheriff of Bradley County, Greeting:

You are hereby commanded to summon John Hardwick and Charles
F. Hardwick, if to be found in your County to appear before
our Circuit Court to be holden for the (P-89) County of Bradley at the Court house in Cleveland on the 2nd Monday of May
next, To answer David Harland of a plea that they under ----
him the sum of Two hundred & Sixty seven dollars Thirty & one
fourth cents, which to him they owe and from him unjustly detain to his damage one hundred dollars, Herein fail not, and
have you them there This writ Witness - Henry Price, Clerk
of our said Court, at office in Cleveland on the 2nd Monday
of January 1838, and of American Independence the 62.

                    Henry Price, Clerk

State of Tennessee   )
)
Bradley County   )   Circuit Court, May Term 1838.

    David Harlan, by attorney, complains of John Hardwick
& Charles F. Hardwick who has been summond by the Sheriff
of Bradley County, of a Plea that they render unto him the
sum of Two hundred and sixty seven dollars & thirty and one
fourth cents which to him they owe and from him unjustly
detained.

    For that whereas heretofore to wit: on the Twentieth day
of September in the year of our Lord One Thousand eight hundred & Thirty six at to wit: in the County aforesaid the
said defendants made executed and delivered their certain
promissory note in writing to the said plantiff signed by
the Style and description of J. & C. F. Hardwick, meaning
thereby John Hardwick & Charles F. Hardwick the date aforesaid and which promissory note is now here to the Court shown
wherein & whereby the said defendants promised on ot before
the first day of November 1837. They promised to pay to the
said plantiff or bearer the sum of two hundred & sixty seven
dollars & Thirty one & fourth cents for value received, yet
the said defendants not regarding their said promises and

undertaking so made(P-90) as aforesaid hath not paid the
aforesaid sum of Two hundred and sixty seven dollars and
Thirty and one fourth cents at any Time before or since then
said promossory notes fell due, or any part thereof to the
said plantiff, or any other person although often thereunto
requested so to do at to wit: in the County aforesaid but
to pay the same or any part thereof, the said defendants
hath hitherto wholy neglected and refused and still doth neglect and refuse to pay the same or any part thereof to the
damage of the said plantiff one hundred dollars and therefore
he sues and hath pledges to prosecute.

                        Jarnagan & Bradford
                        Atts. for Plantiff

State of Tennessee   )   Circuit Court
)
Bradley County   )   May Term 1838

                        Daavid Harland   )
)
                            vs   Debt.   )
)
                        John Hardwick & Charles F. Hardwick)

     The said defendants comes into open Court and craves
oyers of the writing declared upon in the plantiffs declaration mentioned which is read to them in the following words
and figures to wit: On or before the 1st day of November
1837, We promise to pay David Harland, or bearer, Two hundred and sixty seven dollars & thirty one & ¼ cts. for value
received. This 20th September 1836.

Witness --   J. & C. F. Hardwick
W. H. White

     All of which being read and heard by said defendants the
said defendants for plea say that the said plantiff, his
action aforesaid ought to have and maintain because they
say that they have well and truly paid said sum of Two hundred and sixty seven dollars & thirty and one fourth cents
to the ---(P-91) said plantiff upon the day the same fell
due, and that they pray may be inquired of by the County.

                        Levi Trewhitt, Att. for Defts.
And the Plantiff
doth the like.

                        Jarnagan & Bradford, for Platff.

          April Term , 1839

David Harland   )
)
  vs   ) Came the parties by their attorneys
) and also came a Jury of good and
John Hardwick &   ) lawful men to wit: Peter McKinley,
Charles Hardwick) James Butram, Joshua Guin, John B.
                  Caney, Samuel Merrit, John Kennedy,
James Sloan, James Britton, Uriah Shipley, James Haggard,
James C. Areheart, John Borden, who being elected tried and
sworn to well and truly try the issue joined between the
parties on their oath do say they find the defendant hath
not paid the debt in the Plantiffs declaration mentioned
and assess the plantiff damages by reason of the detention
thereof to Twenty four dollars.

It is therefore considered by the Court that the plantiff
recover of the defendant the sum of two hundred & sixty seven
dollars & Thirty one and one fourth cents, the amount of debt
in declaration mentioned together with the further sum of Twenty four dollars damages as aforesaid by the jury and his costs
about his suit in this behalf expended and that he ha ve his
execution.

(P-92)   ----- Bond -----

Know all men by these presents that we William French
and S. Jarnagan, are jointly and severally held and firmly
bound unto John Goodner in the penal sum of Two hundred
and fifty dollars to be void on condition that the said
William French will with effect prosecute a suit by action
of debt which he this day commenced against the said John
Goodner in the Circuit Court for Bradley County or in case
of failure of such prosecution pay and satisfy all costs
and damages as may be awarded against him by our said Court
Witness our hands and seals, This 7th day of April 1838.

William French (Seal)

S. Jarnegan (Seal)

State of Tennessee, To the Sheriff of Bradley County, Greeting:

You are hereby commanded to summons John Goodner if to be found
in your County to appear before our Circuit Court to be holden
for the County of Bradley, at the Court house in Cleveland
on the 2nd Monday of May, next, to answer complaint Campbell Wallace, William B. French, Hugh L. McClung & Ebenezer

Alexander Merchants & partners in Trade, Trading under the
partnership name of Wallace, French and Company, of plea
that he render unto them the sum of Three hundred nine dollars
& Thirty cents which to them he owes and from them unjustly
detains to their damage one hundred and fifty dollars Herein
fail not, and have you them there This writ Witness ---
Henry Price, Clerk of our said Court, at office in Cleveland
the 2nd Monday of January 1838, and of American
Independence the 62.

         Came to hand the 7th April, and executed the same day.

                         James Lauderdale

                            Sheriff.

(P-93)   Circuit Court May Term 1838

State of Tennessee, Bradley County,

     Campbell Wallace, William B. French, Hugh L. McClung &
Ebenezer Alexander, Merchants and Partners in Trade, Trading
under the partnership name of Wallace, French & Co. by attorney complains of John Goodner who being summond by the Sheriff to answer the said plantiffs in a Plea that he render
unto them the sum of Three hundred and nine dollars & Thirty
cents, which to them he owes and from them unjustly detains
For that whereas heretofore to wit: On the Seventh day of
August 1837 at To wit: in the County of Bradley the said defendant made executed and delivered to the said plantiff his
certain promissory note or writing obligatory, signed with
his own proper name and sealed with his seal and which is
now here to the court shown wherein and whereby four months
from the date (meaning the date of said promissory note or
writing obligatory) he promised to pay the said plantiff
under the partnership name of Wallace, French & Co. the said
sum of three hundred and nine dollars & Thirty cents, yet
never the less the said defendant not regarding his said
promise and undertaking has not as yet paid to the said
plantiffs the said sum of Three hundred & nine dollars &
Thirty cents or any part thereof altho often requested so to
do to wit: to pay the same has hither to failed and refused
and still continues to refuse to the damage of said plantiffs
One hundred & fifty dollars wherefore they sue and have pledges &c.

                         Clark, Atto. for Plff.

State of Tennessee, Bradley County

         Circuit Court, May Term 1838

Campbell Wallace, William B. French, Hugh L. McClung &

Ebenezer Alexander is debt - John Goodner, The defendants Attorney comes into open Court and craves oyer of the promissory note declared upon in plantiffs declaration which is made to him in the following words and figures To wit: Dollars 309.30 Four months after date I promise to pay Wallace, French & Co. Three hundred and nine dollars & Thirty cents (P-94) value recieved.

Witness my hand & seal August 7th, 1837.

John Goodner (Seal)

Which being read and heard by said defendant. the said defendant by attorney for plea says that the said Plaintiff's their action afore said ought not to have and maintain because he says that he well and truly paid to the said Plantiffs the sum of Three hundred & nine dolla rs and Thirty cents, upon the day it fell due and this he prays may be inquired of by the County.

Levi Trewhitt

Atto for Deft.

And to Pla ntiff also Clerk, Atto. for Plff.	))	
Campbell Wallace	)	Came the pa rties by their attor-
William B. French	)	neys and also came a Jury of good
Hugh L. McClung &	)	and lawful men to wit: Peter Mc-
Ebenezer Alexander	)	Kinley James Britton, Joshua

Guinn, John B. Coxey, Samuel Merritt, John Sloan, J. Butram, Uriah Shipley, James Haggard, James C. Airheart and John Borden, who being elected tried and sworn to

vs

John Goodner

well and truly the issue between the parties on their oath do say that the defendant hath not paid the debt in the plantiffs declaration mentioned and by reason of the detention thereof assess the plantiffs damage to twenty four dollars and seventy two cents.

It is therefore considered by the Court that the plantiff recover of the defendant the sum of three hundred & nine dollars & Thirty cents the amount of the debt in the declaration mentioned together with the futher sum of twenty four dollars and seventy two cents. The damages aforesaid assessed by the Jury and his cost about his suit in this behalf expended and that he have his execution.

(P-95)   January Term 1837.

```
The State        )
                 )
   vs            )    This day the grand jurors appeared in
                 )    open Court with a bill of indictment
John Carter      )    against the defendant for an assault
                      endorsed by Samuel Howard their fore-
```
man a true bill, which is in the words and figures follow-
ing to Wit: State of Tennessee Bradley County, Circuit
Court January term eighteen hundred and thirty seven.

The grand Jurors in behalf of the State of Tennessee
elected empanneled sworn and charged to enquire for the
County of Bradley, aforesaid upon their oath present that a
certain John Carter, late of said County laborer, on the
seventh day of October, in the year of our Lord one Thousand eight hundred and Thirty six, with force and arms in
the County of Bradley aforesaid an assault did make in and
upon the body of Jesse Poe, then and there being in the
peace of the State to the great damage of the said Jesse
Poe, to the wit: example of all others in like case offending and against the Peace and dignity of the State.

```
   Endorsed to wit:               )    Samuel Frazier
                                  )       Attorney General
The State vs John Carter          )    for the 3rd District
   Jesse Poe, Prosecutor          )
```

Witness for the State sworn in open Court and sent before the grand Jury,

January 12th, 1836

                              Henry Price, Clerk

   A true Bill   Samuel Howard, foreman of the grand
                          Jury. Capias

State of Tennessee, To the Sheriff of Bradley County, Greeting:

We command you to take the body of John Carter if in your
county to be found and him safely keep so that you have him
before the Judge of our Circuit Court to be holden for the
County of Bradley at the Court house in the town of Cleveland
on the first Tuesday after the 2nd Monday of May next to answer a charge of the State exhibited against him by presentment for an assault. Herein fail not, and have them there
this writ.

Witness Henry Price, Clerk of said Court, (P-96) at
office in Cleveland, the 2nd Monday of January, 1837, and
of American Independence 61.

                              Henry Price, Clerk.

Came to hand 30th of January 1837.

Executed 22nd of April by me 1837.

A. A. Clingan, Sheriff

State

vs   Indictment assault & battery.

John Carter   )   This day came the State, by her Attorney
                    general and the defendant in proper per-
son who being charged upon the bill of indictment for plea
says he is not guilty & for his trial puts himself upon the
County and the attorney doth the like,an_d thereupon came
the following Jury good and lawful men to wit: John Kincannon Bartley Benson, Richard Mcfall, John Oneil, John B. Lane
William Parram, Robert Williams, Andrew Coffman, William
Westmoreland, William Night, John McGee & William Wooden,
who having been duly summond tried and sworn the truth to
speak upon the issue joined in this cause upon their oath
aforesaid do say that the defendant is guilty in manner and
form as charged in the bill of indictment.

State   )
)
 vs   )   Came the state by her attorney General
)   and on his motion and affidavit read
John Carter)   for a new trial.

    It is ordered by the Court that notice be served upon
Jesse Poe, and Samuel Dunn, requiring them to appear instantly in Court and show cause why an attatch should not be issued against them for contempt of the Court in said cause.
May 12th 1837.

State   )
)
 vs   )   This day came the State by her attorney
)   genreal and the defendant in proper per-
John Carter)   son and by consent the rule for a new
                  trial is continued until the next term -
Ahd thereupon came the said defendant and acknowledged himself indebted to the State of Tennessee in the sum of two
hundred & fifty dollars to be levied of his goods & chattles
lands (P-97) and Tenements to the use of the State yet to be
void on condition that the said defendant make his personal
appearance before the Judge of the next Circuit Court to be
held for the County of Bradley, at the Court house in the

town of Cleveland on the first day after the second Monday
of September next, and in and before said Court answer a
charge of the State exhibited against him by an indictment
for an assault and not depart the court without leave and
thereupon Levi Carter, into open Court and acknowledged him
self indebted to the State of Tennessee in the sum of Two
hundred and fifty dollars to be levied of his goods and chattles lands & Tenements but to be void on condition that said
defendant appear at the next term of this Court and on Tuesday of said Term; at a Court to be held for the County of
Bradley at the Court house in Cleveland on the 2nd Monday of
September, next to answer a charge to be exhibited against
him by the State and not depart the Court without leave.

----- September 1837 -----

State)) vs)) John Carter)	This day came the State by her Attorney General, and the defendant in proper person and thereupon came on for argument the rule entered in this cause for a new

trial. And upon sufficient reasons appearing to the Court
the verdict is set aside and a new trial is granted in this
cause.

State)) vs)) John Carter)	Defendant appeared in open Court and acknowledged himself indebted to the State of Tennessee in the sum of two hundred & fifty dollars to be levied

of his goods and Chattles, lands and Tenements to the use
of the state yet to be void on condition that he make his
personal appearance before the Judge of our next Circuit
Court, to be held for the County of Bradley at the Court
house in Cleveland on the first Tuesday after the 2nd (P-98)
Monday in January next in and before said Court answer a
charge of the State exhibited against him by indictment for
an assault and not depart the Court without leave; and thereupon came John D. Taynor and acknowledged himself indebted
to the State of Tennessee in the sum of Two hundred and fifty dollars to be levied of his goods and chattles lands and
tenements to the use of the State, yet to be void on condition that the defendant Carter make his peronal appearance
before the Judge of our next Circuit Court to be held for the
County of Bradley at the Court house in Cleveland on the
first Tuesday after the second Monday of January next and in
and before said Court answer a charge of the State exhibited
against him for an assault and not depart the Court without
leave.

January the 9th, 1838.

```
State          )
               )
    vs         )          On affidavit of the defendant ordered
               )          that the Court be continued until the
John Carter    )          next term of this Court and thereupon
                          came the defendant into open Court and
```
acknowledged himself indebted to the State of Tennessee in
the sum of two hundred & fifty dollars to be levied of his
goods and chattles lands and tenements void on condition
that the said defendant make his personal appearance before the
honable Circuit Court for Bradley County at the Court house in
the town of Cleveland, on Tuesday after the second Monday in
May next and answer a charge of the State - exhibited against
him for an assault and do not depart without leave of said
Court.

Whereupon came John D. Traynor, into open Court and acknowledged himself indebted to the state of Tennessee in the
sum of two hundred and fifty dollars to be levied of his goods
and chattles lands and tenements to the use of the state, yet
to be void cn conditions (P-99) that the defendant Carter,
make his personal appearance before the Judge of our Circuit
Court to be held for the County of Bradley at the Court house
in Cleveland on the first Tuesday after the second Monday of
January next, and in & before said Court answer a charge of
the State exhibited against him for an assault and not depart
the Court without leave.

Monday May 14th, 1838

```
The State       )
                )
   vs assault   )          Came the attorney general who prosecutes
                )          for the State and the defendant in proper
John Carter     )          person and by consent of the parties and
                           with the assent of the Court, this cause
```
is continued as on affidavit of the defendant and thereupon
cause the defendant together with John D. Traynor his security and acknowledged them selves jointly and severly indebted
to the State of Tennessee in the sum of Two hundred dollars
to be levied of their respective goods and chattles lands
and tenements but to be void on condition that John Carter
make his personal appearance before the Judge of our Circuit
 Court to be held for the County of Bradley at the Court house
in Cleveland on the fourth Monday of August next then and there
to answer a charge of the State exhibited against him for an
assault and not depart the Court without leave.

August 29th, 1838.

The State   )
)
 vs an assault) Came the Attorney general who prose-
) cutes for the State and the defendant
John Carter   ) in proper person & on affidavit of
           the defendant this cause is contin-
ued and thereupon came Joseph Donohoo, together with the defendant and acknowledged themselves jointly and severely indebted to the State of Tennessee in the sum of two - (P-100)
hundred dollars each to be levied of their respective goods
and chattles lands and tenements to the use of the State but
to be void on condition that John Carter make his personal
appearance before the Judge of our Circuit Court to be held
in the town of Cleveland on the first Wednesday*next and there
& then answer to a charge of the State exhibited against for
an assault, and not depart the Court without leave.
*after the fourth Monday of December
  December 29th, 1838.

The State   )
)
 vs   ) Came the defendant and John D. Traynor
) into open Court and acknowledged thems
John Carter   ) selves severally indebted to the State
           of Tennessee in the sum of Two hundred
& fifty dollars each to be levied on their respective goods
and Chattles lands and tenements to the use of the State but
to be void on condition that the said John Carter shall
make his personal appearance at the next Term of the Circuit
Court to be held for the County of Bradley at the Court house
in Cleveland on the 4th Monday of April next and on Wednesday
of said Term, then and there to answer a charge of the State
exhibited against him for an assault and notdepart the Court
without leave.

  April Term 1839.

 State Assault)
)
 vs   ) Came the attorney general who prosecutes
) for the State and the defendant in his
John Carter   ) proper person who being charged upon
           this bill of indictment for an assault
for plea says he is not guilty, and for his trial puts himself upon the County and the Attorney General doth the like
and thereupon came a jury of good and (P-101)*men to wit:
George M. Haynes, John Borden, James Britton, James Haggard,
Isaac Smith, John W. Kennedy, John Fitzgerald, Robert Shields,
George Reed, William Triplett, Levi Spencer, and Frederick S.
Williams, who being elected tried and sworn to well and truly
try the issue of travis in this cause upon their oaths do
say that the defendant is not guilty of the assault as charged
in said bill. *lawful

It is therefore considered by the Court that the defendant go hence without day and that the Clerk tax the legal
in this cause and certify the same to the County Court for
inspection and allowance.

Friday, August 31st, 1838

The State   )
)
    vs   )   Came the grand jury into open
)   Court and returned with them a
Charles K. Gillespie   )   present against Charles K. Gil-
                                      lespi, for unlawful gaming signed
by all of said grand jury, which is in the words & figures
following to wit: State of Tennessee, Bradley County, Circuit Court August Term eighteen hundred & thirty eight.

The grand jurors in behalf of the State of Tennessee, elected empanneled sworn and charged to enquire for the body of
the County of Bradley aforesaid, upon their oath present that
a certain Charles K. Gillespie, late of said County, labourer
on the first day of August, in the year of our Lord One thousand eight hundred & thirty eight with force and arms in the
County of Bradley, aforesaid, unlawfully did gamble and play
at a certain game of hazzard with cards for twelve & one half
cents good and lawful money of the State of Tennessee, then
and there being bet on hazard so plaid with cards as aforesaid
contrary to the form of the (P-102) statutes in such case made
and provided and against the Peace and dignity of the State
Endorsed to wit:

State   )
)
    vs   )   Found on the testimony of John
)   M. Gifford, Foreman, John Austin
Charles K. Gillespie   )   William ----, Guilford Gattin,
                                      Wm. Thornburgh, N. Barksdale,
James Shaddle, John McNair, J. A. Fletcher, Thomas McCarty,
Peter W. Nash, John Simmons, John Chambers, & Benjamin Maury.

Friday August 31st, 1838.

The State   )
)
    vs   )   Came the defendant Charles K. Gil-
)   lespie into open Court and ac-
Charles K. Gillespie   )   knowledged himself indebted to
                                      the State of Tennessee in the sum
of Two hundred and fifty dollars, to be levied of his goods
& chattles, lands & Tenements but to be void on

condition that he make his personal appearance at the next
term of the Circuit Court to be held for the County of Bradley at the Court house in the town of Cleveland on the first
Wednesday after the fourth Monday of December, next, to answer a charge of the State exhibited against him for unlawful
gameing and not depart the Court without leave, and thereupon came Joseph W. McMillan and acknowledged him self indebted to the State of Tennessee in th sum of two hundred and
fifty dollars to be levied of his goods and chattles lands
& tenements to the use of the State but to be void on condition that Charles W. Gillespie, make his personal appearance
at the next term of the Circuit Court to be held for the County of Bradley, at the Court house in the Town of Cleveland
on the first Monday of December, next, (P-103) and on the first
Wednesday of the Term then and there to answer a charge of the
State exhibited against him for unlawful gameing and not depart the Court without leave.

December Term, 1838

State   )
)
   vs   )   This day came Alexander H. Keith
)   and acknowledged himself indebted
Charles K. Gillespie   )   to the State of Tennessee, in the
                                    sum of Two hundred and fifty dollars
                                    to be levied of his goods and
Chattles lands and tenements to the use of the State yet to be
void on condition that the defendant make his personal appearance before the Judge of our next Circuit Court to be held for
the County of Bradley at the Court house in the town of Cleveland on the 4th Monday of April next and on Wednesday of said
Term in and before said Court, answer a charge of the State
exhibited against for unlawful gameing and not depart the Court
without leave.

                    April Term, 1839.

The State   )
)
   vs   )   Came the Attorney General who
)   prosecutes for the State and
Charles K. Gillespie   )   the defendant by his attorney
                                    James F. Bradford, cannot deny
say that he is guilty as charged in the presentment, and submits to the judgment of the Court.

     It is therefore considered by the court that the defend-
ant for the offence charged in said presentment do forfeit
and to the State of Tennessee a fine of Ten dollars and that
he pay the cost of this prosecution and thereupon the said

James F. Bradford, acknowledged himself the surety of the said Charles K. Gillespie, for the payment of the fine and costs aforesaid.

It is further considered by the Court that the State recover of the said Charles K. Gillespie and James F. Bradford Jointly the fine and costs aforesaid and that execution issue &c.

(P-104)

September Term
1837

The State	)	
	)	
vs	)	This day the grand Jury returned
	)	into open Court a presentment
William Gillian &	)	against the defendants for open
Julia Ann Mays	)	and notorious lewdness signed
		by said grand Jurors, which pre-

sentment is in the words & figures following to wit: State of Tennessee, Bradley County -

Circuit Court September Term, eighteen hundred and thirty seven.

The Grand jurors in behalf of the State of Tennessee, elected empanneld sworn and charged to enquire for the body of the County of Bradley aforesaid upon their oath present that a certain William Gillean late of said County labouer and certain Julia Ann Mays, late of said County, Spinster, being scandelous and evil disposed persons and deviseing contriveing and intending the Morals of the good citizens of the State both male & female to debauch and corrupt on the first day of September in the year of our Lord one thousand Eight hundred and thirty seven, and for a long space of time before that day to wit: Twelve months and more with force and arms in the County of Bradley, aforesaid unlawfully wickedly, openly, notoriously leudly and scandously did have illicit casual sexual intercourse together without being legally married, and the jurors aforesaid upon their oath aforesaid do further present that the said William Gillian and Julia Ann Mays, being such persons as aforesaid on the first day of September in the year of our Lord one thousand eight hundred and Thirty seven, and for a long time before that day - with force and arms in the County of Bradley, aforesaid, unlawfully wickedly (P-105) openly, notoriously lewdly and scandalously, did bed together as husband and wife without being legally married to the great scandal and subversion of religion and good order to the either subversion and ruin of the rites of matrimony to the manifest corruption of good morals. To the evil example of all others

in the like case offending and against the peace and dignity of the State.

Endorsed to wit:

The State vs William Gillian, Julia Ann Mays found on the
information of Isaac Smith, Thomas W. Back, John Igoe, Tip-
ton O. Wood, Solomon Sunny, William Champon, Francis Starr
James Ecay, Elbert E. Cooper, Thomas W. Back, John Hodges,
William M. Kerr, Isaac Smith, John Allen & Hamilton Mc-
Clatchey

Capias,

State of Tennessee, To the Sheriff of Bradley County, Greeting:
You are hereby commanded to take the bodys of William Gillian
& Julia Ann Mays, if to be found in your County and them saf-
ly keep. So that you have them before the Judge of our Circuit Court at a Court to be held for Bradley County, at the
Court house in Cleveland on the 2nd Monday of January next,
then and there to answer a charge of the State exhibited
against them by an indictment for notorious lewdness, and
have you then and there this Writ, Witness Henry Price, Clerk
of our said Court at office in Cleveland the 2nd Monday of
September A. D. 1837.

Henry Price, Clerk.

Executed   William Gillian, Julia Ann Mays, the 14th
December, 1837,

Wm. Rogers, D. S.

(P-106) ---- Lewdness ----

The State   )
)
   vs   )   As on affidavit of the defendant
)   this cause is continued untill the
William Gillean &   )   next term of this Court and there-
Julian Ann Mays   )   upon cause the defendant together
                            with John Hess & Daniel Clark
their securities and acknowledged themselves indebted to the
State in the sum of two hundred and fifty dollars each, to
be levied of each of their goods and chattles lands and Tenements void on condition that the said defendants make their
personal appearance before the honorable Circuit Court for
Bradley County at the Court house in the town of Cleveland
on the first Tuesday after the second Monday in May next and
answer the charge of the State exhibited against them for
lewdness ~~exhibited against them for lewdness~~ and do not depart the Court with out leave.

May Term, 1838

The State   )
)
    vs   )   In this came the Attorney General
)   who prosecutes for the State and
William Gillean &   )   by leave of the Court the forfeiture
JuliarAnn Mays   )   taken against the defendant at this
                          term of the Court is set aside and
by consent of the parties this cause is continued untill next
Term of this court: Thereupon came into Court William Gillean
and Elijah Mays and acknowledged themselves indebted jointly
and severally to the State of Tennessee in the Sum of five
hundred dollars to be levied of their respective goods and
chattles lands and tenements to the use of the State of Tennessee, yet to be void on condition that the said defendant
William Gillean shall make his personal appearance before
the Judge of our Circuit Court to be held for the County of
Bradley at the Court house in Cleveland on the first Wednesday after the fourth Monday of (P-107) August next, then and
there to answer a charge of the State exhibited against him
for lewdness, and not depart the Court without leave.

    August Term 1838.

The State   )
)
    vs   )   Came the attorney General who pro-
)   secutes for the State and this cause
William Gillean &   )   is continued on affidavit of Isaac
Julia Ann Mays   )   Smith and thereupon came Enoch Wil-
                          son together with the defendant who
acknowledged themselves indebted jointly and severally to the
State of Tennessee in the Sum of Two hundred and fifty dollars
each to be levied of their respective goods and chattles lands
and tenements but to be void on condition that the said William Gillean and Julia Ann Mays make their personal appearance
before the Judge of the Circuit Court at a Court to be held
for the County of Bradley at the Court house in Cleveland
on the first Wednesday after the fourth Monday in December,
next, then & there to answer a charge of the State exhibited
against them for lewdness, and not depart the Court without
leave.

    December Term 1838

The State   )
)
    vs   )   This day came Hiram Grimmet into
)   open Court and acknowledged himself
William Gillean &   )   indebted to the State of Tennessee
Julia Ann Mays   )   in the sum of two hundred and fifty

dollars to be levied of his goods and chattles lands and tenements but to be void on condition that the defendants William Gillean do make their personal appearance at the next term of the Circuit Court to be held for the County of Bradley at the Court house in Cleveland on the fourth Monday of April next and on Wednesday of said Term then and there to answer a charge of The State exhibited against them and not depart the Court without leave.

(P-108)   April Term 1839.

State   )
)
     vs   )   By order of the Court this cause
)   is dismissed from the docket.
William Gillean   )

The attorney general came to prosecute on behalf of the State and the defendant in proper person and the attorney General dismissed this cause and thereupon William Gillean one of the defendants confess judgment for the costs of the prosecution.

It is therefore considered by the Court that the State of Tennessee recover of the said William Gillean, the costs of this prosecution so as aforesaid confessed and that execution issue.

---- May Term 1838 ----

The State   )
)
     vs   )   The grand Jurors for the State appeared
)   in open Court and returned a bill of
John W. Kennedy   )   indictment against the defendant en-
William Wooden   )   dorsed thereon a true bill by Daniel
John Hays   )   Buckner, there foreman, which indict-
Thomas Wooden   )   ment is in the words and figures fol-
                             lowing to wit: State of Tennessee,
Bradley County Circuit Court, May Term - Eighteen hundred & Thirty eight.

The grand jurors, in behalf of the State of Tennessee elected empannelled sworn and charged to enquire for the County of Bradley, aforesaid, upon their oaths present that a Certain John W. Kennedy, William Wooden, John Hays, & Thomas Wooden, late of said County, labourers, unlawfully rououtsly and virtually assembled them selves together to break the peace of the State and being so assembled on the sixth day of

February, Eighteen hundred & Thirty eight, with force and
arms in the County of Bradley aforesaid, unlawfully ----
& virtously did make an assault in & upon the body of one
Stephen Scott, then and there being in the peace of the
State, and did there (P-109) and then unlawfully routous-
ly and riotously beat bruise wound and ill treat the said
Stephen Scott and the Jurors aforesaid upon their oath aforesaid do futher present that the said John W. Kennedy, William Wooden, John Hays, and Thomas Wooden on the said sixth
day of February eighteen hundred and Thirty Eight, with force
and Arms in the County of Bradley aforesaid did make an assault in and upon the body of the said Stephen Scott, and did
then and there beat bruise wound and ill treat the said Steph-
en Scott to the great damage of the said Stephen Scott to the
evil example of all others in like case offending and against
the Peace and dignity of the State.

> Samuel Frazier, Attorney General
> for the 3rd solicitorial district

Endorsement --

The State vs John W. Kennedy, William Wooden, John Hays, &
Thomas Wooden, Stephen Scott, *Hamilton Carter, James Finley,
James Farmer and Elias Price, Witnesses for the State, sworn
in open Court and sent before the grand jury. *prosecutor

May 16th, 1838.   Henry Price, Clerk

A true bill Daniel Buckner, forman of the grand Jury.

Capias ---

State of Tennessee, To the Sheriff of Bradley County, Greeting:
you are hereby commanded to take the bodys of William Wooden
& Thomas Wooden if to be found in your County and them safely keep so that you have them before the judge of our Circuit
Court at a Court to be held for Bradley County at the Court
house in Cleveland on the fourth Monday of August next on the
3 day, then and there to answer the charge of the State exhibited against them by an indictment for an affray, and have
you them and there.

This writ Witness, Henry Price, Clerk of our said Court
at office in Cleveland the 2nd Monday of May A. D. 1838.

> Henry Price, Clerk

(P-110) Came to hand 29th May, 1838, and executed on the
body of Wm. Wooden, and Thomas Wooden, this 4th June 1838.

> James Lauderdale, Sheriff.

Appearance Bond

State of Tennessee, Bradley County,

I, James Lauderdale, Sheriff in and for the County aforesaid
having on the 4th day of June 1838, arrested the body of Wm.
Woodden, and Thomas Wooden, by virtue of a capias, issued from
the Circuit Court of said County, commanding me to take the
body of said Wm. Woodden & Thomas Wooden to answer a charge of
the State exhibited against them by indictment for an affray
Thereupon the said Wm. Wooden and Thomas Wooden, defendant
together with Samuel Lane & I. B. Russell, security before me
James Lauderdale, Sheriff as aforesaid acknowledged themselves
jointly and severally indebted to the State of Tennessee, in
the sum of two hundred and fifty dollars each to be levied of
their goods and chattles lands and tenements respectively;
but to be void on condition, the said Wm. Wooden and Thomas
Wooden, shall make their personal appearance before the Judge
of the Circuit Court, at a Court to be held for the County
aforesaid at the Court house in Cleveland on the first Wednesday after the 4th Monday of August next, To answer the said
charge of the State exhibited against them as aforesaid, and
then and there abide by, perform and satisfy the Judgment of
said Court thereon to be rendered, and not depart the Court
without leave.

		his
James Lauderdale	)	Wm X Woodden (Seal)
Sheriff	)	mark
		his
		Thomas X Woodden (Seal)
		mark
		Samuel Lane (Seal)
August Term, 1838		I. B. Russell (Seal)

The State   )
)
)
   vs   )   Came the attorney General who prosecutes
)   for the State and the defendant in proper
Wm. Woodden   )   person, and this cause is continued on af-
                     fidavit of the defendant and thereupon
came the defendant William Wooden, and (P-111) Samuel Lane
his security who acknowledged themselves jointly and severally to be indebted to the State of Tennessee in the sum
of two hundred and fifty dollars to be levied of their respective goods and chattles lands and tenements to be void
on condition that the defendant Wm. Woodden, makes his personal appearance before the Judge of the Circuit Court to
be held for the County of Bradley, at the court house in the
Town of Cleveland, on the first Wednesday after the fourth
Monday of December, next, then and there to answer a charge
of the State exhibitied against him by indictment and not
depart the Court without leave.

The State   )
)
    vs   )   Came the attorney general who prose-
)   cutes for the State and this cause is
Thomas Woodden   )   continued on affidavit of William Wood-
                              den and thereupon came Samuel Lane and
William Wooden, into open Court and acknowledged themselves
jointly and severally to be indebted to the State of Tennessee in the sum of Two hundred and fifty dollars to be void
on condition that Thomas Woodden, make his personal appearance before the Judge of the Circuit Court at a Court to be
held for the County of Bradley at the Court house in the
town of Cleveland on the first Wednesday of the fourth Monday in December next, then and there answer a charge of the
State exhibited against him and not depart the Court without leave.

        December Term, 1838

State   )
)
    vs. affray   )   Came the Attorney general who prose-
)   cutes for the State and by consent
William Woodden   )   of the parties and with the Consent of
                              the Court this cause is continued un-
till the next Term of this Court, Whereupon came the defendant and John Beaty, into open Court and acknowledged themselves
indebted to the State of Tennessee that is to say the said defendant William Woodden in the sum of Two hundred and fifty
dollars and the said John Beaty in the sum of (P-112) Two
hundred and fifty dollars each to be levied of their respective goods and Chattles, lands & Tenements but to be void
on condition that the said William Woodden do make his personal appearance at the next term of this Circuit Court to
be held for the County of Bradley at the Court house in
Cleveland, on the 4th Monday of April, next and on Wednesday
of said Term, then and there to answer a charge of the State
exhibited against him for an affray, and not depart the Court
without leave.

The State   )
)
    vs affray   )   Came the Attorney general as well as
)   the defendant in proper person and
Thomas Woodden   )   by consent and with assent of the
                              Court this cause is continued, Where-
upon came the defendant Thomas Wooden, and John Beaty, into
open Court and severally acknowledged themselves indebted to
the State of Tennessee in the sum of Two hundred and fifty
dollars each to be levied of their respective goods and Chattles lands and tenements but to be void on condition that the
said Thomas Woodden do make his personal appearance at the

next term of the Circuit Court to be held for the County of
Bradley at the Court house in Cleveland on the 4th Monday
of April next and on Wednesday of said Term then and there
to answer a charge of the State exhibited against him for
and assault and battery and not depart the Court without
leave.

April Term, 1839.

The State	)	
	)	
vs	)	Came the attorney general who pros-
		ecutes for the State as well as the
William Woodden &	)	defendants in their own proper per-
Thomas Woodden	)	sons who being charged upon the bill
		of indictment says they are not

guilty as charged in said bill and for their trial put themselves upon the County and the attorney general doth the like
whereupon came a Jury of good and (P-113) lawful men to wit:
Charles Dodd, Robert Hood, John Towns, Joseph Billingsly,
John McMinn, William Parrian, John Carter, James Webb, John
Ervin, William McMillan, Vernon Coe,& Uriah Shipley, who being elected tried and sworn and charged the truth to speak
in the premises upon their oath do say that the defendants
are not guilty in Manner and form as charged in said bill of
indictment, It is therefore considered by the Court that the
defendants go hence without day and that the Clerk tax the cost
in this behalf expended and certify the same to the County
Court for inspection and allowance.

September, 1837.

The State	)	
	)	
vs	)	This day the Grand Jury returned into *a
	)	bill of indictment against the defendant
John Rains	)	for an assault and battery endorsed by
		their foreman a true bill: which in-

dictment is in the words and figures following to wit:
State of Tennessee, Bradley County, Circuit Court, September Term Eighteen hundred and Thirty seven. *Court

The grand Jurors in behalf of the State of Tennessee
elected impanneled sworn and charged to enquire for the
County of Bradley aforesaid, upon their oath present that
a certain John Rains late of said County, labourer, on the
7th day of March in the year of our Lord one Thousand eight
hundred and Thirty seven with force and arms in the County
of Bradley, aforesaid and assault did make in and upon the
body of one Jesse Wimpy, then and there being in the peace
of the State and did then and there beat bruise wound and

ill treat him the said Jesse Wimpy to the great damage of the said Jesse Wimpy to the evil example of all others in like case offending and against the peace and dignity of the State.

                        Samuel Frazier, Attorney
                        General for 3 solicitorial
                        districts

(P-114)   Endorsement ---

The State   )
)
    vs   )   Jesse Wimpy, prosecutor,
)   Isaac Wimpy, a Witness for the State
John Rains   )   sworn in open Court and sent before the
                       grand Jury, September 14th, 1837.

                   Henry Price, Clerk

    A true bill John Igoe, foreman of the grand Jury.

    ----- Capias -----

State of Tennessee, to the Sheriff of Bradley County, Greeting: You are hereby commanded to take the body of John Rains, instantly if to be found in your County and him safely keep , so that you have him before the Judge of our Circuit Court now sitting for Bradley County, at the Court house in Cleveland then and there to answer the charge of the State exhibited against him by an indictment for an assault and battery;

    And have you them and there this wit: Witness - Henry Price, Clerk of our said Court, at office in Cleveland the 2nd Monday of January A. D. 1838.

                        Henry Price
                        Clerk.

    Endorsement, Came to hand 9th of January, 1838. The within is executed by --- this 9th of January, 1838.

                   A. A. Clingan, Shff.

State   )
)
    vs   )   On affidavit of the defendant ordered by
)   the Court that this cause be continued
John Rains   )   until the next term of this Court. Where-
                       upon came the defendant with William Fores-
ter his security and severally acknowledged themselves to owe and be indebted to the State of Tennessee in the sum of two hundred and fifty dollars each to be levied of each of their

goods and chattles, lands and tenements void on condition
that the said defendant John Rains ~~make the said defendant~~
~~John Rains,~~ make his personal appearance before the honorable
Circuit Court for Bradley County at the Court house in the
town of Cleveland on the first Tuesday after the second Monday of May next and answer a charge of the (P-115) State,
against him for an assault and battery and do not depart the
Court with out leave of said Court and came Jesse Wimpy, Prosecutor in said cause into Court in his proper person, and acknowledged himself to owe and be indebted to the State of
Tennessee, in the sum of Two hundred and fifty dollars to be
levied of his goods & Chattles, lands & tenements void on condition that he make his personal appearance before the honorable
Circuit Court for Bradley County at the Court house in the town
of Cleveland on the first Tuesday after the second Monday in
May next and prosecute and give evidence in the case, The
State against John Rains, and do not depart without leave of
said Court.

May Term 1838.

The State   )
)
   vs   )   Came the State by her attorney General
)   and the defendant in proper person and by
John Rains   )   consent of the parties and with the as-
                      sent of the Court this cause is continued
on affidavit of the defendant untill the next term and thereupon came the defendant together with William Forester his
security and acknowledged themselves jointly and severally
indebted to the State of Tennessee in the sum of Two hundred
and fifty dollars to be levied of their goods and chattles
lands and tenements, but to be void on condition that the
defendant John Rains make his personal appearance before
the judge of our Circuit Court to be held for the County of
Bradley at the Court house in the town of Cleveland on the
first Tuesday after the fourth Monday of August, next, then
to answer a charge of the State by an indictment for an assault and battery and not depart the Court without leave.

August Term 1838

(P-116)   August Term, 1838.

State   )
)
   vs A. B.   )   Came the State by her attorney General
)   who prosecutes on behalf of the State
John Rains   )   and the defendant in proper person and
                      this cause is continued on affidavit of
the defendant.

Came Jesse Wimpy, and acknowledged him self indebted to the State of Tennessee, in the sum of Two hundred and fifty dollars to be levied of his goods & chattles, lands and tenements to be void on condition that he make his personal appearance before the Judge of a Circuit Court at a Court to be held for the County of Bradley at the Court house in Cleveland on the first Wednesday after the fourth Monday of December next to prosecute and give evidence on behalf of the State against John Rains .

The State   )
)
  vs   ) Came John Rains the defendant in his own
) proper person and acknowledged himself
John Rains   ) indebted to the State of Tennessee in
                the Sum of Two hundred and fifty dollars
to be levied of his goods and chattles, lands and Tenements but to be void on condition that he make his personal appearance before the Judge of the Circuit Court to be held for Bradley County at the Court house in the town of Cleveland on the first Wednesday after the fourth Monday of December next, then & there to answer a charge of the State exhibited against him by an indictment for an assault and battery, and not depart the Court without leave. And thereupon came Hiram Grimmet and John Griggsly, and acknowledged themselves jointly and severally indebted to the State of Tennessee in the sum of two hundred and fifty dollars to be levied of their respective goods and chattles land and Tenements, but to be void on condition that the*make his personal appearance before the Judge of the Circuit Court to be held for Bradley County at the Court house in the town of Cleveland, on the first Wednesday after the fourth Monday of December next, then & there to answer a charge of the State exhibited against him by an indictment for an assault and not depart the Court without leave. *defendant

December Term, 1838

The State   )
)
  vs A. & B.) Came the attorney General as well as the
) defendant in proper person and by consent
John Rains   ) and with the assent of the Court this
                cause is continued.

Whereupon came the defendant and William Woodden & Thomas Woodden into open Court and acknowledged themselves indebted to the State of Tennessee that is to say the said defendant in the sum of two hundred and fifty dollars and the said William & Thomas Woodden in the sum of two hundred and fifty dollars to be levied of their respective goods, and chattles, lands and tenements but to be void on condition that John Rains makes his personal appearance at the

next term of the Circuit Court to be held for the County of
Bradley at the Court house in Cleveland on the 4th Monday of
April next, and on Wednesday of said term then and to answer
a charge of the State exhibited against him for an assault
and battery and not depart the Court without leave,and thereupon came Jesse Wimpy into open Court and acknowledged himself
indebted to the State of Tennessee in the sum of Two hundred
and fifty dollars to be levied of his goods and chattles lands
and tenements but to be void on condition that he makes his personal appearance at the next term of the Circuit Court to be held
for the County of Bradley at the Court house in Cleveland on the
4th Monday of April next and on Wednesday of said then and there
to prosecute and give evidence on behalf of the State against
John Rains for an assault and battery and not depart the Court
without leave. (P-118) Circuit Court, April Term, 1839

The State	)	The attorney General came to prosecute on be-
	)	half of the State and also comes the defend-
vs	)	ant in proper person, who being charged upon
	)	the bill of indictment for plea says he is not
John Rains	)	guilty and for his trial puts himself upon the
		County and the attorney General doth the like

and thereupon came a jury of good and lawful men to wit: John
Fitzgerald, Robert H. Allison, Isaac Glenden, William Clark,John
Copelin, Benjamin Hawkins, Robert Shields, James Weaver,James
Massey, Frederick,S. Williams,James Haggard & John F. Larrison
who being elected tried and sworn to well and truly try the issue joined between the State of Tennessee and the defendant on
their oaths say the defendant is guilty as charged in the bill of
indictment. It is therefore considered by the Court that the defendant for the offence charged in said bill of indictment do forfeit and pay to the State of Tennessee a fine of Twenty five dollars, and pay the costs of this prosecution and remain in custody of the Sheriff till the fine and costs are paid or secured
to be paid and that he give security in the sum of five hundred
dollars to be of good behavior towards all the good citizens of
the State of Tennessee and especially to one Jesse Wimpy,for the
space of Twelve months ensueing and thereupon came into Court
here, William Forester,William Woodden, Alexander Webb,and Thomas Woodden, who acknowledged themselves the securities of the
said John Rains for the payment of the fine and costs aforesaid.

It is further considered by the Court that the State of Tennessee recover of the said John Rains,William Forester,William
Woodden,Alexander Webb,and Thomas Woodden,the fine and costs
aforesaid and that execution issue,and also said John Rains,
William Forester, William Woodden, Alexander Webb,and Thomas
Woodden,jointly and severally acknowledged (P-119) themselves
indebted to the State of Tennessee in the sum of five hundred
dollars to be levied of their respective goods and chattles,
lands and tenements but to be void if the said John Rains shall
for the space of twelve months next ensueing be of good behavior towards all the good

citizens of the State of Tennessee and especially toward one
Jesse Wimpy.

Circuit Court August Term, 1839.

Came the attorney General who prosecutes for the State
and by leave of the Court enters a note ---- in this cause
and thereupon came John Rains, defendant, together with
William Forester & Alexander A. Clingan, and acknowledged
and say that judgment may be entered against them jointly
for the cost of this suit.

It is therefore considered by the Court that the State
of Tennessee recover of the said John Rains defendant and
the said William Forester & Alexander A. Clingan, securities
the cost of this suit. ~~To confessed as aforesaid for which
execution may issue.~~ So confessed as aforesaid for which
execution may issue.

Circuit Court, May Term, 1838.

The State)
)
  vs Gaming) The grand Jury appeared in open
) Court and returned a presentment
John F. Gillespie) against the defendant signed by
) all of said grand Jury. Which
presentment is in the words & figures following to wit:

  State of Tennessee, Bradley County
  Circuit Court, May Term, eighteen
    hundred and Thirty Eight.

The grand Jurors in behalf of the State of Tennessee,
elected empanneled charged and sworn to enquire for the
County of Bradley, aforesaid upon their oath present that
John F. Gillespie late of said County, Attorney at law, on
the sixteenth day of April in the year of our Lord one thousand eight hundred and Thirty eight, with force and arms in
the County of Bradley, aforesaid, unlawfully did gamble and
play at a Certain game (P-120) of hazard with cards for fifty
cents good and lawful money of the State of Tennessee, and
of the United States. There and then being bet on hazard at
and upon said game of hazard so plaid with cards aforesaid
contrary to the form of the Statutes in such case made and
provided and against the peace and dignity of the State.

Endorsement ---

The State vs John F. Gillespie

Found on the information of John Suggart, Daniel Buckner, foreman of the grand Jury, John I. Cate, Charles Cate, Richard Dean, Sampson H. Prowell, Amos Potts, John Mathews, Wm. Henry, Henry Swisher, Wm. D. Kelly, Joseph Deavenport, Elbert E. Cooper, A. H. Teener,

Capias ---

State of Tennessee, Bradley County.

To the Sheriff of Bradley County, Greeting: You are hereby commanded to take the body of John F. Gillespie, if to be found in your County, and him safely keep. So you have him before the Judge of our Circuit Court at a Court to be held for Bradley County at the Court house in Cleveland, on the 4th Monday of August next, then and there to answer a charge of the State exhibited against him by indictment for unlawful gameing.

And have you then and there this writ, Witness -- Henry Price, Clerk of our said Court, at office in Cleveland, the 2nd Monday of May, A. D. 1838.

Henry Price, Clerk.

Came to hand the said day issued and executed on the boddy of John F. Gillespie.

The 31st May 1838.

James Lauderdale,

Sheriff.

Appearance Bond ---

State of Tennessee, Bradley County.

I, James Lauderdale, Sheriff, in and for the County aforesaid, having on this 31st day of May 1838, arrested the body of John F. Gillespie, by virtue of a Capias -- isued from the Circuit Court of said County, commanding me to take the body of said John F. Gillespie, to answer a charge of the State exhibited against him by indictment*the said John F. Gillespie, is defendant, together with Nicholas S. Peck, security, before me, James Lauderdale, Sheriff as aforesaid acknowledged themselves jointly and severally indebted to the State of Tennessee, in the sum of five hundred dollars each, *for unlawful gambling, thereupon

to be levied of their goods and chattles lands and Tenements respectively; but to be void on condition the said
John F. Gillespie, shall make his personal appearance before the said Judge of the Circuit Court, at a Court to be
held for the County aforesaid at the Court house in Cleveland on the first Wednesday after the 4th Monday of August
next to answer the charge of the State exhibited against him
as aforesaid and then and there abide by, perform and satisfy the Judgment of said Court thereon to be rendered, and
not depart the Court without leave.

John Lauderdale   )   John F. Gillespie (Seal)
    Shff.   )   Nicholas S. Peck (Seal)

Circuit Court August Term
1838 ---

State   )
)
   vs Gaming   )   Came the State by her attorney
)   General, who prosecutes on behalf
John F. Gillespie   )   of the State and the defendant,
                                in proper person, and this cause is
continued as on affidavit of the defendant and there upon
came the defendant John F. Gillespie, and Levi Trewhitt,
Charles K. Gillespie, his securities, and acknowledged themselves indebted Jointly and severally to the State of Tennessee in the sum of two hundred and fifty dollars to be (P-122)
levied of the respective goods and Chattles, land, and tenements, to be levied on conditions that defendant John F. Gillespie, make his personal appearance to the Judge of the Circuit Court, at a Court to be held for the County of Bradley
at the Court house in the town of Cleveland on the first
Wednesday after the fourth Monday in December, next. Then
and there to answer a charge of the State exhibited against
him by presentment and not depart the Court without leave.

Circuit Court D. T. 1838

The State   )
)
   vs Gaming   )   Came the defendant and James F.
)   Bradford into open court and ac-
John F. Gillespie   )   knowledged themselves severally
                                indebted to the State of Tennes-
see in the sum of two hundred and fifty dollars, each to
be levied of their respective goods and chattles lands and
tenements but to be void on condition that the said John
F. Gillespie shall make his personal appearance at the next
term of the Circuit Court to be held at the Court house in
Cleveland on the 4th Monday of April next, and on Wednesday
of said Term, then and there to answer a charge of the State

exhibited against him for unlawful gameing and not depart
the Court without leave.

Circuit Court April 1839

The State   )
)
   vs Gaming   )   The attorney General comes who
)   prosecutes for the State and also
John F. Gillespie)   comes the defendant in proper person
                          who can not but say he is guilty
as charged in the presentment and submits to the Judgment of
the Court.

It is therefore considered by the Court the defendant for *
the said presentment do pay to the State (P-123) of Tennessee a fine of Ten dollars and pay the costs of this prosecution and thereupon came into Court here Levi Trewhitt, and
James F. Bradford and acknowledged them selves the sureties
of the said John F. Gillespie, for the fine and cost aforesaid. *the offence charged in

It is therefore further considered by the Court that the
State of Tennessee, recover of the said John F. Gillespie
and Levi Trewhitt, and James F. Bradford the fine and costs
aforesaid and the execution issue.

August Term 1838.

The State   )
)
   vs   )   The grand Jury appeared in open Court
)   and returned and indictment for an as-
Jemimah Reed   )   sault and battery in this case indorsed
                         thereon a true bill, by John Austin, their
                         foreman, which indictment is in the words
and figures following to wit:

State of Tennessee, Bradley County, Circuit Court, August Term Eighteen hundred and thirty Eight.

The grand jurors, in behalf of the State of Tennessee
elected impanneled sworn and charged to inquire for the County of Bradley aforesaid, upon their oath present present
that a certain Jemimah Reed late of said County, Spinster,
on the twenty fifth day of June in the year of our Lord one

Thousand eight hundred & Thirty Eight, with force and arms
in the County of Bradley aforesaid did make an assault in
and upon the body of one Samuel Dunn, and did there and then
beat, bruise, wound and ill treat the said Samuel Dunn, to the
great damage of the said Samuel Dunn, to the evil example
of all others in like case offending and against the peace
and dignity of the State.

Samuel Frazier,

Attorney General for the 3
Solicitorial District.

(P-124)
(P- Endorsement -----

The State vs Jemimah Reed, Samuel Dunn, Prosecutor,
Samuel Dunn, Emoly Fisher, Witnesses for the State sworn in
open court and sent before the grand Jury August 31st, 1838.

Henry Price, Clerk

Capias -----

State of Tennessee, To the Sheriff of Bradley County, Greeting: You are hereby commanded to take the body of Jemimah
Reed, if to be found in your County and her safley keep
so that you have her before the Judge of our Circuit Court
at a Court to be held for Bradley County at the Court house
in Cleveland on the 4 Monday of December next on the 3 day
of said Term then and there to answer the charge of the
State exhibited against her by an indictment for an assault
and battery, and have you then and there this Writ:

Witness Henry Price, Clerk of our said Court
at office in Cleveland the 4 - Monday of August A. D. 1838.

Henry Price, Clerk,
Came to hand 5th October 1838. Executed by arresting the
within defendant and bond taken for his appearance, this 6th
6th day of October 1838.

John Hughes,

Dept. Sheriff.

Appearance Bond,

We, Jemimah Reed, Abraham Barnes, & Mark Black, acknowledge our selves indebted to the State of Tennessee that is to

say; Jemimah Reed, in the sum of two hundred and fifty dollars the said Abraham Barnes, and Mark Black, in the sum of One hundred and twenty five dollars, to be levied of respective goods & chattles lands and tenements but to be void on condition that the said Jemimah Reed shall make her personal appearance before the Judge of the Circuit Court to be held at the Court house in Cleveland on the -- Wednesday after the 4 - Monday of December next, then and there to (P-125) answer a charge of the State exhibited against her by indictment for an assault and battery and abide by , perform and satisfy the Judgment of the Court or surrender her self to prison and not depart thence without leave first had & obtained.

        Given under hands and seals this 6th October 1838.
                                       her
    John Hughs,   )   Jemimah X Reed (Seal)
)   mark
      Dept Shff.   )
)   Abraham Barnes (Seal)
)   Mark Black (Seal)

        December Term 1838.

The State   )
)
    vs A. & B.   )   Came the attorney General who prose-
)   cutes for the State and by consent
Jemima Reed   )   and with the assent of the Court
                         this cause is continued as on affidavit
of the defendant, whereupon came George Reed into open Court
and acknowledged him self indebted to the State of Tennessee
in the sum of two hundred & fifty dollars to be levied of his
goods and chattles, lands and Tenements but to be void on condition that the said Jemima Reed do not make her personal appearance at the next term of the Circuit Court to be held for
the County of Bradley at the Court house in Cleveland on the
4th Monday of April next and on Wednesday of said Term then
and there to answer a charge of the State exhibited against
her for an assault and battery and not depart the Court with
out leave.

        April Term, 1839

State   )
)
    vs   )   The attorney general who prosecutes on
)   behalf of the State comes and also comes
Jemima Reed   )   the defendant in proper person and on mo-
                     tion of the attorney general and with l
leave of the Court a nolle prouqui is entered in this cause.

It is therefore considered by the Court that the defendant go hence and the Clerk tax the costs of this prosecution
and certify a complete copy thereof to the County Court of
(P-126) Bradley County for the order and allowance of said
Court.

The State   )
)
   vs   )   Came the grand Jury for the State
)   into open Court and returned a bill
Samuel Dunn   )   of indictment against Samuel Dunn
Ezekiel Dunn   )   and others for riot and assault, in-
Madison Dunn   )   dorsed thereon a true bill by John
James Mathes   )   Austin their foreman, which indict-
Harlen Mathes &   )   ment is in the words and figures
George Mathes   )   following to wit: State of Tennes-
                       see Bradley County Circuit Court
August Term eighteen hundred and thirty eight. The grand
Jurors in behalf of the State of Tennessee elected empanneled sworn and charged to enquire for the body of the County of Bradley, aforesaid, upon their oath present that Samuel Dunn, Ezekiel Dunn, Madison Dunn, James Mathews, Harlen
Mathews, and George Mathews late of said County labourers,
unlawfully --- and rioutsly assembled themselves together
to break the peace of the State of Tennessee, and being so
assembled on the second day of June in the year of our Lord
one Thousand eight hundred & Thirty eight with force and
arms in the County of Bradley, aforesaid, unlawfully rautously and rioutsly did make assault in and upon the body
of one George W. Reed then and there being in the Peace of
the State by then and there besetting the dwelling house
of him the said George W. Reed he the said George W. Reed,
there and then dwelling being and living in said dwelling
house and by them then and there strikeing, pushing and shov-
ing open the door of said dwelling house to the great damage
of the said George W. Reed, to the evil example*and against
the peace and dignity of the State.
(P-127)
And the Jurors aforesaid upon their oath aforesaid do futher
present that the said Samuel Dunn Ezekiel Dunn, Madison Dunn,
James Mathews, Harlen Mathews, and George Mathews, on the
second day of June in the year of our Lord one thousand eight
hundred & Thirty eight, with force and arms in the County of
Bradley aforesaid and assault did make in and upon the body
of the said George W. Reed, by then and there besetting the
dwelling house of him the said George W. Reed there and then
*of all others in like case offending

being living and dwelling in said dwelling house and there
and then living therein to the great damage of the said
George W. Reed, To the evil example of all others in like
case offending and against the peace and dignity of the
State.

                              Samuel Frazier, Attorney General
                                 for the 3 - Solocitorial dis-
                                 drict

        Indictment,

The State vs Samuel Dunn, Ezekiel Dunn, Madison Dunn, James
Mathews, Harlen Mathews & George Mathews, George W. Reed, prosecutor. George W. Reed, Witness for the State sworn in
open Court and sent before the grand Jury, August 27th, 1838.

                        Henry Price, Clerk,
     A true bill, John Austin, foreman of the grand jury.

        Capias --

State of Tennessee, To the Sheriff of Bradley County, Greeting:
You are hereby commanded to take the body of James M. Dunn,
if to be found in your County and him safely keep so that you
have him before the Judge of our Circuit Court, at a Court
to be held for Bradley County at the Court house in Cleveland
on the 4 - Monday of April next, and on the 3 day of said term
then and there to answer a charge of the State exhibited against
him for an assault and battery. And you then and there this
wit. Witness Henry Price, Clerk of our said Court at office in
Cleveland, the 4 - Monday of December, A. D. 1838.

                        Henry Price,

                             Clerk.

(P-128) Came to hand the 25 - January 1839, and executed by
arresting the body of James M. Dunn, on the 25th March 1839
and bail - bond Taken.

                        James A. Bates, D. Shff.

State of Tennessee, Bradley County

I, James A. Bates, Debt. Sheriff, in and for the County aforesaid - having on this day of March arrested the body of James
M. Dunn, by virtue of a Capias issued from the Circuit Court
of said County, commanding me to take the body of said James
M. Dunn, to answer a charge of the State exhibited against
him by indictment for assault and battery. Thereupon the said

James M. Dunn, defendant, together with William Lawson, security, before me James A .Bates, Dept. Sheriff as aforesaid
acknowledged themselves jointly and severally indebted to the
State of Tennessee in the sum of two hundred & fifty dollars
each to be levied of their goods and chattles, lands and tenements respectively; but to be void on condition the said
James M. Dunn, shall make his personal appearance before the
said Circuit Court at a court to be held for the County aforesaid at the Court house in Cleveland on the first Wednesday
after the 4 - Monday of April next, to answer the charge of
the State exhibited against him as aforesaid and then and
there abide by perform and satisfy the Judgment of said Court
theren rendered and not depart the Court*without leave.*thereen

    This 25th day of March, 1839.

Signed sealed   )   James M. Dunn (Seal)
and acknowledged   )
before me this 25th   )   William Lawson (Seal)
day of March   )

James A.Bates, D. Sheriff, of Bradley County.

    August Term -- 1838.

The State   )
)
   vs   )   Came the attorney General who prose-
)   cutes for the State and the defendants
Samuel Dunn   )   Samuel Dunn, Ezekial Dunn, Harlan Math-
Ezekia l Dunn   )   ews, and George (P-129) Mathews, who
Harlan Mathews   )   are the defendants in this cause and
George Mathews   )   John Mathews, and Hiram Grimett, to-
                            gether with them acknowledged them-
selves jointly and severally indebted to the State of Tennessee in the Sum of Two hundred and fifty dollars each to be
levied of their respective goods and chattles, lands and
tenements to the use of the State, but to be void on condition that the defendants Samuel Dunn, Ezekial Dunn, Harlen
Mathews and George Mathews, make their personal appearance
before the Judge of our Circuit,*now in session from day to
day and answer a charge of the State, exhibited against them
by indictment for an a riot and assault and not depart the
Court without leave.   *Court

The State   )
)
   vs   )   Came the attorney general who prose-
)   cutes for the State and the defend-
Samuel Dunn   )   ants in the proper persons who being
Ezeikel Dunn   )   charged upon the bill of indictment for
Harlan Mathews   )   a riot for plea thereto says that they
George Mathews   )   are guilty & submit to the Judgment of

the Court it is therefore considered by the Court that Samuel Dunn for such his offence he pay a fine of Ten dollars and thereupon came John Mathews with the defendant and confessed a judgment for the fine and costs aforesaid, it is therefore considered by the Court that the State of Tennessee recover of the said defendant & John Mathews, his security, the fine and costs aforesaid for which execution may issue.

The State	)	
	)	
vs	)	Came the attorney general who prosecutes for the State and the defendant
	)	
Ezekiel Dunn	)	in his proper person who haveing been charged upon the bill of indictment

and pleaded guilty submits to the judgment of the Court, it is therefore considered by the Court that he pay a fine of Five dollars, and thereupon came John Mathews, with the defendant and confessed a judgment for the fine and costs of aforesaid, it is therefore considered by the Court that the State of Tennessee recover (P-130) of the said defendant and John Mathews his security the fine and costs aforesaid for which execution may issue.

The State	)	
	)	
vs	)	Came the attorney General who prosecutes for the State and the defendant
	)	
Harlen Mathews	)	in his proper person who having been charged upon the bill of indictment

for a riot and pleaded guilty submits to the Judgment of the Court it is therefore considered by the Court that he pay a fine of five dollars and thereupon came John Mathews, with the defendent and confessed a judgment for the fine and costs aforesaid it is therefore considered by the Court that the State of Tennessee recover of the defendant and John Mathews his security, the fine and costs as aforesaid for which execution may issue.

The State	)	
	)	
vs	)	Came the attorney general who prosecutes for the State, and the defend-
	)	
George Mathews	)	in his proper person who haveing been charged upon the bill of in-

dictment for a riot and pleaded guilty submits to the judgment of the Court it is therefore considered by the Court that he pay a fine of five dollars, and there upon came John Mathews with the defendant and acknowledged a judgment for the fine

and costs aforesaid, it is therefore considered by the Court
that the State of Tennessee recover of the defendant and
John Mathews his security, the fine and cost aforesaid for
which execution may issue.

The State   )
)
    vs   )   Came the attorney general who prose-
)   cutes for the State and the defendant
James Mathews   )   in proper person and this cause is
                           continued as on affidavit of the de-
fendant and thereupon came James Mathews, the defendant and
Silas M. Wan, his security and acknowledged themselves indebted to the State of Tennessee, Jointly and severally in
the sum of two hundred (P-131) and fifty dollars, to be levied of their goods and chattles, lands and tenements to be
void on condition that the defendant James Mathews make his
personal appearance before the Judge of our Circuit Court
to be held for the County of Bradley, at the Court in the
town of Cleveland on the first Wednesday after the fourth
Monday in December next, then and there to answer a charge
of the State exhibited against him for a riot and not depart
the Court with out leave.

          Circuit Court December Term. 1838.

The State   )
)
    vs   )   Came the attorney general who prose-
)   cutes for the State as well as the de-
James Mathews   )   fendant in proper person and from suf-
                           ficient reasons disclosed in the af-
fidavit of George Reed, this is continued whereupon came
the defendant and John Mathews into open Court who severally
acknowledged themselves to be indebted to the State of Tennessee as follows, that is to say the said defendant in the
sum of two hundred and fifty dollars and the said John Mathis in the sum of two hundred and fifty dollars each to be levied of their respective goods and Chattles lands and tenements
but to be void on condition that the said James Mathews, do
not make his personal appearance at the next term of the Circuit Court to be held for the County of Bradley at the Court
house in Cleveland on the 4th Monday of April, next and on
Wednesday of said term then and there to answer a charge of
the State exhibited and not depart the Court without leave.

          April Term, 1839.
(P-132)
The State   )
)
    vs Riot   )   Came the attorney general who prosecutes

James M. Dunn &) for the State as well as the defendant
James Mathis) in their proper person who being charged
         on the bill of indictment for plea there-
to says they are not guilty and of that puts themselves upon
the County and the Attorney General doth the like and thereupon came a Jury to wit: Joseph Billingsley, Daniel Clark,
Isaac Edwards, John Ervin, Josiah Price John Towns, John Mc-
Minn, Thomas Haydon, Bales Ladd, Issac Huffaker, Benjamin
Hawkins & Levi Spencer, all good and lawful men who being elected tried and sworn to well and truly try the issue joined
between the State of Tennessee and the defendants on their
oath do say that the defendants are not guilty in manner* of
indictment.   *and form as charged in the bill

It is therefore considered by the Court that the defendants
to go hence without day and that the clerk tax the cost in
this behalf expended and certify the same to the County Court
for inspection and allowance.

_____

_____

_____

The State   )
)
 vs Tipling   ) The grand jury appeard in open
) Court and returned a presentment
Robert S. Brashears) against the defendant for keep-
           ing a Tipling house signed by
all of said grand Jury, which presentment is in the words
and figures following to wit:

State of Tennessee, Bradley County, Circuit Court

   April Term, Eighteen hundred and Thirty nine.

The grand Jurors in behalf of the State of Tennessee, empanneled sworn and charged to enquire for the County of Bradley
aforesaid upon their oaths present that a certain Robert S.
Brashears late of said County, labourer, on the second day
of March in the Year of our Lord one Thousand eight hundred
& Thirty nine, and on divers other days and times with force
and arms (P-133) in the County of Bradley aforesaid unlawfully did vend and sell by retail in quantities less than one
quart, a certain kind of spiritous liquors called whiskey,
and and other kinds of spiritous liquors to one James Long,
and to divers other persons and the Jurors aforesaid upon
their oath aforesaid do futher present that the said Robert
S. Brashears on the second day of March in the year of our
Lord one Thousand eight hundred & Thirty nine and on divers
other days with force and Arms in the County of Bradley aforesaid unlawfully did vend and sell by retail certain kind of

spiritous liquors to one James Long and to divers other persons and so the Jurors aforesaid upon their oath aforesaid do say that the said Robert S. Brashears, was then and there guilty of keeping a tipling house contrary to the form of the statutes in such case made and provided and against the peace and dignity of the State.

Presentment --

The State vs Robert S. Brashears, found on the information of James Long, Wm. Grant, James Long, E. Spriggs, Elias Hutchison, James A. Fletcher, Benjamin McCarty, J. R. Mee, Alfred Davis, John Anderson, Lewis Pearse, Joseph Seabourn, Thomas W. Back, Alex Perry.

Capias --

State of Tennessee

To the Sheriff of Bradley County, Greeting: You are hereby commanded to take the body of Robert S. Brashears, instantly, if to be found in your County, and him safely keep so that you have him before the Judge of our Circuit Court now sitting for Bradley County, at the Court house in Cleveland then and there to answer a charge of the State exhibited against him for keeping a Tipling house and have you then and there this writ,

Witness - Henry Price, Clerk of our said Court, at office in Cleveland the 4th Monday of April, A. D. 1839.

Henry Price, Clerk

(P-134)
Came to hand and executed in full this 25th day of April 1839.

James Lauderdale, Sheriff.

Circuit Court April Term 1839.

The State	)	
vs Tipling	)	Came the attorney General who prosecutes for the State as well
Robert S. Brashears	)	as the defendant, in his proper person who being charged by present-

ment for keeping a tipling house for plea thereto says that because he is guilty he will not contend but submits to the Judgment of the Court, And that for such his offence he pay a fine of one dollar and all lawful costs in this behalf expended and that execution issue accordingly.

State of Tennessee,   )   To the Sheriff or any constable
)   of said County, I command you to
Bradley County   )   summons Mark Black, and Sampson
                              Dotson, to appear before me or
some other Justice of said County, to answer the complaint
of Isaac Glandon, of a plea of Trespass with force and arms
for breaking & entering a certain cornfield, lying near Hi-
wassee River, called the Bird field, and taking and carrying
a way a quantity of corn of the value of fifty dollars.

For that the said Mark & Sampson did on the 22nd day of
Oct. 1838, in the County aforesaid then said Mark and Sampson with force and arms by themselves and servants did break
and enter the said cornfield, called the Bird field on Hi-
wassee River, of said Isaac and then and there did forcia-
bly take and carry a quantity of corn to wit: fifty bushels the property of the said Isaac of the value of fifty
dollars and then, there other wrongs done contrary to the
(P-135) peace of said State and to the damage of said Isaac
the sum of money aforesaid.

This 23rd day of October, 1838.

Wm. H. Strain (Seal)

Justice of the peace for said County

Isaac Glanden vs Mark Black, Sampson Dotson

Case in ---- Came to hand the 24th Oct. 1838, This day
summoned 4 witnesses on the behalf of the plantiff, and
also 4 of the above witnesses of the behalf of the defendant Oct. the 26th 1838, and also the 2 defendants above named
and set for trial on the 27th Oct. 1838, before B. F. Taylor,
Esqr.

Witness -   James A. Bates, D. S.

Sutton Atty. George Reed, Tobitha Black, A. Barnes , John
Reed, John Mee, all of the above witnesses summond. John
Mee, David Clark, Wm. Black, Alfred Davis, James Dotson,
resummond the 2 defendants Mark Black and Sampson Dotson
& 13 witnesses summond to appear before B. F. Taylor, Esqr.
at at his own house on the 3rd November for Bradley County
This 2nd Nov. 1838.

James A. Bates, D. Shff.

A bill of the cost accrued thereon for summoning the 2
defendants three times each 50 cents $3.00 -

For summoning 8 witnesses the first time, 8 the second
time 25 cents each Witness $4.00 for summoning 13 witnesses
the third day $3.25 this amount $10.25 Sheriffs cost, Justice

fees 25c. Witness for the plantiff Noah Fisher, Harlen Mathews, John Mathews, J.Woodall, James M. Dunn, Summond the above witnisses all this 3rd Nov. 1838.

James A. Bates, Dept. Shff.

It is considered by me that the plantiff pay all cost in this case --

2nd Nov. 1838.

Benjamin F. Taylor, Justice of the Peace.

Petition ---

To the worshipful justice of the peace in and for the County of Bradley, and State of Tennessee the petition of Isaac Glandon, a citizen of said County. (P-136) of Bradley and State aforesaid your petitioner would beg leave to show to your worships that he purchased some months ago from Ezewal H. Dunn and Harlen Mathews a certain crop of corn which was then ungathered in the County and State aforesaid and paid them a valuable consideration and took a transfer in writing of the said crop and promises which transfer vested the right to the crop in petition but not withstanding all that when petitioner attempted to take posession of and gather the corn as was his duty petitioner was prevented by one Mark Black, and Sampson Dotson, who said they purchased the land and crop from an Indian by the name of Bird, who was a native and who had no right after the 23rd day of May to any part of the Cherokee Nation petitioner would further show that Black & Dotson, took posession of the houses after Dunn, and Mathews, went there and they, Dunn & Mathews, took possession on the 2nd day of June last sometime after the Indian claim expired Dunn & Mathews went on the 3rd day of June as petitioner positively charges to ploughing and took posession of all the farm, and positively declares that there was nobody in posession of the field but themselves on the 5th day of June 1838, petitioner would futher show to you worships that with out regard to Justice the said Black and Dotson, proceeded to gather the crop which was worth $30. or more but petitioner forbid them doing so and positively stated that the crop was his but the Black & Dotson disregarding all the principles of justice and right went on and gathered and is useing the corn, petitioner in order to obtain his rights sited them before Benjamin Taylor an acting justice of the peace in and for said County of Bradley and State aforesaid on a damage warrant and had the cause tried and made all proof necessary to have gained his case but not with (P-137) standing, the proof that was had the justice disregarding all the principals of justice and rights give judgment against petitioner for the cost of suit which is something like $35. petitioner prayed an appeal from the

Judgment to the Circuit Court at Cleveland, Bradley County
Tennessee, on the day the cause was tried.
------- on the 3rd day of this month and went in time to give
security and good and sufficient security was offered but it
was not taken by the justice of the peace and so the matter
stands and without the intervention of your worships the execution ~~of your worships the execution~~ will be placed in the
hand of the deputy Sheriff, James Bates, and petitioner proer-
ty sacraficed to pay an unjust judgment and petitioner loose
his debts.

The premises considered your petitioner prays your worships to grant said petition and direct to the Clerk of the
Circuit Court of Bradley to-issud writs:of supersidias & Cer-
tiorai and directed to the justice and other to the deputy
Sheriff of said County &c. to bring the papers in the Court
of next Circuit Court at Cleveland, Bradley County Tennessee
upon a new trial may be had in the premises and justice may
be done as in duty bound he will ever pray.

This the first application for supersedias and certiorari
ever asked for in this case.

John Dunn, Justice of the peace

James Shaddle, Justice of the peace

State of Tennessee   )
)
Bradley County   )   Personally appeared before me John
                         Dunn an acting justice of the peace
in and for the County & State aforesaid Isaac Glandon, and
made oath that the matters as stated in the foregoing petition
that of his own knowledge are true, and that on the information of others are true to the best of his knowledge and be-
lief sworn to & subscribed before me this 17th day of November, 1838.

Isaac Glandon

John Dunn
 Justice of the Peace

(P-138)
To the Clerk of Bradley County, Circuit Court Tennessee, let
writs of supersedia and certiorari issue according to the
prayr of Petitioner, petitioner giving bond and security as
the law directs.

This the 17th day of November, 1838.

James Shadle, justice
of the Peace

John Dunn, justice
of the Peace

Certiorari

State of Tennessee, To Benjamin F. Taylor, one of the justices of the peace for the County of Bradley, Greeting:
Whereas Mark Black and Sampson Dotson, lately complained of
and recovered a judgment against Isaac Glandon, for cost
and all for certain reasons being desirous that the record
of that suit should be certified to us do hereby command
you to enclose all the papers relative to said suit under
your hand and seal distinctly and plainly together with
this writ and transmit the same to a Court to be held by
the judge of the Circuit Court of law and equity for the
County of Bradley at the Court house in Cleveland on the 4th
Monday in December next in order that our said Court may do
therein what of right and according to law ought to be done.

Witness - Henry Price, Clerk of our said Court, at office
in Cleveland the 4th Monday of August, A. D. 1838 and of
American Independence 63rd.

Henry Price, Clerk.

State of Tennessee, To the Sheriff and his deputy James A.
Bates, and all other officers of the County of Bradley Greeting: You are hereby commanded that from all other proceedings
upon a Judgment for costs obtained by Mark Black and Sampson
Dotson recovered against Isaac Glandon, before Benjamin F.
Taylor one of the Justices of the peade in and for Bradley
County you desist and altogether supercede as the same by our
writ of Certiorari, is removed to our circuit Court of Bradley
County and you are also hereby commanded to notify the said
Mark Black, and Sampson Dotson to appear before the judge of
our Circuit Court at a court to be held for the County aforesaid at the Court house in Cleveland, on the fourth Monday
of December next, then and there to prosecute the said suit
and have you then there this writ:

Witness, Henry Price, Clerk of our said Court at office in
Cleveland the 4th Monday of August 1838, and of American Independance 63 -

Came to hand 3rd December 1838, executed the within by
summoning Mark Black and Sampson Dotson, to appear at our
next circuit Court for December Term, 1838, to prosecute
a suit carried up by certiorari wherein a case between
I. G. Glandon, M. Black, S. Dotson, James A. Bates, D. Sheriff.

Executed in full December 18th, 1838.

James A. Bates, D. Sheriff of
Bradley County,

Circuit Court December Term, 1838.

Isaac Glandon   )

    vs   )   Certiorari

Mark Black &   )   Came the defendants by their attorney
Sampson Dotson   )   and on motion a rule is granted them
                   to shew cause why the writs of Certior-
ari - in this cause should be dismissed.

Isaac Glandon   )

    vs   )   Certirorai -

Mark Black &   )   Came the parties by their attorneys
Sampson Dotson   )   and on consideration of the rule here-
                   tofore taken upon the plantiff to shew
cause why the writs of Certirorai in this cause should not
be dismissed, it is ordered by the Court that said rule be
discharged.

April Term, 1839

(P-140)   Damage Suit.

Isaac Glandon   )

    vs   )   This day came the parties by attorneys
                   and there upon came the following Jury
Mark Black and   )   of good and lawful men to wit:
Sampson Dotson   )

                   1-Robert A. Farmer, 2-Daniel J. Staf-
ford, 3-Joseph L. Igoe, 4-Hyram Brandon, 5-John F. Larrison,
6-Isaac Smith, 7-George W. Cate, 8-Noah Fisher, 9-Robert H.
Ellison, 10-Elias Price, 11-William Park, 12-John W. Kennedy
who having been duly summoned elected tried and sworn the
truth to speak in the matter in dispute between the parties
upon their oath afore said do say that they find for the defendants it is therefore considered by the Court that the
plantiff, take nothing by his warrant but the defendants,
go hence and recover of the plantiff therein costs in this
behalf expended for which execution may issue.

August Term, 1838.

The State vs John W. Webb, Came the grand jury into open Court

and returned a presentment against John W. Webb, for unlawful gaming signed by all of said grand jury which presentment is in the words and figures following, to Wit,

State of Tennessee, Bradley County, Circuit Court, August
Term, Eighteen hundred & thirty Eight.

The grand Jurors in behalf of the State of Tennessee elected empanneld Sworn and charged to enquire for the body of
the County of Bradley, aforesaid, upon their oath present
that a Certain John W. Webb, late of said County labourer,
on the first day of August in the year of our Lord, one thousand eight hundred and thirty eight with force and Arms in
the County of Bradley, aforesaid unlawfully did gamble and
play at a certain game of hazard with cards, for twelve and
one half cents, good and lawful money of the United States,
being then and there bet and hazarded at and upon said game
of hazard so plaid with (P-141) cards as aforesaid contrary
to the form of the statutes in such case made and provided
and against the peace and dignity of the State.

Presentment - The State vs John W. Webb, Found on the information of John M. Gifford, John Austin, foreman of the
grand Jury, Peter W.Nash, Wm. Thornburgh, N. Barksdale, James
Shadle, John McNair, J. A. Fletcher, Thomas McCarty, John
Simmons, John Chambers, Benjamin Murry, William Turner, Guilford Gattin.

Capias ----

State of Tennessee, To the Sheriff of Bradley County, Greeting:
You are hereby commanded to take the body of John W. Webb, if
to be found in your County, and him safely keep, so that you
have him before the Judge of our Circuit Court at a Court
to be held for Bradley County, at the Court house in Cleveland on the 4th Monday of December next, on the 3rd day of
said Term then and there to answer a charge of the State exhibited against him by presentment for unlawful gameing and
have you then and there this writ.

Witness, Henry Price, Clerk of our said Court, at office
in Cleveland, the 4th Monday of August, A. D. 1838.

Henry Price, Clerk

Came to hand the 5th October , 1838.-

Executed the within by arresting the body of John W.
Webb, on the 19th Oct. 1838, and appearance bond taken.

James A. Bates, D. Sheriff

Appearance Bond.

State of Tennessee   )
)
Bradley County   )   We, John W. Webb, and William D.
                               Smith acknowledged our selves in-
debted to the State of Tennessee the said John W. Webb, in
the sum of two hundred and fifty dollars and W. D. Smith
in the sum of two hundred and fifty dollars, each to be void
if the said John W. Webb shall appear before the Judge of
the Circuit Court at the Court house in the town of Cleveland
in Bradley County, on the fourth Monday in December next to
answer(P-142) the State of Tennessee on a charge of unlawful
gameing and abide by such sentence as shall be pronounced
by said Court in the premises or surrender himself into custody and not depart without leave of the Court.

    This 19th day of October, 1838.

                    J. W. Webb (Seal)

                    Wm. D. Smith (Seal)

    Signed and acknowledged before me this 19th October,
1838.

                    James A. Bates, D. Sheriff

    December Term 1838.

The State   )
)
    vs Gameing   )   Came the attorney General who prosecutes
)   for the State as well as the defendant
John W. Webb   )   in proper person, who being charged on
                               the presentment says he cannot deny
but that he is guilty in Manner and form as charged therein
and submits to the Judgment of the Court.

    It is therefore considered by the Court that for such his
offence he is fined the sum of Ten dollars and that he pay
the costs of this prosecution and that he be taken by the
sheriff, and remain in Custody until the fine and cost are
paid or security given therefore.

    Whereupon came John M. Gifford into open Court and
agrees that Judgment may be entered against him Jointly
with the defendant for the fine and costs aforesaid.

    It is therefore considered by the Court that the State
of Tennessee recover of the defendant and the said John M.

Gifford his security the fine and costs aforesaid for which an execution may issue.

August Term, 1838

The State	)	
	)	
vs	)	Came the grand Jury into open
	)	Court and returned a present-
William L. Liddle	)	ment against the defendant for
		unlawful gameing signed by all of

said grand Jury, which presentment is in the words and figures following to wit:

(P-143)
State of Tennessee, Bradley County, Circuit Court, August Term Eighteen hundred and Thirty eight.

The grand Jurors in behalf of the State of Tennessee, elected empanneled sworn and charged to enquire for the body of the County of Bradley, aforesaid upon their oath present that a certain William L. Liddle, late of said County labourer on the first day of August in the year of our Lord one thousand eight hundred and Thirty eight, with force and arms in the County of Bradley aforesaid, unlawful- ly did gamble and play at a certain game of hazard with cards for twelve and one half cents, good and lawful money of the State of Tennessee, then and there being bet and hazarded at and upon said game of hazard so plaid with cards as afore- said, contrary to the form of the Statutes in such case made and provided and against the peace and dignity of the State. found on the testimony of John M. Gifford, John Austin, fore- man of the grand Jury, William Vernon, Guilford Gattin, Wm. Thornburgh, N. Barksdale, James Shadle, John McNair, J. A. Fletcher, Thomas McCarty, Peter W. Nash, John Simmons, Jm Chambers, Benjamin Murry.

Capias ----

State of Tennessee, To the Sheriff of McMinn County, Greeting: You are hereby commanded to take the body of William L. Liddle, if to be found in your County, and him safely keep so that you have him before the Judge of our Circuit Court at a Court to be held for Bradley County, at the Court house in Cleveland on the 4th Monday of December next, and on the 3rd day of said Term then and there to answer a charge of the State exhibited against him by pres- entment for unlawful gameing and have you then and there this writ, Witness - Henry Price, Clerk of our said Court at office in Cleveland the 4th Monday of August, A. D. 1838.

Henry Price, Clerk,

Came to hand the 5th Oct. 1838.

Executed on the 14th (P-144) day of December, 1838.

R. M. Newman, D. Sheriff

Appearance Bond ----

State of Tennessee, McMinn County

I, R. M. Newman, deputy Sheriff in and for said County aforesaid, having on this 14th day of December arrested the body of William L. Liddle, by virtue of a capias issued from the Circuit Court of Bradley County commanding me to take the body of said William L. Liddle to answer a charge of the State exhibited against him by presentment for unlawful gambling thereupon said William L. Liddle, defendant together-er with John C. Mullay, Security, before me R. M. Newman, deputy sheriff as aforesaid, acknowledged themselves Jointly and severally indebted to the State of Tennessee in the Sum of Two hundred and fifty dollars each to be levied of their goods and chattles, lands and tenements respectively; but to be void on condition the said William L. Liddle, shall make his personal appearance before said Circuit Court, at a Court to be held for the County aforesaid at the Court house in Cleveland on the fourth Monday of December next to answer the said Charge of the State exhibited against him as afore-said and then and there abide by perform and satisfy the judg-ment of said Court thereon to be rendered and not depart the Court without leave.

William W. Liddle,

John C. Mullay

Test
R. M. Newman

December Term ---

The State	)	
vs Gameing	)	Came the attorney General, who prosecutes for the State as well
William L. Liddle	)	as the defendant in proper person who being charged upon the pre-

sentment says he can not deny but that he is guilty in man-ner and form as charged therein and submits to the judgment

of the Court, it is therefore considered by the Court that
for such his offence he pay a fine of Ten dollars and also
pay the costs of this prosecution, and that he (P-145) be
taken by the sheriff and remain in Custody untill the fine
and costs aforesaid are paid.

Whereupon came John M. Gifford into open Court and
agrees that judgment may be entered against him jointly
with the defendant for the fine and costs.

It is therefore considered by the Court that the State
of Tennessee, recover of the said defendant and the said
John M. Gifford his security the fine and costs aforesaid
for which execution may issue.

State   )
)
    vs   )   Came the grand jury into open Court
)   and returned a presentment against
John C. Mullay   )   John C. Mullay, for unlawful gameing
                      signed by all of said grand Jury:
Which presentment is in the words and figures following to
wit: State of Tennessee, Bradley County, Circuit Court,
August Term eighteen hundred and thirty Eight.

The grand jurors in behalf of the State of Tennessee,
elected empanneled sworn and charged to enquire for the
body of the County of Bradley, aforesaid upon their oath
present that a certain John C. Mullay, late of said County
labouer, on the first day of August in the year of our Lord
One Thousand eight hundred and Thirty eight with force and
arms in the County of Bradley, aforesaid, unlawfully did
gamble and play at a certain game of hazard with cards for
Twelve and one half cents good and lawful money of the State
of Tennessee being then and there bet and hazarded at and
upon said game of hazard so plaid with cards aforesaid, contrary to the form of the statutes in such case made and provided and against the peace and dignity of the State.

Found on the testimony of John M. Gifford, Foreman,
John Austin, William Thornburgh, William Vernon, Guilford
Gatlin, N. Barksdale, James Shadle, John McNair, J. A. Fletch-
er, Thomas McCarty, Peter W. Nash (P-146) John Simmons, Jm
Chambers, Benjamin Murry.

Capias ----

State of Tennessee, To the Sheriff of McMinn County, Greeting:

You are hereby commanded to take the body of John C. Mullay
if to be found in your County - him safely keep, so that
you have him before the Judge of our Circuit Court, at a Court
to be held for Bradley County at the Court House in Cleveland
on the 4th Monday of December next, then and there to answer
a charge of the State exhibited against him by presentment
for unlawful gameing.

And have you then and there this Writ:

Witness - Henry Price, Clerk of our said Court, at office in Cleveland the 4th Monday of August A. D. 1838.

Henry Price, Clerk

Came to hand 13th, Sept, 1838.

J. T. Reed, D. Sheriff,

Executed and bond taken 13th Sept, 1838,

J. T. Reed, D. Sheriff for
McMinn County

Appearance Bond,

State of Tennessee, McMinn County, I, James T. Reed,
deputy sheriff in and for the County aforesaid, having on
this 13th day of September, 1838, arrested the body of John
C. Mullay, by virtue of a Capias issued from the Circuit Court
of Bradley County commanding me to take the body of said John
C. Mullay to answer a charge of the State exhibited against
him by presntment for unlawful gameing - Thereupon said John
C. Mullay defendant together with James S. Bridges, secubity,
before me James T. Reed, deputy sheriff, as aforesaid acknowledged themselves jointly and severally indebted to the State
of Tennessee in the sum of Two hundred and fifty dollars each
to be levied of their goods and chattles, lands and Tenements
respectively but to be void on condition the said Jonn C.
Mullay, shall make his personal appearance before our said
Court at a Court to be held for the County aforesaid at the
Court house in Cleveland, (P-147) on the fourth Monday of December, next, to answer the charge of the State exhibited against
him as aforesaid and then and there abide by perform and satisfy the judgment of said Court thereon to be rendered and not
depart the Court without leave.

John C. Mullay

James S. Bridges

Test.
J. T. Reed, D. Sheriff

December Term, 1838.

The State   )
)
 vs Gameing) Came the attorney general who prose-
) cutes for the State as well as the
John C. Mullay) defendant, in proper person who being
          charged upon the presentment says he
cannot deny but that he is guilty in manner and form as charged
therein and submits to the judgment of the Court, it is therefore considered by the Court that for such his offence he pay
a fine of ten dollars and also pay the costs of this prosecution and he be taken by the sheriff and remain in custody u
untill the fine and costs are paid or security given.

Therefore, whereupon, came John M. Gifford into open Court
and agrees that judgment may be entered against him jointly
with the defendant for the fine and costs aforesaid, it is
therefore considered by the Court that the State of Tennessee
recover of the defendant and the said John M. Gifford, his
security the fine and costs aforesaid for which execution may
issue.

August Term

State   )
)
 vs   ) Came the grand jury into open
) Court and returned a present-
Hamilton B. Gather) ment against Hamilton B. Gather,
         for unlawful gameing, signed by
all of said grand jury; which presentment is in the words
and figures following to wit:

 State of Tennessee, Bradley County, Circuit Court,
 August Term Eighteen hundred and thirty eight.
(P-148)
 The grand Jurors in behalf of the State of Tennessee,
elected empanneld, sworn and charged to inquire for the body
of the County of Bradley, aforesaid, upon their oath present
that a certain Hamilton B. Gather, late of said County labourer, on the first day of August in the year of our Lord
one thousand eight --- and thirty eight, with force and arms
in the County of Bradley, aforesaid unlawfully did gamble
and play at a certain game of hazard with cards for twelve
and one half cents, good and lawful money of the United States

being then and there bet and hazarded at and upon said game of hazard so plaid with cards, aforesaid contrary to the form of the statutes in such case made and provided and against the peace and dignity of the State.

Presentment found on the testimony of John M. Gifford, Foreman, John Austin Wm. Thornburgh, William Vernon, Guilford Gatlin, N. Barksdale, James Shadle, John McNair, J. A. Fletcher, Thomas McCarty, Peter W. Nash, John Simmons, Jm Chambers, Benjamin Murry,

Capias ---

State of Tennessee, To the Sheriff of Bradley County Greeting: You are hereby cmmanded to take the body of Hamilton B. Gather, if to be found in your County and him safely keep, so that you have him before the Judge of our Circuit Court at a court to be held for Bradley County at the Court house in Cleveland on the 4th Monday of December next, on the 3rd day of said Term, then and there to answer a charge of the State exhibited against him by presentment for unlawful gameing.

And have you then and there this writ,

Witness - Henry Price, Clerk of our Said Court, at office in Cleveland the 4th Monday of August A. D. 1838.

Henry Price, Clerk.

Appearance Bond ---

State of Tennessee, Bradley County. I, James A. Bates, D. Sheriff in and for the County aforesaid having on this 12th day of November 1838. arrested the body of I. B. Gather, (P-149) by virtue of a capias issued from the Circuit Court of said County commanding me to take the body of said I. B. Gather to answer a charge of the State exhibited against him by presentment for unlawful gameing, Thereupon the said H. B. Gather defendant together with John F. Gillespie & N. T. Peck, security, before me James A. Bates, Sheriff as aforesaid, acknowledged themselves jointly and severally indebted to the State of Tennessee in the sum of two hundred and fifty dollars each to be levied of their goods and chattles lands and tenements respectively but to be void on condition the said H. B. Gather shall make his personal appearance before the said Circuit Court at a Court to be held for the County of aforesaid at the Court house in Cleveland on the first Wednesday after the 4th Monday of December next to answer the said charge of the State, exhibited against him as aforesaid and then and there abide

by perform and satisfy the Judgment of said Court there on
to be rendered and not depart the Court without leave.

before me this 12th November, 1838.

H. B. Gather   (Seal)

J. T. Gillespie (Seal)

James A. Bates, D. Sheriff of Bradley
    County.

December Term 1838.

The State	)
	)
vs Gameing	) Came the attorney general who pro-
	) secutes for the State, as well as
Hamilton B. Gather	) for the defendant in proper person
	who being charged upon the present-

ment says he cannot deny but that he is guilty in manner and
form as charged therein and submits to the Judgment of the
Court it is therfore considered by the Court that for such
his offence he pay a fine of Ten dollars and also that he pay
the costs of this prosecution and that he be taken by the
Sheriff and remain in custody untill the fine and costs are
paid or security given therefore Whereupon came John M. Gifford into open Court and agrees that Judgment may be rendered
against him jointly with the defendant for the fine and costs
aforesaid.

It is therefore considered by the Court that the State
of Tennessee recover of the defendant (P-150) and the said
John M. Gifford, his security the fine and costs aforesaid
for which an execution may issue.

September Term 1838.

The grand jurors appeard in open Court and brought with
them a presentment against the defendant for unlawful gameing signed by all of said grand jury.

Which presentment appears in the Words and figures, Towit:
State of Tennessee, Bradley County, Circuit Court August term

In the year of our Lord One thousand eight hundred and Thirty Eight.

The grand Jorors in behalf of the State of Tennessee elected empanneled, sworn & Charged to enquire for the County of Bradley aforesaid upon their oath present that a certain Frederick A. Kance, late of said County, laborer, on the twentieth day of August, in the year of our Lord one Thousand eight hundred and Thirty eight, in the County of Bradley, aforesaid, unlawfully did gamble, with force and arms and play at a certain game of hazard with cards, commonly called faro, for one dollar, good and lawful money of the State of Tennessee, being then there bet and hazarded at and upon said game of hazard, so plaid as aforesaid with cards contrary to the form of the statutes in such case made and provided and against the peace and dignity of the State.

Presentment -- Found on the testimony of John M. Gifford Foreman - John Austin, Peter W. Nash, N. Barksdale, James Shadle, Wm. Thornburgh, Benjamin Murry, John Simmons, Guilford Gatlin, Jm Chambers, William Vernon, J. A. Fletcher, John McNair, Thomas McCarty.

Capias ---

State of Tennessee, To the Sheriff of McMinn County, Greeting: You are hereby commanded to take the body of Frederick A. Kance, if to be found in your County and him safely keep, so that you have him before the Judge of our Circuit Court at a Court to be held for Bradley County at the Court house, (P-151) in Cleveland on the 4th Monday of December next then and there to answer the charge of the State exhibited against him by presentment for unlawful gameing.

And have you then and there this writ,

Witness, Henry Price, Clerk of our said Court at office in Cleveland the 4th Monday of August, A. D. 1838.

Henry Price, Clerk

Executed on F. A. Cants, on December 1838.

Wm. McKamy, Dept. Sheriff

State of Tennessee, McMinn County,

This day we, F. A. Kants and Samuel C. Agnew, all of the County of McMinn, and State of Tennessee, acknowledge our selves indebted to the State of Tennessee, in the following sum to wit: The said F. A. Kants in the sum of two hun-

dred and fifty dollars, and the said Samuel C. Agnew, his
security in the sum of two hundred and fifty dollars to be
levied of their respective goods and chattles, lands and
Tenements to the use of the State but to be void on condition that the said F. A. Kants doth make his personal appearance before the Judge of the next Circuit Court, to be
held for Bradley County at the Court house in Cleveland on
the first Wednesday after the fourth Monday in December next,
Then and there to answer a charge that the State of Tennessee
exhibited against him by indictment for unlawful gambeling
and then and there abide by and perform the judgment of the
Court thereon to be given, and not depart said Court without
leave.

Then this obligation to be void otherwise to remain in
full force and effect.

Given under our hands and Seals

This 8th December, 1838

F. A. Kance (Seal)

S. C. Agnew (Seal)

Test
William McKamey
    Dept. Sheriff

(P-152(December Term, 1838

The State   )
)
    vs Gameing   )   Came the Attorney general, who
)   prosecutes for the State, as well
Frederick A. Kance   )   as the defendant in proper person
                                  and by consent and with the as-
sent of the Court this cause is continued untill the next
term.

Whereupon came the defendant and George Westmoreland,
and John Irwin, into open Court and severly acknowledged
themselves indebted to the State of Tennessee that is to
say the said defendant in the Sum of two hundred and fifty
dollars and the said George Westmoreland and John Erwin in
the sum of twohundred and fifty dollars to be levied of
their respective goods to be levied of their respective ge
and chattles, lands and tenements but to be void on condition that the defendant do make his personal appearance at
the next term of the Circuit Court to be held for Bradley
County, at the Court house in Cleveland, on the 4th Monday
of April, next, and on Wednesday of said Term, then and there
to answer a charge of the State exhibited against him for un-

lawful gameing and not depart the Court without leave.

April Term 1839.

The State   )
)
  vs   ) The attorney general comes who
) prosecutes for the State and
Frederick A. Kance) moved the Court for leave to
           enter a nole proequi in this cause
           which is granted it is therefore
considered by the Court that the defendant go hence and that
the Clerk tax the legal cost of this prosecution and certify
a complete copy of the same to the County Court for order
and allowance of said Court.

(P-153)   May Term, 1838.

The State   )
)
  vs A.B.   ) The grand jury for the State returned
) into open Court and brought with them
Isaac White   ) a bill of indictment against the defend-
          ant indorsed thereon a true bill - by
Daniel Buckner, their foreman, which indictment appears in
the words and figures following, to wit: State of Tennessee
Bradley County, Circuit Court, May Term, Eighteen hundred and
thirty Eight.

  The grand Jurors in behalf of the State of Tennessee el-
ected empanneled sworn and charged to enquire for the County
of Bradley aforesaid upon their oath present that a certain
Isaac White late of said County laberer on the third day of
March in the year of our Lord One thousand eight hundred and
Thirty eight with force and arms in the County of Bradley,
aforesaid an assault did make in and upon the body of John
Jones, and then being in the peace of the State and did then
and there, beat bruise wound and ill treat him the said John
Jones, to the great damage of him the said John Jones, to the
evil example of all others in like case offending and against
the peace and dignity of the State.

Samuel Frazier, Atto General
For the 3 - Solisatorial & ---

Indictment,

Thomas Jones, prosecutor --

John Jones, Samuel Giddion, Absolom,Coleman, Witnesses
for the State sworn in open Court and sent before the grand

jury.   May 14th, 1838.

Henry Price, Clerk

A true bill, Daniel Buckner, foreman of the grand jury

(P-154)   Appearance Bond ---

State of Tennessee, Bradley County

Be it remembered on the 15th day of March in the year of our
Lord One thousand*and thirty eight, personally appeared before me, Soloman Sunny, an acting justice of the peace, Isaac White and David R. White and Eden White and acknowledged
themselves to stand justly indebted to the State of Tennessee
that is to say the said Isaac White in the sum of five hundred dollars and the said David White and Eden White in the
sum of two hundred and fifty dollars each, to be levied of
their respective goods and chattles lands and tenements but
to be void if the said Isaac White shall make his personal
appearance before the Judge of our Circuit Court at a Court
to be holden for said County at the Court house in Cleveland
on the second Monday of May next, Then and there to answer
the State of Tennessee upon a charge of an assault and battery upon the body of John Jones and abide by such sentence
as shall be pronounced in the premises and not depart said
Court untill discharged by due course of law.   *eight hundred

Acknowledged before me the date above written.

Isaac White   (Seal)

David White (Seal)
                    his
Eden White X   (Seal)
                   mark

Attest ---

Solomon Sunny,
    Justice of the Peace

The State   )
)
    vs A. B.   )   Came the State by her attorney general
)   and thereupon came into open Court
Isaac White   )   Eden White, and David White and ac-
                       knowledged themselves indebted to the
State of Tennessee in the sum of two hundred and fifty dol-
lars to be levied of their respective goods and chattles,

lands (P-155) and tenements but to be void on condition that
Isaac White make his personal appearance before the Judge
of our next Circuit Court to be held for the County of Bradley at the Court house in Cleveland on the first Wednesday
after the fourth Monday in August next, and not depart the
Court without leave.

The State	)	
	)	
vs A. B.	)	Came the Attorney General who prosecutes
	)	for the State and the defendant in his
Isaac White	)	proper person and this cause is con-
		tinued on affidavit of the defendant

and thereupon came William White together with said defendant Isaac White, and acknowledged themselves jointly and severally indebeted to the State of Tennessee as follows that
is to say two hundred and fifty dollars each to be levied
of their respective goods and chattles, lands and tenements
to the use of the State but to be void on condition that the
defendant make his personal appearance before the Judge of

the Circuit Court to be held for the County of Bradley at the*
~~County of Bradley~~ on the first Wednesday after the fourth
Monday of December next, and there and then to answer a charge
of the State exhibited against him by indictment for an as-
sault and battery and not depart the Court without leave.
*Court house in Cleveland

The State	)	
	)	
vs	)	Came the State by her Attorney general
	)	who prosecutes for the State and there-
Isaac White	)	upon Thomas Jones came and acknowledged
		himself to owe and be indebted to the

State of Tennessee in the Sum of Twohundred and fifty dollars to be levied of their goods and chattles lands and
tenements to the use of the Court but to be void on condition that he make his personal appearance before the Judge
of the Circuit Court at a (P-156) Court to be held for the
County of Bradley at the Court house in the town of Cleveland on the first Wednesday after the fourth Monday in December, next and prosecute a suit wherein the State is plantiff and Isaac White is defendant and not dePart the Court
without leave on part of the State,

December 25th 1838.

The State	)	
	)	
vs A. B.	)	Came the Attorney genera l who prose-
	)	cutes for the State as well as the

Isaac White   )   defendant in proper person who being
                            charged upon the bill of indictment
says he cannot deny but that he is guilty in manner and
form a_s charged in said bill of indictment and submits to
the judgment of the Court it is therefore considered by the
Court that the defendant for such his offence be fined the
sum of fifteen dollars and futher pay the costs of the prosecution and remain in the Custody of the Sheriff, untill
the fine and costs are paid or security given therefor and
there upon came David Maxwell, into open Court and agrees
that Judgment may be rendered against him jointly with the
defendant for the fine and cost aforesaid it is therefore
considered by the Court that the State of Tennessee recover
of the defendant and David Maxwell his security the fine and
cost aforesaid for which execution may issue.

August Term 1838.

The State   )
)
    vs   )   Came the grand Jury into open
)   Court and returned with them
Carrington Hicks   )   a presentment against Carring-
                              ton Hicks for unlawful gameing
signed by all of said grand Jury which presentment is in
the words and figures following to wit, State of Tennessee
Bradley County, Circuit Court, August Term Eighteen hundred and thirty eight.

The grand jurors in behalf of the State of Tennessee elected impaneled sworn and charged to inquire for the body
of (P÷157) The County of Bradley aforesaid upon their oath
present that a certain Carrington Hicks, late of said County
laborer, on the first day of August in the year of our Lord
One Thousand eight hundred and thirty Eight with force and
arms in the County of Bradley aforesaid, unlawfully did gamble and play at a certain game of hazard with cards for
Twelve and one half cents, good and lawful money of the
State of Tennessee being then and there bet and hazarded at
and upon said game of hazard so plaid with cards as aforesaid
contrary to the form of the statutes in such case made and
provided and against the peace and dignity of the State,
Found on the testimony of John M. Gifford, John Austin, foreman of the grand Jury, Peter W. Nash, Wm. Thornburgh, N.
Barksdale, James Shadle, John McNair, J. A. Fletcher, Thomas McCarty, John Simmons, Jm Chambers, Benjamin Murry, William Vernon, Guilford Gatlin.

Capias ---

State of Tennessee, To the Sheriff of Bradley County, Greeting:

You are hereby commanded to take the body of Carrington Hicks
if to be found in your County and him safely keep, So that
you have him before the Judge of our Circuit Court, at a
Court to be held for Bradley County, at the Court house in
Cleveland, on the 4th Monday of December, next, on the 3rd
day of said term, then and there to answer a charge of the
State exhibited against him by presentment for unlawful gameing, and have you then and there ~~to answer a charge of the
State exhibited against him by presentment for unlawful
gameing, and have you th~~ this writ: Witness - Henry Price
Clerk of our said Court at office in Cleveland, the 4th Mon-
day of August A. D. 1838.

                    Henry Price, Clerk

     Executed the within by arresting the body of Carrington
Hicks this 19th October, 1838, and appearance bond taken.
                              James A. Bates, D. Shff.

(P-158)   Appearance Bond   ----

State of Tennessee, Bradley County, I, James A. Bates, deputy sheriff, in and for the County aforesaid, having on this
third day of December arrested the body of Carrington Hicks
by virtue of a Capias, issued from the Circuit Court of Bradley County, commanding me to take the body of said Carrington
Hicks to answer a charge of the State exhibited against him
by indictment for unlawful gameing thereupon the said Carrington Hicks defendant together with Nat C. Smith, security, before me James A. Bates, D. Sheriff, as aforesaid acknowledged
themselves jointly & severally indebted to the State of Tennessee in the sum of One hundred dollars each to be levied of
their goods and Chattles, lands and tenements, respectively
but to be void on condition the said Carrington Hicks, shall
make his personal appearance before the said Circuit Court
a Court to be held for the County aforesaid at the Court
House in Cleveland, Bradley --- on the first Wednesday after
the 4th Monday of December, next, to answer the charge the
State exhibited against him as aforesaid, And then and there
abide by perform and satisfy the judgment of said Court
thereon to be rendered and not depart the Court without leave.

                    (C. W. Hicks (Seal)
                    (
                    (Nat Smith   (Seal)

     Assigned ---
     sealed and acknowledged before me this 3rd day of Decem-
     ber, 1838.

                    James A. Bates, D. Sheriff
                       of Bradley County

               December Term, 1838.

State   )   Presentment for gaming
)
    vs   )   This day came the State, by his
)   Attorney general and by leave of
Carrington Hicks   )   the Court entered a Nolle prosequi
                      and thereupon came John F. Gilles-
pie and Thomas J. Campbell, and confessed judgment for the
cost in this behalf expended, it is therefore considered
by the Court that the said defendant and his bail be discharged from their recoginance and that the State recover
of the said John F. Gillespie and Thomas J. Campbell, the
costs in this behalf expended (P-159) for which execution may issue.

September Term, 1838

The State   )
)
    vs   )   The grand Jurors appeared in open
)   Court and brought with them a pres-
John C. Mullay   )   entment against the defendant for
                    unlawful gameing signed by all said
grand jury, State of Tennessee, Bradley County Circuit
Court August Term in the year of our Lord one Thousand eight
hundred and Thirty Eight.

The grand jurors in behalf of the State of Tennessee
elected empanneled sworn and charged to inquire for the
body of the County of Bradley aforesaid upon their oath
present that a certain John C. Mullay, late of said County
labourer in the year of our Lord one Thousand eight hundred
and thirty eight, with force and arms in the County of Bradley aforesaid unlawfully did gamble and play at a certain
game of hazard with cards for twenty five cents, good and
lawful money of the State of Tennessee, being then and there
bet and hazarded at and upon said game of hazard so plaid
with cards, as aforesaid contrary to the form of the Statutes
in such case made and provided and against the peace and dignity of the State.

Found on the testimony of Hiram K. Turk, Foreman, John
Austin, Peter W. Nash, N. Barksdale, James Shadle, Wm. Thorn-
burgh, Benjamin Murry, John Simmons, Guilford Gatlin, Jm
Chambers, William Vernon, J. A. Fletcher, John McNair Thomas
McCarty.

Capias,

State of Tennessee, McMinn County, Greeting: You are hereby
commanded to take the body of John C. Mullay, if to be found
in your County and him safely keep, so that you have him before the Judge of our Circuit Court at a Court to be held for
Bradley County at the Court house in Cleveland on the 4th
Monday of December next, then and there (P-160) to answer
a charge of the State exhibited against him by presentment
for unlawful gambeling.

And have you then and there this writ:

Witness Henry Price, Clerk of our
    said Court, at office in Cleveland
The 4th Monday of August A. D. 1838.

                        Henry Price, Clerk

Came to hand 13th Sept. 1838

J. T. Reed, D. Sheriff, for McMinn County

Executed and bond taken 13th September, 1838.

                    J. T. Reed, D. Sheriff.

State of Tennessee, McMinn County, I, James T. Reed, Deputy
Sheriff in and for the County aforesaid having on this 13th
day of September 1838, arrested the body of John C. Mullay
by virtue of a capias issued from the Circuit Court of Bradley County, commanding me to take the body of said John C.
Mullay to answer a charge of the State, exhibited against
him by presentment for unlawful gambeling.

    Thereupon the said John C. Mullay, defendant together
with James S. Bridges security, before me James T. Reed, Deputy Sheriff as aforesaid acknowledged themselves indebted
to the State of Tennessee, in the Sum of two hundred and
fifty dollars each to be levied of their goods and chattles
lands and tenements respectively; but to be void on condition the said John C. Mullay, shall not make his personal
appearance before the said Court at a Court to be held for
the County aforesaid at the Court house in Cleveland, on the
fourth Monday of December, next, to answer the charge of the
State exhibited against him as aforesaid, and then and there
abide by perform and satisfy the Judgment of said Court thereon to be rendered and not depart the Court without leave.

                        John C. Mullay

Test --   )   James S. Bridges
J. T. Reed)

December Term 1838,

The State   )

  vs   )   Came the Attorney general who prose-
)   cutes for the State and leave of the
John C. Mullay   )   Court being had and obtained a Noll
                       porsequi is entered in this cause, it
is therefore considered by the Court that the Clerk (P-161)
tax the costs in this behalf expended and Certify the same
to the County Court for inspection and allowance.

September Term, 1838.

The State   )

  vs   )   The grand jurors appeared in open
)   Court and brought with them a pre-
William Ainsworth   )   sentment*for unlawful gameing
                      Signed by all of said Grand Jurors
which presentment is in the words and figures following towit:

State of Tennessee, Bradley County, Circuit Court, August term
Eighteen hundred and thirty eight.

The grand jurors in behalf of the State of Tennessee elected empanneled sworn and charged to enquire for the County
of Bradley aforesaid upon their oath present that a certain
William Ainsworth, late of said County labourer, on the
Twenty Third day of August in the year of our Lord One Thousand eight hundred and thirty Eight, with force and arms in the
County of Bradley, aforesaid, unlawfully did gamble and play
at a certain game of hazard with cards for twenty five cents
good and lawful money of the State of Tennessee being then and
there bet and hazarded at and upon said game of hazard so plaid
with cards as aforesaid contrary to the Statutes in such case
made and provided and against the peace and dignity of the
State.

Found on the testimony of Hiram K. Turk, Foreman - John
Austin, Peter W. Nash, N. Barksdale, James Shadle, Wm. Thornburgh, John Simmons, Benjamin Murry, Guilford Gatlin, J. M.
Chambers, William Vernon, J. A. Fletcher, John McNair, Thomas McCarty.

Capias ----
*against the defendant

State of Tennessee, To the Sheriff of Bradley County Greeting: You are hereby commanded to take the body of William Ainsworth if to be found in your County, and him safely keep so (P-162) that you have him before the Judge of our Circuit Court at a Court to be held for Bradley County at the Court house in Cleveland on the 4th Monday of December next, and on the 3rd day of said Term, then and there to answer a charge of the State exhibited against him by presentment for unlawful gameing, and have you then and there this writ:

Witness - Henry Price, Clerk of our said Court at office in Cleveland, 4th Monday of August A. D. 1838.

Henry Price, Clerk

Came to hand the same day and executed by arresting the within defendant and appearance bond taken this 8th October 1838.

James Lauderdale,

Sheriff of Bradley County

State of Tennessee, Bradley County,

I, James Lauderdale, Sheriff in and for the County aforesaid, having on this 8th day of October, arrested the body of William Ainsworth, by virtue of a Capias, issued from the Circuit Court of said County commanding me to take the body of said Wm. Ainsworth, to answer a charge of the State exhibited against him by presentment for unlawful gameing

Thereupon, the said Wm. Ainsworth, defendant together with John G. Glass, security before me James Lauderdale, Sheriff as aforesaid acknowledged themselves indebted to the State of Tennessee in the sum of two hundred and fifty dollars each to be levied of their goods and chattles lands and tenements respectively; but to be void on condition the said Wm. Ainsworth shall make his personal appearance before the Judge of our Circuit Court, to be held for the County of aforesaid at the Court house in Cleveland on the first Wednesday after the 4th Monday of December, next, to and to answer the said charge of the State exhibited against him as aforesaid and then and there abide by perform and satisfy the Judgment of said Court there on (P-163) to be rendered and not depart the Court without leave.

William Ainsworth,

J. G. Glass

December Term, 1838.

The State   )
)
 vs   ) Came the Attorney General who pros-
) ecutes for the State and leaving
William Ainsworth) ~~leaving~~ of the Court being had and
           obtained enters a Nolle prosequi
in this cause it is therefore considered by the Court that
the defendant go hence with out day and that the Clerk tax
the legal cost, in this behalf expended and certify the same
to the County Court for inspection and allowance.

May Term, 1837

State   )
)
 vs   ) This day the grand jury for the State
) appeared in open Court and brought
James Harland) with them a bill of indictment against
         the defendant for an assault and bat-
tery endorsed a true bill by Alexander Perry, their foreman
which indictment is in the words and figures following towit:
State of Tennessee, Bradley County, Circuit Court May term
eighteen hundred and thirty seven.

  The grand Jurors in behalf of the State of Tennessee
elected empanneled sworn and charged to enquire for the
body of the County of Bradley aforesaid upon their oath
present that a certain James Harland, late of said County
labourer, on the twenty fifth day of April in the year of
our Lord one thousand eight hundred and thirty seven, with
force and arms in the County of Bradley, aforesaid did
make and assault in and upon the body of one Thomas McNut,
then and there being in the peace of the State, did there
beat bruise wound and ill treat him the said Thomas McNutt
to the great damage of him the said Thomas McNutt, to the
evil example of all others in like case offending and against
the peace and dignity (P-164) of the State,

       Samuel Frazier, Attorney General
        for the 3rd solicitoral
        district.

Thomas McNutt, prosecutor -

A. G. White, Thomas McNutt, Witness for the State sworn in
open Court and sent before the grand Jury.
        Henry Price, Clerk
May 8th, 1837.

Capias ---

State of Tennessee, to the Sheriff of Bradley County -
Greeting: You are hereby commanded to take the body of
James Harland if to be found in your County and him safely keep, so that you have him before the Judge of our Circuit Court at a Court to be held for Bradley County, at
the Court house in Cleveland on the 2nd Monday of September next, then and there to answer a charge of the State
exhibited against him by an indictment for an assault and
battery, and have you then and there this writ, Witness -
Henry Price, Clerk of our said Court, at office in Cleveland
the 2nd Monday of May A. D. 1837.

                         Henry Price,Clerk

    The within is executed by me 20th May, 1837.

                         A. A . Clingan, Sheriff,

    Appearance Bond.

State of Tennessee, Bradley County, We, James Harland, John
D. Traynor and James Bigly, do acknowledge our selves indebted to the State of Tennessee, two hundred and fifty dollars to be levied of our goods and chattles lands and tenements respectively to the use of the State of Tennessee yet
on condition if the said above bound James Harlin do make
his personal appearance before the Judge of our Circuit
Court at a Court to be held at the Court house in the town
of Cleveland on the 2nd Monday of September next, There to
answer a charge that the State exhibited against said Harlin
by indictment and not to depart the said Court without leave.
Herein we set our hands and seals.
This 23rd May, 1837.

                         James Harland (Seal)

                         John D. Traynor (Seal)

                         James Bigley (Seal)

              Attest - A. A. Clingan

(P-165)   January Term, 1838.

State   )
)
   vs   )   On motion of the attorney general an
)   alius Capias, is awarded against the
James Harland   )   defendant.

The State   )
)
  vs   ) Came the attorney General and leave of
) the Court obtained enters a Nolle Prose-
James Harland   ) qui in this cause it is therefore con-
                  sidered by the Court that the Clerk
tax the legal cost in this behalf expended, and certify the
same to the County Court for their inspection and allowance.

August Term, 1838.

The State   )
)
  vs   ) The grand Jury for the State appeared
) in open Court and returned a bill of
George Hambright) indictment against George Hambright
                  indorsed thereon a true bill by
John Austin, their foreman: which indictment is in the words
and figures following to wit: State of Tennessee, Bradley
County, Circuit Court, August term - eighteen hundred and
thirty eight.

The grand jurors in behalf of the State of Tennessee,
elected empanneled sworn and charged to enquire for the body
of the County of Bradley aforesaid upon their oath present
that a certain George R. Hambright, late of said County labourer, on the fourteenth day of July in the year of our Lord
One thousand eight hundred and thirty eight with force and
arms in the County of Bradley aforesaid an assault did make
in and -- William Hammond, then and there being in the
peace of the State and did then (P-166) and there beat
bruise, wound and ill treat the said William Hammond to the
great damage of the said William Hammond, to the evil example of all others in like case offending and against the
peace and dignity of the State.

                        Samuel Frazier, Attorney General
                          for the 3rd Solicitorial district

William Hammond, prosecutor

William Hammond, Witness for the State sworn in open Court
and sent before the grand Jury.
    August 13th, 1838.   Henry Price, Clerk

Capias   ---

State of Tennessee, Bradley County,

To the Sheriff of Bradley County, Greeting: You are hereby
commanded to take the body of G. R. Hambright if to be found
in your County and him safely keep so that you have him before the Judge of our Circuit Court at a Court to be held
for Bradley County at the Court house in Cleveland on the
fourth Monday of December, next, on the 3rd day of said term
then and there to answer a charge of the State exhibited
against him by an indictment for an assault and battery, and
have you then and there this writ: Witness Henry Price, Clerk
of our said Court at office in Cleveland the 4th Monday of
August, A. D. 1838.

Henry Price, Clerk

Came to hand the same issued and executed on G. R. Hambright and bond taken for appearance at Court this 1st October, 1838.

James Lauderdale, Sheriff of
Bradley County.

Appearance Bond,

State of Tennessee, Bradley County, I, James Lauderdale,
Sheriff in and for the County aforesaid, having on this 1st
day of October, 1838 arrested the body of G. R. Hambright
by virtue of a Capias, issued from the Circuit Court of
Bradley County commanding me   (P-167)   to take the body
of said G. R. Hambright to answer a charge of the State exhibited against him by indictment for an assault and battery,

Thereupon the said G. R.Hambright defendant together
with Hugh Hannah and Thomas Hannah, security before me
James Lauderdale, Sheriff as aforesaid acknowledged themselves jointly and severally indebted to the State of Tennessee in the sum of two hundred and fifty dollars each to
be levied of their goods and chattles lands and tenements
respectively, but to be void on condition the said G. R.
Hambright shall make his personal appearance before the
Judge of the Circuit Court at a Court to be held for the
County aforesaid, at the*first Wednesday after the 4th Monday of December, next, to answer the charge of the State exhibited against him as aforesaid.
*Court house in Cleveland on the
And then and there abide by, perform and satisfy the
Judgment of said Court thereon to be rendered and not de-
part the Court without leave.

G. R. Hambright(Seal)

Hugh Hannah (Seal)

Thomas Hannah (Seal)

Attest,
James Lauderdale, Sheriff.

December 1838.

The State   )
)
    vs A. B.   )   Came the Attorney General who
)   prosecutes for the State as
George R. Hambright)   well as the defendant in proper
                             person who being charged on the
bill of indictment says he cannot deny but that he is guilty
in manner and form as charged in said bill of indictment
and submits to the Judgment of the Court it is therefore considered by the Court that for such his offence he pay a fine
of Twenty five dollars and futher pay the costs of this prosecution and be taken by the Sheriff and remain in custody untill the fine and costs are paid or security given therefore.

The State   )
)
    vs   )   May Term, 1838.
)
John Bell   )   For Gameing.

        The grand jury in behalf of the State of
Tennessee appeared in open Court and returned a presentment
against the defendant signed by all of (P-168) said
grand jury; which presentment appears in the words and
figures following to wit: State of Tennessee, Bradley
County, Circuit Court,

        May Term eighteen hundred and thirty eight.

    The grand jurors in behalf of the State of Tennessee
elected empanneled sworn and charged to enquire for the body
of the County of Bradley aforesaid upon their oath present
that a certain John Bell, late of said County labourer, on

the seventeenth day of April in the year of our Lord, One
Thousand eight hundred and thirty eight and on divers other
days and times, with force and arms in the County of Bradley aforesaid, and within the jurisdiction of this honorable Court unlawfully and feloniously did deal at a game
commonly called faro for fifty cents good and lawful money
of the State of Tennessee; and of the United States and other
money bank notes and property bet, staked and hazarded by
one Hiram K. Turk, and other persons on said game of faro
dealt and as aforesaid by the said John Bell, contrary to
the form of the Statue in such case made and provided and
against the peace and dignity of the State.

Found on the testimony of John Suggart, John D. Traynor
who on application of the foreman of the grand jury, were
summond and sworn in open Court and sent before the grand
jury.

Daniel Buckner, foreman of the grand jury, John B. Cate
Charles Cate, Wm. Henry, Joseph Daven port, Elbert Cooper,
Amos Potts, Richard Dean, Henry Swisher, Wm Kelly, Sampson
H. Prowell, John Mathews, A. H. Teenor.

(Capias)

State of Tennessee, to the Sheriff of Bradley County,
Greeting: You are hereby commanded to take the body of John
Bell if to be found in your County and him safely keep so
that you have him before the Judge of our Circuit Court at
a Court to be held for Bradley County, at the Court house in
Cleveland, on the fourth Monday of August, next, on the 3rd
day then and there to answer a charge of the State exhibited
against him by indictment for unlawful gameing, and have you
then and there this writ,

Witness - Henry Price, Clerk of our said Court at office
in Cleveland the 2nd Monday of May, A. D. 1838.

(P-169)   Henry Price, Clerk.

I, James Lauderdale, sheriff, do hereby specially ----
John Burke to execute the within.

This the 27th August, 1838.

Came to hand the same day issued and executed in full
this the 28th August, 1838.

John Burke

The State   )

```
        vs           )    Bradley County Circuit Court
                     )    August Term, 1838.
John A. Bell       )
```

The defendant in his own proper person
comes into Court and being charged in the bill of indictment
in this cause for plea thereto says the State of Tennessee
her prosecution against him ought not to have and maintain
because he says he is a native and citizen of the Cherokee
nation of and not a citizen of the United States as aforesaid States Indians east of the Mississippi, that the said
supposed crime as alledged and set forth in said bill of
indictment if committed at all was committed at the Cherokee Agency east of the Mississippi, within the limits of
the Cherokee, nation, and in the month of April, in the
year of our Lord one thousand eight hundred and Thirty eight

and before the time expired that said Cherokee nation had the
right to occupy and remain upon this territory where said
offence was committed at all under the existing treaties between the United States and said Cherokee, Nation and at a
time when this defendant was not amenable to the laws of the
State of Tennessee, for any crime he might commit within the
limits of said Cherokee nation, and within the Chartered
limits of the State of Tennessee except upon larceny and
murder, as provided in our act of the legislature of the*year
1833; All of wwhich this defendant is ready to verify wherefore he prays judgment if the State of Tennessee ought to
have and maintain her said prosecution &c.
*State of Tennessee passed in the
        (Demurer)

```
The State       )
                )
    vs          )    And Samuel Frazier, the Attorney General
                )    who prosecutes in behalf of the State of
John Bell       )    Tennessee, as to said plea of the said
                     John Bell, by him above pleaded saith that
```
the same and the matters therein contained in manner and
from as the same are above set forth are not sufficient in
law to bar   (P-170)   or preclude the said State of Tennessee from prosecuting said indictment against him the said
John Bell, and that the said State of Tennessee by her Attorney general is not bound by the law of the land to answer the same and this the said Attorney General who prosecutes as aforesaid is ready to verify.

Whereupon for want of a sufficient plea in this behalf
he the said Attorney general for and in behalf of the said
State of Tennessee, prays Judgment and the said John Bell
may be be convicted of the premises in said indictment
specified.

                        Samuel Frazier, Attorney General
                        for the 3rd Solicitorial district.

Joinder in Demurer,
    Jarnagan, Attorney,

        August Term, 1838

            Dealing Faro

The State   )
)
    vs   )   Came the State by her attorney General
)   and thereupon came John Bell and acknowl-
John Bell   )   edged himself indebted to the State of
                      Tennessee, in the sum of one thourand
dollars to be levied of his goods and chattles, lands and
tenements but to be void on condition that he make his personal appearance from day to day before the Judge of our
Circuit Court now setting and there answer a charge of the
State exhibited against him by indictment for dealing faro
and not depart the Court without leave.

    Thereupon came William Johnson and Jesse Mayfield, and
acknowledged themselves Jointly and severally indebted to
the State of Tennessee in the sum of one thousand dollars
to be levied of there goods and chattles lands and tenements to the use of the State. Yet to be void on condition that John A. Bell from day to day appear before the
Judge of our Circuit Court now setting and there answer a
charge of the State exhibited against him for dealing fare
and not depart the Court without leave.

            August Term, 1838

    "Gameing"

The State   )
)
    vs   )   Came the attorney general who prosecutes
)   for the State as well as the defendant
John Bell   )   in his own proper person and the demurer
                     to the defendants plea having been ex-
amined and argument of counsel being had thereon it is
therefore considered   (P-171)   by the Court that the said
demrer be sustained and that defendants plea be overulled
and that the defendant be compelled to plead over to said
indictment and thereupon by consent of the parties and with
the assent of the Court this cause is continued until the
next term of this Court.

            September Term, 1838.

The State   )
)
    vs   )   Came the attorney general who prosecutes

for the State and the said John Bell, having been solemnly
called to come into Court came not but made default and
thereupon Jesse Mayfield and William Johnson who stands bound
by recoginances for the defendants appearance from day to day
at the present Court being solemnly called and required to
come into Court and bring with them the body of the said defendant failed so to do and made default it is therefore considered by the Court that the said Jesse Mayfield and William
Johnson have forfeited to the State of Tennessee, Jointly and
severally the sum of one thousand dollars according to the
tenor and effect of their said recoginance and that sirefa-
cias issue accordingly unless they show cause to the contrary.

December Term, 1838.

The State	)
	)
vs	) Came the attorney general who prosecutes
	) for the State and leave of the Court being
John Bell	) first had and obtained enters a Nolle pro-
	sequi in this cause whereupon came John

Kennedy into open Court and confessed judgment for all the
costs in the prosecution of this cause expended, it is therefore considered by the Court that the State of Tennessee
recover of the said John Kennedy the costs aforesaid for
which execution may issue.

Sirafacias ----

State of Tennessee, To the Sheriff of Bradley County Greeting: Whereas heretofore to wit on the 27th day   (P-172)
of August 1838, in our Circuit Court for the County of Bradley, John A. Bell, acknowledged himself to owe and be indebted to the State of Tennessee in the sum of one Thousand
dollars to be levied of his proper goods and chattles, lands
and tenements to be void on condition that he the said John
A. Bell, should make his personal appearance before said
Court from day to day, there and then to answer the State
on a presentment for dealing faro, and not depart the Court
without leave of said Court. And whereas afterward to wit,
on the first day of September 1838, At the same term of the
Court*and answer said charge - came not but made default and --
*the said John A. Bell having been solemly called to come into
Court

Appeal ----

State of Tennessee)   To any lawful officer of said County
)   to execute and return you are here-
Bradley County   )   by commanded to summons Jacob Buck
                       to appear before me or some other
Justice of the Peace for saidCounty to answer the complainant of William Forsyth of a plea of debt due by ----- herein
fail not and make due return of this warrant given under my
hand and seal this 26th day of January 1839.

                        Jesse Poe, Justice of the Peace

For stay - Benjamin Hawkins

     Endorsement Warrant.

William Forsyth   )
)
     vs   )   Came to hand and summoned Jacob Buck
)   toappear at the Court house in Cleve-
Jacob Buck   )   land before Jesse Poe, at on the 4th
                        January, 1839. this the 4th of Feb-
                        ruary 1839,

                        James   Lauderdale

                        Sheriff of Bradley County

Summons for plantiff James Campbell
        and B. Hawkins.

(P-173)
William Forsyth   )
)
     vs   )   In this cause I give judgment that
)   the plantiff recover forty dollars
Jacob Buck   )   of the defendant that being half
                        the amount of the ---- blame in
partnership and half the cost for which an examination may
issue this 4th February 1839.

                        Jesse Poe

                        Justice of the Peace

Appeal ---

In this cause the defendant prays an appeal to the next
Circuit Court for Bradley County at the Court house in
Cleveland on the 4th Monday of April next, which is granted

him he haveing given bond and security as the law directs.

Jesse Poe, Justice of the Peace

William Forsyth)
)
vs) This day came the parties by their
) attorneys and there upon came a jury
Jacob Buck) of good and lawful men, to wit:
John F. Larrison, George Cate,
Charles Dodd, J. D. Stafford, Mark Black, John W. Kennedy,
Robert H. Allison, Hiram Brandon, Robert A. Farmer, William
Parks, John Carter, and John C. Kennedy, who being duly summond elected tried and sworn the truth to speak upon the
contreversey & maters in dispute between the parties upon
their oath aforesaid, do say that they find for the defendant.

It is therefore considered by the Court that plaintiff
take nothing by his warrant but that defendant go hence and
recover of the plantiff his costs in this behalf expended
for which execution may issue &c.

_____

_____

_____

Writ ----

State of Tennessee,

To the Sheriff of Bradley County, Greeting: You
a_re hereby commanded to summons John ----   (P-174). if
in your county to appear before our Circuit Court to be
held for the County of Bradley, at the Court house in Cleveland on the 4th Monday of December next, to answer William
Ainsworth of a plea of detainer that he render unto him a
Negro boy named Charles, a slave for life of the value of
two thousand dollars which from him he unjustly detains to
his damage two thousand dollars here in fail not and have
you then there this writ,

Witness Henry Price Clerk of our said Court at office
in Cleveland the 4th Monday of August 1838, and of American
Independence the 63rd.

Henry Price, Clerk.

Bond,

Know all men by these presents that we William Ainsworth Adam H. Tener, & Joseph Donohoo, are jointly and severally held and firmly bond John Davis, in the penil sum of two hundred and fifty dollars to be void on condition that said William Anesworth will with effect prosecute a suit by action of ----, which he this day commenced against the said John Davis, in the Circuit Court for Bradley County of in Case of failure of such prosecution pay and satisfy all costs and damage as may be awarded against him by our said Court.

Witness our hands and seals this 28th day of August, 1838.

                    William Anesworth (Seal)

                    A. H. Tener (Seal)

                    Joseph Donohoo (Seal)

        Endorsement -----

William Ainsworth   )
)
      vs   )   Issued August 28th, 1838.
)
John Davis   )

        Came to hand same day issued and executed on the 30th August 1838 in full.

                    James Lauderdale, Sheriff

        Capias ----

State of Tennessee, Bradley County,

To the Sheriff of Bradley County, Greeting:

(P-175) You are hereby commanded to take the body of John Davis if in your County to be found and him safely keep so that you have him before the Judge of our next Circuit Court to be held for the County of Bradley at the Court house in Cleveland on the 4th Monday of December, next, to answer William Ainsworth, of a plea of ---- to his damage two thousand dollars a suit at issue in said Court.

        herein fail not and have you then there this writ:

        Witness Henry Price, Clerk of our said Court at office in Cleveland the 4th Monday of October 1838.

Henry Price,
Clerk

Affidavit ----

State of Tenne ssee   )
)
Bradley County   )   This day personally appeared be-
                            fore me, Henry Price, Clerk of
the Circuit Court of Bradley County, William Anesworth, and
made oath in due form of law the Cause of action mentioned
in the foregoing writ against John Davis, is just and that
the said defendant John Davis, as I am informed & believe
is about to remove his property beyound the jurisdiction
of this Circuit Court of Bradley County State of Tennessee
sworn to and subscribed in my Clerks office this 8th day of
October, 1838.

                    (William Anesworth.

Test,   )
Henry Price, Clerk   )

     Endorsement Capias No. 36.

William Answorth   )
)
      vs   )   Issued October the 8th 1838.
)
John Davis   )

     Came to hand the same day Issued and executed by arrest-
ing the within John Davis and appearance bond taken October
10th 1838.

                    James Lauderdale,

                    Sheriff for Bradley County.

     Bond.

     Know all men by these presents that we John Davis, Fran-
cis D. Kelly, William Raper,   (P-176)   and Jesse Poe are
held and firmly bound unto James Lauderdale the Sheriff of
Bradley County in the penel sum of two thousand dollars to
be levied of our goods and chattles lands and tenements
for the payment of which we bind our selves and each of
our heirs, respectfully severally with our seals and dates
this the 11th day of October, 1838.

The condition of the above obligation is such that
whareas the above bound John Davis has this day been arrested by the said James Lauderdale, high Sheriff for the
County of Bradley.

Attest of Capias -------- at the suit of*John Davis to
answer the said William Anesworth of a plea of detence for
the detanie of one negro boy now if the said John Davis
should make his personal appearance before the Judge of our
next Circuit Court, to be held for the County of Bradley, and
answer the said plea and if condemned in said action pay and
satisfy such judgment or surrender him self a prisnor or that
they do the same for him then the above obligation is to be
void and nul otherwise to remain in full force and effect.

John Davis   (Seal)

F. D. Kelly (Seal)

William Raper (Seal)

Jesse Poe   (Seal)

Assignment -----

I, James Lauderdale, Sheriff of Bradley County, do as-
sign the within condition or obligation to William Anesworth
the plantiff therein named his executors administrators to
be sued for according to the statutes in such case made and
provided.

In witness whereof I have hereunto set my hand and Seal
this the 17th day of November, 1838.

James Lauderdale, Sheriff

(P-177)   Decleration --

State of Tennessee   )   Circuit Court
)
Bradley County   )   December Term, 1838.

William Anesworth, by his attorney complains of John
Davis, in Custody of the Sheriff of Bradley County of a
plea that he render unto him a negro boy named Charles a
slave for life of the value of Two thousand dollars which
from him he unjustly detains, For that whereas the said
plantiff on the 1st day of August, 1838, at the County of
Bradley, aforesaid was lawfully posessed as of own property of the aforesaid negro boy Charles of the value afore-
*William Anesworth against the said

said and being so lawfully possesed he the said plantiff
afterwards to wit on the day and year aforesaid at the
County of Bradley aforesaid Casually lost the said negro
boy Charles out of his posesion and the same afterwards
to wit, on the day of and year aforesaid at the County of
Bradley, aforesaid came to the*defendant by finding yet the
defendant well knowing the said negro boy Charles, to be
the property of him the said plantiff and of right to belong and appertane to him the said plantiff altho requested
hath not as yet delivered the said negro boy Charles to the
said plantiff but to deliver the said boy to the plantiff
hath hitherto wholly neglected and refused and still doth
neglect and refuse to the damage of the plantiff two thousand
dollars and therefore he sus pledges &c.
*Possesion of the

>   Jarnagin & Bradford
>
>   Attorneys for Plantiff.

Plea ---

And the said defendant comes and defends the wrong and
injury when &c. & for plea says the plantiff his action
aforesaid ought not to have and maintain because he says
that he the said defendant doth not detain the said negro
(P-178)   boy Charles in the said declaration ---- in manner and form as the said plantiff hath above thereof complained against him and of this he the said defendant puts
himself upon the County.

>   Trewhitt, Atty for defendant

and the Plantiff also Jarnagin &c.

William Anesworth   )
)
    vs   )   Came the parties by their attorneys
)   and thereupon came on to be argued
John Davis   )   the rule heretofore to show cause
                          why the instrument entered in this
cause should be set aside and after argument of Council and
----   deliberation thereon by the Court.

It is considered by the Court that ~~said considered by
the Court that~~ said rule be discharged and that the defendant go hence and recover of the plantiff his costs.

John Davis   )   On motion of A. H. Tenor and Joseph Dono-
)   hoo by Attorney and it appearing that
    vs   )   an Execution had wrongfully issued against

William Ainsworth   )   them the said A. H. Tener, and Joseph Donohoo, and that said Tener and Donohoo has paid the
money & as this paid said Examination wrongfully issued
against them as aforesaid.

It is therefore considered by the Court that the said
examination be quashed and that the Clerk of this Court into whose hands the money collected as aforesaid by virtue
of said Executor ---- shall refund and pay back to the said
A. H. Tener & Joseph Donohoo, the Money wrongfully paid by
them as aforesaid.

State   )
)
   vs   )   The grand Jury for the State appeared
)   in open Court and returned a present-
Hiram K. Turk   )   ment for unlawful gameing against said
                        defendant which said presentment is
signed by all of said Grand Jury   (P-179)   which presentment is in the words and figures following to wit,

State of Tennessee

Circuit Court May Term, Eighteen hundred and Thirty Eight

The grand jury in behalf of the State of Tennessee,
Elected empanneled sworn and charged to enquire for the
body of the County of Bradley aforesaid upon their oath
present that a Certain Hiram K. Turk, late of said County
labourer on the sixteenth day of April in the year of our
Lord one thousand eight hundred and Thirty eight with force
and arms in the County of Bradley aforesaid unlawfully did
gamble and play at a certain game of hazard with cards for
fifty cents good and lawful money of the State of Tennessee
and of the United States, being then and there bet and hazarded at and upon said game of hazard so plaid with cards
as aforesaid contrary to the form of the statutes in such
case made and provided and against the peace and dignity of
the State.

Endorsement No. 18.

Presentment The State vs Hiram K. Turk.

Found on testimony of John Shugarts, Daniel Buckner, Fore-
man of the grand Jury, John B. Cate, Charles Cate, Richard
Deen, Sampson H. Prowel, Amos Potts, John Mathews, William
Henry, Henry R. Swisher, William D. Kelly, Joseph Devenport,
Elbert E. Cooper A. H. Tener.

State of Tennessee,

          To the sheriff of Bradley County, Greeting, You
are hereby commanded to take the body of Hiram K. Turk if
to be found in your County and him safely keep so that you
have him before the Judge of our said Circuit Court at a
Court to be held for Bradley County at the Court House
(P-180) in Cleveland on the fourth Monday of August next,
and on the 3rd day of said term then and there to answer the
charge of the State Exhibited against him by presentment for
unlawful gameing and have you then there this writ:

Witness - Henry Price, Clerk of our said Court at office
in Cleveland, the 2nd Monday of May A. D. 1838.

                    Henry Price, Clerk

     Endorsement   Capias ---

The State   )
)
   vs   )   Issued May 22nd 1838.
)
Hiram K. Turk   )   Came to hand same day issued and ex-
                        ecuted on the boddy of H. K. Turk, on
                        the 30th May, 1838.

               James Lauderdale, Sheriff,

     State of Tennessee   )
)
     Bradley County   )   James Lauderdale, Sheriff in
                               and for the County of Bradley
aforesaid having on the 31st day of May1838, arrested the
body of Hiram K. Turk, by virtue of a Capias issued from the
Circuit Court of said County, commanding me to take the body
of the said Hiram K. Turk, to answer a charge of the State
exhibited against him by presentment for unlawful gameing.

     Thereupon the said Hiram K. Turk, defendant together
with Nicholas Peek, surety before me James Lauderdale, Sheriff as aforesaid acknowledged themselves jointly and severally indebted to the State of Tennessee in the sum of five
hundred dollars each to be levied of their goods chattles
lands and tenements respectively but to be void on condition

the said Hiram K. Turk make his personal appearance before
the Judge of the Circuit Court at a Court to be held for
the County aforesaid at the Court house in Cleveland on
the first Wednesday after the 4th Monday of August next, to
answer a charge of the State exhibited against him as aforesaid and then and there abide by preform and satisfy the judgment of said Court thereon to be rendered and not depart the
Court without leave.

> H. K. Turk   (Seal)
>
> Nicholas Peek   (Seal)
>
> James Lauderdale, Sheriff

(P-181)   Circuit Court August Term, 1838.

State   )
)
   vs   )   Came the attorney general who prosecutes
)   for the State as well as the defendant
Hiram Turk   )   in his own proper person, and this cause
                     is continued as on afidavit of the At-
                     torney general for the State Samuel Fra-
zier and thereupon came the defendant Hiram K. Turk into
open Court and Joseph Donohoo, his security and acknowledged themselves indebted to the State of Tennessee each
in the sum of two hundred and fifty dollars to be levied
of their respective goods and chattles lands and tenements
but to be void on condition that the defendant Hiram K. Turk
make his personal appearance at the next Term of the Circuit
Court to be held for the County of Bradley at the Court house
in Cleveland, on the first Wednesday after the 4th Monday in
December next then and there to answer a charge of the State
Exhibited against him by presentment for unlawful gameing
and not depart the Court without leave.

> December Term
> 1838.

State   )
)
   vs   )   Gameing ---
)
Hiram K. Turk   )   Came the attorney general who prose-
                       cutes for the State and Hiram K. Turk
                       haveing been solemnly called to come
into Court as he was bound to do to answer the State of Tennessee on a presentment pending against him for unlawful gameing, came not but made default and Joseph Donohoo, also having been solemnly called to come into Court and bring with

him the body of Hiram K. Turk to answer said charge came
not but made default.

It is therefore considered by the Court that the Joseph Donohoo, for the default aforesaid do forfeit and pay
to the State of Tennessee, the sum of (P-182) two hundred
and fifty dollars according to the tenor and effect of his
said recognizance entered into by him at the last term of
this Court unless he shows good and sufficient cause to the
Contrary at the next term of this Court and that Serafacias
issue to warn him.

                        April Term, 1839.

State   )
)
    vs   )   Gameing ----
)
Hiram K. Turk   )   Came the attorney general who prose-
                            cutes for the State and leave of the
Court first being had and obtained a Nole proseque is entered
in this cause and there came Joseph Donohoo into open Court
and confessed a judgment for all the costs in this cause.

It is therefore considered by the Court that the State
of Tennessee recover of the said Joseph Donohoo all the
costs in this behalf for which execution may issue.

    Sie Fa ---

State   )
)
    vs   )   Came the attorney General who prose-
)   cutes for the State sets aside the
Hiram K. Turk   )   forfet in this cause and thereupon
                            came Joseph Donohoo, into Court and
confessed a judgment for all costs in this.

It is considered by the Court that the State of Tennessee, recover of the said Joseph Donohoo for which execution may Issue.

                    _____

                    _____

The State   )   The grand Jury appeard in open Court and
)   returned a bill of indictment against the
    vs   )   defendant for unlawfully retailing spiri-
                     tous liquors endorsed by their foreman
*therefore   *all costs in this behalf expended

William Grant, a true bill which indictment is in the words
and figures following to wit:

State of Tennessee, Bradley County, Circuit Court, April
Term   (P-183)   Eighteen hundred and thirty nine.

The grand jurors in behalf of the State of Tennessee
elected empannelled sworn and charged to enquire for the
body of the County of Bradley aforesaid upon their oath
present that a certain David Leuty, late of said County
labourer on the tenth day of March in the year eighteen
hundred and thirty nine, and on divers other days with no
force and arms in the County of Bradley aforesaid upon their
oath present that a certain David unlawfullly did vend and
sell in quantities less than one quart a certain kind of
spiritous liquors called whiskey and other kinds of spiritous liquors to one Elam Johnston and to divers other persons and the jurors aforesaid upon their oath aforesaid upon
their oath aforesaid do further present that the said David
Leuty on the said tenth day of March in the year of our Lord
one thousand eight hundred and thirty nine and on divers
other days with force and arms in the County of Bradley aforesaid unlawfully did vend and sell by retail a certain kind of
spiritous liquors called whiskey and other kind of spiritous
liquors to to one Elam Johnston, and to divers other persons
and so the jurors aforesaid upon their oath aforesaid do say
that the said David Leuty was then and there guilty of keeping a tipling house contrary to the form of the statutes in
such case made and provided and against the peace and dignity
of the State.

                    Samuel Frazier, Attorney General
                       for the 3rd Solicitorial district

    Endorsement -----

    Indictment - The State vs David Leuty

    A ndrew B. Foster, prosecutor, George W. Selvedge, Wit-
ness for the State.

    Sworn in open Court and sent before the grand Jury.

April the 29th, 1839.

                    Henry Price, Clerk

A true bill, William Grant, Foreman of the grand Jury.
    A pril Term, 1839.

State   )   Tipling ---
)
    vs   )   Came the attorney General who prosecutes for
David Leuty)

the State and the defendant in his own proper person who says
he cannot deny but that he is guilty (P-184) in manner
and form as charged in the indictment and submits to the judgment of the Court.

It is therefore considered by the Court that the defendant for the offence aforesaid pay the State of Tennessee a
fine of one dollar and the costs of this prosecution, and
therefore came in the Court George W. Selvedge and acknowledged him self the Security of the said defendant for the
fine and cost aforesaid,

It is therefore considered by the Court that the State
of Tennessee recover of the said defendant and George W.
Selvedge his security the fine and cost aforesaid for which
Execution may Issue.

State   )
)
  vs   ) Gameing -----
)
John S. Smith) The Grand Jury for the State appeared
          in open Court and returned a bill of
indictment against the defendant for unlawful gameing indorsed there on a true bill, by John Austin their foreman
which is in the words and figures following to wit:

State of Tennessee) Circuit Court
) August Term 1838
Bradley County)

         The grand jury in behalf of the
State of Tennessee elected empanneled sworn and charged to
enquire for the body of the County of Bradley aforesaid upon their oath present that a certain John S. Smith late of
said County labourer, on the twenty second day of August in
the year of our Lord One thousand eight hundred and Thirty
eight, with force and arms in the County of Bradley aforesaid unlawfully did gamble and play at a Certain game of
hazard with cards for one Round about boat worth two dollars
good and lawful money of the United States being there and then
bet and hazarded at and upon said game of hazard so played -
(P-185) with cards as afore said contrary to the form of
the statutes in such case made and provided and against the
peace and dignity of the State.

Samuel Frazier, Attorney General
for the 3rd Solisitorial
district.

Endorsement ----

Indictment -- The State vs John S. Smith, John Fitzgerald, prosecutor, John Fitzgerald, Witness for the State, sworn in open Court and sent before the grand Jury,

August 28th, 1838.

Henry Price, Clerk

A true bill, John Austin, foreman of the Grand Jury.

Capias ---

To the Sheriff of Bradley County, Greeting: You are hereby commanded to take the boddy of John Smith, Instantly if to be found in your County and him safely keep so that you have him before the Judge of the Circuit Court now setting for Bradley County at the Court house in Cleveland then and there to answer a charge of the State executed against him by Indictment for gameing and have you then and there this writ,

Witness - Henry Price, Clerk of our said Court at office in Cleveland this 4th Monday of August, 1838.

Henry Price, Clerk.

Endorsement --

Capias --

The State	)	
	)	
vs	)	Issued August the 28th 1838.
	)	
John S. Smith	)	Came to hand 28th August 1838, and Executed in full 29th August 1838.

S. M. Ulan, Dept. Sheriff.

I do hereby dept. S. M. Ulan, to execute this --- 28th August 1838.

James Lauderdale, Sheriff.

August Term, 1838.

State   )

```
        vs          )       Gameing
                    )
John S. Smith       )       Came the Attorney General who    (P-186)
                            prosecutes for the State and the de-
fendant in his proper person and this cause is continued
untill the next as on affidavit of the defendant and there-
upon came the defendant John S.Smith with Abraham Barns, his
security who acknowledged themselves to be indebted to the
State of Tennessee in the sum of two hundred and fifty dol-
lars each to be levied of their goods chattles and lands
chattles void on condition that the defendant John S. Smith
make his personal appearance before the Judge of our Cir-
cuit Court to be held for the County of Bradley at the Court
house in Cleveland on the first Wednesday after the 4th Mon-
day of December next, then and there to answer a charge of
the State Exhibited against him by presentment for unlawful
gameing and not depart the Court without leave.
```

December Term, 1838.

```
State               )
                    )
        vs          )       Gameing ---
                    )
John Smith          )       Came the Attorney General as well as the
                            defendant in proper person and by consent
this cause is continued untill next term.
```

    Whereupon came the defendant and Mark Black who acknowl-
edged themselves indebted to the State of Tennessee in the
Sum of two hundred and fifty dollars each to be levied of
there goods and Chattles, lands and tenements void on condition that the defendant make his personal appearance at
the next term of the Circuit ---- to be held for the County
of Bradley at the Court house in Cleveland on the ~~Court house~~
4th Monday of April next and on Wednesday of said Term, then
and there to answer a charge of the State exhibited against
him for unlawful gameing and not depart the Court without
leave.

```
(P-187)             April Term 1839.

State               )
                    )
        vs          )       Gameing  ---
                    )
John S. Smith       )       Came the attorney General who prose-
                            cutes for the State, as well as the
defendant in his own proper person who being charged upon
the presentment for plea thereto says he is not guilty and
of that he puts him self upon the County and the Attorney
General doth the like and there upon came a Jury To wit:
```

Arnett Shields, James Massey, John Hayse, John D. Price,

Samuel Samples, Robert Weatherly, John F. Larrison,Isaac
Smith, Charles Dood, Robert Woody, Absolom Colman and Thomas Taylor, being elected tried and sworn to well and truly
the issue joined between the State of Tennessee and the defendant on their oath do say that the defendant is guilty in
manor and form as charged in the presentment.

It is therefore considered by the Court that the defendant for said offence pay to the State of Tennessee of fine
of Ten dollars and the costs in this behalf expended for
which execution may Issue &c.

State   )
)
   vs   )   Gameing ---
)
John S. Smith   )   Came the Attorney General and there-
                              upon came Mark Black and acknowledged
himself the security of the defendant for the payment of
the fine and cost heretofore adjudged against the defendant and in this cause it is therefore considered by the
Court that the State of Tennessee recover of the said defendant and Mark Black his surety the fine and costs so as
aforesaid confessed and that execution Issue.

_____

_____

_____

State   )
)
   vs   )   Tipling --
)
John Fitzgerrel   )   The grand Jury appeared in open
                              Court and returned a presentment against
(P-188)   the defendant for keeping a Tipling house signed
by all of said grand Jurys which is in the words and figures
following to wit:

State of Tennessee   )
)
Bradley County   )   Circuit Court August Term Eighteen
                             hundred and Thirty Eight

The grand jury in behalf of the State of Tennessee,
Elected empanneled sworn and charged to enquire for the body
of the County of Bradley aforesaid upon their oath present
that a certain John Fitzgerrel, late of said County labourer,
on the twenty seventh day of August Eighteen hundred and Thirty Eight and on divers other days with force and arms

in the County of Bradley aforesaid did vend and sell by retail in quantities less than one quart a certain kind of
spiritous liquors called whiskey and other kinds of spiritous liquors to one John S. Smith and to divers other persons and so the grand Jury aforesaid upon their oath aforesaid do say that the said John Fitzgerrel was then and there
guilty of keeping a Tipling house contrary form of the Statutes in such case made and provided and against the peace
and dignity of the State.

Samuel Frazier, Attorney general
for the 3rd Solisatorial district

Endorsement --

Indictment - The State vs John Fitzgerald, John S. Smith
prosecutor, Witness for the State sworn in open Court and
sent before the grand jury.

August 31st, 1838.　　　　　Henry Price, Clerk.

A true bill, John Austin, foreman of the grand jury.

Capias ---

State of Tennessee -

　　　To the Sheriff of Bradley County, Greeting: You
are hereby commanded to take the body of (P-189) John
Fitzgerral, if to be found in your County and him safely
keep so that you have him before the Judge of our Circuit
Court to be held --- Bradley County at the Court house
in Cleveland on the 4th Monday of December next and on the
3rd day of said term, then and there to answer a charge of
the State exhibited against him by an indictment for Tipling and have you then & there this writ, Witness Henry
Price Clerk of our said Court at office in Cleveland the
4th Monday of August, 1838.

Henry Price,
Clerk.

Endorsement -

Capias -

The State vs John Fitzgerral issued September 6th 1838,
came to hand the 6th September, 1838.

Executed by arresting the boddy of the within defendant
and bond taken for his appearance this 6th day of October
1838.

John Hughs, Dept. Sheriff.

Bond --

We, John Fitzgerrel, Thomas Skelton & William Poe acknowledged our selves indebted to the State of Tennessee that is to say John Fitzgeral in the sum of two hundred and fifty dollars and the said Thomas Skelton, and William Poe, in the sum of one hundred and twenty five dollars to be levied of their respective goods and chattles lands and tenements but to be void on condition that the said John Fitzgeral, make his personal appearance before the Judge of the Circuit Court at a Court to be held at the Court house in Cleveland on the 1st Wednesday after the 4th Monday of December, next, then and there to answer a charge of the State exhibited against him by indictment for Tipling and abide by and preform and satisfy the judgment of the Court or surrender himself to prison, and not depart thence without leve had and   (P-190) obtained.

Given under our hands and seals this 6th October, 1838.
                              his
                    John X Fitzgerel (Seal)
                         mark

                    William Poe   (Seal)

December Term
     1939

State   )
)
   vs   )   Tipling ---
)
John Fitzgerrel   )   Came the attorney General who prose-
                           cutes for the State as well as the
defendant in his own proper person and this Cause is continued until the next term by consent and there upon came
the defendant together with John Walker and William Poe, who
acknowledged them selves Jointly indebted to the State of
Tennessee in the sum of two hundred - to be levied of their
goods and chattles lands and Tenements but to be void on condition that John Fitzgeral make his personal appearance at
the Court house in Cleveland at a Court to be held on the
4th Monday of April next, and on Wednesday of the Term, then
and there to answer a charge of the State Exhibited against
him by indictment for keeping a Tipling house and not depart
the Court without leave.

April Term, 1839

State   )
)
   vs   )   Tipling

Came the attorney General who prose-cutes for the State as well as the defendant in his own proper person who being charged upon the bill of Indictment for plea says he is not guilty and for his trial puts himself upon the County and the Attorney General doth the like and thereupon came a jury of good and lawful men towit: (P-191) Charles Dodd, Robert Hood Absolam, *John Towns, Joseph Billingsly, John McMinn, Uriah Shipley, Joshua Stafford, Isaac Huffaker, Thomas Smith, James Haggard, Hiram Brandon, who being elected tried and sworn to well and truly try the Issue --- between the State of Tennessee and the defendant on their oath say the defendant is guilty in maner and form as charged in the bill of Indictment. *Coleman

It is therefore considered by the Court that the defendant pay to the State of Tennessee a fine of one dollar and the costs of this prosecution and remain in the custody of the Sheriff until fine and costs are paid or Security given therefore and thereupon came in to Court Isaac Smith and acknowledged himself security for the defendant for the payment of the fine and cost.

It is therefore considered by the Court that the State of Tennessee recover of the defendant and Isaac Smith his security the fine and cost aforesaid, and that execution issue accordingly and C.

John Fitzgeral)

State of Tennessee)
)
vs)
)
William Poe)

Came the Grand jury into open Court and returned a presentment against the defendant for un-lawful Gameing signed by all of said Grand jury which is in the words and figures, following --

To wit:

(P-192)
State of Tennessee) Circuit Court
) August Term
Bradley County) Eighteen hundred and Thirty Eight

The grand Jurors, in behalf of the State of Tennessee

elected empaneled sworn and charged to enquire for the boddy
of the County of Bradley aforesaid upon their oath present
that a certain William Poe, late of said County labourer,
on the fifteenth day of August in the year of our Lord one
Thousand eight hundred and Thirty Eight, with force and arms
in the County of Bradley, aforesaid unlawfully did gamble
and play at a certain game of hazard with cards for one
pair of shoes and ---- shirt of the value of one dollar and
fifty cents good and lawful money of the State being then
and there bet and hazarded at and upon said Game of hazard
so played as aforesaid Contrary to the form of the statutes
in such case made and provided and against the peace and dignity of the State.

Endorsement ----

Presentment ----

The State)
)
vs) Found on the testimony of John S. Smith
) Foreman, James Shaddle, Thomas McCarty,
William Poe) Gilford Gatlin, William Thornburg, Benjamin Murry, N. Barksdale, J. A. Fletch-
er, JM Chambers, John McNear, Peter W. Nash, William Vernon,
John Simmons.

Capias ----

State of Tennessee,

To the Sheriff of Bradley County Greeting: You are
hereby commanded to take the boddy of William Poe, if to be
found in your County and him safely keep so that you have him
before the Judge of our Circuit Court at a Court to be held
for Bradley County at the Court house in Cleveland on the
4th Monday of December next, and on the 3rd day of said term.

Then and there to answer a charge of the State Exhibited
against him by a presentment for unlawful Gameing and have
you then and there this writ:

Witness - Henry Price, Clerk of our said Court at
office in Cleveland the 4th Monday of August, A. D. 1838.

Henry Price

Clerk.

(P-193) Endorsement - Capias --

The State   )
)
   vs   )   Issued September the 5th 1838.
)
William Poe   )   Came to hand the 6th September 1838,
                      Executed by arresting the within de-
fendant and bond taken for his appearance this the 6th day
of October, 1838.

John Hughs

Deputy Sheriff

Bond ----

We, William Poe, John Fitzgeral and James McCallister, acknowledge ourselves indebted to the State of Tennessee that is to say William Poe in the sum of two hundred and fifty dollars and said John Fitzgeral and James McCallester in the sum of one hundred and Twenty five dollars each to be levyed of our goods and chattles lands and tenements but to be void on condition that the said William Poe shall make his personal appearance before the Judge of the Circuit Court to be held at the Court house in Cleveland on the 1st Wednesday after the 4th Monday of December next, then and there to answer a charge Exhibited against him by Present- ment for unlawful gameing and abide and preform and satis- fy the Judgment of the Court or surrender him self to pris- on and not depart the Court without leave first had and obtained.

Given under our hands and seals

this 6th day of October, 1838.
                    his
              William X Poe (Seal)
                 mark
               his
             John X Fitzgeral (Seal)
               mark
             James McCallester (Seal)

John Hughes   )
)
   Dept Sheriff)

Circuit Court December Term, 1838.

State   )

vs   )   Came the State by his Attorney General
)   and the defendant in his proper person
William Poe   )   and by the Consent of the parties this
)   Cause is continued until next Term of
this Court and thereupon came the said defendant to gether
with John Walker, who acknowledged them selves indebted to
the State of Tennessee jointly in the sum of two hundred
and fifty dollars, to be levied of there respective goods
and chattles   (P-194)   lands and tenements to the use
of the State yet to be void on condition that William Poe,
make his personal appearance before the Judge of our next
Circuit Court to be held for the County of Bradley at the
Court house in Cleveland on the 4th Monday of April next
and on Wednesday of said Term and in and before said Court
answer a charge of the State exhibited against him by an
indictment for a misdemeanor & not depart the Court without leave.

Circuit Court April Term, 1839.

State   )
)
   vs   )   Gameing   ----
)
William Poe   )   The attorney General comes to prosecute
                        on behalf of the State and comes the
defendant in proper person, and on motion of the attorney
General and for reasons appearing to the sattisfaction of
the Court a Nole proseque is entered in this cause.

    It is therefore considered by the Court that the De-
fendant go hence without day and that the Clerk Tax the
legal Costs in this cause and certify the same to the County Court for inspection and allowance.

_____

_____

_____

State   )
)
   vs   )   Gameing   ----
)
Frederick A. Kance   )   The Grand Jury appeared in open
                            Court and returned a presentment

against the defendant for unlawful Gameing Signed by all of
said Grand Jury which is in the words and figures following
to wit:

State of Tennessee   )
)   Circuit Court, August Term
Bradley County   )   Eighteen hundred and Thirty Eight.

The grand jurors in behalf of the State Elected empaneled
sworn and charged to enquire for the body of the County of
Bradley aforesaid, upon their oath aforesaid present that a
Certain Frederick A. Kance, late of said County, labourer on
the fifteenth day of August (P-195) in the year of our
Lord One thousand Eight hundred and Thirty Eight with force
and arms in the County of Bradley aforesaid unlawfully did
Gamble and play at a Certain game of hazard with cards comon-
ly called Faro one dollar good and lawful money of the State
of Tennessee being then and there bet and hazarded at and upon said game of hazard so played with cards aforesaid contrary to the forms of the Stattutes in such case made and provided and against the peace and dignity of the State.

Endorsement   ---   Presentment

The State vs Frederick A. Kance found on the Testimony
of Hiram K. Turk, Foreman, John Austin, Peter W. Nash, William Thornburgh, N. Barksdale, James Shaddle, John Simmons,
Benjamin Murry, Gilford Gatlin, Jm Chambers, William Vernon,
J. A. Fletcher, John McNair, Thomas McCarty.

Capias   ---

State of Tennessee,

To the Sheriff of Bradley County, Greeting: You are hereby
commanded to take the boddy of Frederick A. Kance if to be
found in your County and him safely keep so that you have
have him before the Judge of the Circuit Court at a Court to
be held for Bradley County at the Court house in Cleveland
on the 4th Monday of December next and on the 3rd day of said
Term then and there to answer a charge of the State exhibited
against him by presentment for unlawful Gameing and have you
then there this writ

Witness - Henry Price, Clerk of our said Court at office
in Cleveland the 4th Monday of August, 1838.

                    Henry Price, Clerk

Endorsement   ----

Capias ----

The State vs Frederick A. Kance, issued September 7th 1838,
Executed on the F. A. Kance on the 8th of December 1838.

                    Wm. McKamy, Dept. Sheriff.

  Bond ----

State of Tennessee   )
)
McMinn County   )   This day we F. A. Kance, Samuel
                                 C. Agnew, (P-196) All of the
County of McMinn, and State of Tennessee, acknowledged our
selves indebted to the State of Tennessee in the following
sums to wit: The said F. A. Kance, in the sum of two hundred and fifty dollars and S. C.Agnew, his security in the
sum of two hundred and fifty dollars to be levyed of the
goods chattles lands and tenements to the use of the State
but to be void on condition that the said F. A. Kance make
his personal appearance before the Judge of the Circuit
Court a Court to be held for Bradley County at the Court
house in Cleveland on the first Wednesday after the 4th
Monday in December next then and there answer a charge of
the State of Tennessee exhibited against him by an Indictment for unlawful gameing and then and there abide by and
preform the Judgment of the Court thereon to be given and
not depart said Court with out leve then this obligation
is to be void otherwise to be and remain in full force and
effect

        Given under our hands and seals

        this 8th Day of December, 1838

                            F. A. Kance (Seal)

                            S. C. Agnew (Seal)

Wm McKamy, Dept. Sheriff.

                        December Term, 1838.

State   )
)
    vs   )   Gameing ----
)
Frederick A. Kance   )   Came the attorney General who pro-
                                 secutes for the State as well as
the defendant in his own proper person and by consent and

with the assent of the next term of this Court Whereupon came the defendant and George Wesmoreland and John Irven into open Court and severly acknowledged themselves indebted to the State of Tennessee that is to say the said defendant in the sum of two hundred and fifty dollars and the (P-197) said George Wesmoreland and John Irven in the sum of two hundred and fifty dollars to be levied of their respective goods and chattles and tenements but to be void on condition the defendant make his personal appearance at the next term of the Circuit Court to be held for Bradley County at the Court house in Cleveland on the 4th Monday of April next and on Wednesday of the Term then and there answer a charge of the State Exhibited against him for unlawful Gameing and not depart the Court without leave.

Circuit Court -

April Term, 1839

State)
)
vs) Gameing ---
)
Frederick A. Kance) The attorney General comes to prosecute on behalf of the State and moved the Court for leve to enter a Nole proseque, in this cause which is granted.

It is therefore considered by the Court that the defendant go hence and that the Clerk Tax the legal costs in this cause and Certify the same to the County Court for inspection and allowance.

_____

_____

_____

The State)
)
vs) Gameing ---
)
Lewis A. Glass) The Grand Jury appeared in open Court and returned a presentment against the defendant for unlawful Gameing, Signed by all of said Grand Jury, Which is in the words and figures following to wit:

State of Tennessee) Circuit Court

Bradley County   )   August Term
                         Eighteen hundred and Thirty Eight.

The grand jurors in behalf of the State of Tennessee, elected
empanneled sworn and charged to enquire for the body of the
County of Bradley aforesaid upon their oaths prosent that a
Certain Lewis A. Glass,   (P-198)   late of said County
labourer on the 12th day of August in the year of our Lord
one thousand Eight hundred and Thirty Eight with force and
arms in the County of Bradley aforesaid did Gamble and play
at a certain game of hazard with cards for one dollar good
and lawful money of the State being then and there bet and
hazarded at and upon said Game of hazard so played with
cards as aforesaid contrary to the form of the Statutes iin
such case made and provided and against the peace and dignity of the State

          Endorsement - Presentment ---

The State   )
)
    vs   )   Found on the testimony of John S.
)   Smith Foreman -- John Austin, James
Lewis A. Glass   )   Shaddle, N. Barksdale, Thomas Mc-
                         Carty, Peter W. Nash, Wm Thornburgh
J. A. Fletcher, Gilford Gatlin, Jm Chambers, John Simmons
John McNair, William Vernen, Benjamin Murry

          Capias   ----

The State of Tennessee

     To the Sheriff of Bradley County Greeting: You are
hereby commanded to take the body of Lewis A. Glass if to
be found in your County and him safely keep so that you have
him before the Judge of the Circuit Court at a Court to be
held at the Court house in Cleveland on the 4th Monday of
December next and on the first Wednesday of said Term then
and there to answer a charge of the State exhibited against
him by presentment for unlawful Gameing and have you then
there this writ, Witness - Henry Price, Clerk of said Court
at office in Cleveland the 4th Monday of August, 1838.

                    Henry Price, Clerk

          Endorsement - Capias ---

The State vs Lewis A. Glass, issued September the 4th
1838.

Came to hand the same day issued Executed by arresting the within named defendant and taking bond this the 12th day of September 1838.

James Lauderdale, Sheriff.

(P-199)   Bond ---

State of Tennessee, Bradley County,

I, James Lauderdale, Sheriff in and for the County aforesaid having on this 12th day of September 1838, arrested the body of Lewis A. Glass, by virtue of a Capias issued from the Circuit Court of said County commanding me to take the body of said Lewis A. Glass to answer a charge of the State exhibited against him by indictment for unlawful gameing and thereupon the said Lewis A. Glass is defendant together with Jesse Poe, security before me James Lauderdale, Sheriff as aforesaid acknowledged themselves jointly and severally indebted to the State of Tennessee in the sum of two hundred and fifty dollars each to be levied of their goods and chattles lands and tenements respectively but to be void on condition the said Lewis A. Glass, shall make his personal appearance before the Judge of the Circuit Court at a Court to be held for the County aforesaid, at the Court house in Cleveland on the first Wednesday after the 4th Monday in December next to answer a charge of the State exhibited against him aforesaid and abide by perform and satisfy the judgment of said Court there on to be rendered and not depart the Court without leave.

Lewis A. Glass   (Seal)

Jesse Poe   (Seal)

James Lauderdale,

Circuit Court

December Term, 1838.

The State   )
)
     vs   )   Gameing ---
)
Lewis A. Glass   )   Came the attorney General as well
                          as the defendant in his own proper
person and by consent and the assent of the Court this
cause is continued untill the next term whereupon came the
defendant & John Baty and William Childers into open Court

and acknowledged themselves severly indebted to the State of Tennessee, that is to say (P 200)   the said defendant in the sum of two hundred and fifty dollars, and the said John Baty and William Childress in the sum of two hundred and fifty dollars jointly to be levied of their respective goods and Chattles lands and tenements but to be void on condition that the said Lewis A. Glass do make his personal appearance at the next term of the Circuit Court to be held for the County of Bradley at the Court house in Cleveland on the 4th Monday of April next, and Wednesday of the Term then and there to answer a charge of the State exhibited against him for unlawful gameing and not depart the Court without leave.

Circuit Court

April Term, 1839

State   )
)
   vs   )   Gameing ---
)
Lewis A. Glass   )   Came the Attorney General to prose-
                                  cute on behalf of the State and also
came the defendant in proper person and on motion of the Attorney General and from reasons appearing to the sattisfaction of the Court a Nole proseque is entered in this cause.

It is therefore considered by the Court that the defendant go hence and that the Clerk tax the legal Costs in this Cause and Certify the same to the County Court for Inspection and allowance.

State   )
)
   vs   )   Gameing ---
)
William Lowery   )   The Grand Jury appeared in open
                                  Court and returned a presentment
against the defendant for unlawful Gameing Signed by all of said Grand Jury which is in the words and figures following to wit:

State of Tennessee   )   Circuit Court, August Term -
)   Eighteen hundred and thirty eight

Bradley County   )

                         (P-201) The Grand jurors in behalf of the State of Tennessee Elected empaneled sworn and charged to enquire for the body of the County of Bradley aforesaid upon their oath present that a Certain William Lowery late of said County labourer on the first day of August in the year of our Lord One Thousand Eight hundred and thirty eight with force and arms in the County of Bradley aforesaid unlawfuly did gamble and play at a certain game of hazard with cards for twelve and one half cents good and lawful money of the United States, then and there being bet and hazarded at and upon said game of hazard so played with cards as aforesaid contrary to the form of the Statutes in such case made and provided and against the peace and dignity of the State.

         Endorsement - Presentment --

The State   )

    vs   )   Found on the testimony of John M. Gifford, John Auston, foreman of the

William Lowry   )   Grand Jury, Peter W. Nash, William
                         Thornburgh, N. Barksdale, James Sheddle, John McNair, John Simmons, Jm Chambers, Benjamin Murry, Gilford Gatlin, William Vernon.

         Capias ---

State of Tennessee

      To the Sheriff of McMinn County, Greeting: You are hereby commanded to take the body of William Lowery, if to be found in your County and him safely keep so that you have him before the Judge of our Circuit Court at a Court to be held for Bradley County at the Court house in Cleveland on the 4th Monday of December next then and there to answer a charge of the State exhibited against him by presentment for unlawful Gameing, and have you then and there this writ, Witness --

Henry Price, Clerk,   (P-202)   of our said Court at office in Cleveland the 4th Monday of August 1838.

                     Henry Price,

                         Clerk.

Endorsement - Capias --

The State vs William Lowery, issued September the 6th, 1838.

Executed the 15th September, 1838
                    J. T. Reed, Depty Sheriff.

    Bond,

State of Tennessee, McMinn County,

I, James T. Reed Depty Sheriff in and for said County
aforesaid having on this 15th day of September, 1838, arrested the body of William Lowrey, by virtue of a Capias
issued from the Circuit Court of Bradley County commanding
me to take the body of William Lowery to answer a charge
of the State Exhibited against him by presentment for unlawful Gambling thereupon the said William Lowery defendant together with George M. Murrell, Surety before me,
James T. Reed, Dept. Sheriff as aforesaid acknowledged
themselves jointly and severaly indebted to the State of
Tennessee in the sum of two hundred and fifty dollars each
to be leveyed of there goods and chattles lands and tenements
Respectively but to be void on condition the said William Lowery shall make his personal appearance before the said Circuit
Court at a Court to be held for the County aforesaid at the
Court house in Cleveland on the 4th Monday of December next
to answer the said charge of the State Exhibited against
him as aforesaid and then and there abide by preform and satisfy the judgment of said Court thereon to be rendered and
not depart the Court without leave.

                        William Lowery (Seal)

                        George M. Murrell (Seal)

        December Term
            1838

State   )
)
    vs   )   Gameing --
)
William Lowery   )   Came the attorney General who prose-
                                cutes for the State and by consent
and   (P-203)   with the assent of the Court this cause
is continued until the next term of the Court whereupon
came Thomas J. Campbell into open Court and acknowledged
himself indebted to the State of Tennessee, in the sum of
two hundred and fifty dollars to be levied of his goods
and Chattles, lands and tenements but to be void on condition William Lowery shall make his personal appearance
at the next term of the Circuit Court for the County of
Bradley at the Court house in Cleveland on the 4th Monday
of April next and on Wednesday of the Term, then and there
answer a charge of the State Exhibited against him for un-

lawful Gameing and not depart the Court without leave.

Circuit Court April Term, 1839.

State)
)   Gameing ---
vs)
)   The attorney General comes to prose-
William Lowery)   cute on behalf of the State and also
                        the defendant comes in his proper
person and on motion of the attorney General and for reasons
appearing to the satisfaction of the Court a Nole proseque
is entered in this Cause and thereupon the defendant confessed judgment for the costs of this prosecution.

It is therefore considered by the Court that the State
of Tennessee recover of the said defendant the costs in
this behalf expended as confessed aforesaid and that execution issue accordingly &c.

The State)
)
vs A. B.)   The Grand jury appeard in open Court
)   and returned a bill of indictment
Alexander Webb)   against the defendant for an assault
                        and battery endorsed there on a true
bill by William Grant there foreman   (P-204)   Which bill
is in the words and figures following to wit:

State of Tennessee)
)   Circuit Court
Bradley County)   April Term
                        Eighteen hundred and thirty nine.
The grand Jurors in behalf of the State of Tennessee elected
empanneled sworn and charged to enquire for the body of the
County of Bradley aforesaid upon their oath present that
Alexander Webb, late of said County labourer on the Seventeenth day of February in the year of our Lord one thousand
eight hundred and thirty nine, with force and arms in the
County of Bradley aforesaid an assault did make in and upon
the body of one James K. Pate then and there being in the
peace of the State and did then and there beat bruise wound
and ill treat the said James K. Pate to the great damage of

him the said James K. Pate and to the evil example of all
others in like maner offending and against the peace and
dignity of the State.

Samuel Frazier
Attorney General for the
3rd Judetial District.

Endorsment -- Indictment --

State vs Alexander Webb, James K. Pate prosecutor, James
Britton, John Shugart, James Riddle, Witnesses for the State
Sworn and sent before the Grand Jury 23rd April 1839,

Henry Price, Clerk

A true bill   William Grant, fourman
                          of the Grand jury.

Capias ---

The State of Tennessee

    To the Sheriff of Bradley County, Greeting: You are
hereby commanded to take the body of Alexander Webb if in
your County to be found and him safely keep so that you
have him before the Judge of the Circuit Court now setting
for Bradley County at the Court house in Cleveland then
and there to answer a charge of the State exhibited against
him by an indictment for an assault and battery and have
you then and there this writ:
                                              our
    Witness - Henry Price, Clerk, (P-205) of/said Court
at office in Cleveland the 4th Monday of April 1839.

Henry Price, Clerk

    Endorsment - Capias - - - - The State vs Alexander Webb

    Issued 24th April 1839.

    The defendant comes into Court and submits this 24th
April 1839

John Brown, Dept. Sheriff.

    Bond,

Know all men by these presents that we, Alexander Webb,
James Webb

and John Murphy acknowledge ourselves indebted to the State of Tennessee to be leveyed of our goods and chattles, lands and tenements that is to say Alexander Webb, the defendant, in the sum of two hundred and fifty dollars, and James Webb and John Murphy in the sum of one hundred and twenty five dollars each yet to be void if the said Alexander Webb shall make his personal appearance before the Judge of the Circuit Court at the Court house in Cleveland on the first Wednesday after the 4th Monday in April next, there and then answer a charge of the State exhibited against him for an assault and battery upon the body of one James K. Pate, and abide by preform and satisfy the judgment of said Court or surrender himself to custody or they will do it for him.

                    Alexander Webb, (Seal)

                    James Webb (Seal)

                    John Murphy (Seal)

        April Term, 1839.

State   )
)
    vs A. B.   )   Came the Attorney General who prose-
)   cutes for the State and the defendant
Alexander Webb   )   in his own proper person who being
                            charged upon the bill of indictment
for an assault and battery for plea thereto says because he
is guilty he will not contend but submits to the Judgment of
the Court.

        It is therefore considered by the Court that for such
his offence he pay a fine of Ten dollars (P-206) and
that he remain in the care of the Sheriff until fine and
cost is payed or surety given, therefore and thereupon
came John Hayse in to open Court and acknowledged himself
surety for the fine and cost aforesaid.

        It is therefore considered by the Court that the State
of Tennessee recover of the defendant and John Hayse, his
securety the fine and costs aforesaid for which Execution
may issue.

State   )
)
    vs   )   The Grand Jury appeared in open
)   Court and returned a bill of
Alfred Copland &   )   indictment against the defendants
Jabell Parks   )   endorsed thereon a true bill by

William Grant there fourman which is in the words and figures following to wit:

State of Tennessee)
)
Bradley County) Circuit Court April Term Eighteen hundred and thirty nine.

The Grand jurors in behalf of the State of Tennessee impaneld sworn and charged to enquire for the body of the County of Bradley aforesaid upon there oath present that Alfred Copland and Jabell Parks late of said County laborers on the twenty fifth day of December in the year of our Lord One thousand Eight hundred and thirty nine with force and arms in the County of Bradley aforesaid an assault did make in and upon the body of Hannah Horne then and there being in the peace of the State by them and there besetting the dweling house of Riley Horne she the said Hannah Horn being the wife of the said Riley Horn then and there living and being in said dweling house and by then and there throwing Rocks and other messels at upon the top of the said dweling house then the said Hannah Horn then and there living and being in said dweling house and by then and there throwing rocks and other missiles at upon the top of the said dweling house her the said Hannah Horn then and there living and being in said dwelling house, to the evil example of all others in like manner offending and against the peace and dignity of the State.

Samuel Frazier, Attorney General
For the 3rd Solicitorial district

(P-207)   Indictment - Endorsment -

The State vs Alfred Copeland and Jabell Parks, Riley Horn prosecutor, John I Parker, Francis Langly, Thomas Smith William Coker, Samuel Parks, John Copeland

Witness sworn and sent before the Grand Jury the 24th April 1839.

Henry Price, Clerk

A true bill   Wm. Grant Fourman of the
Grand Jury.

Capias ---

State of Tennessee

To the Sheriff of Bradley County, Greeting: You are

hereby commanded to take the bodys of Alfred Copeland and
Jabell Parks instantly if to be found in your County and
them safelay keep so that you have them before the Judge
of the Circuit Court now setting for Bradley County at the
Court house in Cleveland then and there to answer a charge
of the State Exhibited against them by an Indictment for
malicious mischief and have you then and there this writ:

Witness -- Henry Price, Clerk of our said Court at
office in Cleveland the 4th Monday of April 1839.

Henry Price, Clerk.

Endorsment , I James Lauderdale do hereby autherise and
Dept. David Ragen, to execute this writ, this 24th April 1839.

James Lauderdale, Sheriff

Capias --

The State vs Alfred Copeland, Jabell Parks.

Issued 24th of April 1839.

Came to hand the 24th April Executed on Jabell Parks
Alfred Copeland not found this 25th April 1839.

Daniel Ragain, Dept. Sheriff

Bond --

State of Tennessee   )   This day came Alfred Copeland
)   and J. F. Parkes, and John
Bradley County   )   Copeland before me and acknowl-
                           edged themselves to be indebted
                           to the State of Tennessee as

follows to wit:

Alfred Copeland and J. F. Parks in the sum of One hundred
dollars jointly & the said Samuel Parks and John Copeland in
the sum of one hundred dollars jointly and severaly to be
void if said Alfred Copeland and Jabell Parks make their personal appearance at the next term of the Circuit Court of
Bradley County to be held. (P-208) in the town of Cleveland on the 4th Monday of said Term to answer the State
of Tennessee upon a charge of Stoneing of a mile house and
safely keep so that you have them
*Of April next on the first Wednesday

dwelling house and not depart the Court without leave of the same this the 9th day of January 1839.

> A. Copeland (Seal)
>
> J. F. Parks (Seal)
>
> Samuel Parks (Seal)
>
> John Copeland (Seal)

Circuit Court April Term , 1839.

State

vs

Alfred Copeland &
Jabell Parks

Came the attorney General who prosecutes for the State as well as the defendants who being charged upon the Indictment for plea thereto says they are not guilty and of that they put themselves upon the County and the Attorney General doth the like and thereupon came a jury to wit: Rutherford Rose, Charles Dodd, Robert Hood Absalom Coleman, John Towns, Joseph Billingsley, John Mc-Minn, Uriah Shiply, Joshua Stafford, Isaac Huffaker, James Haggard and Hiram Brandon, who being elected tried and sworn well and truly to try the issue ---- between the State of Tennessee and the defendants upon their oaths do say that the defendants are not guilty in manor and form as charged in the Indictment.

It is therefore considered by the Court that the defendant go hence without day and that the Clerk Tax the legal costs in this cause and certify the same to the County Court for inspection and allowance.

_____

_____

_____

State

vs

John R. Dooling

The grand Jury appeared in open Court and brought with them a presentment against the defendant -- Gameing - Signed by all (P-209) of said grand Jury, which is in the words and figures following to wit:

State of Tennessee   )   Circuit Court
)   August Term
Bradley County   )   Eighteen hundred and Thirty Eight.

The Grand jurors in behalf of the State of Tennessee Elected
empanaled sworn and charged to enquire for the body of the
County of Bradley aforesaid upon there oath present that a
certain John R. Doolin, late of said County labourer on the
fifteenth day of August in the year of our Lord one Thousand eight hundred and thirty eight with force and arms in
the County of Bradley aforesaid unlawfuly did gamble and
play at a certain game of hazard with cards commonly called
Faro, for one dollar good and lawful money of the State of
Tennessee being then and there bet and hazarded at and upon
said game of hazard so played with cards as aforesaid contrary to the form of the statutes in such case made and
provided and against the peace and dignity of the State.

Endorsment - Presentment -

The State vs John R. Dooling

found on the testemony of Hiram K. Turk, Foreman, John
Austin, Peter W. Nash, N. Barksdale, James Sheddle, Wm Thornburgh, Benjamin Murrey, John Simmons, Gilford Gatlin, Jm
Chambers, William Vernon, J. A. Fletcher, John McNair, Thomas McCarty.

Capias   ---

State of Tennessee,

      To the Sheriff of Bradley County Greeting: You
are hereby commanded to take the body of John R. Dooling,
if to be found in your County and him safely keep so that
you have him before the Judge of the Circuit Court at a
Court to be held at Cleveland 4th Monday   (P-210) of
December next and the first Wednesday of said Term, then
and there to answer a charge of the State Exhibited against
him by presentment for unlawful Gameing, and have you then
and there this writ:

Witness - Henry Price Clerk of our said Court at office
in Cleveland the 4th Monday of August, 1838.

                  Henry Price, Clerk

Endorsment - Capias -

The State vs John R. Doolin, Issued September the 7th 1838.

Came to hand the same day issued executed by arresting John D.
Doolin, on the 8th of September, 1838.

John Brown, Depty. Sheriff

Bond ———

State of Tennessee, Bradley County

I, John Brown, Dept. Sheriff in for Bradley County, having on the 6th day of September 1838. Arrested the body of John R. Doolin, by virtue of a Capias issued from the Circuit Court of said County commanding me to take the body of John R. Doolin to answer a charge of the State exhibited against him by presentment for unlawful Gameing Thereupon the said John R. Doolin, is defendant to gather with J. G. Glass suerety before me John Brown, Dept. Sheriff as aforesaid acknowledged themselves jointly and severaly indebted to the State of Tennessee in the Sum of Two hundred and fifty dollars each to be levyed of there goods and Chattles lands and tenements respectively but to be void on condition John R. Doolin make his personal appearance before the Circuit Court at a Court to be held for the County aforesaid at the Court house in Cleveland on the first Wednesday after the 4th Monday of December next to answer a charge of the State Exhibited against him as aforesaid and then and there abdde by preform and satisfy the judgment of said Court thereon to be rendered and not depart the Court without leave.

John R. Doolin (Seal)

James G. Glass (Seal)

(P-211)   Circuit Court

December Term, 1838.

State   )
)
  vs   )   Came the Attorney General who prose-
)   cutes for the State as well as the
John R. Doolin)   defendant in proper person who being
                    charged upon the Presentment says
he can not deny but that he is guilty in manner and form
as charged therein and submits to the judgment of the Court.

It is therefore considered by the Court that for such his offense he pay a fine of Ten dollars and all costs in this behalf expended and that he be taken by the Sheriff and remain inCustody until fine and costs aforesaid be paid or security given therefore, and thereupon came Thomas H. Calloway into open Court together with the defendant and

agreede that -- judgment might be rendered against him
with the defendant jointly for the fine and costs assesed
against the defendant on yesterday being ten dollars and
the costs of this prosecution.

It is therefore considered by the Court that the State
of Tennessee recover of the defendant and Thomas H. Calloway
his surety the fine and costs aforesaid confessed and that
Execution issue accordingly.

State   )

  vs   )   Gameing ---

James A. Lea)   Came the Grand Jury into open Court
               and returned a presentment against
the defendant for unlawful Gameing, Signed by all of said
grand jurors which is in the words and figures following
to wit:

    State of Tennessee   )

    Bradley County   )   Circuit Court,
                      April Term, Eighteen hun-
dred and Thirty nine.

The grand jurors in behalf of the State of Tennessee
elected impaneled sworn and charged to enquire for the body
of the County (P-212) of Bradley aforesaid upon their
oath present that a certain James A. Lea, late of said
County labourer on the Tenth day of January in the year
of our Lord One thousand eight hundred and Thirty nine with
force and arms in the County of Bradley aforesaid unlawfuly
did gamble and play at a certain game of hazard played with
cards for twelve and one half cents good and lawful money
of the State of Tennessee being then and there bet and hazarded at and upon said game of hazard so played with cards
as aforesaid contrary to the form of the statutes in such
case made and provided and against the peace and dignity
of the State.

Endorsment - Presentment -

The State vs James A. Lea, found upon the testimony of

Thomas H. Caloway, William Grant, James Long, Ezekiel Spriggs, James A. Fletcher, Alfred Davis, Joseph Mee, Benjamin McCarty, John Anderson, Lewis Price, Joseph Seabourn, Thomas W. Back, Alex Perry.

Circuit Court

April Term, 1839.

The State	)	
vs	)	Gameing ----
James A. Lea	)	Came the attorney General who prose-

cutes for the State as Well as the
defendant who being charged upon presentment for unlawful
gameing for plea there to say that because he is guilty
he will not contend but submits to the judgment of the
Court.

It is therefore considered by the Court that for such
his offence he pay a fine of ten dollars and all costs in
this behalf expended and that he remain in the Custody of
the Sheriff until fine and costs be paid or surety given
therefore and thereupon came the defendant and William M.
Biggs into open Court and confessed Judgment for the fine
and costs aforesaid.

It is therefore considered by the Court that the State
of Tennessee recover of the defendant and William M. Biggs
the fine and costs as aforesaid confessed and   (P-213)
that Execution issue accordingly.

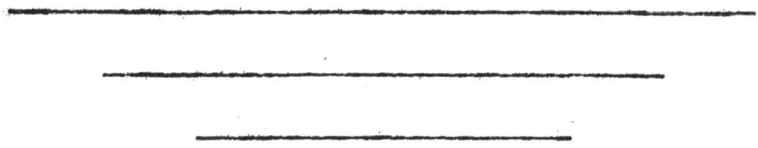

State	)	
vs Sarafacias	)	The Sheriff of Hamilton County, greeting: whare as heretofore
William Windham	)	to wit: On the 30th day of Aug- ust 1838, at to wit: in the Coun-

ty of Bradley, William Windham entered into recognizance
before the Honorable Judge of the Circuit Court whare
upon he acknowledged himself indebted to the State of
Tennessee in the sum of two hundred and fifty dollars to
be levied of his goods and Chattles lands and Tenements
to the use of the State of Tennessee, Yet to be void on

condition that the defendant William Windham, make his personal appearance at the Court house in Cleveland on the first Wednesday after the fourth Monday of December, 1838, And then answer a charge of the State for unlawful Gameing and on this day to wit, At the Circuit Court to be held for the County of Bradley at the Court house in Cleveland on the first Wednesday after the fourth Monday of December 1838. Came on the State by her Attorney General and the said William Windham being solemly called to come into Court and answer said charge, Came not but made default.

It is therefore considered by the Court that the said defendant William Windham has forfeted to the State of Tennessee the sum of two hundred and fifty dollars unless he show sufficient cause to the contrary at the next term of this Court and you are therefore hereby commanded to make known to the said William Windham to be and appear before the Judge of our next Circuit Court to be held for the County of Bradley at the Court house in Cleveland on the first Wednesday after the fourth Monday of April next, to show cause if any there can be why the States (P-214) Execution ought not to have Issued against him for the sum of two hundred and fifty dollars according to the tener and effect of his daid recognizance here in fail not and have you there and then this writ

Witness Henry Price, Clerk of our said Court at office in Cleveland the 4th Monday of December, 1838.

Henry Price, Clerk

Endorsment - Sifa.

The State vs William Windham, Issued the 25th January 1839, Came to hand the 25th February 1839.

Search made up to the 28th of March and not to be found in my County by me E. H. Freeman, Sheriff.

Circuit Court April Term, 1839.

State	)	
	)	
vs Sifa	)	Gameing --
	)	
William Windham	)	Came the Attorney General who prosecutes for the State and by consent

of the parties and with the assent of the Court a Noleproseque is entered in this cause and thereupon came William Windham, and Nathaniel Hayse into open Court and confessed a judgment for the Cause in this behalf expended.

It is therefore considered by the Court that the State of Tennessee recover of William Windham and Nathaniel Hayse his security the costs in this behalf expended for which execution may issue.

State)
  vs Sifa) Came the attorney General who prose-
William Windham) cutes for the State and the defendant
also and on motion and by consent
and with the assent of the Court
the forfeture heretofore entered in this cause is set aside and there upon came William Windham and Nathaniel Hayse in- to open Court and confessed a judgment for this cause.

It is therefore considered by the Court that the State of Tennessee Recover of the defendant and Nathaniel Hayse his security the costs on this behalf exspended for which execution may issue.

(P-215)
State)
  vs Sifac)
Jesse Poe) State of Tennessee to the Sher of
Bradley County Greeting:

Whare as heretofore to wit, on the 30th of August 1838, At to wit: In the County of Bradley, William Wind- ham, and Jesse Poe entered into recognizance before me Judge of the Circuit Court whare upon they acknowledged themselves indebted to the State of Tennessee in the sum of two hundred and fifty dollars, each to be levied of their goods chattles lands and tenements to the use of the State of Tennessee.

Yet to be void on condition that William Windham make his personal appearance at the Court house in Cleve- land on the first Wednesday after the 4th Monday of Dec- ember 1838, and then answer a charge of the State Ex- hibited against him for unlawful Gameing and not depart the Court without leve and on the day to wit, the first Wednesday after the 4th

Monday of December 1838, Came on the Attorney General who
prosecutes for the State and the said William Windham, being solomly called to come in to Court and answer said
charge came not but made default and said Jesse Poe being
solomly called to come into Court and bring with him the
body of William Windham came not but made default.

It is therefore considered by the Court that the Said
Jesse Poe, has forfeited to the State of Tennessee the sum
of two hundred and fifty dollars according to the Tener of
his said recognizance unless he show sufficient cause to
the contrary at the next term of this Court, and you are
therefore hereby commanded to make known to the said Jesse
Poe to be and appear before the Judge of our next Circuit
Court to be held for   (P-216)   the County of Bradley at the
Court house in Cleveland on the first Wednesday after the
4th Monday of April next, 1839, to show cause if any he can
why the States Execution ought not have issued against him
for the sum of two hundred and fifty dollars according to the
tener and effect of his said recognizance herein fail not and
have you then and there this writ,

Witness Henry Price, Clerk of our said Court at office
in Cleveland, the 4th Monday of December, 1838.

Henry Price, Clerk

Endorsement - Sifa

The State vs Jesse Poe

Issued January the 25th, 1839.

Came to hand 6th of April, 1839, Executed by making
known the within to Jesse Poe, the 15th of April, 1839.

James Lauderdale, Sheriff
of Bradley County.

Circuit Court, April Term, 1839.

State   )
)
   vs Sifa   )   The Attorney General comes to prosecute
)   on behalf of the State and on motion
Jesse Poe   )   a Nole proseque is entered in this cause
                   and thereupon came William Windham and
Nathaniel Hays who confessed judgment for the costs of this
prosecution.

It is therefore considered by the Court that State recover of the defendant William Windham, and Nathaniel Hays

who confessed judgment for the costs of this prosecution.

It is therefore considered by the Court that State recover of the defendant William Windham, and Nathaniel Hays the costs so as aforesaid confessed and that execution issue accordingly &c.

State)
)
 vs) Tipling --
)
William Samples) The grand Jury appeared in open
 Court and returned a bill of indictment against the defendant for retailing spirituous Liquors in less quantities than a quart indorsed by their Fourman William Grant, A true bill which is in the words and figures following to wit,

State of Tennessee) Circuit Court
) April Term
Bradley County) Eighteen hundred and thirty nine.

(P-217) The Grand Jurors in behalf of the State of Tennessee elected empaneled sworn and charged to enquire for the body of the County of Bradley upon there oath present that a Certain William Samples, late of said County labourer on the first day of March Eighteen hundred and Thirty nine and on divers other days with force and arms in the County of Bradley aforesaid unlawfuly did vend and sell by retail a certain kind of spiritous Liquers and other kinds of spirituous liquors to one Jacob Russel, and to divers other persons and the jurors aforesaid upon their oath aforesaid do futher present that the said William Samples on the said first day of March Eighteen hundred and Thirty nine and on divers other days and times with force and arms in the County of Bradley aforesaid did unlawfuly vend and sell by retail in quantities less than one quart a certain kind of spirituous liquors cald Brandy, and other kinds of spirituous liquors to one Jacob B. Russell, and to divers other persons and to the Jurors aforesaid upon their oath aforesaid do say that the said William Samples was then and there guilty of keeping a Tipling house contrary to the form of the Statutes in such case made and provided and against the peace and dignity of the State.

Samuel Frazier, Attorney General
for the 3rd Solicitorial
District.

Circuit Court, April Term, 1839.

State   )
)
 vs   ) Tipling
)
William Samples) Comes the Attorney General who prose-
         cutes for the State and the defendant
in proper person and says he cannot deny but that he is guilty in Maner and form as charged (Pages 218 & 219 blank)
(P-220) in the Indictment and submits to the Judgment of
the Court.

  It is therefore considered by the Court that for such
his offence he pay a fine of one dollar and the costs of
this prosecution and thereupon came into Court George W.
Selvidge and acknowledged himself as the security of the
defendant for the payment of the fine and costs aforesaid

  It is therefore considered by the Court that the State
of Tennessee recover of the defendant and George W. Selvedge
his security the fine and costs aforesaid and that Execution
issue.

State   )
)
 vs   ) The grand Jury for the State appeared
) in open Court and returned a bill of
Samuel Dunn &) indictment against Samuel Dunn, Eze-
Harlem Mathes) kiel Dunn & Harlam Mathes Endorsed
         there on a true bill by William Grant
fourman which is in the words and figuers following towit:

State of Tennessee)
)
Bradley County   ) Circuit Court
          April Term - Eighteen hundred and
thirty Nine.. The grand jurors in behalf of the State of

Tennessee elected empaneled sworn and charged to enquire
for the body of the County of Bradley aforesaid upon their
oath present that Samuel Dunn, Harlam Mathes, George Mathes
& Ezekiel Dunn late of said County labourers on the second
day of June, Eighteen hundred and Thirty eight with force
and arms in the county of Bradley aforesaid unlawfuly Rautously and Riotously assembled them selves to brake the
peace of the State of Tennessee and being so assembled afterwards to wit, On the said second day of June in the year
of our Lord One Thousand eight hundred and(P-221) Thirty
nine with force and arms in the County of Bradley aforesaid
unlawfuly ---- and Rioutously comit a vilant trespass upon
the house and premises of One Mark Black by then and there
rautously and riotusly entering in and upon the premises
and ---- of the said Mark Black and then and there with much
force violince and strong hand braking open the doors of
the house of the said Mark Black and then and there unlawfuly Rautously and riotusly entering in to said house and
then and there unlawfuly rautously and riotusly with threat
menewvers and much force and maintaining the possession of
the same to the evil example of all others in like manner
offending and against the peace and dignity of the State.

                    Samuel Frazier, Attorney General
                        for the 3rd Solicitorial District

     Endorsment - Indictment ---

The State vs Samuel Dunn, Harlan Mathes, George Mathes and
Ezekiel Dunn, Mark Black prosecutor, Mark Black Mordicai
Ford, Sampson Dotson, George Reed,

     Witnesses for the State sworn in open Court and sent
before the grand jury the 23rd April 1839.

                    Henry Price, Clerk

     A true bill   Wm Grant, foreman of the
                            grand jury.

     Capias ---

     State of Tennessee

          To the Sheriff of Bradley County Greeting: You are
hereby commanded to take the bodys of Samuel Dunn, Harlam
Mathis George Mathis and Ezekiel Dunn, instantly if to be
found in your County and them safely keep so that you have
them before the Judge of our Circuit Court now setting for
Bradley County at the Court house in Cleveland, then and

there to answer the (P-222) State exhibited against them by an indictment for a Riot and have then and there this writ -

Witness Henry Price, Clerk of our said Court at office in Cleveland the 4th Monday of April, 1839.

Henry Price, Clerk

Endorsment - Capias - Instanter -

State vs Samuel Dunn, and others issued the 23rd April, 1839.

Came to hand the same day Issued Executed by aresting Samuel Dunn, Ezekiel Dunn, and Harlam Mathis but George Mathis is not taken.

James A. Bates, Dept. Sheriff.

Capias --

State of Tennessee

To the Sheriff of Bradley County Greeting: You are hereby commanded to take the body of George Mathis, instantly if in your County to be found and him safely keep so that you have him before the Judge of our Circuit Court, now setting for Bradley County at the Court house in Cleveland then and there to answer a charge of the State Exhibited against him by Indictment for an afray and have you then and there this writ -

Witness - Henry Price, Clerk of our said Court at office in Cleveland the 4th Monday of April, 1839.

Henry Price, Clerk

Endorsment - Capias -

The State vs George Mathis Issued the 23rd of April 1839.

Came to hand the same day Issued Executed by arresting George Mathis and giving him in to Court this 24th April 1839.

James A. Bates, Dept. Sheriff

April Term, 1839.

State   )

)

  vs   )   Came the Attorney General who prosecutes
)   for the State and also for the defendant
Samuel Dunn)   in their proper person who acknowledged
*   themselves indebted to the   (P-223)

State of Tennessee in the sum of two hundred and fifty dollars
each to be levied of there respective goods and chattles lands
and tenements but to be void if said defendants do make there
personal appearance here at the Court house at the present
Term from day to day and answer a charge of the State Exhibited against them for a Riot and not depart the Court without leave and there upon came there into Court, John Mathews
and James A. Bates who solemnly acknowledged themselves to
owe the State of Tennessee the sum of two hundred and fifty
dollars each to be levyed of there respective goods and
Chattles lands and tenements to the use of the State to be
void on condition the defendants Samuel Dunn Ezekiel Dunn
and Ha rlam Mathis do make there personal appearance here
at the Court house at this term from day to day and answer
a charge of the State Exhibited against them for a Riot and
not depart the Court without leave.

State   )

)

  vs   )   A Riot
)

George Mathews)   Came the attorney General who prose-
                cutes for the State and the defendant
George Mathews, also comes in to Court and acknowledges
himself indebted to the State of Tennessee in the Sum of two
hundred and fifty dollars to be levyed of his goods chattles
lands and tenement but to be void on condition said defendant make his personal appearance at the present term of this
Court from day to day and answer a charge of the State exhibited
against him for a Riot and not depart the Court without
leave and there upon Came John Mathews and James M. Dunn
into Court here and acknowledged themselves indebted to the
State of Tennessee in the   (P-224)   sum of two hundred
and fifty dollars each to be leveyed of there goods and
chattles lands and Tenements but to be void on condition
the defendant George Mathews make personal appearance before the Judge of the Circuit Court here, now setting and
answer a charge of the Syate Exhibited against him for a
Riot and not depart the Court without leave.
*& Ezekiel Dunn & Harlam Mathis

    April Term, 1839.

State   )   The attorney General comes to prosecute on
)   behalf of the State and the defendant in
  vs   )   proper person, also comes -- who being
*the *his

Harlam Mathews   )   charged on the Indictment for plea
Samuel Dunn   )   says they are not guilty and the
Ezekiel Dunn &   )   attorney General doth the like and
George Mathews   )   there upon came a jury of good
                             and lawful men to wit:

Herman Brandon, Josiah S. Price, Robert A. Farmer, John W. Kennedy, Thomas Taylor, John Mee, James Hawkins, Daniel J. Stafford, Samuel Lane, Arnett Shields, John F. Larrison & John Kincannon, who being elected tried and sworn to well and truly try the Issue joined between the State of Tennessee and the defendants on trial on there oath say that the defendants Harlin Mathews, Samuel Dunn, and George Mathews are guilty as charged in the Indictment and Ezekiel Dunn is not guilty as Charged in the Indictment

It is therefore considered by the Court that the said Ezikiel Dunn go hence without day and that Harlin Mathews, Samuel Dunn & George Mathews pay a fine of one dollar each and costs in this behalf expended and that they remain in Custody of (P-225 the Sheriff until fine and costs be said or security given therefore and thereupon came the defendants into open Court and brought with them James A. Bates and John Mathews who confesed judgment for the fine and costs aforesaid.

It is therefore considered by the Court that the State of Tennessee Recover of the Defendants and James A. Bates & John Mathews there security the fine and costs aforesaid and that execution Issue accordingly.

_____

_____

_____

The grand Jury appeared in open Court and returned a presentment against the defendant, Adam H. Pitner, for unlawful Gameing which is in the words and figures following to wit:

State of Tennessee   )   Circuit Court
)   April Term, Eighteen hundred and
Bradley County   )   thirty nine.

The grand jurors in behalf of the State of Tennessee elected sworn empenolled and charged to enquire for the body of the County of Bradley aforesaid upon there oath present that a certain Adam H. Pitner late of said County labourer on the twenty eighth day of January, Eighteen hundred and thirty nine with force and arms in the County of Bradley aforesaid unlawfuly did gamble and play at a certain game of Hazard with cards for two dollars and fifty cents paper money of the value of two dollars and fifty cents good and lawful money of the State of Tennessee being then and there bet and hazarded at and upon said game of Hazard so played with cards as aforesaid contrary to the form of the Statuts in such case made and provided and (P-226) against the peace and dignity of the State.

Endorsement -

Presentment -

The State vs Adam Pitner, found on the testimony of Thomas H. Calloway, Wm. Grant, James Lang, Ezekiel Spriggs, James A. Fletcher, Benjamin McCarty, Joseph R. Mee, Alfred Davis, John Anderson, Lewis Pearce, Joseph Seabourn, Thomas W. Back, Alex Perry

Capias -

State of Tennessee

To the Sheriff of Bradley County, Greeting: You are hereby commanded to take the body of Adam H. Pitner Instant - if to be found in your County and him safely keep so as that you have him before the Judge of the Circuit Court now sitting for Bradley County at the Court house in Cleveland then and there answer the charge of the State Exhibited against him by presentment for unlawful gameing and have you then and there this writ,

Witness Henry Price, Clerk of our said Court at office in Cleveland the 4th Monday of April, 1839.

Henry Price, Clerk.

Endorsment - Capias -

The State vs Adam H. Pitner

Issued the 26th of April 1839

Came to hand and executed in full and brought before the Court and the defendant give security the same day Issued James Lauderdale, Shff.

Circuit Court

April Term, 1839.

State   )

    vs   )   Gameing --

)

Adam H. Pitner)   Came the State by his Attorney
                      General and Adam H. Pitner, the
defendant and acknowledged him self indebted to the State
of Tennessee in the sum of two hundred and fifty dollars
to be levyed of his goods and Chattles lands and tenements
but to be void on condition he make his personal appearance
before the Judge of the next Circuit Court to be held for
(P-227) the County of Bradley at the Court house in
Cleveland on the first Wednesday after the fourth Monday
in August next, and answer a charge of the State exhibited
against him by presentment for unlawful gameing and not
depart the Court with out leave, And thereupon came John
C. Kennedy also who acknowledged himself indebted to the
State of Tennessee in the sum of two hundred and fifty
dollars to be leveyed of his goods and Chattles lands and
tenements but to be void on condition that Adam H. Pitner
make his personal appearance before the Judge of the Circuit
Court at a Court to be held at the Court house in Cleveland on the first Wednesday after the 4th Monday of August next and answer a charge of the State Exhibited against
him by presentment for unlawful gameing and not depart the
Court with out leave.

State   )

    vs   )   Gameing --

)

Adam H. Pitner)   The Attorney General comes to prose-
                      cute on behalf of the State and the
defendant comes in proper person and for plea says he is
guilty will not contend. *he

    It is therefore considered by the Court that for such
his offence he pay a fine of Ten dollars and remain in
Custody of the Sheriff untill fine and costs are payed
or security given therefore.

_____

    _____

    _____

(P-228)

William Kerr   )

)

   vs   )   Bond --

)

Samuel McJunkin   )   Know all men by these Presents
that we Samuel McJunkin and John
C. Kennedy are jointly and severaly held and firmly bound
unto William Kerr, Jr. in the penel sum of two hundred
and fifty dollars to be void oncondition Samuel McJunkin
will with effect prosecute a suit by action of Traver,
which he this day commenced against the said William Kerr,Jr.
in the Circuit Court of Bradley County or in case of failure of such prosecution pay and satisfy all costs and damages
as may be awarded against him by our said Court.

    Witness our hands and seals this 10th day of October,
1838.

                      Samuel McJunkin (Seal)

                      John C. Kennedy (Seal)

Test -
Levi Trewhitt

    Writ -

    State of Tennessee,

        To the Sheriff of Bradley County Greeting: You
are hereby commanded to summon William Kerr, Jr., if to
be found in your County to appear before our Circuit Court
to be held for the County of Bradley at the Court house
in Cleveland on the 4th Monday of December next, to answer
Samuel McJunkin of a plea of Trespass on the case of his
damage two hundred dollars, herein fail not and have you
then and there this writ

    Witness - Henry Price, Clerk of our said Court at
office in Cleveland the 4th Monday of August, 1838.

    And of American Independance the 63.

                  Henry Price, Clerk.

    Endorsement - Summons N. 39.

    Samuel McJunkin vs William Kerr, Jr.

    Issued the 10th October, 1838.

Came to hand the same day Issued and Executed in full the

15th of October 1838, on the within defendant.

James Lauderdale, Sheriff for
Bradley County

(P-229)   Declaration -

State of Tennessee	)	Circuit Court
Bradley County	)	December Term, 1838.

Samuel McJunkin, by Attorney, complains of William
Kerr, Jr. Summond by the sheriff of Bradley County of a
plea of Trespass on the case for that whare as heretofore
to wit: On the 9th day of October, 1838, at to wit, in
the County of Bradley aforesaid he was lawfuly posesed as of
his own property of Certain horse beast commonly called a
mare of great value to wit, of the value of one hundred
and fifty dollars and being possesed thereof he the said
plaintiff afterwards to wit, on the day and year last aforesaid at to wit, in the County aforesaid casually lost the
said Mare out of his possesion, and the same afterwards to
wit: on the day and year last aforesaid at to wit: in the
County aforesaid came to the possession of the defendant by
finding yeat the said defendant well knowing the said Mare
to be the property of the said plantiff and of right to belong and appertain to him but contriveing and fradulently
entending craftly and subtly to deceive and defraud the said
plantiff in this behalf hath not as yeat delivered the said
Mare to the said plantiff although often requested so to do
and that he thereto holy refused so to do and afterwards to
wit, on the day and year last aforesaid at to wit, in the
County aforesaid converted and disposed of the said Mare to
his own use to the damage of the said plantiff two hundred
- and therefore he brings his said suit and pledges to prosecute.

Trewhitt, Attorney
For Plantiff.

Plea ---

And the defendant by his attorney and defends wrong and
Injury when &c. and   (P-230)   and for plea says the
plaintiffs action aforesaid against him ought not to have
and maintain because he says he is not guilty of the trover
and convention in the plantiffs decleration mentioned in
manner and form as therein alledged against him and of
this he puts him self on the County.

Campbell & Vandyke, attorneys
For Defendant.

and the plantiff likewise,

Trewhitt, attorney for Plaintiff.

Circuit Court

April Term, 1839.

Samuel McJunkin)
)
    vs   )   This day came the parties by their
William Kerr   )   attorneys and thereupon came the
                      following Jury good and lawful men
to wit: John Towns, Joseph Billingsly, James Britton, Isaac Huffaker, Robert Hood, Absolam Coleman, Uriah Shipley,
Charles Dodd, Samuel Samples, John Murphy, Joshua Stafford,
James Haggard, who having been duly summoned elected tried
and sworn the truth to speak upon the Issue joined by the
parties in this cause upon their oath aforesaid do say they
find that the defendant is not guilty as in his Plea he hath
alledged.

It is therefore considered by the Court that the plantiff take nothing by his writ but that the defendant go
hence without day and recover of the plantiff his costs
about his defence in this behalf expended for which execution may issue.

Samuel McJunkin   )   State of Tennessee
)
    vs   )   To the Sheriff of Bradley
)   County, Greeting:
Right Romines   )
                        (P-231)   You are hereby commanded
to summons Right Romaines if to be found in your County to
appear to appear before the Circuit --- to be held for the
County of Bradley at the Court house in Cleveland on the
4th Monday of August next to answer Samuel McJunkin of a
plea of Trespass on the case to his damage two hundred dollars.

Herein fail not and have you then there this writ.

Henry Price Clerk of our said Court at office in Cleveland the 4th Monday of May, 1838, and of American Independence the 62.

Henry Price, Clerk.

Endorsement - Summons -

Samuel McJunkin vs Right Romines

Issued the 18th August, 1838.

Damages $200.00.

Came to hand the same day issued search made the within defendant not found.
1838
This 25th August,/Jas. Lauderdale, Shff.

Bond ---

Know all men by these presants that we Samuel McJunkin - - - - - - are jointly and severally held and firmly bound unto Right Romines in the penel sum of two hundred and fifty dollars, to be void on condition that the said Samuel McJunkin will with effect prosecute a suit by action Trover which he this day commenced against the said Right Romines, in the Circuit Court of Bradley County or in case of failure of such prosecution pay and satisfy all costs and damages as may be awarded against by our said Court

Witness our hands and seals this 18th day of August 1838.

Test   Samuel McJunkin (Seal)
Levi Trewhitt
                              Steven Scott (Seal)

Alias Summons awarded.

State of Tennessee

To the Sheriff of Bradley County, Greeting: You are hereby commanded as here to fore to Summon Right (P-232) Romines if to be found in your County to appear before our Circuit Court to be held for the County of Bradley at the Court house in Cleveland on the 4th Monday of December next to answer Samuel McJunkin of a plea of Trespass on the case to his damage two hundred dollars, herein fail not and have you then there this writ.

Witness Henry Price, Clerk of our said Court at office in Cleveland the 4th Monday of August 1838, and of American Independence the 62nd.

Endorsment Alias Summons --

Samuel McJunkin vs Right Romines

Issued October the 11th 1838,*Executed in full the same day by making known the within to defendant.

James Lauderdale, Sheriff
of Bradley County.

Declaration -

State of Tennessee	Circuit Court
Bradley County	December Term, 1838.

Samuel McJunkin, by attorney, complains of Right Romines, Summond by the Sheriff to answer the said plantiff of a plea of trespass on the case.

For that whare as the plantiff here to wit, upon the 17th day of August 1838 at to wit, in the County aforesaid was lawfuly possesed as of his own property of one yoke of oxen of great value of one hundred dollars and being so possesed thereoff he the said plantiff afterwards to wit, on the said year last aforesaid at to wit, in the County aforesaid Casually lost the said yoke of Oxen out of his possession and the same afterwards to wit,

Came to the possesion of the said Defendant by finding yeat the said defendant well knowing the said yoke of oxen to be the property of the said plantiff and right to belong and appertaine to him but contriveing and fraudulantly in tending craftly and subtelly to devise and defraud the said plantiff in this behalf hath not as yeat delivered (P-233) the said yoke of Oxen to the said plantiff, although often requested so to do and hath hereto wholly refused so to do and afterward to wit, upon the day and year last aforesaid at to wit, in the County aforesaid convested and depposesed of the said yoke of Oxen to his own use to the damage of the said plantiff two hundred dollars and therefore he brings his said suit and pledges to prosecute.

Trewhitt, Attorney for Plantiff.
*Came to hand the 12th October, 1838.

Circuit Court

December Term, 1838.

Samuel McJunkin)
)
vs) Trover --
)
Right Romines) This day came the plantiff and
having heretofore filed his de-
cleration in this cause and the defendant being solomnly
called and requested to come into Court and defend the
plantiffs suit failed so to do.

It is therefore considered by the court that the
plantiff recover of the defendant his damages in the
plantiffs decleration mentioned to be here after asertained by a Jury of the County.

Circuit Court

April Term, 1839.

Samuel McJunkin) Court of inquiry
)
vs) This day came the plantiff by his
) attorney and there upon came a
Right Romines) Jury of good and lawful men to wit:

(1) Robert A. Farmer (2) Daniel J. Stafford (3) Joseph
L. Igoe (4) Hiram Brandon (5) John F. Larrison (6) Isaac
Smith (7) George W. Cate (8) Noah Fisher (9) Robert H. Elison (10) Elias Price (11) William Parks (12) John W. Kennedy, who having been duly summond elected tried and sworn
will and truly to inquire of and assess the plantiffs damage in this cause who upon there oath aforesaid do say they
assess the plantiffs damage to Seventy dollars

It is therefore considered by the Court that the plantiff Recover of the defendant his damages aforesaid by the
Jury aforesaid -- (P-234) assessed together with the
costs in this behalf expended for which execution may Issue.

_____

_____

_____

State of Tennessee) Circuit Court
)
Bradley County) August Term Eighteen hundred and
Thirty Eight.

The grand jurors in behalf of the State of Tennessee, elected impaneled sworn and charged to inquire for the body of the County of Bradley aforesaid upon there oath present that a certain John Fitzgeral, late of said County labourer on the twenty sixth day of August, Eighteen hundred and thirty eight and divers other days with force and arms in the County of Bradley aforesaid did vend and sell by retail in quantities less than one quart a certain kind of spirituous Liquors called whiskey and other kind of spirituous liquors to one John S. Smith and to divers other persons and so the Grand Jurors aforesaid upon there oath aforesaid so said that the said John Fitzgerrel was then and there guilty of keeping a Tipling house, contrary to the form of the Statutes in such case made and provided and against peace and dignity of the State.

Samuel Frazier,

Attorney General for the Third
Solestorial District.

Witness for the State sworn in open Court and sent before the Grand Jury, August 31st, 1838.

Henry Price, Clerk.

A true Bill,   John Auston, fourman of the
                           Grand Jury.

Capias --

State of Tennessee,

To the Sheriff of Bradley County, Greeting: You are hereby commanded to take the boddy of John Fitzgeral, if to be found in your County and him safely keep so that you have him before the Judge of our Circuit -- at a Court to be held for Bradley County at the Court house in Cleveland on the 4th Monday of December, next and on the 3rd day of said Term then and there to answer the charge of the State   (P-235)   Exhibited against him by Indictment for tipling and have you then and there this writ -

Witness Henry Price, Clerk of our Circuit Court at office in Cleveland the 4th Monday of August A. D. 1838.

Henry Price, Clerk

Endorsment - Capias -

The State vs John Fitzgerrel

Issued September the 6th 1838.

Came to hand the 6th September, 1838, Executed by arresting the within defendant and bond taken for his appearance this 6th day of October, 1838.

John Heights
Dept. Sheriff.

The State   )
)
    vs Felony   )   The attorney General comes to
)   prosecute for the State and the
George W. Maroney)   defendant being brought to the
                      Bar of the Court in the Custady
of the Sheriff of Bradley County and on motion of the Attorney General and for reasons appearing to the satisfaction of the Court a Nole proseque is entered in this cause.

It is therefore considered by the Court that the defendant go hence without day and be discharged and that the Clerk tax the legal costs for the inspection of the Court.

State   )
)
    vs   )   James Lauderdale, Sheriff of
)   Bradley County
George W. Maroney)

Presented in open Court the following account to wit:

To Sheriff Lauderdale for boarding Defendant from the 5th of November 1839, untill the 25th of December 1839, making in all fifty days at 37½ cents per day - - - $18.75

To two turn keys at 50c each   1.00

Sworn to in open Court

James Lauderdale, Sheriff

The State   )
)
    vs Larceny   )   The attorney reported to Court
)   the following bill of cost in
George W. Maroney)   this cause duley certified to
                      be correctly taxed which is in
the words and figures following -

To wit: Clerk Price receiveing   (P-236)   and fileing
one recognizance 25cts - 2 subponeas 25¢ - final Judgment
75¢ - Copy of cost 25¢ one witness --- 6/4- Recording proceedings after final Judgment 162 - 318 3/4
*
Dept Sheriff, Kinsey C. Seabourn one subpoena 25¢

Sheriff James Lauderdale, for boarding defendant from the
fifth of November 1839 till the 25th of December 1839, making in all fifty days at 37½ each day 18.75. Two turn
keys at 50¢ each 1.00

Justice Seabourn for boarding Deft - 50¢

    Attorney General fee - -5.00
                  $28.40

State of Tennessee	)	Circuit Court
	)	August Term
Bradley County	)	Eighteen hundred and thirty Eight.

    The grand Jurors in behalf of the State of Tennessee
elected empaneled sworn and charged to inquire for the boddy
of the County of Bradley aforesaid upon there oath present
that a certain Harris D. Tharp, late of said County labourer on the first day of August, in the year of Our Lord One
thousand eight hundred and Thirty Eight with force and arms
in the County of Bradley aforesaid unlawfully did gamble
and play at a certain game of hazard with cards for twelve
and one half cents good and lawful money of the State of
Tennessee then and there being bet and hazarded at and upon
said game of hazard so played with cards as aforesaid Contrary to the form of the statutes in such case made and
provided and against the Peace and dignity of the State.

    Endorsment - Presentment

    The State vs Harris D. Tharp

Found in the testimony John M. Gifford, Fourman, John Austin, William -----, Gilford Gatlin, William Thornburgh,
*Dept Sheriff, George W. Witt, of hambelon County Serveing
 one subpoena 25¢

N. Barksdale, James Sheddle (P-237) John McNair, Peter
W. Nash, J. A. Fletcher, John Simmons, John Chambers, Benjamin Murry.

Capias --

State of Tennessee,

To the Sheriff of Bradley County, Greeting: You are
hereby commanded to take the body of Harris D. Tharp, if
to be found in your County and him safely keep so that you
have him before the Judge of our Circuit Court at a Court
to be held for Bradley County at the Court house in Cleveland on the 4th Monday of December next, and on the 3rd day
of Said term, then and there to answer the charge of the
State exhibited against him by presentment for unlawful
Gambling and have you then and there this writ,

Witness Henry Price, Clerk of our said Court at office
in Cleveland the 4th Monday of August, A. D. 1838.

Henry Price, Clerk.

Endorsment --

Capias - The State vs Harris D. Tharp,

Issued the 6th - 1838

Came to hand the same day Issued and Executed by arresting
the boddy of Harris D. Tharp, and bond taken for his appearance the 22nd September, 1838.

James Lauderdale, Sheriff

Bond --

State of Tennessee,

Sheriff in and for the County aforesaid having on
this 2nd day of September 1838. Arrested the body of Harris
D. Tharp, by virtue of a capias issued from the Circuit Court
of -- County commanding me to take the body of said Harris
D. Tharp to answer a charge of the State exhibited against
him by presentment for unlawful Gameing and thereupon the
said Harris D. Tharp, defendant together with Joel K. Brown
Security before me James Lauderdale, Sheriff as aforesaid
acknowledged themselves jointly and severaly indebted to the

State of Tennessee in the sum of two hundred and fifty dollars each to be levied of their goods and chattles, lands and tenements respectively but to be void on condition of said Harris D. Tharp shall make his personal appearance before the said Judge of the Circuit Court at a Court to be held for the County aforesaid at the Court house in Cleveland on the first Wednesday after the 4th Monday of December next, to answer the said (P-238)   charge of the State exhibited against him as aforesaid and then and there abide by and preform and satisfy the judgment of said Court thereon to be rendered and not depart the Court without leave.

                              H. D. Tharp (Seal)

                              Joel K. Brown (Seal)

    Witness

    James Lauderdale, Sheriff.

State   )

vs   )   Came the Grand Jury into open Court
)   and returned a presentment against
Harris D. Tharp   )   Harris D. Tharp, for unlawful Gameing signed by all of said Grand Jury.

    December Tern, 1838.

State   )

vs   )   Came the attorney General and this
)   cause is continued till the next
Harris D. Tharp   )   term.

    Whare upon came Spencer Jarnagin into open Court and Acknowledged himself indebted to the State of Tennessee in the sum of two hundred and fifty dollars but to be void on condition that Harris D. Tharp do make his personal appearance at the next term of the Circuit Court to be held for the County of Bradley at the Court house in Cleveland on the 4th Monday of April next, and on the 3rd day of said term then and there to answer a charge of the State exhibited against him for unlawful Gameing and not depart the Court without leave.

    April Term, 1839.

The State   )
)
  vs   )   The attorney General comes to pro-
)   secute on behalf of the State and
Harris D. Tharp   )   moved the Court to enter a Nole
                      Proseque in this cause and with
leve of the Court a Nole proseque is entered and there upon
came the defendant and James Berry and confessed a Judgment
for the cost of th s prosecution.

    It is therefore considered by the Court that the State
of Tennessee Recover of the defendant and James Berry his
Security jointly the costs confessed as aforesaid, and
that Execution Issue and C.

(P-239)
State   )
)
  vs   )   December Term 1838.
)
Andrew Fox   )

    Came the attorney General and reported to the following
bill of cost on the record as being inspected by the and
being correctly taxed which to be issued ----- in the bill
of which is in the words and figures following to wit:

State of Tennessee   )
)
  vs   )   I. Spencer Bevers, Sheriff and
)   Jailer of McMinn County, charge
Andrew Fox,   )   for keeping said Fore in the
                      Jail of McMinn County from the
3rd day of October 1838, till the 25th day of December 1838.
Making in all Eighty four days at 37½ cents per day. $31.50

             Two Turn Keys at 50 cents each   -   1.00

Also for conveying said defendant from the Jail of McMinn
County to the Court house in Cleveland going to and returning from 52 miles at 10 cents per Mile $ 5.20

And two of a guard at 6 cents per mile each   6.24

Due the 25th -- 1838.   11.44

S. Bevers, Account Sworn to.

December Term 1838.

State   )
)
 vs   ) Came the Attorney General who prosecutes
) for the State and leave of the Court
Andrew Fox) · being first had and obtained the Defend-
         ant is discharged from the Custody of the
Sheriff.

      A Nole Proseque -

     April Term, 1839.

The
State   )
)
 vs   ) Came the attonney General and reported
) to the Court the following bill of cost
Andrew Fox) as being correctly Taned which was in-
         spected by the Court and ordered to bd
spread on the record which is in the words and figures following to wit:

  Attorney General fee $5.00

  Clerk Price, one recognizance 25 copey of
  costs 25 final judgment 75 one affadavit
  6/4 Recording proceedings after final judgment 162)293½.

State   ) Spencer Bevers, Sheriff
) and Jailer of McMinn County
 vs   ) For charge of keeping of said defendant
) in the Jail of McMinn County from (P-240)
Andrew Fox) the 3rd day of October 1838, till the 25th
day of December 1838, making in all 84, days at 37½ cents
per day $31.50.

                   31.50
    Two turn keys at 50 cents each $1.00

                   32.50

Also to conveying said defendant from the Jail of McMinn
County to Cleveland 52 Miles going and returning 5.20
     2 of a guard at 6 cents per mile each 6.24
                   11.44

State   )
)
  vs   )   John Brown, Dept. Sheriff of Bradley
)   County
Andrew Fox   )

               Charge for conveying prisoner to Jail
of McMinn County 52 miles going and returning at 10 cents
per mile   5.20.
and 2 of a guard at 6 cents per mile each for the same
distance   6.24

One days boarding Prisoner 37½   .27¼
                                 63.69¼

And it appearing to the Court that the defendant had been confined under a charge of feloney and had been legally discharged from said confinement and from charge.

It is therefore considered by the Court that the foregoing bill of cost which has been reported to court and examined by the amounting to Sixty Three dollars and sixty nine and a fourth cents be paid by the State of Tennessee.

Alexander Webb   )
William Wood   )
  vs   )   Petition
)
Robert H. Ellison)   To the Hornable Chas F. Keith,
                  one of the Judges of the Circuit
Court of law in and for the State of Tennessee.

    The petition of Robert H. Ellison, humble complains and shows to your honor that on or there about the last day of January, last part, a certain Alexander Webb, ----of William Wooden, recovered a judgment against your petitionerfor the sum of twenty dollars debt with costs and intrest before William Forester, a Justice of the peace for Bradley County (P-241) Your petitioner prayed stay of Execution upon said judgment and tenered and give as security for the sum Benjamin C. Jameson, who is and was good and sufficient securety and entirely solvent for all debts and damages that he owed or was otherwise

against him, which security was accepted of by William
Forester, the Justice of the Peace who rendered said judgment and who entered said stay upon his execution Docket,
but so it was may it please your honor the said Plantiff
not withstanding said stay of Execution by said Jameson
as aforesaid on the first day of the present month demanded an Execution of said justice upon said judgment
against your petitioner which the said justice issued not
withstanding he had accepted of the security for the stay
and so entered it upon his official books as he so informed
your Petitioner which Execution so illigally issued as
aforesaid is now leveyed by James Bate Depty Sheriff for
Bradley County upon your petitioners property and your petitioners property will be sold and sacrifised under the
same unless it is superceded your petitioner therefore
prays that writs of certiorari and supersedias be Issued
by the Clerk of the Circuit Court of Bradley County stay-
ing all futher proceedings upon said Execution and that
same be brought up to the next Term of the Circuit Court
for Bradley County that the above state of affords may be
proved to your honor and the said Execution quashed ----
here states and shows to your honor that this is the first
application for writs of certiorari and supercedes in said
cause he therefore prays your honor to grant him writs of
Certiorari and supercedes as afore said of the Circuit
Court of Bradley County and that said Execution may be
quashed,   (P-242)   And your petitioner as in duty bound
will for ever pray.

        February the 19th, 1839, enterlined before signed.

                        Robert H. Ellison

State of Tennessee   )
)
Bradley County   )   This day personally appeared
                                  before me Jesse Poe an acting
Justice of the Peace for Bradley County, Robert H. Ellison
the foregoing petitioner and made oath that the facts set
forth in the foregoing petition as of his own knowledge
are true and those that are not stated as of his own knowledge but upon information he believes to be true.

        Sworn to and subscribed this 19th day of February,1839.

                        Jesse Poe, Justice of the Peace.

State of Tennessee   )
)
Judicial Circuit   )   To the Clerk of Bradley County
                                  in 3rd Judicial Circuit in the
State aforesaid let writs of Certiorari & supercedes Issue
agreeable to the prayer of the foregoing petition upon

209

the petitioner giveing bond and security as the law directs.

Given under my hand this 26th day of February, 1839.

Charles F. Keith, Jd. &c.

Writs -

State of Tennessee

To William Forester, one of the Justices of the peace for the County of Bradley, Greeting: Whareas Alexander Webb, assence of William Wooden lately complained of and recorded a judgment against Robert H. Ellison, for the sum of twenty dollars debt with cost and we for certain reasons being desirous that the record of that suit should be certified to us do hereby command you to enclose all the papers relative to said suit under your hand and seal distinctly and plainly to gether with this writ and transmit the same to a Court to be held by the Judge of the Circuit Court of law and equity for the County of Bradley at the Court house in Cleveland on the 4th Monday of April next, in order that our said Court may do therein of right and wording to have ought to be done.

Witness,

Henry Price, Clerk of our said Court at office in Cleveland the 4th Monday of December, 1838, and of American independence the 63rd.

Henry Price, Clerk.

Endorsment - Certiorari

Alexander Webb, assence of William Wooden vs Robert H. Ellison, Issued March the 4th 1839.

Supercedes,

State of Tennessee

To the Sheriff of Bradley County, Greeting:

You are hereby commanded that from all procedings upon a judgment that Alexander Webb, assence, of William Wooden by virtue there of against Robert H. Ellison, before William Forester one of the Justices of the peace in and for Bradley County you --- and altogether supercede as the same by our writs of certiorari is removed to the Circuit

Court of Bradley County and you are hereby also commanded
to notify the said Alexander Webb, assence of *Wooden to appear before the Judge of our Circuit Court at a Court to
be held for the County aforesaid at the Court house in
Cleveland on the 4th Monday of April next then and there
to prosecute the said suit and have you then and there this
writ Witness Henry Price, Clerk of our said Court at office
in Cleveland the 4th Monday of December 1838, and of American Independence, the 63rd.

                    Henry Price, Clerk.

        Endorsment - Supercedes -

    Alexander Webb, assence of William Wooden vs Robert H.
Ellison, Issued March 4th 1839.

    Notifyed the within Alexander Webb, as herein requested
the 6th day of April 1839.

                    James A. Bate, Dept. Sheriff.

        April Term 1839.

Alexander Webb   )
)
    vs   )   Came the parties by their attor-
)   neys and on the motion of the
Robert H. Ellison   )   Plantiff by his Attorney a rule
)   is granted him to show cause
why the defendants petition should be dismissed.

(P-244)
        Presentment --

State of Tennessee   )   Circuit Court
)
Bradley County   )   April Term, Eighteen hundred and
                              Thirty nine.

    The Grand Jurors in behalf of the State of Tennessee
elected impaneled sworn and charged to enquire for the
body of Bradley County aforesaid upon there oath present
that Russel Lawson and Thomas Igobright late of said County
labours on the tenth day of February in the year of our
Lord one Thousand and Eight hundred and Thirty nine with
force and arms in the County of Bradley aforesaid unlawfuly did gamble and play at a certain game of hazard played
with cards for one dollar good and lawful money of the State
*William

of Tennessee being then and there bet and hazarded at and
upon said game of hazard so played with cards as aforesaid
and the jurors aforesaid upon their oath aforesaid do futher
present that the said Rusell Lawson and Thomas Igobright
on the tenth day of February, Eighteen hundred and thirty
nine with force and arms in the County of Bradley aforesaid unlawfully did gamble and play at a certain game of
hazard played with cards for one dollar paper money of the
Value of one dollar good and lawful Money of the State of
Tennessee, being then and there bet and hazarded at and
upon said game of hazard so played with cards as aforesaid
contrary to the form of the Statutes in such case made and
provided and against the peace and dignity of the State.

Endorsment - Presentment

State   )
)
    vs   No.1.   )   Found on the Testimony of Freder-
)   ick A. Kance, William Grant, James
Russell Lawson &   )   Lang, Ezekiel Spriggs, Elias Hutch-
Thomas Igobright   )   ison, James A. Fletcher, Benjamin
                              McCarty, Joseph Mee, Alfred Davis,
John Anderson, Lewis Perece, Joseph Seabourn, Thomas W.
Back, Alex Perry,

Capias

The State of Tennessee

        To the Sheriff of Bradley County, Greeting:

You are hereby commanded to take the body of Russel
Lawson, if in your County and him safely keep so that you
have him before the Judge of our Circuit Court at a Court
to be held for the County of Bradley at the Court house
in Cleveland on the 4th Monday of August next, and on the
3rd day of said term then and there to answer the charge
of the State exhibited against him by presentment for unlawful gameing and have you then and there this writ,

Witness Henry Price, Clerk of our said Court at office
in Cleveland, the 4th Monday of April, A. D. 1839.

                Henry Price, Clerk.

Endorsment - Capias -

The State vs Russell Lawson

Issued May the 29th, 1839.

Came to hand the 26th of June 1839.

Executed and bond taken this the 25th July 1839.

John A. Bates,

Depty. Sheriff

Bond --

State of Tennessee, Bradley County

I, James A. Bates, Dept. Sheriff in and for the County
aforesaid having this 25th day of July 1839, arrested the
body of Russell Lawson, by virtue of a Capias Issued from
the Circuit Court of said County commanding me to take the
body of said Russel Lawson to answer a charge of the State
exhibited against him by presentment for unlawful gameing,
and thereupon the said Russell Lawson defendant together
with Reynolds Lawson, security before me James A. Bates,
Sheriff, as aforesaid acknowledged themselves jointly and
severly indebted to the State of Tennessee in the sum of
two hundred and fifty dollars each to be levyed of there
goods and chattles lands and tenements respectively, but
to be void on condition the said Russell Lawson shall make
his personal appearance before the said Circuit Court at
a Court to be held for the County aforesaid at the Court
house in Cleveland on the first Wednesday after the 4th
Monday of August next to answer the said charge of the
State exhibited against him as aforesaid and then and
there abide by perform and satisfy the judgment of said
Court thereon to be rendered and not depart the Court
(P-246) without leave signed sealed and acknowledged before me, James A. Bates, Dept. Sheriff of Bradley County
July the 25th, 1839.

Russell Lawson (Seal)

Reynolds Lawson (Seal)

The State	
vs Gameing	The grand Jurors appeared in open Court and returned a presentment against the defendants for unlawful Gameing.
Russell Lawson & Thomas Igobright	
Circuit Court	
August Term, 1839.	

State   )
)
 vs Gameing   ) The attorney General comes to prose-
) cute on part of the State, and also
Russell Lawson   ) the defendant in proper person who
           says he cannot deny but that he is
guilty as charged in the presentment and submits to the
Judgment of the Court.

It is therefore considered by the Court that the defendant for the offence aforesaid pay a fine of ten dollars and that he pay the costs of this presentment and
that he remain in the Custody of the Sheriff untill fine
be paid or that securety given, therefore and thereupon
came Reynolds Lawson and acknowledged him self the security of the said defendant for the payment of the fine and
costs aforesaid.

It is therefore considered by the Court that the State
of Tennessee recover against the said defendant and Reynolds
Lawson, his securety the fine and costs aforesaid confessed and that Execution Issue accordingly.

State   )
)
 vs No. 2.   ) Presentment ---
)
Russell Lawson   ) Circuit Court
) April Term, 1839.
State of Tennessee)
) The grand jurors in behalf of
Bradley County   ) the State of Tennessee, elected
           empaneled sworn and charged to
inquire for the Body of --- ---- (P-247) the County
of Bradley aforesaid upon their oath present that a Certain Russell Lawson, and Berry Ford late of said County
labourer on the fifth day of March in the year of our Lord
one thousand eight hundred and thirty nine with force and
arms in the County of Bradley aforesaid unlawfuly did Gamble and play at a certain game of hazard played with cards
for fifty cents good and lawful money of the State of Tennessee being then and there bet and hazarded at and upon
said game of hazard so played with cards as aforesaid and
the jurors aforesaid upon the oath aforesaid do futher
present ør that the said Russell Lawson and Berry Ford
on the said fifth day of March in the year Eighteen hundred
and thirty nine with force and arms in the County of Bradley aforesaid unlawfuly did gamble and play at a certain

game of hazard played with cards for one dollar paper
money of the State of Tennessee, being then and there
bet and hazarded at and upon the said game of hazard so
played with cards as aforesaid contrary to the form of
the statutes in such case made and provided and against
the peace and dignity of the State.

Endorsment - Presentment --

The State vs Russell Lawson, Berry Ford, on the Testimony
R. A. Kance.

Jurors Names,

William Grant, Ezekiel Spriggs, Elias Hutcherson,
James A. Fletcher, Benjamin McCarty, Joseph Mee, Alfred
Davis, John Anderson, Lewis Pearce, Joseph Seabourn, Thomas W. Back, Alex Perry.

Capias - State of Tennessee,

To the Sheriff of Bradley County, Greeting: You are
hereby commanded to take the body of Russell Lawson, if to
be found in your County and him safely keep so that you
have him before the Judge of our Circuit Court at a Court
to be held for Bradley   (P-248)   County at the Court
house in Cleveland on the 4th Monday of August next, and
on the 3rd day of said Term then and there to answer the
charge of the ---- exhibited against him by presentment
for unlawful gameing and have you then and there this writ,

Witness, Henry Price, Clerk of our said Court at office in Cleveland the 4th Monday of April, 1839.

Henry Price, Clerk.

Endorsment -- Capias --

The State vs Russell Lawson, Issued May the 29th, 1839.

Came to hand the 26th of June 1839. Executed by arresting the body of Russell Lawson and taking bond the 25th
of July 1839.

James A. Bates, Dept. Sheriff.

Bond - State of Tennessee,

To the Sheriff of Bradley County, Greeting: I,
James A. Bates, Dept. Sheriff, in and for the County aforesaid having on the 25th day of July 1839, arrested the Body

of Russell Lawson by virtue of a Capias issued from the
Circuit Court of said County commanding me to take the
body of the said Russell Lawson to answer a charge of the
State, Exhibited against him by presentment for unlawful
gameing and there upon the said Russell Lawson defendant
together with Reynolds Lawson securety before me James A.
Bates Sheriff as aforesaid acknowledged themselves jointly
and severly indebted to the State of Tennessee in the Sum
of Two hundred and fifty dollars each to be levied of their
goods, Chattles, bonds and tenements respectively but to
be void on condition the said Russell Lawson shall make his
personal appearance before the Judge of the Circuit Court
to be held for the County aforesaid at the Court house
in Cleveland on the first Wednesday after the fourth Monday of August next to answer the charge of the State exhibited against him as aforesaid and then and there abide
by thereupon and satisfy the judgment of said thereon to
be rendered and not depart the Court without leave.

(P-249)
Signed sealed and acknowledged in presence of me, this
the 25th day of July 1839.

James A. Bates   )   Russell Lawson (Seal)
   Dept. Sheriff   )   Reynolds Lawson (Seal)

Circuit Court

April Term, 1839.

State   )
)
   vs   Gameing   )   The Grand Jury appeared in open
)   Court and returned a presentment
Russell Lawson   )   against the defendant for unlawful
                          gameing.

Circuit Court

April Term, 1839.

State   )
)
   vs Gameing   )   The Grand Jury appeared in open Court
)   and returned a presentment against
Russell Lawson   )   the defendant for unlawful gameing.

Circuit Court --

August Term, 1839.

State   )

  vs No 2   )   The attorney General comes to prose-
)   cute on behalf of the State and the
Russell Lawson   )   defendant in proper person who says
                     he cannot deny but that he is guilty
in maner and form as charged in the presentment and submits
to the Judgment of the Court

It is therefore considered by the Court that the defendant for the offence charged in said presentment do to
the State of Tennessee the a fine of five dollars and
that he pay the cost of this prosecution and that he remain
in the Custody until fine and costs are paid or secured, and
thereupon came into Court, Reynolds Lawson, and acknowledged
himself the securdty of the said defendant for the payment
of the fine and cost aforesaid.

It is therefore considered by the Court that the State
of Tennessee recover of the defendant and Reynolds Lawson
jointly fine and cost aforesaid and that Execution Issue &c.

Presentment ---

State of Tennessee   )   Circuit Court
)
Bradley County   )   May Term, Eighteen hundred and
                       thirty Eight.

The Grand Jurors in behalf of the State of Tennessee,
elected   (P-250)   impaneled sworn and charged to inquire for the body of the County of Bradley aforesaid upon
their oath present that a certain John L. Simmons, late of
said County labourer on the tenth day of March in the year
of our Lord, One thousand Eight hundred and Thirty Eight.
With force and arms in the County of Bradley, aforesaid unlawfuly did gamble and play at a certain game of hazard
with cards for twelve and one half cents good and lawful money
of the State of Tennessee and of the United States, being then
and there Bet into Court John Simmons, and confessed Judgment for the cost in this cause.

It is therefore considered by the Court that the State
of Tennessee recover of the said John Simmons the cost in

this behalf expended as aforesaid confessed and that Execution Issue &c.

_____

_____

_____

(P-251)
State of Tennessee)
) Indictment --
Bradley County   )

Circuit Court

December Term, Eighteen hundred and Thirty Eight.

The Grand Jurors in behalf of the State of Tennessee elected impaneled sworn and charged to inquire for the Body of the County of Bradley aforesaid upon their oath present that a certain William Peoples late of said County labourer, not having the fear of God before his eyes but being moved and seduced by the Instegation of the Devil on the first day of February in the year of our Lord One thousand Eight hundred and Thirty Eight, with force and arms in the County of Bradley aforesaid and within the Jurisdiction of this honerable Court in and upon one Jane Peoples, then and there being the daughter of him the said William Peoples, did feloniously make an assault and did then and there feloniously have carnel knowledge of her the said Jane Peoples she the said Jane Peoples then and there being the daughter of him the said William Peoples as aforesaid and the Jurors aforesaid upon their oath aforesaid do futher present that the said William Peoples on the said first day of February in the year of Our Lord One Thousand Eight hundred and Thirty Eight with force and armes in the County of Bradley aforesaid in and upon the body of one Jame Peoples then and there being the daughter of the Wife of the said William Peoples did feloniously make an assault and then and there feloniously have carnal knowledge of and sexual intercourse with the said Jane Peoples she the said Jane Peoples then and there being the daughter of the said wife of the said William Peoples and so the Jurors aforesaid upon there oath aforesaid   (P-252)   do say that the said William Peoples was then and there to wit: On the said first day of February in the year of Our Lord One thousand Eight hundred and Thirty Eight, In the County of Bradley aforesaid with force and armes as aforesaid feloniously guilty of ---- Contrary to the form of the statutes in such case made and provided and against the peace and dignity of the State.

                    Samuel Frazier

                    Attorney General for the 3rd
                        Solicitorial District.

Endorsment - A true Bill ---

                    Baldwin Harle, Fourman of
                        the Grand Jury.

Indictment, The State vs William Peoples

Nathan Jones prosecutor, Jame Peoples, Nathan Jones,
Witnesses for the State.

Sworn in open Court and sent before the Grand Jury.

December the 25th 1838.

                    Henry Price, Clerk.

Circuit Court

December Term, 1838.

State   )
)
  vs   )   Came the Grand Jury into open Court
)   and brought with them a bill of in-
William Peoples   )   dictment against the defendant, In-
                            dictment endorsed there on a True
bill by Balden Harle, there foreman.

Circuit Court

December Term, 1838.

State   )
)
  vs   )   Came the Attorney General who prose-
)   cutes for the State and the defend-
William Peoples   )   ant in his own proper person who
                            being named and charged on the bill
of Indictment for plea thereto says he is not guilty in
maner and form as charged therein and for his trial puts
himself upon the County and the Attorney General doth the
like and thereupon to try said Issue, Came a Jury to wit:
James Haggard, Abraham Barnes, Robert Allen   (P-253)

Peter W. Nash, Micheal Helterbrand, Mark Black, John Brannon, Elias Bolar, Thomas Wooden, William Wooden, David Dame, and Alexander A. Clingan, all good and lawful men of the County of Bradley who being elected tried and sworn the truth to speak of and conserning the premeses by consent of the Attorney General and of the said defendant are put under the charge of the Sheriff who is ordered to keep them together in some convenient apartment apart from other citizens and without permiting any other person to have any communication with them until they return to court at the meeting thereof on tomorrow to resume the consideration of this cause and It is ordered that the defendant be taken in the custody of the Sheriff.

Thursday the 27th of December

State   )
)
  vs   )   Came the attorney General who prose-
)   cutes for the State as well as the
William Peoples)   defendant in his own proper person
                   and the same Jury heretofore sworn
in this cause and was placed under the care of the Sheriff and having returned into Court and resumed the considera- tion of this cause on there oath do say that the defend- ant is guilty of Incest in manner and form as charged in the bill of Indictment and the Jurors aforesaid upon there oath aforesaid do futher asecertain and say that the said Wil- liam Peoples for the offence aforesaid shall undergo con- finement in the Jail and penetentiary house of the State of Tennessee for the space of ten years from this day and there upon It is ordered by the Court that the defendant be taken into custody of the Sheriff   (P-254)

State   )
)
  vs   )   Came the Attorney General who prose-
)   cutes for the State as well as the
William Peoples)   defendant in proper person and there-
                   upon it is demanded of him the said
William Peoples if he has or knows of any thing why the Court should not procede to Judgment thereof against him according to law who nothing futher sayth then as before he hath said, It is therefore considered by the Court that the said William Peoples for the offence aforesaid do under- go confinement at hard labour in the Jail and penitentiary house of the State of Tennessee for the term of ten years commencing on the 27th day of December 1838, and that the Sheriff convey him fourth with to said Jail and penitentiary house and that he take two of a guard for his safe convey- ance and it is futher ordered by the Court that the said Defendant William Peoples pay the cost of this prosecution for which Execution Issue and that the Clerk make out and

certify a copy of this Judgment to the keeper of the Penitentiary.

The State   )

vs   )   Indictment --

James H. Bridges   )   State of Tennessee

Bradley County

Circuit Court April Term Eighteen hundred and Thirty nine.

The Grand Jurors in behalf of the State of Tennessee elected impaneled sworn and charged to enquire for the Body of the County of Bradley aforesaid and upon there oath present that a certain James H. Bridges late of said County labourer on the first day of March Eighteen hundred and Thirty nine and of divers other days with force and armes in the County of Bradley aforesaid did vend and sell by retail in quantities less than one quart a certain kind of spiritous Liquors called whiskey and other kinds of spirituous liquors to one Benjamin Albert and divers other persons and the jurors aforesaid upon their oath aforesaid do futher present that said James H. Bridges, on the said first day of March, Eighteen hundred and thirty nine and on divers other days did unlawfuly vend and sell a certain kind of spirituous liquors called whiskey to one Benjamin Albert and to divers other persons and so the jurors aforesaid upon there oath aforesaid do say that the said James H. Bridges was then and there guilty of keeping a tipling house contrary to the form of the statuts in such case made and provided and against the peace and dignity of the State

Samuel Frazier, Attorney General
for the Solicitorial District.

Endorsment - A true Bill, Wm Grant, Foreman of the Grand Jury, Indictment --

The State vs James H. Bridges, William H. Strane, prosecutor, James Bates, and Rutherford Rose, Wincen Rose, Witnesses for the State sworn and sent before the grand Jury April the 25th, 1839.

Henry Price, Clerk.

Capias --

State of Tennessee

To the Sheriff of Bradley County Greeting: You are here
by commanded to take the body of James H. Bridges if to be
found in your County and him safely keep so that you have
him before the Judge of our Circuit Court at a ourt to be
held for Bradley County at the Court house in Cleveland on the
4th Monday of August next and on the 3rd day of said Term then
and there to answer a charge the State exhibited against him
by presentment for Tipling and have you then and there this
writ:

Witness Henry Price, Clerk of our said Court at office
in Cleveland, the 4th Monday of April, 1839.

Henry Price, Clerk.

Capias - Endorsment -

The State vs James H. Bridges Issued May the 27th, 1839.

Came to hand same day Issued.

Executed by arresting   (P-256)   James H. Bridges,
and Bond taken this 18th day of July 1839.

James A. Bates, Dept. Sheriff,

Bond, State of Tennessee, Bradley County.

I, James A. Bates, Dept. Sheriff, in and for the County
of Bradley having on this 18th day of July 1839, arrested
the body of James H. Bridges, by virtue of a Capias Issued
from the Circuit Court of said County commanding me to take
the body of said James H. Bridges to answer a charge of the
State exhibited against him by presentment for Tipling and
thereupon the said James H. Bridges, defendant together
with R. S. Pervine, Security before me James A. Bates, Dept.
Sheriff, as aforesaid acknowledged them selves jointly and
severaly indebted to the State of Tennessee in the sum of
two hundred and Seventy five dollars each to be levied of
their goods and chattles, lands and Tenements respectively
but to be void on condition the said James H. Bridges shall
make his personal appearance before the said Court at a
Court to be held at the Court house in Cleveland on the
first Wednesday after the 4th Monday of August next, to
answer a charge of the State exhibited against him aforesaid and then and there abide by preform and satisfy the

judgment of said Court there on to be rendered and not depart the Court without leave.

Signed and acknowledged in the presence of

James A. Bates, Dept. Sheriff.

James H. Bridges (Seal)

R. S. Pervine (Seal)

State   )
)
   vs Tipling   )   Circuit Court
)
James H. Bridges   )   April Term, 1839.

The grand Jury appeared in open Court and returned a bill of Indictment against the defendant Indorsed by their foreman, Wm Grant, a true bill.

Circuit Court

August Term, 1839.

State   )
)
   vs Tipling   )   Came the attorney General who prose-
)   cutes for the State and the defend-
James H. Bridges   )   ant in proper person who being
                                        charged upon the bill of Indictment
keeping a tipling house for plea says that because he is guilty he will not contend but submits to the Judgment of the Court.

It is therefore considered by the   (P-257)   Court that for such his offence he pay a fine of five dollars and all lawful costs in this behalf expended and there upon came the defendant together with James A. Bates and confessed a judgment for the fine and cost aforesaid.

It is therefore considered by the Court that the State of Tennessee recover of the defendant and James A. Bates, his securety, the fine and costs as aforesaid confessed for which Execution may Issue.

Indictment --

State of Tennessee   )
)   The Grand Jurors in behalf of
Bradley County   )   the State of Tennessee Elected
                               impaneled sworn and charged to
enquire for the body of the County of Bradley aforesaid
upon there oath present that a Certain Alfred Conner, Hamilton Biggs and Allen C. Biggs, late of said County labourers on the nineteenth day of April, Eighteen hundred
and Thirty nine with force and armes in the County of Bradley aforesaid unlawfuly notoriously and Riotously assembled themselves together to Brake the peace of the State
and being so assembled on the said nineteenth day of April
Eighteen hundred and thirty nine, with force and armes in
the County of Bradley aforesaid unlawfuly riotously and notoriously did attempt to pull down and then and there unlawfuly riotously and ---- did pull down and demolish the
walls of a Spring house then and there belonging to me John
N. Taylor, to the great damage of the said John N. Taylor
to the evil example of all others in like case offending
and against the Peace and dignity of the State.

                        Samuel Frazier, Attorney General
                          for the 3rd Solicitorial District.

Endorsment - A true Bill -

        Wm Grant, Foreman of the Grand jury.   (P-258)

Indictment -

    The State vs Alfred Conner, Hamilton Biggs, Allen C.
Biggs, John N. Taylor, prosecutor, John N. Taylor, Hyram
F. Taylor, Witnesses for the State sworn and sent before
the grand Jury, April 27th, 1839.

                        Henry Price, Clerk.

    Capias --

State of Tennessee,

    To the Sheriff of Bradley County Greeting: You are
hereby commanded to take the bodys of Alfred Conner, Hamilton Biggs, Allen C. Biggs if to be found in your County
and them safely keep so that you have them before the Judge
of our Circuit Court at a court to be held for the County
of Bradley at the Court house in Cleveland on the 4th Monday of August next, and on the 3rd day of said Term then

and there to answer the charge of the State exhibited
against them by an Indictment for a riout and have you
then and there this writ,

Witness - Henry Price, Clerk of our said Court at office in Cleveland, the 4th Monday of April, 1839.

Henry Price, Clerk,

Endorsment - Capias --

The State vs Alfred Conner, Hamilton Biggs, Allen C. Biggs,
Issued May 27th, 1839.

Executed by arresting Alfred B. Conner, Hamilton Biggs,
and Allen C. Biggs.

This 12th July, 1839.

John S. Oneil, Dept. Sheriff.

Bond --

We, Alfred Conner, Hamilton Biggs, and Allen C. Biggs
and William M. Biggs, acknowledge our selves indebted to
the State of Tennessee, as follows - the said Alfred Conner, Hamilton Biggs, and Allen C. Biggs, the sum of two
hundred and fifty dollars each and the said William N. Biggs
in the sum of one hundred and Twenty five dollars to be void
on condition that the said Alfred Conner, Hamilton Biggs and
Alfred Biggs, shall appear before the Judge of the Circuit
Court at the Court house in the town of Cleveland in the
County of Bradley on the first Wednesday after the 4th Monday of August at the Circuit Court there to be held to answer
the State of Tennessee by Indictment for Riout and abide by
such sentence as shall be given by said (P-259) Court
in the premeses or surrender themselves into the Custody
of the Court and not depart the Court without leave of the
Court given under our hands this the 12th day of July 1839.

Hamilton Biggs (Seal)

Allen C. Biggs (Seal)

William M. Biggs (Seal)

Alfred Conner (Seal)

Circuit Court

April Term, 1839.

State   )
)
    vs   )   The Grand Jury came into Court and
)   returned a bill of Indictment against
Alfred Conner   )   the defendants indorsed <u>at True Bill</u>
Hamilton Biggs   by William Grant there foreman.
Allen C. Biggs

        Circuit Court

        August Term, 1839.

The State   )
)
    vs   )   Indictment --
Hamilton Biggs   )
Alfred Conner   )   For a Riot --
Allen C. Biggs

     The attorney General comes to prosecute on part of the
State & the defendants in proper person who being charged
upon the bill of Indictment for plea says they are not
guilty and for their trial puts them selves upon the County
and the Attorney General doth the like. And thereupon came
a Jury to wit: Moses Fergison, Benjamin Francisco, John
Kincannon, Greenbury Denton, John Murphy, John Raper, George
M. Salley, John Allen, Benjamin Hawkins, Jeptha Randolph,
Lucieon Goodwin, and Robert Allen, all good and lawful citizens of Bradley County who being Elected tried and sworn
to try the Issue found between the State of Tennessee, and
the said defendants upon there oath say are guilty in manner and form as charged in the bill of Indictment.

     It is therefore considered by the Court that the de-
fendant Alfred Conner, for the offence aforesaid pay to the
State   (P-260)   of Tennessee a fine of Ten dollars and
that he pay the cost of this prosecution and remain in
Custody till the fine and costs are paid or secured whare
upon William M. Biggs, came into Court acknowledged himself the security of the said Alfred Conner for the payment of the fine and cost aforesaid.

     It is therefore considered by the Court that the State
of Tennessee recover of the said defendant and William Biggs
jointly the fine and costs aforesaid and that Execution
Issue &c.

     It is also considered by the Court that the defendant
Hamilton Biggs, for the appearence aforesaid pay a fine of
Five dollars to the State of Tennessee, that he pay the
Costs of this prosecution and remain in Custody till fine
and costs are paid or made sure, and therefore came William M. Biggs and acknowledged him self the security of the
said Hamilton Biggs, for the payment of the fine and costs

aforesaid.

It is therefore considered by the Court that the State of Tennessee recover of the said Defendant and William M. Biggs his surety the fine and costs aforesaid and that Execution Issue and C. and also, It is considered by the Court that the defendant Allen C. Biggs, for the offence aforesaid pay a fine to the State of Tennessee of Five dollars and the costs of his prosecution that he remain in custody till fine and costs are paid or secured and thereupon William M. Biggs came into Court and acknowledged himself the securety of the said Allen C. Biggs, for the payment of the fine and cost aforesaid.

It is therefore considered by the Court that the defendant Allen C. Biggs and William M. Biggs, his security jointly pay the fine and costs to the State of Tennessee and that Execution Issue &c.

Sirafacias ---

The State   )
)
    vs   )   State of Tennessee
)
James Riddle   )   to the Sheriff of Bradley County,
                              Greeting: whare as heretofore
to wit: (P-261)   On the -- day of December, 1838.
James Lauderdale, high Sheriff of Bradley County, returned into Court a subpoena issued by the Clerk duly Executed upon James Riddle requesting him to appear in Court and give Evidence against unlawful Gamblers before the Grand Jury whareupon came the State by his attorney General and the said James Riddle, being solomnly called to come in to Court and give Evidence against unlawful Gamblers before the Grand Jury came not but made default --

It is therefore considered by the Court that the said James Riddle has forfited to the State the sum of two hundred and fifty dollars unless he show good and sufficient cause to the contrary at the next term of this Court, and you are therefore hereby commanded to make known to the said James Riddle to appear before the Judge of our next Circuit Court to be held for the County of Bradley at the Court house

in Cleveland on the 4th Monday of April next, and on the
5th day of said term to show cause if any there can why
the States Execution ought not to Issue against him for
the sum of twohundred and fifty dollars according to the
tenner and effect of this said subpoena here in fail not
and have you then there this writ,

Witness Henry Price, Clerk of our said Court at office
in Cleveland this 4th Monday of December, 1838.

Henry Price, Clerk,

Endorsement - Sifa -

The State vs James Riddle, Issued January the 31st 1838.
Came to hand the 9th February 1839. Made known the within
to James Riddle the same day came to hand -

James Lauderdale, Sheriff.

Circuit Court April Term, 1839.

State   )
)
  vs Sifa   ) Came the attorney General who prose-
) cutes for the State and the defendant
James Riddle   ) in proper person and the ---- hereto-
                    fore entered in this cause against
(P-262)   the defendant is set aside and thereupon came
James Riddle, the defendant and confessed judgment for all
costs in this cause.

It is therefore considered by the Court that the State
of Tennessee render of the said James Riddle all the costs
in this behalf Expended for which Execution may Issue.

Know all men by these presents that we, Thomas J. Barnes
Abraham Barnes, and George W. Reed are held and firmly bound
unto James M. White, James Crofford, Andrew Carr, James
F. Lane, John D. Harr, William G. Snodgrass, Asley Cox, and
Samuel Dunn in the penel sum of two hundred and fifty dollars to be void on condition that the said Thomas J. Barnes
by Abraham Barnes, his Guardian will with effect prosecute

a suit by action of Trespass on the case which he this
day commenced a gainst the said James M. White, James Crofford Andrew Carr, James F. Lane, John D. Harr, William G.
Snodgrass, Asul Cox, and Samuel Dunn, in the Circuit Court
of Bradley County or in case of failure of such prosecution
pay and sattisfy all costs and damages as may be awarded
against him by our said Court.

Witness our hands and Seals this the 2nd day of August
A. D. 1838.

                    Thomas J. Barnes   (Seal)

                    Abraham Barnes   (Seal)

                    George W. Reed,   (Seal)

State of Tennessee

     To the Sheriff of Bradley County, Greeting:

                                          You are
hereby commanded to Summon James M. White, James Crofford
Andrew Carr, James F. Lane, John D. Harr, William G. Snodgrass, Asly Cox, and Samuel Dunn, if to be found in your
County to appear before our Circuit Court to be held for
the County of Bradley at the Court house in Cleveland on the
4th Monday of August next there to answer Thomas J. Barnes
of a plea of Trespass to his damage of five Thousand dollars
(P-263)   Here in fail not, and have you then there this
writ -

     Witness - Henry Price, Clerk of our said Court at of-
fice in Cleveland the 4th Monday of May, 1838, and of American Independance the 62nd.

     Endorsment --

     Summons - Thomas J. Barnes by Abraham Barnes vs Father
and Friend vs James White, James Crofford, Andrew Carr,
James F. Lane, John D. Harr, William G. Snodgrass, Asly
Cox, and Samuel Dunn.

     Issued August the 2nd, 1838.

     Came to hand the 4th of August, 1838.

     Executed by summoning - James M. White, James Crofford,
James F. Lane, John D. Hair, Samuel Dunn, Andrew Carr, and
William Snodgrass and Asley Cox, not found - this 13th
August 1838.

James Lauderdale, Sheriff.

Decleration --

State of Tennessee   )   Circuit Court

Bradley County   )   December Term, 1838.

    Thomas J. Barnes, under the age of Twenty one years
who sues by his next friend Abraham Barnes by his attorney
complains of James White, James Crofford, Andrew Carr, James
F. Lane, John D. Hair, William Snodgrass, and Samuel Dunn
who have been summoned to answer of a plea of trespass for
this that the said defendants on the twenty fifth day of
June 1838 at the County of Bradley aforesaid with force and
arms seized and tuck into there custody and keeping the said
plantiff and with force and armes then and there kept detained and imprisoned the said plaintiff against his will
and consent for a long space of time, to wit: for the space
of five hours and then and there forced the said plaintiff
to go and travel a long distance with them to wit, the distance of five Miles and other wrongs to the said plantiff
then and there did against the peace and dignity of the
State and to the damage of the plaintiff five Thousand dollars and   (P-264)   therefore he sues and Pledges &c.

              Campbell & Vandergriff

              J. F. Gillespie, Att. for Plaintiff.

    Plea, defendant by his Attorney comes into Court and
defends the force and -- when and whare and says the plaintiff his action against him ought not to have and maintain
because they say they are not guilty in maner and form as
plaintiff in decleration has alledged against them and of
this they put themselves on the County.

              Jarnagin & Bradford

              Atts. for Defendants.

And the Plaintiff doth like.

              Campbell & Gillespie,

              Attys. for Plaintiff.

    Circuit Court, April Term, 1839.

Thomas J. Barnes, by his next friend

vs   )   Came the parties by their Attorneys
)   and on motion this cause is continued
James M. White   )   as on afidavit of the plaintiff till
)   next term.

Circuit Court

August Term, 1839.

Thomas J. Barnes, by next   )
   friend Abraham Barnes   )
)
)
      vs   )   Came the parties by there
)   Attorneys and thereupon
James M. White   )   came a Jury of good and
)   lawful men to wit:

Isaac Smith, John W. Kennedy, William Thornburry, Robert Allen, Jeremiah Brandon, William Thornhill, Benjamin
Hawkins, Samuel Merrit, Moses Fergison, John Kincannon,
Allen Blevens and Benjamin Francisco, who being elected
and sworn and tried to well and truly to try the Issue
Joined between the parties upon their oath do say they find
the defendant Samuel Dunn guilty of the Tresspass with force
(P-265)   and armes as in the plaintiffs Decleration mentioned and assesses the plaintiffs damage by reason thereof
to twenty five dollars.

It is therefore considered by the Court that the plaintiff recover of the defendant Samuel Dunn, the sum of Twenty
five dollars as assessed by the Jury aforesaid and his costs
about his suit in this behalf expended and that he have his
Execution and the Jury aforesaid on their oath above said
do futher say that the defendants James M. White, James Crofford, Andrew Carr, James F. Lane, John Hair & William Snodgrass are not guilty as in the pleadings they hath alledged.

It is therefore considered by the Court that the said
last named defendants go hence and be discharged and recover
of the plaintiff their costs of there defence in this behalf
expended for which an execution may Issue

      Indictment   )

State of Tennessee   )   Circuit Court

Bradley County   )   August Term, Eighteen hundred and
                                     thirty nine.

The grand jurors in behalf of the State of Tennessee
Elected Impaneled sworn and charged to inquire for the body

of the County of Bradley, aforesaid, upon the oath present
that a certain John Cockram late of said County labourer
on the fourteenth of June in the year of our Lord One thousand Eight hundred and thirty nine with force and armes
in the County of Bradley aforesaid and within the jurisdiction of this Honerable one bay horse of the value of two
dollars good and lawful money of the State of Tennessee
then and there being the goods and chattles of one George
Baker, faloniously did steal take and carry away from and
out of the possesion of the said George Baker, contrary
to the form of the statutes in such case made and provided
and against the peace and dignity of the State.

(P-266)   Samuel Frazier, Attorney General
                                    for the 3rd Solisetorial
                                    District.

          Endorsment - Indictment -

The State   )
)
    vs   )
)
John Cockram   )

     George Baker, prosecutor - Malone Carter, George Baker,
Alman Guinn, Thomas Duther John Grimes, William Bowling,
Joseph Bowling, Witnesses for the State sworn in open Court
and sent before the grand Jury -

     28th August, 1839.

                         Henry Price, Clerk.

     Not a true bill - Abraham Lilard, Fourman of the Grand
Jury.

          Horse Stealing -

State   )
)
    vs   )   Came the grand Jury into open
)   Court and returned a bill of
John Cockram   )   Indictment against the defend-
Robert Shields &   )   ants
Samuel Carter   )
                         Indorsed, not a true bill by
William Grant, there foreman.

The State   )
)
    vs   )   On charge of Horse Stealing

Robert Shields   )   This day came the Attorney Gener-
John Cockram &   )   al who prosecutes for the State &
Samuel Carter   )   by the assent of the Court enters
                               a Nole proseque in this cause, It
is therefore considered by the Court that the defendants
be discharged from their said recognizance and that they
go hence without day -

Petition -

To the Honorable Chas. F. Keith, Judge of the Third
juridical Circuit of the Circuit Courts of law in and for
the State of Tennessee.

The Petition of Samuel McJunken, represents and s
shows to your honor that a judgment was recorded against
him in favor of J. D. Traynor, on the 23rd day of June
1838 - by Jessee Poe, Esquire, one of   (P-267)   the
justices of the Peace in and for the County of Bradley
& State of Tennessee for sixty seven dollars & ninety
seven cents debt and seventy five cents cost your petitioner believeing that the said Judgment unjust and he
would have appealed from the same but at the time of its
rendition he was in the service of the United States as
a volunteer sailor and that he could not obtain permition
from his commanding officer to be absent from the post
so as to take an appeal in the time prescribed by law. To
these your honor that great injustice has been done to your
petitioner and that the merits of this controversy are with
him he would further state that the demand on which the
judgment complained of is grounded on or given out of a
store account which account was filed with the warrant in
this cause, the whole account was for seventy two dollars
and Eighty four cents & a half, with a credit of four dollars and eighty seven cents the amount debt for which the
judgment aforesaid was rendered your petitioner further
represents that the account on its face shows Sixty six
and one fourth cents was got by your petitioner and that
much of the account he acknowledged to be correct and just
but the ballance of the account amounting to fifty two dollars Eighteen and a fourth cents your petitioner denys the
justice of -- It appears from the account that articals
consisting chiefly of wine, Beer, whisky & Brandy, Crack-
ers Roesin, Cheese and articles of like character and in
small quantitys and at divers times was got of the said
Traynor by your petitioners son Tillman, Your petitioner
avers that the said Tillman never was authorised by your
petitioner to pledge his   (P-268)   credit for the purchase of those articles and futher that they werenot necessary to the Education or clothing of the said petitioners
son but were wholly unnecessary and your petitioner futher
states that he never promised said Traynor that he would
pay an account of his sons contracting to ammount greater

than three or four dollars, Tillman, the son of your petitioner is a minor Execution on said judgment has been Issued on one mare and colt and filley the property of your Petitioner to sattisfy said unjust judgment therefore your petitioner considers him self ingered --- and prays that your honor order writs of Certiorari and superceeds to Issue to remove the proceedings in said cause into the Circuit Court of Bradley County at this next term to be held in the Court house in Cleveland that a new trial may be had and justice according to law adminstered to your petitioner and that all further proceedings in said cause may be stayed and superseded this the first application for a superseder in this cause unless your honer should consider the paper hereto attached marked A - such as on application this paper was never presented to the Circuit Clerk for official action or there was no counsel to whom your petitioner could apply for advice and if this paper should prevale your honor grants the said writs he will be with out any stay and his property sacraficed on said judgment to sattisfy a claim that those should not be entitled or covetious of ---The premises was due order the writs granted your petitioner as in duty bound will ever pray.

Samuel Mc Junken

State of Tennessee   )

Bradley County   )   Personally appeared before
                          Jesse Poe, acting Justice of
the peace in and for   (P-269)   the County and State aforesaid Samuel McJunkin, and made oath in due form of law that the facts set fourth in the fourgoing petition or of this knoledge of the Petitioner or he believes to be true.

Samuel McJunkin

Sworn to and subscribed before me this 30th day of July A. D. 1838.

Jesse Poe, Justice of the Peace

State of Tennessee   )

Third Judicial Circuit   )

       To the Clerk of the Circuit Court of Bradley County and State aforesaid let writs of certiorari and super-

cedias Issue according to the prayer of the foregoing
petitioner or the parties giveing bond and securety as
directed by law given under my hand the 2nd day of August 1838.

Charles F. Keith, Judge &c.

Bond ---

Know all men by these presents that we Samuel McJunkin, John C. Kennedy and John Hardwick of Bradley County
and State of Tennessee are executors and adminstrators are
held and firmly bound unto John D. Traynor, his heirs,
executors adminstrators or assigns in the sum of one hundred and thirty Seven dollars to be void on condition that
the said -- shall present with effect a writ of certiorari
by him this day obtained to remove the proceedings of a
suit which John D. Traynor, as plaintiff and Samuel McJunkin is defendant from before Jesse Poe, the Justice of the
Peace into our Circuit Court for the County of Bradley or
in case of failure therein preform whatever judgment shall
be awarded and rendered by said Court in said Cause or in
case said certiorari shall be dismissed by said Court for
Informality or want of form or sufficient substance or for
any other cause pay and sattisfy such judgment as shall be
given by said Court, against him.   (P-270)

Witness our hands and seals this --- day of ---

Samuel McJunken (Seal)

John C. Kennedy (Seal)

John Hardwick (Seal)

Certioraris --

State of Tennessee   )   To Jesse Poe, a Justice of the
)   Peace for the County aforesaid
Bradley County   )   whare as John D. Traynor, lately
                                  before Jesse Poe ----- of and
recovered a judgment against Samuel McJunkin for Sixty
dollars and we for certain reasons being desirous that the
record of that suit should be dertified to us do hereby
command you to enclose all the papers relative to said suit
under your hand and seal destinctly and plainly together
with this writ, and Transmit the same to a Circuit Court
to be held by the Judge of the Circuit Court of law and
Equity for the County of Bradley at the Court house in Cleveland on the fourth Monday of August 1838, in order that our
said Court may do therein what of right and according to

law ought to be done.

Witness - Henry Price, Clerk of our said Court at office in Cleveland the 4th Monday of May, 1838 and of American Independence the 62nd.

Henry Price, Clerk

Endorsment -

John D. Traynor vs Samuel McJunkin

Issued August the 6th 1838.

To the Judge of the Circuit Court of the County of Bradley, Tennessee.

In obediance to the within writ, I have Enclosed all the papers in my possession in relation to the said suit being the warrent and amount filed with the same and the Judgment on said warrant in this cause whare in John D. Traynor is Plaintiff and Samuel McJunkin is defendant given under my hand and seal this 6th day of August A. D. 1838.

Jesse Poe (Seal)
Justice of the Peace

(P-271)
Supercedes --

State of Tennessee)
)
Bradley County)

To the Sheriff and all lawful officers of said County of Bradley, Greeting: You are hereby commanded that from all other proceedings upon a Judgment for sixty ~~sum ed dollars~~ sum od dollars obtained before Jesse Poe, one of the Justices of the Peace for Bradley County you desist and altogether supercede as the same by our Circuit Court for the County of Bradley and you are also commanded to notify the said John D. Traynor, to appear before the Judge of our said Circuit Court at a Court to be held for the County aforesaid at the Court house in Cleveland on the fourth Monday in August 1838 - Then and there to answer the said suit and have you then and there this writ - Witness - Henry Price, Clerk of our said Court at office in Cleveland the 4th Monday in May 1838, and of American Independence the 62nd.

Henry Price, Clerk

Endorsment - Supersedes -

John D. Traynor, vs Samuel McJunkin

Issued August the 6th, 1838

Came to hand the same day Issued & Summond John D. Traynor this the 10th July 1838.

James Lauderdale, Sheriff.

Certiorari

December Term, 1838.

John D. Traynor)
)
vs) This day came John Hardwick and John
) C. Kennedy into open Court and under
Samuel McJunkin) took for the defendant and say in
case he fail to prosecute his said
Certiorari with effect or on failure there of dose not pay
and sattisfy all costs and damages which may be awarded
against him that they will pay it for him.

April Term, 1839.

John D. Traynor)
)
vs) Came the parties by there attorneys
) and an afedavit of the plaintiff
Samuel McJunkin) this cause is continued untill next
(P-272) term, and a commission is
awarded him to take the deposition Abraham Humphries a
citizen of Moore County and Lewis Wills, a citizen of the
State of Massorie by giveing the defendant at least thirty
days notice as to Wills and ten days at Humphries.

August Term, 1839.

John D. Traynor)
)
vs) Certiorari
)
Samuel McJunkin)

The parties by there attorneys appear and on motion

of the plaintiff by his attorney Levi Trewhitt, a Nole
proseque is entered in this cause.

It is therefore considered by the Court that the defendant go hence and recover of the plaintiff his costs
about his defence in this behalf expended and have Execution &c.

Warrant --

State of Tennessee   )
)
Bradley County   )   To any lawful officer in and for
                               the County of Bradley you are
hereby commanded to summons Isaac Swan to appear before me
or some other Justice of the Peace for said County to answer the complaint of Joseph L. Swan, for the nun payment
of a sum under one hundred dollars, due by account here in
fail not, given under my hand and seal this 4th day of February 1839.

                        Jesse Poe   (Seal)
                           Justice of the Peace for Bradley
                           County.

Summond for Plaintiff

Henry Price   )
)
John Swan   )
)
James Britton &   )
)
Levi Spencer   )
)
Eliza Price   )

     Endorsment -- Warrant

Joseph Swan   )
)
     vs   )   Issued Feb. 4th 1839.

Isaac Swan   )   Came to hand the same day Issued exe-
                    cuted for trial the 9th of February
1839, before Isaac Day,

                    G. W. Selvedge, Const.

(P-273)   Judgment entered against the defendant for debt -

                                                15.00

        Sheriff cost   1.75
        One Witness claims his attendance   .25
        Justus Judgment   .25

    By me Jesse Poe, Justice of the Peace, this 19th
        February, 1839.

    Appeal Bond

State of Tennessee   )
)
Bradley County   )   We, J. N. Swan, and Henry Brown
                             acknowledge ourselves indebted
to Joseph Swan, his heirs Executors adminstrators and assigns in the sum of Thirty dollars, but to be void if the
said J. N. Swan shall well and truly prosecute with effect
to appear which he has this day prayed and obtained to our
next Circuit Court to be held for said Circuit Court to be
County at the Court house in Cleveland on the 4th Monday
of April next, from a Judgment Rendered by Jesse Poe a Justice of the Peace for said County for the sum of fifteen
dollars debt and damage and the further sum of two dollars
and twenty five cents*if he shall well and truly pay and
sattisfy the Judgment of the Circuit Court in case there is
a Judgment rendered by said Court against him given under
my hand and seal this 21st February, 1839.

                      J. N. Swan (Seal)

                      Henry Brown (Seal)

Jesse Poe, Justice   )
    of the Peace   )

    Appeal April Term, 1839.

Joseph Swan   )
)
    vs   )   By consent of parties this cause is
*costs

Isaac Swan   )   continued untill the next term.

    Appeal August Term, 1839.

Joseph Swan   )
)
    vs   )   The parties by there Attorney appear
)   and by consent and with leave of the
Isaac Swan   )   Court this cause is continued till
                         next term.

(P-274)   Bond

    Know all men by these presents that we, Shearwood
Orsburn and John D. Traynor, are jointly and severlly
held and firmly bound unto John Cline, William M. Shaw
and others in the penal sum of two hundred and fifty dollars to be void on condition that the said Shearwood Orsburn will with effect prosecute a suit by action of Trespess which he this day commenced against John Cline, and
others in the Circuit Court of Bradley County or in case
of failure of such prosecution pay and satisfy all costs
and damages as may be awarded against him by our said
Court.

    Witness our hands and seals this 3rd day of July 1838.

                        (Shearwood Orsburn (Seal)
                        (
                        (J. D. Traynor (Seal)

Test -

Henry Price.

    -        Writ -

State of Tennessee   )   To the Sheriff of Bradley
)   County, Greeting: You are
Bradley County   )   hereby commanded to summons
                            John Cline to be and appear
before the Judge of our next Circuit Court to beheld for
the County of Bradley at the Court house in Cleveland on
the 4th Monday in August next to answer Shearwood Orsburn
of a plea of Trespes with force and armes to his damage
one thousand dollars here in fail not and have you then
and there this writ.

    Witness, Henry Price, Clerk of our said Court at office
in Cleveland the 4th Monday of May, 1838.

                    Henry Price, Clerk.

Witness for the plantiff, John D. Traynor and Levi Trewhitt.

Endorsment No. 33

Summons - Shearwood Orsburn vs John Cline, William Shaw and others.

Issued 3rd day of July 1838 to August Term, 1838.

Came to hand the 4th July 1838 and Executed by summoning John Cline this the 5th July 1838.

John Lauderdale, Sheriff

Decleration -

State of Tennessee   )   Circuit Court
)
Bradley County   )   August Term, 1838.

Shearwood Orsburn, by Attorney complains of John L. Cline, who is summoned by the sheriff by the name of John Cline to answer the said plantiff of a plea of trespass with force and armes

For that the said defendant upon the 1st day of April 1838, At to wit, in the county aforesaid with force and armes broke and entered the dwelling house of the said plantiff and seized took and carried away from and out of said dwelling divers household goods and kitchen furniture to wit, Five feather beds and furniture of the value of one hundred dollars one clock of the value of fifty dollars, All proper goods & chattles of the said plantiff and then and there with force and armes broke rent tore and destroyed and wholly ruined the same untill it was of no value and other wrongs to the said plantiff then and there did against the peace and dignity of the state, and to the damage of the said plaintiff two hundred and fifty dollars and also for that the said defendant aforesaid to wit, upon the same day and year last mentioned aforesaid at to wit, in the County with force and armes seized took and carried away from and out of the possession of the said plaintiff divers other house hold goods and kitchen furniture to wit one fether bed & furniture of the value of one hundred dollars one table of the value of two twenty five dollars all the proper goods and chattles of the said plantiff and then and there greatly broke rent and tore destroyed and lessened in value the same and other wrongs to the said plantiff then and there did against the peace and dignity of the State and to   (P-276)   the damage of the said plantiff two hundred and fifty dollars, and also for that the said defendant on the --- day and year last aforesaid at to wit, in the County aforesaid with force and armes broke and entered a certain other dwelling house of the said plaintiff situated in the County aforesaid and there and then ejected exspeled put out and removed the said plantiff and his family from the possesion use own --- and enjoying of the said dwelling house and kept and continued them ejected exspeled put out and removed for al long space of time to wit from them hitherto whare by the said plaintiff for and during all that time lost and was deprived of the use and benifit of his said dwelling house to wit in the County aforesaid and other wrongs to the said plaintiff then and there did against the peace and dignity of the State and to the damage of said plaintiff one thousand dollars and therefore he brings his suit and pledges to prosecute.

                    Trewhitt, Atty. for Plaintiff

        Plea --

        And the said defendant by his attorney comes into Court and defends the force and injury when and whare and says the plaintiff his action against him ought not to have and maintain because he says he is not guilty in manner and forms as plaintiff in declaration hath alledged against him and of this he puts him self on the County and the plaintiff likewise.

                    Jarnagin & Bradford

                    Attys for defendant.

Levi Trewhitt,
    Atty. for Plaintiff.

        August Term, 1838

Sherwood Orsburn   )
)
    vs   )   Came the parties by their attorneys
)   and from reasons appearing to the
John L. Cline   )   sattisfaction of the from the af-
                          fedavit of Spencer Jarnagin time
is given the defendant to plead   (P-277)

        Circuit Court

        December Term 1838.

Sherwood Orsburn)
)
vs)   This day came Levi Trewhitt, Esqr.
)   Attorney for the plaintiff and sug-
John L. Cline)   gested the death of the said
)   plain tiff upon the record.

Circuit Court, April Term, 1839.

Sherwood Orsburn)
)
vs)   This day came Thomas Orsburn the
)   Executor of the plaintiff whare
John L. Cline)   death was suggested at the last
)   Term and brought with him into
open Court letters testementry to him granted by the County Court of Bradley County and by his Attorney moved the
Court to revive this cause in his name as Executor aforesaid which is accordingly done.

April Term, 1839.

Thomas Orsburn, Executor)
   of Sherwood Orsburn, Dest.)
)
)
vs)   The parties by there At-
)   torneys appear and by
)   consent and with assent
John L. Cline)   of the Court this cause

is continued till next term.

December Term, 1839.

Thomas Orsburn, Executor)
   of Sherwood Orsburn)
)
)
vs)   The parties by their attor-
)   neys appear and also a Jury
)   of good and lawful men to
John L. Cline)   wit, Henry Richards, John
Mee, William Camp, Henderson Thatch, John Fulks, Josiah
Johnston, Adam H. Tener, John Goodner, John W. Kennedy, Andrew Stephens, Edward Austin, and Isaac Edwards who being
elected tried and sworn to well and truly try the Issue
joined between the   (P-278)   parties on there oath say
that the defendant is guilty of the tresspes and force in
the plaintiffs decleration mentioned in manner and form as
the said plaintiff hath declared and assess the plaintiffs

damage by reason thereof to Fourhundred and seventy five dollars.

It is therefore considered by the Court that the plantiff recover of the defendant the sum of Four hundred and Seventy five dollars the damage so as aforesaid affixed by the Jury and the costs about his suit in this behalf Expended and have Execution.

Tuesday 31st December, 1839.

Thomas Orsburn, Executor)
  of Sherwood Orsburn)
)
  vs) The defendant by his at-
) torney appeared and moved
John L. Cline) the Court for a new Trial
  to be entered to show why
a new Trial should be granted which rule is granted.

Thursday 2nd, January, 1840

Thomas Orsburn, Executor)
  of Sherwood Orsburn)
)
  vs) The parties by their attor-
) neys appear and the rule
John L. Cline) heretofore granted in this
  cause to the defendant to
show cause why a new trial should be had in this cause being argued by counsel.

It is considered by the Court that said rule be discharged.

_____

_____

_____

Indictment --

The State)
)
  vs) State of Tennessee
)
Thomas J. Davis) Bradley County
*cause

Circuit Court, August Term, Eighteen hundred and Thirty nine.

The Grand Jurors in behalf of the State of Tennessee elected empaneled sworn and charged (P-279) to enquire for the body of the County of Bradley aforesaid upon there oath present that a Certain Thomas J. Davis late of said County labourer on the 12th day of February in the year of one thousand eight hundred and thirty nine with force and armes in the County of Bradley aforesaid and within the jurisdiction of this Hounerable Court one guelding of the value of One hundred and thirty dollars good and lawful money of the State of Tennessee, and of the United States then and there being the goods and Chattles of one Samuel Foreman a native of the Cherokee Nation of Indians falaciously did steal take and carry away from and out of the possesion of the said Samuel Foreman, to the great damage of the said Samuel Foreman to the evil example of all othere in like case offending contrary to the form of the Statute in such case made and provided and against the peace and dignity of the State.

Samuel Frazier,

Attorney General for the Third Solictorial district.

Endorsment - Indictment

The State vs Thomas J. Davis.

Alexander A. Clingan prosecutor. Alexander Clingan, Lewis Williams Marvel Dunken, Veny Johnson.

Witness for the State, Sworn and sent before the grand Jury, August the 28th, 1839.

Henry Price, Clerk

A true Bill - Abraham Liland, Foreman of the Grand Jury.

Edward Cooper, Phillip Davis William Davis,

Circuit Court May Term, 1838.

The State   )
)
    vs   Horse Stealing   )   Spencer Bevers, Sheriff of

Thomas J. Davis   )   McMinn County brought into Court
                             the body of Thomas J. Davis, who
was ordered into the Custody of the Sheriff of Bradley
County.

(P-280)   May Term 1838.

State   )
     vs   )
Thomas J. Davis   )   Horse Stealing

                             The grand Jury for the State appeared
in open Court and brought with them a bill of Indictment Endorsed a true Bill by Daniel Buckner, there fourman, Spencer Bevers, Sheriff and Jailer for McMinn County for keeping said defendant in Jail from the 6th day of March 1838,
to the 14th day of May 1838, making in all 70 days at 37cts.
per day $26.25.

        Also to conveying said defendant from Athens, McMinn
County Jail to Cleveland Bradley County fifty two miles
going and returning at 10¢ per mile $5.20
        Also 2 of a guard at 6 cents Per Mi.   6.24
            Two turn keys at 50¢ each   1.00
                                             _____

                                    $38.69

    And it further appearing to the Court that there is no
Jail in Bradley County and that the defendant was commited
to McMinn County Jail for safe keeping.

    It is therefore considered by the Court that the above
bill of cost be certified to the State of Tennessee according to an act of the General Assembly in such case made and
provided and that the same be turned in the bill of Cost.

        May Term, 1838.

The State   )
     vs   )   Horse Stealing
Thomas J. Davis   )

                             Came the Attorney General who prose-
cutes for the State and the defendant in his own proper person who being charged upon the Bill of Indictment and for
plea says that he is not guilty as charged upon the Bill
of Indictment and for plea says that he is not guilty as
charged in said bill of Indictment and for his trial puts him
self uppon the County and the Attorney General   (P281)
Doth the like and it appearing to the satisfaction of the
Court from the affidavit of the defendant that he cannot
come safely to trial at the present term of this Court on
account of the present Excitement against him It is there
fore considered by the Court that this cause be continued
untill the next term of this Court.

August Term 1838.

State)
vs) Horse Stealing
Thomas J. Davis)

      Came the attorney General who prosecutes for the State and this cause is continued on affidavit of the defendant and there upon came the said defendant Thomas J. Davis and acknowledged him self to be indebted to the State in the sum of One thousand dollars to be leveyed of his goods and chattles lands and tenements to the use of the State and void on condition that he make his personal appearance before the Judge of the Circuit Court at a Court to be held for the County of Bradley at the Court house in Cleveland on the first Wednesday in ~~Cleveland on the first Wednesday~~ after the fourth Monday in December next then and there to answer a charge of the State against him for Horse Stealing and do not depart this Court without leve and there uppon came Phillip Davis Sr. and Phillip Davis, Jr. and John Welbourn and acknowledged them selves jointly and severly to be indebted to the State of Tennessee in the Sum of one thousand dollars to be leveyed of these goods and Chattles lands and tenements to be void on condition Thomas J. Davis make his personal appearance before the Judge of the Circuit Court at a Court to be held for the County of Bradley at the Court house in Cleveland on the first Wednesday after the fourth Monday in December, next,   (P-282)   then and there to answer a charge of the State Exhibited against him for Horse Stealing and not depart the Court without leve.

State)
vs) Horse Stealing
Thomas J. Davis)

      Came the attorney General who prosecutes for the State and thereupon came Lewis Williams and acknowledged himself to be indebted to the State of Tennessee in the sum of two hundred and fifty dollars to be leveyed of his goods and Chattles lands and tenements to be void on condition that he make his personal appearance before the Judge of the Circuit Court to be held for the County - Bradley at the Court house in the town of Cleveland on the first Wednesday after the fourth Monday of December next and give Evidence in behalf of the State against Thomas J. Davis, on a charge of Horse Stealing, and not depart the Court without leve.

Circuit Court, December, 1838.

The State)

```
     vs                )      Horse Stealing
Thomas J. Davis        )
```

Came the Attorney General who prosecutes for the State and there upon came Marvel Dunken acknowledged himself indebted to the State of Tennessee in the sum of two hundred and fifty dollars to be levied of his goods anc chattles lands and tenements void on condition that he make his personal appearance before the Judge of the Circuit Court at a Court to be held for the County of Bradley at the Court house in the town of Cleveland on the first Wednesday after the fourth Monday in December next and give evidence in behalf of the State against Thomas J. Davis on a charge of Horse Stealing and not depart the Court with out leave.

Circuit Court, December, 1838.

```
The State              )
    vs                 )      Horse Stealing
Thomas J. Davis        )
```

Came the Attorney General who prosecutes for the State and the defendant being solemnly called to come into Court and answer a charge of the State exhibited against him for Larceny came not but made default It is therefore considered by the Court that the said Thomas J. Davis for the default aforesaid do forfit and pay to the State of Tennessee the sum of one thousand dollars according to the tener and effect of his said recognizance entered into by him at the last term of thisCourt unless good and sufficient reason to the contrary is shown at the next term of this Court and that serafacious Issue to warnt him.

```
State                  )
    vs                 )      Serafacias
Phillip Davis, Sr.     )
Phillip Davis, Jnr.    )      Came the attorney General who
and John Wilburn       )      prosecutes for the State and
                              Thomas J. Davis being solemnly
```
called and requested to cum into Court as he was this day bound to do and answer a charge of the State of Tennessee came not but made default and the said Phillip Davis, Senr. and the Phillip Davis, Jnr. and John Wilburn also -- being solemnly called to come into Court and bring with them the body of Thomas J. Davis to answer said charge came not but made default.

It is therefore considered by the Court that said Philip Davis, Senr. and Phillip Davis Jnr. and John Wilburn doth forfeit to the State of Tennessee.

April Term, 1839.

State	)	
vs	)	Serfacias
Phillip Davis, Jnr.	)	
Phillip Davis, Snr. &	)	Came the Attorney General
John Wilburn	)	who prosecutes for the State
		and also comes into Court

(P-284)   Phillip Davis, Senr. Phillip Davis Jnr. and John
Wilburn, and brought with them the body of Thomas J. Davis
and in open Court surrendered him in to the Custody of the
Sheriff of Bradley County who is ordered by the Court to
take charge of him and on motion the forfeit heretofore entered in this cause against the Bail - is set aside by leve
the Court and the said Phillip Davis, Snr. Phillip Davis, Jnr..
and John Wilburn, confess Judgment for all costs that have
accrued in this behalf.

It is therefore considered by the Court that the State
of Tennessee render of the said Phillip Davis, Snr. Phillip
Davis, Jnr. and John Wilburn jointly the costs so as aforesaid confessed by them and Execution Issue &c.

State	)	
vs Sifa	)	Came the attorney General who pros-
Thomas J. Davis	)	ecutes on behalf of the State and
		the defendant being brought to the
		bar by the Sheriff on motion and

by consent of the attorney General and with leve of the
Court the forfet heretofore taken in this cause is set a-
side and there upon came Phillip Davis, Snr. Phillip Davis,
Jnr. and John Wilburn, together with the defendant confeses
judgment for all costs that have accrued in this behalf.

It is therefore considered by the Court that the State
of Tennessee recovered of the said defendants the costs
as aforesaid confessed and that Execution Issue &c.

The State	)	
vs	)	Indictment Grand Larceny
Thomas J. Davis	)	
		The attorney General comes to prose-
		cute on behalf of the State and the

said Thomas J. Davis is brought to the barr in the Custody
of the Sheriff of Bradley County and the said   (P-285)
Thomas J. Davis, being arranged and charged on said bill of
Indictment pleads not guilty to the same and for his trial
puts himself upon the County and the Attorney General doth
like and thereupon to try said Issue Came a Jury to wit -
William Poe, A. Aken, John Caplan, Charles Dodd, Robert H.
Allison, James Massey, Alman Guinn, Daniel J. Stafford,
George Wesmoreland, Isaac Glandon, Daniel Anderson and John
F. Larrison all good and lawful men of the County of Bradley.

Who being elected tried and sworn to well and truly try
and true ----- make between the good people of the State
of Tennessee and the said defendant on their oath do say
the defendant Thomas J. Davis is guilty of the Larceny
as charged in said bill of Indictment and the Jury aforesaid*do futher ascertain and say that the said Thomas J.
Davis for the offence aforesaid shall undergo confinement
in the Jail and Penetenteary house of the State for the
space of four years.

        April Term, 1839.

State   )
   vs   )   The Attorney General reported to
Thomas J. Davis)   Court the following bill of Cost
                     which was inspected by the Court
                     and ordered to be spread on the
record to wit -

The State   )   Sheriff Lauderdale
   vs.   Feleney   )   5th March, 1838.
Thomas J. Davis   )   To boarding defendant 1 day at
                            37½ to conveying prisoner to
                            Athens Jail from Cleveland and
returning 52 - miles at 10 cents per mile $5.20 two of a
guard same distance 6 cents per mile 6 24 who had been committed to Athens Jail by Jesse Poe,   (P-286)   Justice
of the Peace which was ordered to be taxed in the bill of
costs --

State   )
   vs   )   Came the attorney General who prose-
Thomas J. Davis)   cutes for the State and also the de-
                     fendants council and the defendant
                     being brought to the Barr and there-
upon came on the rule heretofore entered in this cause to
be argued to show cause when a new trial should be had in
this cause and after argument of councel and mature decleration of the Court, It is considered by the court that said
rule be made absolute and a new trial to be granted the defendant in this cause.

        August Term, 1839.

The State   )
   vs   )   The Sheriff of McMinn County appeared
Thomas J. Davis   )   and surrendered the body Thomas J.
                         Davis, of the defendant in open Court
                         and the said defendant is thereupon
ordered into the Custody of the Sheriff of Bradley County.

        August Term, 1839.
*on their oath aforesaid

The State   )
    vs   )   The Attorney General comes to prose-
Thomas J. Davis   )   cute on behalf of the State and
                           Thomas J. Davis, is brought to the
                           bar of the Court in Custody of the
Sheriff of Bradley County and on motion of the Attorney
General and for reasons appearing to the satisfaction of the
Court a Nole proseque is entered in this cause and the said
Thomas J. Davis remanded to the County Jail of Bradley County
and that the Clerk Tax the ~~cost for the Inspection~~ of the
(P-287)   cost for the Inspection of the Court.

    Circuit Court August Term, 1839.

State   )
    vs Larceny   )   Indictment for grand Larceny
Thomas J. Davis   )

                           The grand Jury appeared and returned
                           into open Court a bill of Indict-
ment against the defendant for Horse Stealing endorsed by
their fourman Abraham Lillard A true bill.

    August term 1839.

State   )
    vs   )   Indictment for Larceny --
Thomas J. Davis   )

                           The Attorney General comes to
                           prosecute on behalf of the State
                           and the said Thomas J. Davis is
brought to the bar of the Court by the Sheriff of Bradley
County and the said Thomas J. Davis being arranged and
charged on said bill of Indictment pleads not guilty to
the same and for his trial puts him self upon the County
and the attorney General doth the like and there upon comes
a Jury to wit -

    John Anderson, Abraham McKissick, John Green, Green-
bury Denton, Alexander Murfey, David Holmes, William Gilliland, John Esman, William Fergerson, William Kelley, Preston Parker and Buonepart Mapels good and lawful men citizens of Bradley County who being elected tried and sworn
the truth to speak of and conscerning the premses and the
Jury not having a greed are put under the charge of the Sheriff James Lauderdale who is Instructed by the Court to keep
them together in some convenant apartment seperately and
apart from other citizens and not permit any other persons
to have any conversation with them until there return into
Court at meeting of the Court tomorrow to resume the consideration of this cause Order that the said Thomas J. Davis
be remanded to Jail   (P-288)

State   )   Horse Stealing
   vs   )
Thomas J. Davis)   The Attorney General comes to
                    prosecute on behalf of the State
                    and the defendant is brought to
the bar of the Court in custada of the Sheriff of Bradley
County and the Jury heretofore sworn having returned into
Court and resumed the consideration of this cause on there
oath do say that the said defendant Thomas J. Davis is
guilty of the feloniously taking and carring a way of a
certain sorrel Horse of the good and chattles of Samuel
Foreman in maner and form as charged in the bill of Indictment and the Jurors aforesaid upon there oath aforesaid
do futher ascertain and say that the said Thomas J. Davis
for the offence aforesaid shall undergo confinement in the
Jail and penitentiary house of this State for the space of
four years and the said defendant is remanded to Jail.

State   )
   vs   )
Thomas J. Davis)   James Berry, produced in open Court
                    and proved his account for thirty
                    four days furnished the Jury in this
cause at twenty five cents each 600 which account is allowed and ordered to be spred of record filed and taxed in
the bill of cost.

State   )
   vs   Larceny)   John Brown, Dept. Sheriff for
Thomas J. Davis)   Bradley County produced in open
                    Court and proved his account for
                    Conveying the said defendant from
Cleveland to Athens and returning 52 miles at 10 cents per
mile   . $5.20

     & two of a guard at 6cts.
                     each $6.24

which account is allowed and ordered   (P-289)   to be
filed and taxed in the bill of Cost. $11.44

State   )
   vss   )   James Lauderdale, Sheriff, proves
Thomas J. Davis)   his account in open Court for board-
                    ing the defendant 4 days at April
                    Term, 1839, at 37½ cents per day
$1.50 conveying the defendant from Cleveland to Athens Jail
McMinn County and returning 52 miles at 10 cents per mile
                                             $5.20
          Two of a guard at 6 cents each $6.24

to boarding Defendant at August Term, 1839,

    Eight days at 37½ cents per day $3.00
    Eight Turn keys at 50 cents each $4.00
  Which is allowed by the Court and ordered to be
taxed in the bill of cost $19.94

State   )
  vs   )   The defendant comes and assigns the
Thomas J. Davis   )   following reasons in arest of Judg-
              ment, It does not appear of record
              that the Bill of Indictment upon
which the defendant is convicted was returned into open
Court by the grand Jury for the State for this and for other
reasons apparent upon the record the defendant pays the Judgment be arested and the defendant discharged and the record
being inspected by the Court and no other reasons appearing
It is considered by the Court that said reasons in arest of
judgment filed as aforesaid be over ruled and the defendant
having nothing further to say why the Court shall not pro-
ceede to Judgment and Execution thereof against him according to law then as before he hath said It is therefore considered by the Court that said Thomas J. Davis for the offence aforesaid do undergo confinement at hard labour in the
Jail and Penitentiary house.   (P-290)   of this State for
the Term of four years commencing on the 31st day of August
1839, that he be rendered infemaus and incompetent of being
Examined as a witness in any of the Courts of this State,
and that he pay the costs of this prosecution for which execution may issue.

    And also that the Sheriff summons two of a guard to as-
sist in conveying said Defendant to the said jail and Penitentiary house of this State there to be delivered over
by him to the said Sheriff to the keeper of said jail and
Penitentiary house within a reasonable time from this day
and date.

_____

Indictment -

State of Tennessee   )   Circuit Court, August Term
)   Eighteen hundred and Thirty nine.
Bradley County   )
            The grand Jurors in behalf of the
           State of Tennessee, elected em-
paneled sworn and charged to enquire for the body of the

County of Bradley aforesaid upon there oath present that a
Certain Edward Williams late of said County, labourer and
acertain Moses H. Ayers, late of said County labourer on
the first day of May in the year of Our Lord One thousand
eighteen and thirty nine, with force and armes in the County of Bradley, aforesaid and within the jurisdiction of
this Honerable Court, one piece of Iron of the value of
two dollars and fifty cents goodsand lawful money of the
State of Tennessee Then and there being the goods and Chattles of James A. Fletcher, feloniously did steal take and
carry away from and out of the posession of the said James
A. Fletcher, and the jurors aforesaid upon their oath aforesaid do futher present that the said Edward Williams and the
said Moses H. Ayers, being persons of evil name and fame and
dishonest Conversation and common byers and receivers of
Stolengoods on the first day of May in the year of Our Lord
(P-291)   One thousand Eightehundred and thirty nine, with
force and Armes in the County of Bradley, aforesaid, one
piece of Iron of the value of two dollars and fifty cents
good and lawful money of the State of Tennessee then and
there being the goods and chattles of James A. Fletcher by
a certain evil disposed person to the jurors aforesaid
yeat unknone then lately before feloniously stolen of the
same evil disposed purson feloniously fraudulantly did --
and have with intent to deprive the true owner there of
they the said Edward Williams and Moses H. Ayers then and
there well knowing and each of them well knowing the said
goods and chattles to have been felonously stolen contrary to the form of the Stattute in such case made and provided and against the peace and dignity of the State.

                    Samuel Frazier, Attorney General
                         for the third Solicitorial
                         District

Endorsment - Indictment -

The State vs Edward Williams, and Moses H. Ayers,
James A. Fletcher, Prosecutor

James A. Fletcher, Wm. H. Davis, Baker Armstrong,
George A. Boler, Robert H. Pharris, Abraham H. Hagler,
Robert Stephenson, Witnesses for the State sworn in open
Court and sent before the Grand Jury, August the 28th 1839.

                    Henry Price, Clerk

A True Bill - - Abraham Lillard, Fourman of
                    the Grand Jury.

Circuit Court August Term, 1839.

State)
vs) Indictment
Edward Williams)
& Moses H. Ayers) Petet Larceny

     The grand Jury appeared in open
Court and returned a bill of Indictment against the defendants for Petet Larceny -

   Endorsed by their fourman Abraham Lillard,

     A True Bill

     August Term, 1839.

State)
 vs) Petet Larceny
)
Edward Williams) The sheriff of McMinn County appeared
        and surrendered the* (P-292) of the
        said Edward Williams in open Court
and thereupon the*Edward Williams was ordered into the custody of the Sheriff of Bradley County -

   Spencer Bevers, Sheriff and Jailor for McMinn County
charged for keeping the said Williams in the Jail of Mc-
Minn County from the 21st of June 1839, untill the 26th of
August, 1839. Making in all sixty seven days at 37½ cents

              25.12½

      Two turn keys at 50cts ea. 1.00

     To conveying said Williams from
     Athens Jail to Cleveland and re-
     turning 52 Miles at 10 cents Per
     Mile   5.20

     Two men of a guard at 6 cents
     Per Mile   6.24
              _____

              37.56½

   Also Spencer Bevers, Sheriff and jailer of McMinn
County appeared in open Court and surrendered the body
of Moses H. Ayers, and the said Defendant was ordered
into the custoda of the Sheriff of Bradley County also
for keeping said defendant Ayers in the Jail of McMinn
County from the 19th of June 1839, untill the 26th of
*Body *said

August 1839, making in all 69 - days at 37½ cents $25.87½

      And two turn keys at 50 cents each   1.00

      Also to conveying said Ayers from Athens
        Jail to Cleveland and returning 52
        miles at 10 cents per mile   - $5.20

      Two men of a guard the same distance
        at 6 cents per mile each $6.24

                                     $38.31½

State	August Term, 1839.
vs	
Edward Williams	To Sheriff Lauderdale

To boarding Defendant four days at 37½cents p
                           per day $1.50

     To four turn keys at 50 cents each $2.00

                                    $3.50

State	To James Lauderdale,
vs	Sheriff
Moses H. Ayers	

For boarding Defendants Ayers, four days at 37½
                     cents per day $1.50

     To four turn keys at 50 cents each $2.00

                                    $3.50

State	G. W. Selvedge
vs	a Constable
Edward Williams	

Appeared in open Court and proved his account for conveying the defendant   (P-293)   from Cleveland, Bradley
County to Athens Jail and returning 52 miles at 10 cents
per mile $5.20

     and two of a guard at 6 cents each
       the same distance $6.24

                                    $11.44

      Also conveying the defendant Moses H. Ayers
        from Bradley County Cleveland to Athens

Jail Mc Minn County and return-
ing 52 Miles at 10 cents per mile $5.20

and two of a guard at 6 cents per mile the
same delivered $6.24
                                      _____
                                      $11.44

     Which accounts ware allowed by the Court and ordered
to be spred on the record and taxed in the bill of cost
in this cause.

     Circuit Court August Term, 1839.

State   )   Petet Larceny
     vs   )
Edward Williams   )   The attorney General on behalf of
& Moses H. Ayers   )   the State and the said defendants
                        Edward Williams and Moses H. Ayers
are brought to the bar of the Court in the Custody of the
Sheriff of Bradley County who for plea say they are not
guilty and for their trial puts themselves upon the County
and the Attorney General doth the like and there upon came
a jury to wit:

     David Wies William Thornhill, Jeptha Randolph, Lancas-
ter Randolph, John H. Roberts, Senr. Joshua Guinn, Elias
Petner, John Kincannon, Herman Grimett, William M. Biggs,
Joel Coffee, and John McGhee all good and lawful men citizens of the County of Bradley who being elected sworn and
charged the truth to seek of and conserning the premeses
on there oath do say that the defendants are not guilty
in Maner and form as charged in the bill of Indictment.

     It is therefore considered by the court that the said
defendants go hence with out day and that the State of Tennessee pay his own costs incurred in this prosecution and
that the Clerk tax the legal Cost for the Inspection of the
Court
(P-294)
     Indictment --

STATE OF TENNESSEE   )   Circuit Court
)
BRADLEY COUNTY   )   August Term, 1839.

     The Grand Jurors in behalf of the State of Tennessee
elected empaneled sworn and charged to enquire for the
body of the County of Bradley aforesaid upon there oath
present that a Certain Henry Gasaway, late of said County
labourer on the fifteenth day of March in the year of our

257

Lord one thousand Eight hundred and Thirty nine with force
and armes in the County of Bradley aforesaid and within the
jurisdiction of this Honerable Court one cow beast called
a Heifer of the value of ten dollars and fifty cents good
and lawful money of the State of Tennessee, then and there
being the goods and chattles of one Isaac Smith, feloniously did steal stake and carry away from and out of the possession of the said Isaac Smith contrary to the form of the
Statutes in such case made and provided and against the
Peace and dignity of the State.

Samuel Frazier,

Attorney General for the Third Solicitorial
District.

Endorsment   -   Indictment

The State vs Henry Gasaway

Isaac Smith, Prosecutor

Isaac Smith, Gabriel Dawson, Levi Brotherton, James Lawson,
Russell Lawson, John ONeal Witnesses for the State sworn
in open Court and sent before the Grand Jury - August the
29th 1839.

Henry Price, Clerk,

Not a true Bill

Abraham Lillard, Foreman of the grand Jury.

Circuit Court

August Term, 1839 -

State   )
   vs   )   The Grand Jury appeard in open
Henry Gasaway)   Court and returned a bill of Indictment
                    against the defendant, Henry Gasaway
                    for Larceny

     Indorsed not a true Bill
          by Abraham Lillard
(P-295)
     August Term, 1839.

The State   )   The Attorney General comes to prosecute

vs

Henry Gasaway   )   on behalf of the State and the defendant comes into Court in proper
person and the Grand jury having
heretofore returned into Court a bill of Indictment against
the said defendant for Larceny endorsed by there foreman
Abraham Lilard not a true Bill and there being nothing
further appearing aginst the defendant, It is considered
by the Court that he go hence without day and be discharged
from his recognizance and the Clerk Tax the cost for the
Inspection of the Court.

State   )   August Term, 1839.
   vs   )
Henry Gasaway   )   To boarding defendant four days
                       at 37½ cents per day $1.50

                       To two turn keys at 50 cents
                       each   1.00
                                                   _____
                                                   $2.50

Indictment -

STATE OF TENNESSEE   )   Circuit Court
)
BRADLEY COUNTY   )   August Term --
                            In the year of our Lord One
                            thousand Eight hundred and
thirty Eight.

    The Grand Jurors in behalf of the State of Tennessee
elected empaneled sworn and charged to enquire for the
body of the County of Bradley aforesaid upon their oath
present that a certain Wasaha an native Cherokee late of
said County labourer, not having the fear of God before
his eyes but being moved and seduced by the instigation
of the Devil on the seventh day of July in the year of our
Lord One thousand Eight hundred and Thirty Eight, with
force and armes in the County of Bradley aforesaid and with
in the jurisdiction of this Honerable Circuit Court in and
upon the body of one Kenesaha then and there being in the
peace of God and the State of Tennessee faloniously willful-
ly delibertly maliciously premeditatedly and with malice
afore thought did make an   (P-296)   assault and that the
said Wasaha a certain pistol of the value of Ten dollars

then and there loaded and charged with gunpowder and one
leaden bullet which said Pistol he the said Wasaha, then
and there in his right hand had and held to against and
upon the said Kenesaha, then and there felonously wilfully deliberately maliciously premeditatedly and with malice
aforethought did shoot and discharge and that the said Wassaha with the said leaden bullet out of the Pistol aforesaid then and there by force of the gun powder and that
sent fourth as aforesaid the said Wassaha in and upon the
left breast of him the said Kenesaha then and there feloniously wilfully deliberately meliciously premeditatedly
and with malice of four thought did strike penetrate and
wound injuring to the said Kenssaha then and there with
the said leaden bullet So as aforesaid that discharged and
sent fourth out of the Pistol aforesaid by the said Wassaha in and upon the left breast of him the said Kenesaha
one mortal wound of the depth of seven inches and of the
breadth of two inches of which said mourtel wound the said
Kenesaha then and there instently died and so the Jurors
aforesaid upon their oath aforesaid do say that the said
Wassaha the said Kenesaha in Maner and form aforesaid feloniously wilfully deliberately maliticiously premeditatedly and with malice aforethought did kill and murder and
did then and there feloniously wilfully deliberately maliciously premeditately and with malice afourthought commit Murder in the first degree contrary to the form of
the statute in such case made and provided and against the
peace and dignity of the State.

                    Samuel Frazier, Attorney General
                       for the 3rd Solicitorial District
                       of the State of Tennessee

Endorsment - Indictment

The State vs Wassaha, Abraham Gregg, prosecutor, Hiram Blan-
ton, Jesse Cristy (P-297) Witness for the State, sworn in
open Court and sent before the Grand Jury August the 30th
1839.

                    Henry Price, Clerk

A true bill John Auston, fourman of the Grand Jury.

Spencer Bevers, Sheriff and Jailer of McMinn County produced in Court an account sworn to in Court for keeping Wassaha, a Cherokee Indian, in the Jail of McMinn County which
account being certifyed by the Attorney General as correctly
taxed is therefore ordered by the Court to be spred of record
which is in the words and figures following to wit:

State of Tennessee) Spencer Bevers, Sheriff and Jailer of Mc-
     vs   ) Minn County for keeping said Wassaha, a
Wassaha   ) Cherokee Indian in the Jail of McMinn
                 County from the 3rd day of September

ber 1838, to the 25th day of December making one hundred
and fourteen days at 37½ cents per day $42.75

                    Two turn keys at 50 cents each   1.00
                                                            _____
                                                             $43.75

December 25th   S. Bevers, Sheriff and
                                 Jailor of McMinn County

State of Tennessee   )
    vs   )   I, Spencer Bevers, Sheriff of the
Wassaha   )   County of McMinn Charge for con-
                            veying Wassaha from the Jail of
                            McMinn County to Cleveland , Brad-
ley County and return 52 miles at 10 cents per mile
making $5.20

                    Two of a guard the same distance at
                         6 cents per mile each   6.24
                                                            _____
                                                             $11.44

        December the 25th 1838.

            S. Bevers, Sheriff.
(P-298)
The State   )   The grand Jury for the State appeared in
    vs   )   open Court and returned a bill of Indict-
Wassaha   )   ment against Wassaha, indorsed thereon
                      a True bill by John Austin, there four-
                      man.

        August Term, 1838 -

State   )
    vs   )   Murder
Wassaha, an Indian   )
                               Came the Attorney General who
                               prosecutes for The State as
well as the defendant in his own proper person who being
Charged upon the bill of Indictment for plea thereto says
he is not guilty and of this he puts him-- upon the County and the Attorney General doth the like and thereupon
an affidavit of the defendant this cause is continued ~~this~~
~~cause is continued~~ till Tomorow morning.

        Saterday, August Term, 1838.

State   )
    vs   )   From reasons appearing from the affidavit
Wassaha   )   of the defendant this Cause is continued

untill the next Term of this Court and it further appearing to the sattisfaction of this Court that there is no
Jail in Bradley County It is ordered by the Court that the
sheriff of Bradley County Convey the defendant to the Jail
of McMinn County for safe keeping untill the next term of
this Court or be otherwise discharged by a ----- of law and
that the Clerk of this Court make out a copy of this record
and Transmit the same to the keeper of the County Jail of
McMinn County.

April Term, 1839.

State	)	
vs	)	Came the Attorney General who
Wassaha, an Indian	)	prosecutes for the State and
		with the assent of the Court
		enters a Nole proseque in this

Cause.

The Attorney General reported to Court the following
bill of cost which being inspected   (P-299)   by the Court
is ordered to be spred on the record and taxed in the bill
of costs in this case.

August Term, 1839.

State	)	
vs	)	To conveying prisoner from Cleveland to
Wassaha	)	Athens and returning 52 miles at 10 cents
		per mile $5.20

To two of a guard the same distance
      at 6 cents per mile $6.24

To boarding defendant two days
      at 37½ cents per day   .75

To James Lauderdale $12.19

Sworn to and subscribed in open Court

April 26th, 1838.

Henry Price, Clerk

Which bill of cost being examined by the Attorney General and reported by him to be correctly taxed and was
inspected by the Court and ordered to be spred on the record and taxed in the bill of cost in this cause.

State of Tennessee   )
)

Bradley County   )   To any lawful officer to execute
                                  and return Greeting: You are
                                  hereby commanded to summons
Jesse C. Moore to appear before me or some other Justice
of the peace in and for said County to answer George Thomason in a plea of Trespess on the case taken and converting
to his own use money that he collected on a note given by
John Coon & Lewis Baly payable to George Thomason, to his
damage Thirty dollars here in fail not.

      Given under my hand and seal this the
           10th July 1838.

                    William H. Strane
                    Justice of the Peace.

Summons for the Plaintiff)
)

John Thomason   )

Endorsment - Damage Warrant

George Thomason vs Jesse C. More

Came to hand the 10th of July 1838

      Executed in full and set for trial the same day that
it came to hand before William H. Strane, Judgment.
I give
    /Judgment in this cause in favor of the plaintiff for
Eighteen dollars and thirty cents and the costs of said
suit.

      This 10th day of July, 1838.

      Twenty five cents - Witness, Wm. H. Strane.

(P-300)   from which Judgment the defendant prays an appeal
to the next Circuit Court which to him is granted upon the
Deft. given bond and suerety which was done this 10th day
of July, 1838.

                    Wm. H. Strane, J. P.

      Justice fee for Judgment 25 cents
      Appeal bond 50 cents
      Sheriffs fee 75 cents

      Bond --

Know all men by these Presents, that we, Jesse C. More and Thomas Skelton are held and firmly bound unto George Thomason in the sum of fifty dollars to be void if Jesse C. More shall prosecute with effect and appeal this day taken ~~taken~~ to the next Circuit Court for Bradley County from a Judgment of Wm H. Strane, a Justice of the Peace for said County in favor of George Thomason, against him for $18.30 cents.

Shall prosecute said appeal suceesfuly or in case of failure shall comply with and preform the Judgment of said Court.

This 10th day of July, 1838.

                         Jesse C. More   (Seal)

                         Thomas Shelton (Seal)

Witness,   )

William H. Strane, Justice   )
    of the Peace.   )

December Term, 1838.

George Thomason	)	Appeal Cause
vs	)	This day came the Plaintiff by his
Jesse C. More	)	Attorney and upon his motion a

rule is granted him to show cause
why this cause should be stricken

from the docket.

December Term, 1838.

Goerge Thomason	)	
vs	)	Came the parties by their Attorneys
Jesse C. More	)	and from sufficient reasons appear-

ing to the sattisfaction of the Court
from the affidavit of the defendant
the rule heretofore entered in this cause to strike this
cause from the Docket is continued over till the next term
and a Rule is granted the defendant to amend the pleadings
before the Justice of the Peace so as to not delay the trial
at the next term.

(P-301)   December Term, 1839.

George Thomason	)	Appeal
vs	)	
Jesse C. More	)	The parties by there Attorney appear

and a jury of good and lawful men
citizens of Bradley County to wit;

Henry Richardson, John Mee, William Camp, Henderson Thach,

John Fulks, Josiah Johnston, Adam H. Tener, John Goodner, John W. Kennedy, John Collins Edward Auston and Isaac Edwards who being elected tried and sworn to well and truly try the maters in dispute between the parties on there oath say the defendant is guilty of taking and converting to his own use the money that he had collected as the plantiff in his warrant hath aledged and by reason thereof assesses the Plaintiff damage to Eighteen dollars and Thirty cents being the amount of the Justiceses judgment.

It is therefore considered by the Court that the plaintiff recover of the defendant and his suerety Thomas Skelton the sum of Eighteen dollars and thirty cents the damages so as afore assesed by the Jury aforesaid being the Judgment of the Justice of the Peace together with the further sum of Three dollars and thirty cents being the intrest at 12¢ per anum on the sum afore said from the date of the renditian of said Judgment before said Justice up to this time and the costs about his suit in   this behalf expended and have his Execution &c.

Bond --

George Bowman)
      vs   )
John G. Glass)

Know all men by these presents that we George Bowman and Thomas Elderage, are Jointly and severly held and firmly bound unto John G. Glass in the penal sum of two hundred and fifty dollars to be void on condition that the said George Bowman will with effect prosecute a suit by action of Debt. which he this day commenced against the said John G. Glass, in the Circuit   (P-302) Court of Bradley County or in case of failure of such prosecution pay and sattisfy all costs and damages as may be awarded against him by of our said Court Witness our hands and seals this the 21st day of February 1839.

Thomas Elderage (Seal)

George Bowman (Seal)

By Jeptha Browder (Seal)

Test   )   Writ
Levi Trewhitt)

To the Sheriff of Bradley County, Greeting: You are

hereby commanded to summon John G. Glass if to be foounde
in your County to appear before our Circuit Court to be
held for the County of Bradley at the Court house in Cleveland on the 4th Monday of April next - answer George Bowman of a plea that he render unto him the sum of Six hundred and forty six dollars and Eighty Seven Cents which to
him he owes and from him unjustly detains to his damage
two hundred and fifty dollars here in fail not and have
you then there this writ -

Witness Henry Price, Clerk of the Circuit Court at
office in Cleveland the 4th Monday of December 1838, and
of American Independence the 63.

Henry Price, Clerk.

Endorsment --

George Bowman vs John G. Glass, Issued 21st of February, 1839.

Came to hand the 23rd February, 1839.

Summond John G. Glass, the same day came to hand.

James Lauderdale, Sheriff

Decleration --

State of Tennessee   )   Circuit Court
)
Bradley County   )   April Term, 1839.

George Bowman, by Attorney complains of John G. Glass,
who has been summond by the Sheriff &c. to answer the said
plaintiff of a plea that he render unto him the sum of six
hundred and forty six dollars and Eighty seven cents which
to him he owes and from him unjustly detains For that
whare as heretofore to wit on the 10th day of December, 1836
At to wit in the County of   (P-303)   Bradley aforesaid
the said Defendant made Executed signed sealed and delivered
to the said Plaintiff his certain writen obligation and now
shows to the Court here the date whereof is the same day and
year last where in and whereby the said defendant promised
twelve months after date (Meaning twelve months after the
date of said writen obligation to pay to the Plantiff Six
hundred and forty six dollars and Eighty seven cents with
intrest from the present date (Meaning intrest from the date
of said writen obligation for value received - Yet the said
Defendant although after requested so to do hath not as yet
paid the said sum of Six hundred and forty six dollars and
Eighty seven cents The sum above demanded 6 with Intrest
there on or any part there of to the said Plaintiff but to

pay the same or any part there of to the said plaintiff
he the said defendant hath hitherto wholey refused and
still refuses so to do to the damage of the said Plaintiff two hundred fifty dollars and therefore he brings his
suit and pledges to prosecute.

Trewhitt, Attorney for Plaintiff

Plea --

George Bowman   )
        vs   )   The defendant by attorney comes and
John G. Glass   )   defends the wrong and Injury when
                        and whare &c. and for plea says
                        said plantiff this action against
him ought not to have and maintain because he says he paid
the debt in the decleration mentioned before Issuance of
the original writ in the cause and of this he puts him self
upon the County and the Plaintiff likewise Trewhitt, Attorney for Plantiff.

Circuit Court, December Term 1839.

George Bowman   )
        vs   )   The parties by their attorneys appear
John G. Glass   )   and thereupon came a jury of lawful
                        men to wit:

Thomas McMinn, Henderson Thach, Henry Ritchards, John
Mee, Josiah Johnston, John Fulks, Absalom Coleman, John Igoe,
(P-304)   Robert Williams, Joseph R. Mee, Nathan Stafford and John Anderson, who being elected tried and sworn
to well and truly try the Issue joined between the parties
upon there oath say that the defendant hath not paid the debt
in the plaintiffs decleration Except the sum of Sixteen dollars and Eighty cents and assess the Plaintiffs damage for
the detention thereof to one hundred and thirty dollars and
forty cents.

It is therefore considered by the Court that the plaintiff Recover of the defendant the sum of Six hundred and
Thirty dollars and seven cents the residue of the debt in
the Plaintiffs decleration mentioned together with further
sum of One hundred and thirteen dollars and forty cents.
The damages assessed by the Jury aforesaid and the costs
about his suit in this behalf expended and have his Execution &c.

267

        Know all men by these presents that we John Tucker
and John G. Glass are jointly and severly held and firmly bound unto William Triplett in the penel sum of two
hundred and fifty dollars to be void on condition that
the said John Tucker will with effect prosecute a suit
by action of Trespess on the case which he this day commenced against the said William Triplett in the Circuit
Court for Bradley County or in case of failure of such
prosecution pay and sattisfy all costs and damages as
may be awarded against him by our said Court Witness our
hands and seals this the 29th day of December, 1838.

                        John Tucker   (Seal)

                        J. G. Glass   (Seal)

        Writ -   State of Tennessee

        To the Sheriff of Bradley County, Greeting: You are
hereby commanded to summons William Triplett, if to be
found in your County to appear before our Circuit Court
to be held for the County of Bradley at the   (P-305)
Court house in Cleveland on the 4th Monday of April next
to answer John Tucker, of a plea of Trespess on the case
of his damage nine hundred dollars, here in fail not and
have you then there this writ

        Witness   Henry Price, Clerk of our said Court at
office in Cleveland the 4th Monday of December, 1838, and
of American Independence the   ---

                        Henry Price, Clerk.

        Endorsment No. 31   Summons

        John Tucker vs William Triplett

        Damages $900.00   Issued 29 December, 1838.

        Came to hand the 6th of February 1839.

        Executed - Summond William Triplett the 8th Feb-
            ruary, 1839.

                        James Lauderdale, Sheriff.

Decleration -

STATE OF TENNESSEE   )   Circuit Court

BRADLEY COUNTY) April Term, 1839.

John Tucker by attorney complains of William Triplett
who has been summond by the Sheriff of a plea of Trespess
on the case for that whare as heretofore to wit - on the --
day of December 1839, at to wit in the County aforesaid
at the special Instence and request of him the said defendant he the said plaintiff Bargained with said Defendant to
buy of him the said defendant a preferance right or occupent clame that he the said defendant falsley represented
that he had and held into and upon the North East quarter
section of land of section Thirty of Township third and in
the first Range West of the Bases line in the Ocoee District
in Bradley County and he the said defendant then and there
falsly and fraudulently represented to the said plaintiff
that he the said defendant had the entire occupent claim
upon the aforesaid quarter section of land and he the said
Plaintiff confideing in the said false representation of
him the said defendant he the said Plaintiff did purchase
of and from the said Defendant the preferance or occupent
right to the center quarter section of land aforesaid
(P-306) for and in consideration of which he the said
Plaintiff paid to the said defendant a large sum of Money
to wit, the sum of thirteen hundred dollars good and lawful money of the United States of America and in consideration of which he said defendant promised that he the said
planetiff should have the entire occupent right to the
aforesaid quarter section of land and to put him the said
Plaintiff in possesion peaceably of the hole of said quarter section and the plantiff in a fact avers that he the
said defendant was not the true owner of the entire occupent clame or preferance right to the hole of said quarter
section of land but the Plaintiff in fact says that one
William Williams was justly and rightfuly entitled to and
was the true owner as an occupent to one half of the aforesaid quarter section of land or had the joint intrest with
the said defendant in the right to enter said quarter section and the said plaintiff in fact saith that the said
defendant by means of the premises on the day and year
aforesaid at to wit in the County aforesaid falsley and
fraudenlantly Issued him the said plantiff in the sale
of the occupent right to the aforesaid quarter section of
land whareby the said plaintiff was greatly injured and
was forced to pay out a large sum of money to wit the sum
of nine hundred dollars to the said William Williams in
order to procure the entire occupent right in and to the
aforesaid quarter section of land at to wit in the County
aforesaid and for this that afterwards to wit on the same
day and year last aforesaid at to wit in the County aforesaid the said plaintiff and the said defendant agreed to
and with each other of and concerning the occupent claim

or preferance right to the North Ea_st quarter section of
land Section Thirty Township Third and Range first, west
(P-307)   of the Bases line in the Ocoee District in the
County of Bradley and he the said Plaintiff agreed to pay
to the said defendant in consideration of the entire occupant right to the entire quarter section of land aforesaid a large sum of Money to wit, The sum of thirteen
hundred dollars good and lawful money of the United States
and the said defendant did then and there falsly and
fraudulantly represent to the said Plaintiff the said defendant had and held the entire occupant right or clame
to the aforesaid quarter section of land whare as in truth
and in fact the said plaintiff avers that he the said defendant had the occupant right only to one half of the
aforesaid quarter section of land by mens of which the said
Plaintiff was put to great trouble and exspence in procur-
ing the occupent right to the other half of the said quarter section so that he could procure a title therefore and
was compeled to lay out and exspend a large sum of money
to wit - The sum of nine hundred dollars good and lawful
money in purching and secureing the occupent right to the
other half of said quarter and afterwards to wit on the same
day and year last aforesaid and faithfully promised to pay
him the said plaintiff the aforesaid sum of money where-
ever he the said defendant should in there afterwards requested at to Wit in the County aforesaid and for this that
whare as hereto fore to wit on the same day and year last
aforesaid at to wit in the County aforesaid then said defendant was indebted to the said plaintiff in a large sum
of Money to wit in the sum of Nine hundred dollars good and
lawful money of the United States of America advanced to and
for the use of him the said defendant in purchasing an occupant clame for him the said defendant in and upon   (P308)
the North East quarter section of land of section Thirty
of Township Third in the fourth range West of the Bases
line in the Ocoee District and at the special Instance and
request of him the said defendant and for an nother sum of
Ninehundred dollars said acct and Expended to and for the
use of him the defendant and at the special instance and
request of him the said defendant and being so indebted in
consideration thereof afterwards to wit on the same day
and yaar last aforesaid at to wit in the County aforesaid
he the said defendant undertook and then and there faithfully promised to pay the said plaintiff the defendant several sums of Money when ever he the said defendant should
be thereunto afterwards requested and whare as afterwards
to wit on the same day and year last aforesaid at to wit
in the County aforesaid the plaintiff and the said defendant with each other for the Sale by the defendant to the
plaintiff for the occupent clame or right to a quarter
section of land situate lying and being in the County of

Bradley aforesaid in the Ocoee District for and in consideration of a large Sum of Money to wit the sum of Thirteen hundred dollars thereafter to be paid by the said plaintiff to the said defendant which said sum of money the said plaintiff then and there afterwards paid to the said defendant and the said defendant in consideration thereof he the said defendant undertook and faithfully promised and agreed that he the said defendant was the true and only owner of the whole of the occupant clame on said quarter section of land and that he had a right to sell and dispose of the occupant right to the whole thereof and that no other person else had any claim right or title thereto and the plaintiff in fact avers that the said defendant was not the sole owner of the occupant right or claim to said quarter section of land at the time (P-309) of the sale by the said defendant to the said plaintiff but on the Contrary thereof one William Williams was the owner of one half part or mostly thereof by means of which said false and fraudulant representation of the said defendant to the said plaintiff the said plaintiff was compaled to purchase of said Williams his occupant claim to one half of the aforesaid quarter section of land and was compeled to pay said Williams Nine hundred dollars therefor which said sum of money the said Defendant ought to have paid to said Williams to fulfil and secure the said defendants contract and agreement with the said plaintiff and afterwards to wit on the same day and year last aforesaid at to wit in the County aforesaid he the said defendant then and there undertook and faithfuly promised to pay to the said planetiff the aforesaid Sum of Money whenever he the said defendant should be thereunto afterwards requested, Yeat the said defendant not regarding his aforesaid several promises and undertakings so made as aforesaid but contriveing and intending to cheat and defraud the said planetiff in this behalf the said Defendant has not paid the aforesaid several sums of Money or any part thereof although often requested so to do and still doth fale and refuse at to wit in the County aforesaid to the damage of the said Plaintiff Nine hundred dollars and therefore he sues and hath pledged to prosecute.

Jarnagin & Bradford,

Attorneys for Planetiff.

Plea

Bradley County Circuit Court

April Term, 1839.

And the defendant by his attorney cums and defends the

wrong and injury when &c. and for Plea says the plantiff
is action aforesaid against him ought not to have and mantain   (P-310)   because he says he is not guilty in maner and form as the plantiff in declareing hath thereof
complained against him and of this he puts himself upon
the Country.

Campbell & Vandyke

Attorneys for Defendant
And the Planetiffs also.

Jarnagan & Bradford
    Attorneys for Plaintiff

Circuit Court

April Term, 1839.

John Tucker   )
    vs   )   Came the parties by there Attor-
William Triplett   )   neys and on motion of the defend-
                             ant and for reasons appearing to
                             the sattisfaction of the Court
a commetion is awarded him to take the deposition of Peter
W. Nash and ----- White before sum Justice of the peace for
Bradley County on giveing the Plantiff five days notice
of the time and place of taking the same.

Circuit Court

August Term, 1839.

John Tucker   )
    vs   )   The parties by there attorneys
William Triplett   )   appear and by consent this cause
                             is continued untill the next Term.

Circuit Court

December Term
    1840

John Tucker   )
    vs   )   The parties by there attorneys
William Triplett   )   appear and also cums a Jury of
                             good and lawful men to wit -

    John Goodner, Henry Richards, John Mee, Charles Cate,
James Campbell, Joseph Seabourn, John Igoe, Joseph McAn-
drew, Isaac Huffaker, Josiah Johnston, John Fulks and
Mathew Winkler, who being elected tried and sworn to well

and truly try the Issues Joined between the parties are
by consent of the parties and with   (P-311)   leve of
the Court Respited from Rendering these judgment till
tomorrow morning.

Thursday January 2nd, 1840.

John Tucker   )
    vs   )   The parties by there Attorneys ap-
William Triplett   )   pear and the Jury who was on yesterday
                          evening respited from rendering
                          there verdict in this cause have-
ing appeared in Court and resumed the consideration of this
cause on there oath do say that the defendant is not guilty
of the wrongs and Injury in the plaintiffs decleration mentioned as in pleading he hath alledged.

It is therefore considered by the Court that the defendant go hence and recover of the Plaintiff his costs
about his defence in this behalf exspended and have Execution &c.

And the attorney for the Plantiff moves the Court for a
rule to show cause why a new trial should be had in this
cause which is granted him and the said rule being argued
by council and understood by the Court

It is considered by the Court that said Rule be Discharged

Attachment

STATE OF TENNESSEE   )   Personally appeared before me
)   Samuel Howard one of the acting
BRADLEY COUNTY   )   Justices of the Peace in and
                             for said County and James Mc-
                             gurgen, Defendant and sayeth
that Daniel O'Conner and Brazel are jointly indebted to
him Sixty five dollars and the said O'Conner & Brazel hath
removed there selves out of the County or so conseled them
selves that the ordinary process of law cannot be served
on them.

Sworn to and subscribed before me this 11th day
    of October, 1839.

(P-312)   Samuel Howard (Seal)
                             Justice of the Peace for
                             Bradley County.

                              his
                    James X Mcgurgen (Seal)
                             mark

Bond --

STATE OF TENNESSEE   )
)   Know all men by these presents that
BRADLEY COUNTY   )   we James Mcgurgen and John D. Tray-
                                    nor all of the County and State afore-
said are held and firmly bound unto
Daniel O'Conner and Martin Brazel defendants in the sum of
one hundred and thirty dollars to be leveyed of our Respective goods and chattles lands and tenements for the payment
of which we bind our selves our heirs executors and adminstrators &c. jointly and severaly sealed with our seals and
assigned with our names this 10th October 1839.

     The condition of the above obligation is such that
whare as the above bound James Mcgurgen hath sued out an
attachment against the Estate of Daniel O'Conner and Martin
Brazel for the sum of Sixty five dollars and hath obtained
the same returnable before me or some other Justice of the
Peace for said County.

     Now if the said James Mcgurgen shall prosecute his suit
with effect or in case of failure shall well and truly pay
a nd sattisfy the said O'Conner & Brazel all such costs
and damages as shall be awarded and recovered against the
said James Mcgurgen his heirs assignes in one suit or suits
that may hereafter be brought for wrongfuly serving out
said attachment then the above bond or obligation to be
void other wise to remain in full force and effect the day
and date above writen.
                                      his
     Witness   James X McGurgen (Seal)
                                     mark

                            John D. Traynor (Seal)

     Writ of Attachment

          State of Tennessee

               To any lawful officer for Bradley County -
Greeting: whare as James Mcgurgen hath complained on
(P-313)   oath to me Samuel Howard one of the Justices
of the Peace for said County that Daniel O'Conner and
Martin Brazel are justly indebted to him to the amount
of Sixty five dollars and also oath having been made that
the said Daniel O'Conner and Martin Brazel hath removed
or is about to remove out of your County or so absent or

conseal them selves that the ordeney prossess of law cannot be served on them and that said James Mcgurgen haveing given bond and surety according to the derections of
the act of the General assembly in such cases made and
provided I command you that you attach the estate of the
said O'Conner & Brazel or so much thereof on seurety or
shall be of value sufficient to sattisfy said debt and cost
according to the complaint and such estate so attached in
your hands to secure or so to provide that the same may
be to further proceeding thereon   before me or the Judge
of the Circuit Court at the Court house in Cleveland on the
fourth Monday of December next so as to compel the said Daniel O'Conner and Martin Brazel to appeal and answer the
above complaint of the said James Mcgurgen when and whare
you shall make known how you shall have Executed this writ

        given under my hand and seal this 10th day of October
1839.

                        Samuel Howard   (Seal)
                        Justice of the Peace

        Endorsment - Writ of attachment

        James McGurgen for the use of J. D. Traynor.

        Messers Brazel & O'Conner, Came to hand and attached
one sorrel Horse & one cart and cart Harnes.

        This 11th of October, 1839.

                        James Lauderdale, Sheriff

        Decleration

STATE OF TENNESSEE   )   Circuit Court
)
BRADLEY COUNTY   )   December Term, 1839.

                        James Mcgurgen by his attorney
complains of Daniel O'Conner and   (P-314)   Martin
Brazel partners and Contractors on the Highwasey Railroad
who are attached of there goods and Chattles &c. to answer
of a plea of Trespes on the case for that whare as heretofore to wit on the day of in the year of Our Lord One thousand Eight hundred and Thirty --- at to wit in the County
aforesaid the said Defendants are indebted to the said plantiff in a large sum of money to wit the sum of one hundred
dollars good and lawful money of the United States of America

for goods ware merchandise sold and delivered by the said
Plaintiff to the said Defendants at the speceal instance and
request of them the said Defendants and being so indebted
they the said defendants afterwards to wit on the same day
and year last aforesaid at to wit in the County aforesaid
then and there undertook and faithfuly promised to pay to
the said plaintiff the aforesaid sum of One hundred dollars,
when ever they the said defendants should be afterwards thereunto Irequested, Yeat though often requested the said Defendants have not yeat paid to the said Plaintiff the aforesaid
sum of one hundred dollars or any part thereof but wholey neglects and refuses so to do to the damage of the said Plantiff
of one hundred and fifty dollars and there fore he sues and
hath given pledges to prosecute.

John T. Coffee, Attorney for Plaintiff

December Term 1840

James Mcgurgen vs Daniel O'Conner & Martin Brazeal	The plantiff by his attorney John T. Coffee appears and the defendants being solomnly called to come in to Court and defend the suit brought against them by the plaintiff Came not but made default

It is therefore considered by the Court that (P-315) Plaintiff recover of the defendants there damage sustained by reason of the menperformence of the promises and assumption in
plantiffs decleration mentioned but because It is unknown to
the Court what damages the plaintiffs hath sustained therefore
let a Jury cum to enquire thereof at the next term.

Indictment --

STATE OF TENNESSEE BRADLEY COUNTY	Circuit Court, December Term, 1839. The Grand Jurors in behalf of the State of Tennessee elected empaneled sworn

and charged to enquire for the body of the County of Bradley
aforesaid upon there oath present that Edward Edwards and Isaac Brewer late of said County Labourers on the sixteenth day
of November in the year of Our Lord one thousand Eight hundred
and thirty nine with force and armes in the County of Bradley
aforesaid an assault did make in and uppon the body of one Hubbart Cate then and there being in the peace of the State and
did then and there beat bruise wound and ill treat him the said
Hubbart Cate, to the great damage of him the said Hubbart Cate
to the Evil example of all others in like maner offending and
against the Peace and dignity of the State.

Samuel Frazier, Attorney General for
the 3rd Solicitoreal District

Endorsment - Indictment
The State vs Edward Edwards & Isaac Brewer

Hubbart Cate, prosecutor

Hubbard Cate, John Simmons, Jackson Simmons, Joseph B. Mix, Alexander Long, Senr, Jameson Jenkins,

Witnesses for the State sworn and sent before the Grand Jury 24th December, 1839, December Term, 1839.

H. Price, Clerk

Endorsed a true Bill

The State   )
   vs   )   The Grand Jury appeared in open
Edward Edwards   )   Court and returned a bill of Indict-
Isaac Edwards   )   ment against the defendants for an
                        assault and Battery endorsed by there
                        fourmen, Abraham H. Haglar, a true
                        Bill.

Circuit Court

December Term, 1839.

The State   )
   vs A. B.   )   The attorney General cums to prose-
Edward Edwards   )   cute on behalf of the State and the
                        defendant in proper person who says
                        he cannot deny but that he is guilty
as charged in the bill of Indictment and submits to the
Judgment of the Court.

It is therefore considered by the Court that the defendant for his offence pay a fine to the State of Tennessee
of Three dollars and pay the costs of this prosecution and
thereupon came John Simmons into open ---- here and acknowledged him self the securety of the said defendant for the
payment of the fine and costs aforesaid

It is therefore considered by the Court that the State
of Tennessee recover of the said defendant and his scurety
jointly the fine and costs aforesaid and that Execution
Issue &c.

Indictment --

STATE OF TENNESSEE   )
)   Circuit Court
BRADLEY COUNTY   )

December Term, Eighteen hundred and thirty nine.

The grand jurors in behalf of the State of Tennessee elected empaneled sworn and charged to enquire for the body of the County of Bradley aforesaid upon there oath present that a certain Isaac (P-317) Edwards late of said County labourer on the sixteenth day of November in the year of our Lord One Thousand Eight hundred and Thirty nine with force and armes in the County of Bradley aforesaid an assault did make in and upon the body of one Hubbard Cate then and there being in the peace of the State and did then and there beat bruise wound and ill treat him the said Hubbard Cate to the grate damage of the said Hubbard Cate to the Evil Example of all others in like case offending and against the peace and dignity of the State.

> Samuel Frazier, Attorney General
> for the 3rd Solisatoreal
> District.

Endorsment --

The State vs Isaac Edwards

Hubbard Cate, Prosecutor

Hubbard Cate, John Simmons, Jackson Simmons, Joseph B. Hicks Alexander D. Long, Senr., Jameson Jinkens, Witnesses for the State Sworn in open Court and sent before the grand Jury 24th of December 1839.

> H. Price, Clerk.

A true Bill, Abraham Hagler, fourman of the Grand Jury.

Circuit Court

December Term, 1839.

The State) The Grand Jury appeared in oppen
vs) Court and returned a bill of In-
Isaac Edwards) dictment against defendant for an
assault and battery endorsed by
there foreman Abraham Hagler

A true Bill

Circuit Court December Term, 1839.

```
The State              )
       vs              )     The attorney General cums to prose-
Isaac Edwards          )     cute for the State and also cums the
                             defendant in proper person who says
                             he cannot deney but that he is guilty
in maner and form as charged    (P-318)    In the bill of
Indictment and submits to the Judgment of the Court.
```

It is therefore considered by the Court that the defendant for his offence pay to the State of Tennessee a fine of Ten dollars and the Costs of this prosecution and remain in custada of the Sheriff untill fine and costs be paid or securety given therefor whare upon Jackson Simmons came into Court and acknowledged himself the suerety of the said defendant for the payment of the fine and costs aforesaid.

It is therefore considered by the Court that the State of Tennessee recover of the said defendant and Jackson Simmons jointly the fine and costs aforesaid and that Execution Issue &c.

Indictment --

```
STATE OF TENNESSEE     )     Circuit Court
                       )
BRADLEY COUNTY         )     December Term
                       )       Eighteen hundred and Thirty
                                nine
```

The Grand Jurors in behalf of the State of Tennessee elected empaneled sworn and charged to enquire for the body of the County of Bradley aforesaid upon there oath present that Edward Edwards and Isaac Brewer, late of said County labourers on the sixteenth day of November in the year of our Lord one thousand Eight hundred and Thirty nine With force and armes in the County of Bradley aforesaid an assault did make in and upon the body of one Hubbard Cate then and there being in the peace of the State and did beat Bruise wound and ill treat him the said Hubbart Cate, to the evil example of all others in like case offending and against the peace and dignity of the State.

> Samuel Frazier, Attorney General
>   for the 3rd Solisatorial
>   District

Endorsment -- Indictment

The State vs Edward Edwards and Isaac Brewer, Hubbard Cate, prosecutor Hubbard Cate, John Simmons   (P-319)   Jackson

Simmons, Joseph B. Hix, ^Alexander Long, Jemison Jenkins, Witnesses for the State sworn in open Court and sent before the Grand Jury 24th of December 1839.

H. Price, Clerk.

A true Bill

Abraham W. Hagler, fourman of the Grand Jury.

State of Tennessee,

To the Sheriff of Bradley County Greeting, you are hereby commanded to take the body of Isaac Brewer Instantly if to be found in your County and him safely keep so that you have him before the Judge of the Circuit Court now setting for Bradley County at the Court house in Cleveland then and there to answer the charge of the State Exhibited against him by an indictment for an assault and Battery and have you then there this writ

Witness Henry Price, Clerk of our Circuit Court at office in Cleveland the 4th Monday of December A. D. 1839.

Henry Price, Clerk.

Endorsment - Capias

The State vs Isaac Brewer, Issued the 24th December 1839, Came to hand the same day Issued Executed by arresting the body of Isaac Brewer and bringing him into Court.

James A. Bates, Dept.

Circuit Court

December Term 1839.

State   )
  vs   )   The Grand Jury appeared in Court and
Isaac Brewer   )   returned a Bill of Indictment against
                    the defendant for an assault and
                    Battery endorsed by there foreman

A true Bill

Circuit Court

December Term, 1839.

State   )
  vs   )   The Attorney General comes to prose-
Isaac Brewer   )   cute for the State and the defendant
                    in proper person who being charged
                    upon the bill of Indictment for an

assault and batry for says because he is guilty he will not
(P-320)   Contend but submits to the Judgment of the
Court.

It is therefore considered by the Court that for such
his offence he pay a fine of one dollar and the costs of
this prosecution and thereupon came John Fulks and acknowledged him self securety for the payment of the fine and costs
aforesaid.

It is therefore considered by the Court that State of
Tennessee Recover of the defendant and John Fulks his sure-
ty the fine and costs aforesaid for which Execution may
Issue.

Indictment

STATE OF TENNESSEE   )
)   Circuit Court
BRADLEY COUNTY   )   December Term, Eighteen hundred
                                and thirty nine.

The grand jurors in behalf of the State of Tennessee
elected impaneled sworn and charged to enquire for the body
of the County of Bradley aforesaid upon there oath present
that a Certain Alexander Long, Senior, late of said County
labourer on the seventeenth day of November, Eighteen hundred and Thirty nine with force and armes in the County of
Bradley aforesaid an assault did make in and upon the body
of one Isaac H. Edwards, then and there being in the Peace
of the State and did then and there beat bruise wound and
Ill treat him the said Isaac H. Edwards to the great damage of the said Isaac H. Edwards to the evil example of
all others in like case offending and against the Peace and
dignity of the State.

                         Samuel Frazier

                         Attorney General for the
                         3rd Solicatorial District.

Endorsment - Indictment

The State vs Alexander Long, Senr.

Isaac H. Edwards, prosecutor

Isaac H. Edwards, Jackson Simmons, Witnesses for the State sworn and sent before the Grand Jury December the 24th 1839.

                    Henry Price, Clerk

    A true Bill

    Abraham   (P-321)   W. Haglar, foreman of thegrand Jury.

        Capias --

State of Tennessee,

        To the Sheriff of Bradley County, Greeting: You are hereby commanded to take the body of Alexander Long, Senr. Instantly if to be found in your County and him safely keep so that you have him before the Judge of our Circuit Court now sitting for Bradley at the Court house in Cleveland then and there to answer the charge of the State exhibited against him by an indictment for an assault & batrey and have you there and then this writ

        Witness - Henry Price, Clerk of our said Court at office in Cleveland, the 4th Monday of December A. D. 1839.

                    Henry Price, Clerk.

        Endorsment - Capias

The State vs Alexander Long, Senr.

        Issued December the 24th 1839.

        Came to hand the same day Issued executed by arresting the body of Alexander Long and bringing ~~into Court 25th of December 1839~~ in to Court 25th of December 1839.

                    James A. Bates, Dept. Shff.

        Circuit Court

        December Term, 1839.

The State   )
    vs   )
Alexander Long, Sr.   )   The Grand Jury appeared in open

Court and returned a bill of Indictment against the defendant for an assault and batery indorsed by their foreman Abraham W. Hagler.

A true Bill --

Circuit Court

December Term, 1839.

The State   ) Indictment
vs   )
Alexander Long, Senr.) An assault and batrey.

The Attorney General Comes to prosecute for the State and the defendant in proper person who says he cannot deny but that he is guilty as charged in the bill of indictment and submits to the judgment of the Court

It is therefore considered by the Court that the defendant for such his offence pay a fine of three dollars and pay the costs of this prosecution and Joseph Bayley came into (P-322) Court here and acknowledged himself the Shuerety of the defendant for the payment of the fine and costs aforesaid.

It is therefore considered by the Court that the State of Tennessee recover of the defendant and Joseph Bayley his securety the fine and costs aforesaid and that Execution Issue &c.

Indictment --

State of Tennessee) Circuit Court
)
Bradley County) December Term, Eighteen hundred
         and thirty nine

The Grand Jurors in behalf of the State of Tennessee elected empaneled sworn and charged to inquire for the body of the County of Bradley aforesaid upon their oath present that Preston Bedwell Calep Bedwell, Hubard Cate and John Bedwell, Senr. late of said County labourers on the sixteenth day of November, Eighteen hundred and thirty nine with force and armes in the County of Bradley aforesaid an affray did make by them and their fighting in a public place together with one Alexander P. Gremett to the Grate Terror of the Citizens then and there assembled to the evil Example of all others in like case offending and against the peace and dignity of the State.

> Samuel Frazier, Attorney General
> for the 3rd Solicitoral
> District

Endorsment - Indictment

The State vs Preston Bedwell, Caleb Bedwell, Hubberd Cate, John Bedwell,Senior, Isaac H. Edwards, Prosecutor,

Isaac Edwards, Jackson Simmons, John Simmons, Witnesses for the State

Sworn and sent before the Grand Jury

December the 24th, 1839.

> Henry Price, Clerk

A true Bill --

Abraham H. Hagler, fourman of the Grand Jury.

Capias

The State	)	State of Tennessee
vs	)	
Preston Bedwell	)	To the Sheriff of Bradley County,
Hubberd Cate &	)	Greeting:
John Bedwell	)	

* You are hereby commanded to take the bodys of Preston (P-323) Bedwell, Caleb Bedwell, Hubberd Cate, John Bedwell, Senr. Instantly if to be found in your County and them safely keep so that you have them before the Judge of the Circuit Court now sitting for Bradley County at the Court house in Cleveland then & there to answer a charge of the State Exhibited against them by an Indictment for an affray and have you then and there this writ

Witness, Henry Price, Clerk of our said Court at office in Cleveland the 4th Monday of December, 1839.

> Henry Price, Clerk.

Endorsment - Capias

The State vs Preston Bedwell, Caleb Bedwell, Hubberd Cate, John Bedwell, Issued December the 24th, 1839.
*Caleb Bedwell

Came to hand the same day Issued Executed by arresting the bodys of Preston Bedwell, takeing Bond & Caleb Bedwell, and taking bond Hubberd Cate, and bringing into Court and appearance bond John Bedwell, bringing him into Court and entering recognezence.

James A. Bates, Dept, Shff.

Bond --

State of Tennessee, Bradley County, I, James A. Bates, Dept. Sheriff in and for the County aforesaid having on this 24th day of December, 1839. Arrested the body of Preston Bedwell, by virtue of a capias Issued from the Circuit Court of said County commanding me to take the body of said Preston Bedwell to answer a charge of the State Exhibited against him by Indictment for an affray and there upon the said Preston Bedwell, defendant together with John Bedwell, Senr. Scurety before me James A. Bates, Dept. Sheriff as aforesaid, acknowledged themselves jointly and severally indebted to the State of Tennessee in the sum of two hundred & fifty dollars each to be leveyed of their goods and chattles lands and Tenements respectively but to be void on condition the said Preston Bedwell shall make his personal appearance before the Judge of the Circuit Court at a Court to be held at the Court house in Cleveland on the first Wednesday after   (P-324)   the 4th Monday December next to answer the charge of the State Exhibited against him as aforesaid and then and there abide by preform and satisfy the Judgment of said Court thereon to be rendered and not depart the Court without leve.

Preston Bedwell, (Seal)

John Bedwell (Seal)

Signed sealed   )
acknowledged before   )
me this 24th day of   )
December, 1839.   )

James A. Bates, Dept. Sheriff
of Bradley County.

Circuit Court, December Term, 1839.

The State   )   The Grand Jury appeard in open Court and

vs)
Preston Bedwell)
Calib Bedwell)
Hubberd Cate &)
John Bedwell, Senr.)

returned a bill of Indictment against the defendants for an affray Endorsed by there four-man, Abraham H. Hagler,

A true Bill -

Circuit Court

December Term, 1839.

The State)
    vs   an affray)
Preston Bedwell)

The attorney General comes to prosecute for the State and the defendant in proper person who being charged upon the bill of

Indictment for plea says he is not guilty and for his trial puts himself upon the Country and the Attorney doth the like and thereupon came a jury of good and lawful men of Bradley County to wit:

John Hannah, H. Turner, Henderson Thatch, James Haggard Ezekiel Spriggs, Adam H. Tener, William Kemp, John Fulks, Josiah Johnston John Igou, Basely H. Lowery and John Hard-wick who being elected tried and sworn to well and truly try the Issue between the State of Tennessee and the said defendant on there oath say the defendant is guilty as charged in said bill of Indictment.

State)
    vs affray)
Preston Bedwell)

The attorney General comes to prose-cute on behalf of the State (P-325) and the defendant in proper person and the jury who was on yesterday empaneled and sworn in this cause

having found the defendant guilty as charged in said Indict-ment as appears of record, It is therefore considered by the Court that for such his offence he the said defendant shall pay the State of Tennessee a fine of fifteen dollars and pay the costs of this prosecution and be in custada till the fine and costs are paid or securety given and John Bedwell, Senr. Comes and acknowledges himself the securety of the defendant for the payment of the fine and costs afore-said.

It is therefore considered by the Court that the State of Tennessee recover of the defendant and John Bedwell, Sr. his securety the fine and costs aforesaid and that Execu-tion Issue.

286

Caleb Bedwell, Bond.

State of Tennessee, Bradley County, I, James A. Bates, Dept. Sheriff in and for the County of aforesaid having on this 24th day of December arrested the body of Caleb Bedwell by virtue of a capias Issued from the Circuit Court of said County commanding me to take the body of said Caleb Bedwell to answer a charge of the State Exhibited against him by Indictment for an affray thereupon the said Caleb Bedwell, defendant together with William Blare, Securety before me James A. Bates, Debt. Sheriff as aforesaid acknowledged themselves jointly and severaly indebted to the State of Tennessee in the sum of two hundred and fifty dollars each to be leveyed of their goods and chattles lands and Tenements respectively but to be void on condition the said Caleb Bedwell shall make his personal appearance before the said Court at a Court to be held for the County aforesaid at the Court house in the town of Cleveland on the first Wednesday after the 4th Monday of December next to answer the said charge of the (P-326) State Exhibited against him as aforesaid and then and there abide by and preform and satisfy the Judgment of said Court there on to be rendered and not depart the Court without leave.

Caleb Bedwell (Seal)

Wm. Blair (Seal)

Circuit Court

December Term, 1839.

The State   )
    vs an affray)   The attorney General comes to
Caleb Bedwell   )   prosecute on behalf of the State and
                       the defendant comes in proper per-
                       son who being charged on the bill
of Indictment say he cannot deny but that he is guilty of an affray as charged and submits to the Judgment of the Court. It is therefore considered by the Court that he the defendant for his offence pay a fine of three dollars to the State of Tennessee and pay the costs of this prosecution and remain in custody till the fine and costs be paid or securety given therefore and John Bedwell, Senr. comes into Court here and confessed a judgment as securety of the said defendant for the payment of the fine and costs aforesaid.

It is therefore considered by the Court that the State of Tennessee recover of the said defendant and his said securety jointly the fine and costs aforesaid and that Execution Issue.

Circuit Court

December Term, 1839.

The State)
  vs an affray)   Came the attorney General who
Hubbard Cate)   prosecutes for the State and
                      defendant in proper person who
                      being charged upon a bill of
Indictment for an affray for plea says he is not guilty
and for his trial puts himself upon the Country and the
Attorney General doth the like and thereupon came Joseph
B. Hicks with the defendant and acknowledged themselves
jointly indebted to the State of Tennessee in the sum of
two hundred and fifty dollars to be leveyed of there goods
and Chattles lands   (P-327)   and tenements to be void on
condition that the said Hubbard Cate make his personal
appearance from day to day at the present term of the Court
and answer a charge of the State Exhibited against --- by
Indictment for an affray and not depart the Court without
leave.

Circuit Court

December, Term, 1839.

State)
  vs affray)   Came Hubbard Cate the defendant in
Hubberd Cate)   this cause who submited at the pres-
                      ent term of the Court and was fined
                      in the sum of five dollars for an
affray and who has remained on his recognizance untill
the payment or securety for the payment of the fine and
costs of this prosecution for said affray and for reasons
appearing to the Court four dollars of the fine are remit-
ted and Silas M. Wan, in proper person comes and acknowledges himself the Shurety of the said defendant for the
payment of the fine and costs aforesaid.

It is therefore considered by the Court that the State
of Tennessee recover of the defendant and Silas M. Wan,
his securety the fine and costs aforesaid and that Execution Issue &c.

Circuit Court, December Term, 1839.

State)
  vs an aFray)   Comes the attorney General who
John Bedwell, Senr.)   prosecutes for the State and
                      the defendant comes in proper
person who being charged on the bill of Indictment says he

cannot deny but that he is guilty of an afray as charged
and submits to the Judgment of the Court.

It is therefore considered by the Court that the defendant for such his offence pay to the State of Tennessee
a fine of three dollars and pay the costs of this prosecution   (P-328)   and be in custada till the fine and
costs are paid or securety given and Caleb Bedwell came into Court here and acknowledged himself the securety of the
said defendant for the payment of the fine and costs aforesaid.

It is therefore considered by the Court that the State
of Tennessee recover of the defendant, John Bedwell and
Caleb Bedwell his Securety the fine and costs aforesaid
and that Execution Issue &c.

    Indictment

State of Tennessee   )   Circuit Court
)
Bradley County   )   December Term, Eighteen hundred
                                and thirty nine

    The Grand Jurors in behalf of the State of Tennessee
elected empaneled sworn and charged to enquire for the
body of the County of Bradley aforesaid upon there oath
present that a certain Preston Grimett late of said County labourer on the sixteenth day of November Eighteen hundred and Thirty nine with force and armes in the County of
Bradley aforesaid an aFray did make by them and there fighting together with one Preston Bedwell in a public place
to the Terror of the people there and then assembled to
the evil Example of all others in like case offending and
against the peace and dignity of the State

                        Samuel Frazier, Attorney General
                            for the 3rd Solisatorial District.

    Endorsement   -   Indictment

The State vs Preston Grimett

    Preston Bedwell, Prosecutor

    Preston Bedwell, Jackson J. Dodd, Witnesses for the
        State

    Sworn and sent before the Grand Jury 6th of December
1839.

                H. Price, Clerk

A true Bill

Abraham H. Hagler, fourman of the Grand Jury.

(P-329)   Capias

State of Tennessee

To the Sheriff of Bradley County, Greeting: You are hereby commanded to take the body of Preston Grimett Instantly if to be found in your County and him safely keep so that you have him before the Judge of our Circuit Court now setting for Bradley County at the Court house in Cleveland then and there to answer a charge of the State Exhibited against him by an Indictment for an afray and have you then and there this writ.

Witness   Henry Price, Clerk of our said Court at office in Cleveland the 4th Monday of December, 1839.

Henry Price,   Clerk

Endorsment   Capias

The State vs Preston Grimet

Issued December the 26th, 1839.

Executed by arresting the body of Preston Grimett and binding him to Court this the 28th December, 1839.

James A. Bates, Dept. Shff.

Circuit Court

December Term, 1839.

State   )
   vs an afray   )   The Grand Jury appeared in open
Preston Grimett)   Court and returned a bill of In-
                     dictment against the defendant
                     for an afray endorsed thereon
by Abraham H. Hagler, there fourman. A true Bill.

Circuit Court

December Term, 1839.

State   )   The attorney comes to prosecute for the State

vs an affray   )   and defendant comes in proper per-
Preston Grimet   )   son who being charged on the bill
                         of Indictment says he cannot deny
                         but that he is guilty in maner and
form as charged and submits to the judgment of the Court.

It is therefore considered by the Court that for his
offence he pay a fine of ten dollars - pay the costs of
this prosecution and   (P-330)   be in Custada untill fine
and costs be paid or secured and thereupon Isaac Edwards
comes into Court and acknowledged himself the security of
the said defendant for the payment of the fine and costs
aforesaid.

It is therefore considered by the Court that the State
of Tennessee recover of the defendant and his securety
Isaac Edwards the fine and costs aforesaid and that Execution Issue &c.

Know all men by these presents that we Samuel Lane,
and J. B. Russell are jointly severally held and firmly bound
unto Harris D. Tharp and John Ross, in the penel sum of two
hundred and fifty dollars to be void on condition that the
said Samuel Lane which has this day complained will with effect prosecute a suit by action of Trespess on the Case which
he this day commenced against the said Harris D. Tharp and
John Ross, in the Circuit Court of Bradley County or in case
of failure of such prosecution pay and sattisfy all costs
and damages as may - awarded against him by our said Court

Witness our hands and seals this 12th day of November
1838.

                    Samuel Lane (Seal)

                    J. B. Russell (Seal)

Teste -   )
Henry Price   )
Writ -   )

State of Tennessee

To the Sheriff of Bradley County, Greeting: You
are hereby commanded to summon Harris D. Tharp & John Ross
if to be found in your County to appear before our Circuit

Court to be held for the County of Bradley at*the 4th Monday of December next, to answer Samuel Lane of a plea of Trespesse in the case to his damage   (P-331)   two hundred dollars here in fail not and have you then there this writ

Witness   Henry Price, Clerk of our Circuit Court at office in Cleveland the 4th Monday of August 1838, and of American Independence the 63 -

Henry Price, Clerk

Endorsment   Writ No 22

Samuel Lane vs Harris D. Tharp & John Ross, Issued November 12th 1838.

Came to hand 14th November 1838. Executed by summoning John Ross & Harris D. Tharp, on the 21st November, 1838.

James A. Bates, Dept. Sheriff
of Bradley County/

Decleration

State of Tennessee   )   Circuit Court

December Term, 1838.

Samuel Lane, by Attorney complains of Harris D. Tharp and John Ross summond by the Sheriff &c. to answer the Plaintiff of a plea of Trespess on the case for that whareas heretofore to wit, on the 1st day of November, 1838. The said defendants was indebted to the said Plaintiff in the Sum of Eighty Eight dollars & Thirty five cents for meets and drinks and other necesarys by the said Plaintiff before that time found and provided at the special Instance and request of the said defendants for divers persons and being so indebted they the said defendants in consideration there of afterwards to wit on the day and year last aforesaid undertook and faithfully promised the said Plaintiff to pay him the said sum of money when they should be thereunto afterwards requested and for that whare as afterwards to wit upon the same day and year last aforesaid at (P-332)   To wit in the County aforesaid the said defendants was indebted to tha said Plaintiff for meets and Drinks and other necessarys before that time found and provided at the special Instance and request of the said Plaintiff for divers persons and being so indebted they the said defendants *the Court house in Cleveland

undertook and then and there faithfully promised the said
plaintiff to pay him so much money as the said last mentioned meet, Drink and other necessarys was reasonably worth
when they the said defendants should be thereunto afterwards
requested and the said plaintiffs avers that the last mentioned det &c. there necessaries at the time of the delivery
thereof was reasonably worth the futher sum of Eighty Eight
dollars and twenty five cents.

To wit upon the day and year last aforesaid at to wit
in the County aforesaid whareof the said defendants afterwards to wit upon the day and year last aforesaid to wit
in County aforesaid had notice Never the less the said defendants not regarding there said several promises and undertakings but entertaining and fraudulantly intending
craftly and sublity to deceive and defraud the said plaintiff in this behalf hath not as yeat paid the said saveral
sums of money or any part thereof or either of them or any
part thereof to the said Plaintiff although of ten requested so to do to wit on the day and year last aforesaid at
to wit in the County aforesaid but the said defendant to
pay him the sum with hereunto wholly neglected and refused
and still neglects and refuses to the damage of the plaintiff two hundred dollars and therefore he brings his suit
and pledges to prosecute.

Trewhitt, Attorney
For Plaintiff

(P-333)
Defendant by his attorney cums into Court and defends
the wrong and injury where and when and says the Plaintiff
his action against them ought not to have and mantain because they say they did not assume and undertake as plaintiff in declareing hath alledged against them and of this
they put themselves upon the Country

And the Plaintiff doth the like)
Trewhitt, Atts for Plaintiff)

Jarnagin & Bradford   )
Attos. for Defendants)

Circuit Court

April Term, 1839.

Samuel Lane   )
vs   )   Came the parties by there Attorneys
Harris D. Tharp &   )   and by consent of the parties and
John Ross   )   with assent of the Court this
                         cause is continued untill the
                         next Term.

Circuit Court

December Term, 1839.

Samuel Lane   )
vs   )   The parties by there attorneys
Harris D. Tharp &)   appear and a Jury of good and
John Ross   )   lawful men cums to wit:

                         Abraham H. Haglar, George
Colville, Robert Hood, Robert H. Pharris, James M. Henry,
John Dunn, John K. Ross, John Tucker, Robert S. Brashears,
William Parks, John Igou and Middleton Lane, who being
elected tried and sworn to well and truly try the issue
joined between the parties on there oath say the defendant
Harris D. Tharp did not assume and undertake in Maner and
form as the plaintiff hath declared against him and the
jurory aforesaid on there oath aforesaid does futher say
that the defendant John Ross, did assume and undertake in
Maner and form as the plaintiff hath declared against him
and assesses the Plaintiffs damage   (P-334)   by reason
thereof to Eighty Eight dollars.

     It is therefore considered by the Court that the De-
fendant Harris D. Tharp go hence and recover his costs and
that the plaintiff recover of the defendant John Ross, the
sum of Eighty Eight dollars the damages so as aforesaid assessed by the jury and his costs about his suit in this behalf Expended and have Execution &c.

     The Same Term.

Samuel Lane   )
vs   )   The defendant John Ross, by his
John Ross &   )   Attorney appears and moves the
Harris D. Tharp)   Court for a rule be entered to
                       show cause why a new   trial this
                       cause should be had which rule is
granted.

     At the same Term of Court.

Samuel Lane   )   The parties by there Attorneys
vs   )   appear and the rule heretofore
John Ross &   )   entered in this Cause by the de-
Harris D. Tharp)   fendants attorney to show cause
                       why a new trial should be had being
                       argued by Council and understood by
the Court.

     It is considered by the Court that said rule be discharged.

George Bowman   )
    vs   )   Know all men by these Presents that
John G. Glass   )   we, George Bowman and Thomas Elderage
                        are jointly and severaly held and firm-
                        ly bound unto John G. Glass in penal
sum of two hundred and fifty dollars to be void on condition
that the said George Bowman will with effect prosecute a
suit by action of Debt. which he this day commenced against
the said John G. Glass in the Circuit Court of Bradley
County or in case of failure   (P-335) of such prosecution
pay and sattisfy all costs and damages as may be awarded
against him by our said Court

    Witness our hands and seals, this 21st day of February
1839.

        Test   )   Thos. Elderage (Seal)
        Levi Trewhitt)   George Bowman (Seal)
                              By Jeptha Bowman (Seal)

    Writ

    State of Tennessee

            To the Sheriff of Bradley County Greeting: You
are hereby commanded to summon John G. Glass if to be found
in your County to appear before our Circuit Court to be held
for the County of Bradley at the Court house in Cleveland
on the 4th Monday of April, next, to answer George Bowman
of a plea that he render unto him the sum of Six hundred
and forty six dollars and Eighty seven Cents which to him
he owes and from him unjustly detains to his damage two hundred and fifty dollars herein fail not and have you then
there this writ:

    Witness   Henry Price, Clerk of our Circuit Court at
office in Cleveland the 4th Monday of December, 1838, and
of American Independence the 63rd.

                        Henry Price, Clerk.

    Endorsment -   Summons

295

George Bowman vs John G. Glass

Issued 21st February 1839.

Came to hand the 23rd of February, 1839.

Summond John G. Glass, the same day came to hand

James Lauderdale
Sheriff

Trewhitt, Atty)
For Plaintiff)

Declaration

STATE OF TENNESSEE)
)
BRADLEY COUNTY)

Circuit Court

April Term, 1839.

(P-336)

George Bowman, by Attorney complains of John G. Glass, who
of John G. Glass, who has been summoned by the Sheriff &c.
To answer the said Plaintiff of a plea that he Render unto
him the sum of Six hundred and forty six dollars and Eighty
Seven cents which to him he owes and from him unjustly detains For that whereas heretofore to wit on the 10th day of
December 1836, at to wit in the County of Bradley aforesaid
The said defendant made Executed Signed sealed and delivered
to the said Plaintiff his certain writting obligation and
now showes to the Court here the date when of is the same
day and year last wherein and whereby the said Defendant
Twelve months after date (Meaning twelve months after the
date of said writing obligatry to pay to the said plantiff
Six hundred and forty Six dollars and Eighty Seven cents
with Intrest from the date of said writing obligatrey for
value received.

Yeat the said Defendant although often requested so to
do hath not as yeat paid the said Sum of Six hundred and
forty Six dollars and Eighty Seven cents the sum above demanded with Intrest thereon or any part thereof to the said
Plantiff but to pay the same thereof to the said Plaintiff
he the said Defendant hath hitherto wholey refused and still
refuses so to do to the damage of the said Plaintiff two
hundred and fifty dollars and therefore he brings his suit

and pledges to prosecute.

Trewhitt, Attorney
for Plaintiff

Plea

George Bowman   )
      vs   )   The defendant
John G. Glass   )   by attorney

        Comes and defends the wrong and injury when and where &c. and for plea says said plaintiff his action against him   (P-337)   ought not to have and maintain because he says he paid the debt in the decleration mentioned before the Issue of original writ in this Cause and of this he puts himself upon the Country.

And the Plaintiff doth   )   Jarnagin &
    the like.   )   Bradford, attorney
)   for Defendant
    Trewhitt, Atty.   )
      for Plaintiff   )

Circuit Court

December Term, 1839.

George Bowman   )
      vs   )   The parties by there Attorneys ap-
John G. Glass   )   pear and thereupon came a jury of good and lawful men to wit - Thomas McMinn Henderson Thach, Henry Richards, John Mee, Josiah Johnston, John Fulks, Absalam Colman, John Igou Robert Williams, Joseph R. Mee, Nathan Stafford, and Daniel Anderson, who being elected tried and sworn to well and truly try the Issue joined between the parties upon their oath say the defendant hath not paid the debt in the Plaintiffs decleration mentioned.

Except the Sum of Sixteen dollars Eighty cents and assesses the plaintiffs damage for the detintion there of to one hundred Thirteen dollars and forty cents.

It is therefore considered by the Court that the Plaintiff recover of the defendant the sum of Six hundred and Thirty dollars and seven cents the resedue of the debt in the plaintiffs decleration mentioned together with the further sum of one hundred and thirteen dollars and forty cents the damage assessed by the jury as aforesaid and the costs about his suit in this behalf exspended and have his Execution   (P-338)

Bond

Know all men by these presents that we William Hammond & Levi Trewhitt are jointly and severaly held and firmly bound unto Benjamin Hambright in the penal Sum of two hundred and fifty dollars to be void on condition that said William Hammond will with effect prosecute a suit by action of Tresspess with force and armes which he this day commenced against the said Benjamin Hambright in the Circuit Court of Bradley County or in case of failure of such prosecution pay and sattisfy all costs and damages as may be awarded against him by our said Court

Witness our hands and seals this 6th day of April, 1839.

William Hammond   (Seal)

Levi Trewhitt   (Seal)

Writ

State of Tennessee

To the Sheriff of Bradley County, Greetings: You are hereby commanded to summon Benjamin Hambright if to be found in your County to appear before our Circuit Court to be held for the County of Bradley at the Court house in Cleveland, on the 4th Monday of April, next, to answer William Hammond of a plea of Tresspess with force and armes to his damage One thousand dollars,

Herein fail not, and have you then there this writ

Witness Henry Price, Clerk of our said Court at office in Cleveland, the 4th Monday of December, 1838, and of American Independence the 63rd.

Henry Price, Clerk.

Emdorsment   -   Summons

William Hammond vs Benjamin Hambright

Issued the 6th of April, 1839.

To May Term Tresspess Damage $1000.00 came to hand the 8th of April 1839.

Executed by summoning Benjamin Hambright the 9th of April, 1839.

James Lauderdale, Sheriff
of Bradley County

Trewhitt, Attorney
for Plaintiff

(P-339)   Decleration

State of Tennessee	)	Circuit Court
Bradley County	)	April Term 1839

William Hammond, by attorney complains of Benjamin Hambright who has been summoned by the Sheriff &c. to answer the said plaintiff of a plea of Tresspass with force and armes &c.

For this that the said defendant on the first day of March 1839, and on divers other days and times between that day and the day of the commencement of this suit with force and armes &c. broke and entered the close of the said Plaintiff of which the said Plaintiff was rightfully and lawfully possesed situated lying and being in the County of Bradley aforesaid and then and there by force and strong hand threw down the fence of the said Plaintiffs also then and there entered into the field and close of the said plaintiff and with feet of horses oxen and cattle trod down and spoiled the erth & soil of the said Plaintiffs also then and there with other horses & oxen and plows plowed up and spoiled the Erth & soil of said plaintiffs belonging to said close also then and there choped up & cut into trees of hickory & oak in said close belonging to said Plaintiff also then & there ejected exspelld put out and removed the said Plantiff from the possession use occupation of his said field & close of Ground and kept and continued him so ejected Exspeled put out and removed for a long space of time to wit for the space of thirty days and from thence hitherto wholey the said Plaintiff for and during all the time lost and was deprived of the use benifit and enjoyment of his said field and close of ground and other wrongs and injuries to the said Plaintiff then and there did   (P-340)   against the peace of the State and to the damage of the said Plaintiff one thousand dollars and therefore he brings his suit and pledges to prosecute.

Trewhitt, Attorney for Plaintiff.

Plea --

And he the defendant by Attorney comes and Defends the
wrong and injury when and whare &c. and says said plaintiff
his action against him ought not to have and maintain because he says he is not guilty in maner and form as said
plaintiff ~~in maner and form as said plaintiff~~ in his said
declaration has thereof complained against him and this he
prays may be enquired of by the County

April 27th, 1839.

Gillespy, Attorney
For the Defendant

And the Plaintiff likewise
Threhitt attorney for Plaintiff

Circuit Court

April Term, 1839.

William Hammond   )
    vs   )
Benjamin Hambright)

This day came the parties by
there attorneys and by consent
this cause is continued till the
next term.

Circuit Court

December Term, 1839.

William Hammond   )
    vs   )
Benjamin Hambright)

The parties by there attorneys
appear and a Jury of good and
lawful men came to wit:

Absolom Colman, Josiah Johnston, Henderson Thatch, Edward Austin, Amos Potts, Samuel Moroon, Jackson Simmons,
Daniel Anderson, John G. Reuble, Armsted Bredwell, Joseph
Land and John Fulks, who being Elected tried and sworn to
well and truly try the Issue joined between the parties
on their oath say that the defendant   (P-341) is not guilty
of the trespess with force and armes in the Plaintiffs Decleration mentioned in manner and form as said plaintiff
in declareing hath Elledged therefore.

It is considered by the Court that the defendant go
hence without day and recover of the Plaintiff all costs
in this behalf exspended for which an Execution may Issue.

Indictment

STATE OF TENNESSEE	)	Circuit Court
BRADLEY COUNTY	)	August Term, Eighteen hundred and thirty nine

The Grand jurors in behalf of the State of Tennessee
Elected empaneled sworn and charged to enquire for the
body of the County of Bradley aforesaid upon their oath
present that a certain Joshua Cresong late of said County
labourer on the first day of July in the year of our Lord
one thousand and Eight hundred and Thirty nine, with force
and armes in the County of Bradley aforesaid and within the
jurisdiction of this Honerable Court one mare of the value
of One hundred dollars good and lawful money of the State
of Tennessee and of the United States/,then and there being
the goods and chattles of William McCarty feloniously did
steal take and carry away from and out of the possesion of
the said William McCarty, Contrary to the form of the Stattute in such case made and povided and against the peace and
dignity of the State.

                    Samuel Frazier, Attorney General
                        for the Third Solicitorial
                        District.

Endorsment   -   Indictment

The State vs Joshua Cresong

William McCarty, Prosecutor

William McCarty, James M. Edmondson, James M. Henry.

(P-342)   Witness is for the State sworn in open Court
and sent before the Grand jury August the --- 1839.

                    Henry Price, Clerk.

A true Bill   Abraham Lillard, Fourman of the
                        Grand Jury.

Circuit Court

August Term, 1839.

The State   )
  vs   ) The Grand Jury appeared and returned
Joshua Cresong) here into open Court a Bill of In-
          dictment for Grand Larceny against
          the State endorsed by their Fourman

Abraham Lillard

A True Bill

State   )
  vs   ) Indictment for Grand Larceny
Joshua Cresong)

The Attorney General comes to prosecute on behalf of
the State and the said Joshua Cresong is brought to the
barr of the Court in Custody of the Sheriff of Bradley
County and the said Joshua Cresong being araigned and
charged on said bill of Indictment pleads not guilty to
the same and for his trial puts himself upon the Country
and the Attorney doth the like and thereupon affidavit of
the defendant this cause is Continued till next term,
and he remanded to the common Jail of Bradley County there
to remain untill he give security in the sum of one thousand dollars with two good securitys each in the sum of
Five hundred dollars each or untill he beg discharge by
a due corse of law.

   Circuit Court

   December Term, 1839.

State   )
  vs   ) Larceny --
Joshua Cresong)

       The attorney General who prosecutes
       for the State for the Third Judetial
District comes and the Defendant Joshua Cresong is brought
to the Barr of the Court in the Custody of the Sheriff of
Bradley County, and the said Defendant being arranged and
Charged on said bill of Indictment pleads not guilty to the
same and for his trial puts himself upon the Country and
the Attorney (P343) General doth the like.

  And thereupon to try said Issue comes a Jury to Wit:

  Abraham McKissick, A. Thomas, William Triplett, Barcla
H. Lowery, James Carr, Edward Austin, James Massey, Sims
Harris, James Britton, Jacob Ruth, Jeptha, Randolph and
Elias Pitner all good and lawful men Citizens of Bradley

County, who being elected tried and sworn the truth to
speak upon Issue joined on there oath say that the said
Joshua Cresong is guilty of the Feloneous taking and carrying away of a certain bay mare of the goods and Chattles of William McCarty in Manner and form as charged in the
bill of Indictment and the jurors aforesaid upon there oath
aforesaid do futher asertain and say that the said Joshua
Cresong for the offence aforesaid shall undergo confinement in the Jail and Penetenteary house of this State for
the space of Three years, ordered that the said defendant
be remanded to Jail.

State   ) Larceny --
 vs   )
Joshua Cresong) The attorney General Comes into
         Court and reported the following
         bill of costs as being correctly
taxed which was ordered by the Court to be spred on the
record taxed in the bill of costs in this cause which is
in the words and figures following to wit, The State of
Tennessee to Thomas Edmondson, special Deptity constable
for conveying said defendant from Jasper to Cleveland going to and returning 120 Miles at 10 cents per mile $12.00

One of a guard the same distance at 6 cents per mile $7.20

  Sworn to in open Court December the 26th 1839.

    Henry Price, Clerk.

    Thomas Edmondson

(P-344) Circuit Court

   December Term, 1839.

The State   )
 vs   ) Indictment for
Joshua Cresong)   Horse Stealing

 The attorney General for the third soliciterial District comes to prosecute on behalf of the State and the
said Joshua Cresong is brought to the Bar of the Court in
Custody of the Sheriff of Bradley County and a Jury to wit:

 Abraham McKissick, Adenyah Thomas, William Triplett,
Barcla H. Lowery, James Carr, Edward Auston, James Massey,
Sims Harris, James Britton, Jacob Ruth, Jeptha Randolph,
and Elias Petner, who were on the first Thursday of the
present Term of this Court elected tried and sworn in this

cause having returned a verdict of guilty against the said
Joshua Cresong and having futher asertained and said that
for his offence he shall undergo confinement in the Jail
and Penetenteary house of this State for the space of three
years and it is now therefore further demanded of the said
Joshua Cresong, If he has or knows of any thing to say why
the Court shall not proceed to judgment and Exeution thereof against him according to law who nothing further saith
then as before he hath said

It is therefore considered by the Court that the said
Joshua Cresong, for the offence aforesaid do undergo Confinement at hard labore in the Jail and Penetenteary house
of this State for the Term of Three years commencing from
the first Thursday of the Twenty Sixth day of December
Eighteen hundred and Thirty nine, that he be rendered in-
famous and incapebel of being examined as a Witness in any
of the Courts of this State and that he pay the Costs of
this prosecution for which Exeution may Issue and also
that the Sheriff of Bradley County summon two of a guard
to assist in conveying said Joshua Cresong (P-345)   to
the said Jail and Penetenteary house there to be delivered
over by him the said Sheriff to the keeper there of within
a reasonable time from this day and date.

Larceny --

State	)	
vs	)	James Lauderdale, Esq. produced in
Joshua Cresong	)	open Court the following account
		Certifyed by the Attorney General
		as being Correctly taxed and sworn

to in open Court to wit, Sheriff Lauderdale, for boarding
defendant from the 20th of July 1839 Untill 4th January 1840.

making in all 167 days at 37½ cents per day $62.62½

To 8 Turn keys at 50 cents each ——   4.00

                                                      $66.62½

State of Tennessee   )   To the Sheriff of Bradley County
)   You are hereby commanded to take
Bradley County   )   the body of the said Edward Aus-
                                 tin if in your County to be found
                                 and him safely keep untill he pay
and sattisfy a judgment which Thomas McCallie obtained against

him before the Judge of the Circuit Court for the County aforesaid on the 22nd day of April, 1839, for the sum of Thirty Six dollars and Seventy Cents damage and the further sum of ten dollars and fifty seven cents costs and the costs of this writ one dollar or untill he shall be discharged by a due Course of law given under my hand at office this 11th day of December, 1839.

Henry Price, Clerk.

Endorsment --

Thomas McCallie vs Edward Austin

Issued December the 20th, 1839.

Came to hand the 24th December, 1839.

Serch made the same day arested the defendant Bond and Security taken for Prison bonds.

John Brown, Depty Sheriff

(P-346)   Bond --

State of Tennessee	)	We, Edward Austin, John Auston
	)	and Alexander A. Clingan acknowl-
Bradley County	)	edged our selves indebted to

James Lauderdale, Sheriff of Bradley County in the Sum of ninety Eight dollars and Eighty cents, But to be void on dondition that said Edward Auston who has been taken into Custody of the said Sheriff and commited to Prison on a Capias ad respondendom in favor of Thomas McCallie for the sum of Thirty Six dollars and seventy cents damage and the further sum of ten dollars and fifty seven eents costs and also the costs of this Caca shall remain and continue within the Prison bounds of said County and not escape out of the same before he shall have paid damage and costs or be otherwise discharged according to law

given under our hands seals this 24th day of December 1839.

E. Auston   (Seal)

John Auston   (Seal)

A. A. Clingan   (Seal)

Circuit Court, December Term, 1839.

305

Thomas McCallie)
   vs)   The Plaintiff and Defendant in
Edward Auston)   proper person and on motion of
      Thomas J. Campbell, Attorney,
      Came Joseph R. Mee, John Auston,
Jesse Mee, and Alexander A. Clingan together with the defendant and confessed judgment for the damages and costs
in this cause

    It is therefore considered by the Court that the Plain-
tiff recover of the said defendant and his securetys the
said Joseph R. Mee, John Austin, Jesse Mee and Alexander A.
Clingan, the sum of Thirty Six dollars and seventy cents
the amount of damage aforesaid for which a judgment has
been heretofore rendered in this Court together with the
further sum of one dollar and forty six cents intrest due
on said Judgment and all costs that have accrued in this
Cause   (P-347)   and the plaintiff agrees to stay the
Exacution for the space of Six Months and it appearing to
the Court that said Defendant has been arested on a casa
in this cause and has given bond and securety to keep the
Prison Bonds.

    It is considered by the Court that he go hence & be
discharged therefrom.

_____

Writ

State of Tennessee)   To any lawful officer to exe-
)   cute and return you are hereby
Bradley County)   commanded to summons Phillip
      Coffel to appear before me or
      some other Justice of the piece
for said County to answer the complaint of Derias Browder
in a plea of debt due by note of hand under twenty dollars
here in fail not

    given under my hand and seal this the 1st day of March
1841.

           Joseph Seabourn
           Justice of the Peace

Endorsment

Debt Warrant Derias Browder vs Phillip Coffel

Executed and returned for trial on the 2nd day of March 1841, before

Samuel George, Esqr.

K. C. Seabourn, Const.

Judgment against the defendant for $19.75 cts. beside the futher sum of 75 cents for costs serving warrant

50 cents

Judgment   25 cents

Samuel George
Justice of the Peace

Execution

STATE OF TENNESSEE   )   To any lawful officer of said
)   County, Greeting: Whare as
BRADLEY COUNTY   )   Diras Browder did on the 2nd
                                  day of March, 1841 before me
                                  Samuel George one of the acting
Justices of the Peice in and for said County recovered a Judgment against Phillip Coffel for the sum of nineteen dollars and seventy cents together with the   (P-348) futher sum of Eighty seven and a half cents for costs which said judgment was staid by John Brimer, and the security for stay of Execution had the amount of said Judgment to pay and thare is now a chance for property of the said Phillip Coffel and this is thare fore to command of the goods and chattles lands and tenements of the said Phillip Coffel if to be found in your County you cause to be made the aforesaid sums of Money with legal intrust on said Judgment * and commission on this Execution here in fail not and have you the said Moneys ready to render to the Plaintiff as the law dyrects.

given under my hand and seal

this the 24th August, 1841.

Samuel George
Justice of the Peace

Endorsment

Derias Browder   )   Received of the within fourteen
and also your fees

vs   )   dollars ten cents the 6th of July
Phillip Coffel   )   1841.

                    Came to hand the same day Issued
No personal property of Phillip Coffel to be found in my
County.

         Levied on a track of land of the Defendant lying in*
said County the East corner of the North West quarter section ten said to be 40 acres town ship 3rd Range 2 West of
the Basis line in the Ocoee District August 24th 1841.

                     A. A. Clingan
                     Sheriff.

     Writ

STATE OF TENNESSEE   )   To any lawful officer to Exe-
)   cute and return Summons J. R.
BRADLEY COUNTY   )   Wells to appear before me or some
                         other Justice of the Peace in and
                         for said County to answer the
complaint   (P-349)   of Barrett & Earnest for the use of
McClung & French & Co. of a plea of debt due by note

         Given under hand and seal this the 3rd day of February
1841.

                     Davis Preddy
                     Justice of the Peace

     Endorsment

Barratt & Earnest   )
      vs   )   Executed and for tryal on the
J. R. Wells   )   12th February, 1841, before

         J. R. Mee, Esqr.

     Judgments   )   J. W. Earnest Dept Sheriff
(P-349)
Barrett & Ernest   )
     vs   )   Judgment debt $87.76
Robert Wells   )
                    Cost   .75

                    J. R. Mee, J. P.
*Bradley County District 11th in

Execution

STATE OF TENNESSEE   )
)   To any lawful officer of said
BRADLEY COUNTY   )   County, Greeting:

          Whereas Barrett & Earnest for
the use of McClung & French & Co. on the 11th day of February 1841, before me J. R. Mee, one of the acting Justices
of the Peace in and for said County recovered a judgment
against J. R. Wells, for the sum of Eighty seven dollars
and seventy six cents to geather with the further sum of
Eighty seven and a half cents for castze you are therefore
hereby commanded that of the Goods and chattles lands and
tenements of the said J. R. Wells if to be found in your
County made the aforesaid sum of money with legal intrest
on said Judgment and also your fees and commissions on this
Execution.

          Here in fail not and have you the said moneys ready
to render to there Plaintiff as the law dyrects

          Given under my hand and seal this 18th day of February
1841.

                    (Joseph R. Mee,
                    (J. P. for Bradley County

          Endorsment --

Barrett & Earnest   )
     vs   )
J. R. Wells,   )

     (P-350)
     Judgment $87.76

     Intrust 1.75

     Collecting fee 3.58

     Costs 87½
                                        _____
                                        93.96½

          No goods & chattles to be found in my County of J. R.
Wells, Levied upon two town lots No 9 & 91 of the defendants
lying in Bradley in Charleston and said to contain three
fourths of an acre more or less each, February 20th, 1841.

               J. W. Earnest, Depty Sheriff.

It is therefore considered by the Court that the town lots Levied on afforesaid be sold to satisfy the plantiffs Execution.

Issued and the Justices, Judge & the cost of this motion for which an order of sale Issue.

Warrant

STATE OF TENNESSEE)	To any lawful officer to execute
)	and return summond J. R. Wells
BRADLEY COUNTY)	to appear before me or some other

Justice of the Peace in and for said County to answer the complaint of E. Barden in a plea of debt due by note given under my hand and seal this 16th day of January, 1841.

Davis Preddy)
Justice of the Peace)

Endorcement

E. Barden)
vs)   Executed and ready for tryal on the
J. R. Wells)   30th January, 1841, before

J. R. Mee, Esq.

F. W. Earnest
Depty Sheriff

Judgment

E. Barden)
vs)   Debt $61.33
J. R. Wells)   Coat .. .. .75

Execution

J. R. Mee, J. P.

STATE OF TENNESSEE)   To any lawful officer of said
BRADLEY COUNTY

County Greeting:

Where as Elisha Barden, on the 30th day of January 1841 (P-351) Before me J. R. Mee, one of the acting Justices of the Peace in and for said County Recovered a Judgment against J. R. Wells, for the sum of Sixty one dollars and thirty three cents together with the further sum of Eighty Seven and a half cents costs, You are therefore hereby commanded that of the goods and chattles lands and tenements of the said J. R. Wells, if to be found in your County and if not then of the goods and chattles lands and tenements of the said you cause to be made the aforesaid sum of money with legal intrust on said Judgement and also your fees and commissions on this execution

Here in fail not and have you the said moneys ready to render to the plantiff as the law directs

given under my hand and seal

this the 18th day of February, 1841

Joseph R. Mee
Justice of the Peace for
Bradley Co.

Endorsment

No.
E. Barden   )   The goods chattles to be found in my
    vs   )   County of J. R. Wells levied on two
J. R. Wells   )   town lots No. 9 & 91 of the defendants
                      lying in Bradley County and in Charles-
                      ton and said to contain three fourths
of an acre more or less each.

February 20th, 1841.

F. W. Earnest
Depty Sheriff.

It is thereupon considered by the Court that the land levied on as aforesaid condemed and sold as the law directs to satisfy the Plantiffs execution Issued on the Justices Judgment aforesaid and the costs on this motion and that an order of sale issude.

Court then adjourned till tomorrow morning nine o'clock.

Charles F. Keith

(P352) Warrant

STATE OF TENNESSEE	)	To any lawful officer to exe-cute and return Summons J. R. Wells, to appear before me or some other Justice of the Peace in and for said County to answer
BRADLEY COUNTY	)	

the complaint of William Felts in a plea of debt due by note

Given under my hand and seal

this the 6th day of February, 1841.

Davis Preddy
Justice of the Peace

Endorsement

William Felts vs J. R. Wells	)))	Executed and for tryal on the 9th February 1841, before J. R. Mee, Esqr.

F. W. Earnest, Debt, Sheriff

Judgment

William Felts vs J. R. Wells	)))	Debt .. .. $60.33 Cost .. .. .75

J. R. Mee, J. P.

Execution

STATE OF TENNESSEE	))	To any lawful officer of said County Greeting:
BRADLEY COUNTY	)	On the 9th day of February, 1841, before me, J. R. Mee, one of the

acting Justices of the Peace in and for said County recovered
a Judgment against J. R. Wells for the sum of Sixty dollars
and thirty three cents together with the further sum of
Eighty Seven and a half cents for costs you are therefore
hereby commanded that of the goods and chattles lands and
tenements of the said J. R. Wells if to be found in your
County you cause to be made the aforesaid said sum of Money with legal intrust on said Judgement and also your fees

and commission on this execution here in fail not and have
you the said moneys ready (P-353)   to render to the
plaintiff as the law directs

Given under my hand and seal this 18th day of February
1841.

J. R. Mee, Justice of the Peace
for Bradley County

Endorsement

Wm. Felts   )   No goods and Chattles to be found in
     vs   )   my County of J. R. Wells, Levied on
J. R. Wells   )   two town lots No. 9 & 91, of the de-
                        fendants lying in Bradley and in Charles-
                        ton and said to contain three forths of
an acre more or less each February 20th, 1841.

F. W. Earnest,
Debt. Sheriff

It is therefore considered by the Court that the town
lots levied on aforesaid be condemned and sold as the law
directs to satisfy the plantiffs Execution Isude upon the
Justices Judgment and an order of the sale Isuded.

Warrant

STATE OF TENNESSEE   )
)   To any lawful officer to Execute
BRADLEY COUNTY   )   and return Summons J. R. Wells to
                               appear before me or some other
                               Justice of the peice in and for
said County to answer the complaint of Zacharias Martin of
a Plea of Debt due by note.

Given under my hand and seal this 19th day of January
1841.

Davis Preddy,
Justice of the Peace.

Endorsement

Zacheriah Martin   )
     vs   )   Judgment
J. R. Wells   )
                           Debt $46.03½

Cost 75

J. R. Mee, J. P.

STATE OF TENNESSEE   )   To any lawful officer of said
)   County, Greeting: Where as
BRADLEY COUNTY   )   Zacheriah Martin, on the 30th
                             of January 1841 before me J. R.
                             Mee, one of the acting Justices
of the Peace in and for said County recovered of Judgment
against J. R. Wells for the sum of Forty six dollars and
two and a half cents together with the futher sum of Eighty
seven and a half cents for costs you are tharefore hereby
commanded that of the goods and Chattles lands and tenements of the said J. R. Wells, if to be found in your County
you cause to be made the aforesaid sum of money with Legal
Intrest on said Judgment and also your fees and commissions
in this Execution here in fail not and have you the said
money ready to render to the Plaintiff as the law directs.

     given under my hand and seal

     this 18th day of February 1841.

                       Joseph R. Mee, Justice of the Peace
                       for Bradley County.

     Endorsment

Zacheriah Martin   )
    vs   )   No goods and chattles to be found
J. R. Wells   )   in my County of J. R. Wells, Lev-
                         ied on two town lots No. 9 & 91
                         of the defendants lying in Brad-
ley County and in Charleston & said to contain three forths
of an acre more or less each

     February the 20th, 1841

                F. W. Earnest
                Depty Sheriff

     It is therefore considered by the Court that the land
levied on be sold as the law directs to satisfy the Plaintiffs Execution.

     Isude upon the Justices Judgement and the costs of
this motion that an order of sale Issued.

(P-355)   Warrant

STATE OF TENNESSEE   )   To any lawful officer to Exe-
)   cute and return.
BRADLEY COUNTY   )

                             This is to command you to som-
                             mons Samuel Crosslen, Thomas
Johnston and ---- Morgan to appear before any acting Justice of the Peace for said County to answer the Complaint
of Thomas G. Stuart, William & John B. Carmichail pardners
in trade, traiding under the Ferm name and Stile of Stuart
& Carmichail in a plea of debt due by note one hundred dollars here in fail not

     Given under my hand and seal this the 29th day of
January, 1841.

                    Joseph Mitchel
                    Justice of the Peace

     Indorsement

Stewart & Carmichail   )   Executed and for tryal the
        vs   )   12th January 1841 before
Samuel Crosslin, and   )   James Mitchell, Esqr. by sum-
Thomas Johnson,   )   moning Thomas Johnson and Sam-
                             uel Crosslin.

               Samuel Blevins,
               Constable

     Judgement

     Judgment is given in favor of the plantiffs for $80.78
cents debt $1.25 Damage $4.00 dollars cost of suit $1.25
cents

     given under my hand and seal

     This 12th day of January, 1841

                    James Mitchell
                    Justice of the Peace

STATE OF TENNESSEE   )
)
BRADLEY COUNTY   )   To any lawful officer to Execute
                             and return these are to command

you that of the goods and chattles lands and tenements of
Samuel Crosslen, Thomas Johnson and Morgan if to be found
in your County you make the sum of Eighty Six dollars and
three cents for which Thomas G. Stewart and William and
John B. Carmichal, Pardners in Trade, Tradeing under the
firm name and stile of Stewart & Carmichael   (P-356)

Recovered a Judgement on the 12th day of January, 1841.

before me Joseph Mitchell, an acting Justice of the
Peace for said County also the further sum of your fees
and all lawful cost and intrust.

Here in fail not and have you this writ returned as
the law directs.

Given under my hand and seal

This 16th day of January, 1841.

                    Joseph Mitchell,
                    Justice of the Peace.

Fi Fa on No. 535   )
)
Stewart & Carmichael   )
        vs   )   Levied this Execution and
)   seven head of hogs the 16th
Crosslen, Johnson and   )   of January, 1841.
Morgan   )

                    Sold the 7 Hogs for four dol-
                    lars. Bid by T. Crosslen.
        Levied this Execution on one sorrel Horse, one sorrel
mare and seven Hogs the 2nd February, 1841, and for sale
the 20th.

Relevied pr alias the 8th, March, 1841.

                    Samuel Blevins.

Judgment

For debt $80.78

For Intrust 4.00

Cost 1.37½
                               _____
                               86.15½
Received on the within
    January 22nd, 1841 $25.00

Received by sale of Hogs, Feb. 2nd   4.00

Received Cash Feb. 2nd.   .75

                             $29.75

Cr. By cash	$25.00	
" " "	61.15½	
" Two sums)	.75	
" One dollar)	1.00	
" D -- Bond	60.40	
By sale	$64.97½	
----------	4.00	
	60.97½	

(P-357)

STATE OF TENNESSEE   )   To any lawful officer to Execute
)   and return these are tharefore
BRADLEY COUNTY   )   as hath heretofor ben that of
                              the goods and chattles lands
                              and tenements of Crosslen, John-
son and Morgan if to be found in your County You make the
sum of Eighty Six dollars and three cents for which Thomas
G. Stewart, John B. & William Carmichael, pardners in trade
Tradeing under the name and stile of Stewart and Carmichael
recovered a Judgement on the 12th day of January, 1841,

Before me, Joseph Mitchell, an acting Justice of the
peace for said County also the further sum of your fees and
all lawful costs and intrust here in fail not and have you
this writ returned as the law dyrects

given under my hand and seal

this 8th day of March, 1841.

                          Joseph Mitchell,
                          Justice of the Peace.

1st Alies fi fa

Stewart & Carmichael   )
     vs   )   Search made and no per-
Morgan, Crosslin & Johnson   )   sonal property of the

defendant to be found in my County.

Levied this fi fa on the east half and the North West corner of section 14 South east quarter and the North east corner of the North East quarter of 14 in township four and range two west of the Basis line in the Ocoee District

This the 11th day of March, 1841.

It being the land of Thomas Johnson, one of said defendants.

Samuel Blevins,
Constable.

Judgement

For debt $60.97½

Alies .. .. .12½

(P-358)
It is therefore ordered and adjudged by the Court that the land levied on as aforesaid be exsposed to sail as the law dyrects to satisfy the Plaintiffs Judgement and rendered by the Justice aforesaid, and the cost of the said on order of sale Issue.

Warrant

STATE OF TENNESSEE)
) To any lawful officer of said
BRADLEY COUNTY) officer of said County:

You are commanded to summons Jacob Rinkle to appear before me or some other Justice of the Peace for said County to answer the Complaint of Willford Rucker in a plea of debt due by a note of hand for One hundred and ninety five dollars.

Herein fail not Given under my hand and seal May 25th 1839.

Thomas Taylor,
Justice of the Peace.

Endorsement

Willford Rucker   )
      vs   )   Executed by acknowledgement
Jacob Rinkle   )

Judgement

This day the within was confessed due the Plaintiff one hundred and ninety five dollars

Confessed before me on this 26th day of May, 1839.

                    Thomas Taylor,
                    Justice of the Peace

Fi Fa

STATE OF TENNESSEE   )
)
BRADLEY COUNTY   )   To the Sheriff or Custable of
                                said County, I command you
                                that of the goods and Chattles
lands and tenements of Jacob Rinkle, if to be found in
your County, you make the Sum of One hundred and ninety
five dollars and the Coats of suit   (P-359)   to satisfy a Judgment that Willford Rucker, obtained against him
before me on the 26th day of May, 1839, and pay over the
sum as the law dyrects this the 27th day of May, 1841.

                    Thomas Taylor,
                    Justice of the Peace

Endorsement

    Fi Fa

Willford Rucker   )
      vs   )   Came to hand same day Issued.
Jacob Rinkle   )
                           Levied the within 28th May, 1841.

On one colt - 1 cow and yearling - ten head of hogs -
three geese - four head of sheep - one kettle as the property of Jacob Rinkle, and sold on the tenth of June, 1841,
as the law dyrects amounting to fourteen dollars eighteen
and three forths cents and no more personal property to
be found in my County, This the 10th June, 1841.

                    D. D. Taylor.

Levy on Land

Levied the within on forty acres of Land the South west
corner of section 27. Township one Range two west of the
Basis line in the Ocoee District.

There being no more personal property to be found in
my County, this the 10th of June, 1841.

D. D. Taylor

Constable.

Received on the within, fourteen dollars sixty eight
and three forths cents

This 10th day of June, 1841.

D. D. Taylor,
Const.

It is therefore considered by the Court that the land
Levied on as aforesaid be sold to satisfy the Plantiffs
Judgement Rendered by the Justices as afore said and the
costs of this motion and order of sale Issue.

(P-360)

STATE OF TENNESSEE	)	
	)	To any lawful officer in and
BRADLEY COUNTY	)	for said County, you are hereby commanded to summons John Carr, to appear before me or some

other Justice of the Peace for said County to answer the complaint of E. & A. N. Pitners, for the non Payment of a sum
under ten dollars due by note given under my hand and seal

This 14th day of May, 1839.

Jesse Poe,

Endorsement for Bradley County

E. & A. N. Pitners	)	
vs	)	Executed and for tryal the 15th
John Carr	)	of June, 1839, before Jesse Poe.

George W. Selvedge,
Constable.

Judgement

Judgement Entered against the defendant

Debt and Intrust $8.86

Cost fee   .50

Judgement by me 15th June 1839   .25

                    Jesse Poe
                        Justice of the Peace.

        Fi Fa

STATE OF TENNESSEE   )
)   To any lawful officer, Greeting:
BRADLEY COUNTY   )

    Whare as Elias & A. N. Pitners, did on the 15th day of
June, 1839, before me Jesse Poe, one of the acting Justices
of the Peace in and for said County, Recovered a Judgment
against John Carr, for the sum of Eight Dollars and eighty
six cents togeather with the further sum of Eighty seven
and a half cents you are therefore hereby commanded that
of the goods and chattles lands and tenements of the said
John Carr, If to be found in your County you cause to be
made the aforesaid   (P-361)   Sum of money with legal
Intrust on said Judgement and also your fees and commissions
on this Execution.

    Here in fail not and have you the said moneys ready to
render to plantiff as the law directs

    given under my hand and seal

    This 10th day of June, 1841

                    Jesse Poe,
                        Justice of the Peace

E. & A. N. Pitners   )
      vs   )   Came to hand the same day Issued
John Carr   )
                            No goods & Chattles to be found
in my County of John Carr, Levied upon a tract of land of the
defendant lying in the second District of Bradley County
and said to contain forty acres, south east corner of South
East quarter section two Township 2nd Range 1st East of the
Basis line in the Ocoee District, This 12th June, 1841.

                    A. A. Clingan, Sheriff

It is thereupon ordered and adjudged by the Court that the land levied on as a fore stated be sold as the law directs to satisfy the plantiffs execution.

Issude upon the Justices Judgement as aforesaid and that an order Issue.

The State)
vs)
John Spencer &)
William Spencer)

Came the Grand Jury into open Court and returned a bill of Indictment against the defendant for a felon indorsed by their foreman Samuel Howard a true bill, which bill of

Indictment is in the words and figures

STATE OF TENNESSEE)
)
BRADLEY COUNTY)

Circuit Court

August Term, Eighteen hundred and forty one

The grand jury   (P-362)   In behalf of the State of Tennessee elected impanneled sworn and charged to inquire for the County of Bradley aforesaid upon their oath present that William Spencer and John Spencer, late of said County Labours on the twenty seventh day of July in the year of Our Lord one thousand eight hundred and forty one, with force and armes in the County of Bradley aforesaid and with in the Jurisdiction of this honorable Court feloniously unlawfully and maliciously did make an assault --- upon the Boddy of Wm. R. Lavender, then and there being in the peace of the State being in and did then and thare feloniously unlawfully and maliciously put out the left eye of him the said William R. Lavendar, contrary to the forms of this State in such case made and provided and against the peace and dignity of the State.

> Samuel Frazier,
> Attorney General for the
> 3rd Solisotorial District

Indictment

The State)
vs)
Wm. Spencer &)
John Spencer)

William R. Lavender
Prosecutor

William R. Lavender Witnesses for

the State, sworn in open Court and sent before the Grand Jury, August 24th, 1841.

Henry Price, Clerk.

A true Bill, Samuel Howard, foreman of the Grand Jury.

Tuesday August 24th, 1841.

State)
   vs)   Came the attorney General who
Wm. & John Spencer)   prosecutes for this State and
                       the defendant in their answer
                       proper person together with
Levi Spencer who acknowledge themselves in debeted to the State of Tennessee as follows to wit, the said John Spencer and the said Wm Spencer, defendants in the sum of Five hundred dollars jointly and Levi Spencer in the sum of Five (P-363) hundred dollars to be levied of their respective goods and chattles lands and tenements to the use of the State but to be void if the said William Spencer and John Spencer shall make their personal appearance before the Judge of the Circuit Court now setting for the County of Bradley at the Court House in the town of Cleveland from day to day and answer a charge of the State exhibited against them by Indictment for a felony and not depart the Court with out leave first had and obtained.

The State)
   vs)   Assault & Battery
John Spencer)
Wm. Spencer)   Came the Grand Jury into open Court
                       and returned a bill of indebtment
                       against Defendant for an assault &
Battery indorsed by their foreman.

Samuel Howard, Foreman

A true Bill

The State)
   vs)   Assault & Battery
John Spencer &)
William Spencer)   Came into open Court, Levi Spencer,
                       who acknowledges himself indebted
                       to the State of Tennessee in the
sum of two hundred and fifty Dollars to be levied of his goods and chattles lands and tenements to the use of the State but to be void on condition that John Spencer and

and Wm. Spencer shall make theire personal appearance before the Judge of the Circuit Court at the Court house in the town of Cleveland on the first Wednesday after the fourth Monday of December next thare and then to answer a charge of the State exhibited against them by Indibtment for an assault and Battery and not depart the Court with out leave, (P-364) and thare upon came William Lavender into open Court and acknowledged himself indebted to the State of Tennessee in the sum of two hundred and fifty Dollars to be levied of his Goods and Chattles lands and Tenements to the use of the State, but to be void if he shall make his personal appearance before the Judge of the Circuit Court at the Court house in the town of Cleveland at the Court house in Bradley County thare and then and thare Prosecute and give evidence on part of the State against the Defendants and not depart the Court without leave.

The State	)	
vs	)	Assault & Maliciously knocking out
John Spencer &	)	the Eye of William Lavendar
William Spencer	)	

Came the attorney General who prosecutes for the State and by leave of the Court enters a Nola procique in this Cause.

It is thare upon considered by the Court that the Clerk take the legal cost in this cause for the Inspection of the Court.

The State	)	
vs	)	Felon — Knocking out the Eye of
John Spencer &	)	Wm. R. Lavender.
Wm. Spencer	)	

The attorney General reported to Court the following Bill of Cost which has been examined and duly certified and ordered to be recorded which is in the words as follows to wit,

Attorney General S. Frazier $3.00, H. Price, Clerk Issueing an Capias 75 cents, three recognizances in Court 25 cents each 75 cents, Judgement final 75 cents, complete copy of cost (P-365) Recording proceedings after final Judgement, Issueing one sifa 12½ cents, $162½ Debt, Sheriff James Donoho two arrests $4.50, one dollar each $2.00
$9.59

I certify that I have examined the foregoing Bill of
Cost and the same is ----

December 29th, 1841.

> Samuel Frazier, Atty General
> for the 3rd Soli. District.

I have examined the foregoing Bill of cost and certify
the same to be legally exelerntly taxed.

> Charles F. Keith &c.

And it appearing to the satisfaction of the Court that
there has been hear to fore a Nole proseque entered in this
cause, It is therefore considered by the Court the same be
paid by the Treasuer of the State of Tennessee, the foregoing Bill of Cost amounting to nine dollars and fifty cents.

Assault

The State	)	
vs	)	Came the attorney General who prose-
John Spencer &	)	cutes for the State and the cause
William Spencer	)	is continued until the next term

of this Court and came Levi Spencer
who acknowledges him self indebted
to the State of Tennessee in the sum of Three hundred dollars to be levied of his goods and chattles lands and tenements to the use of the State but to be void if John Spencer
& William Spencer shall make there personal appearance before the Judge of the Court at the Court House in Cleveland
on the first Wednesday after the 4th Monday in April next
County of Bradley then and there answer a charge of the
State exhibited against them by Indictment for an assault
and not depart the Court with out leave.

Assault & Battery

The State	)	
vs	)	This day came the attorney General
John Spencer &	)	and by leave of the Court enters a
Wm. Spencer	)	Nola Prosequi in this cause

It is thereupon ordered by the Court
that the Clerk Certify the cost on this cause to the County
Court for payment.

The State)
 vs   ) Came the Grand Jury into open Court
Wm. D. Dillion) and returned a bill of Presentment
       against the Defendant retailing
       spiritious liquers signed by all
of said Grand Jury which Bill of Presentment is in the
words and figures to ---

STATE OF TENNESSEE) Circuit Court
)
BRADLEY COUNTY) August, Eighteen hundred and
         forty one.

  The Grand Juries in behalf of the State of Tennessee,
elected impanelled sworn and charged to enquire upon their
oath present that William D. Dillion, late of said County
labourer on the Tenth day of July, Eighteen hundred and
forty one with force and armes in the County of Bradley
aforesaid unlawfully did vend and sell by retail in quantities less than one quart a certain kind of spirituous
liqueurs called french Brandy to one Robert Mathews, contrary to the form of the Statutes in such case made and
provided and against the Peace and dignity of the State.

   Presentment

The State   ) Found on the information of
 vs   ) Robert Mathews
William D. Dillion)
(P-367)
    Names of Grand Jury:

  Samuel Howard, Baker Armstrong, John Berk, Joseph Mc-
Andrew, Isaac Smith, John F. Davis, Robert Mathews, James
Shadle, J. A. Dearmond, James Grisham, Joseph Seabourn,
S. B. Cathey, E. Edwards.

STATE OF TENNESSEE)
) To the Sheriff of Bradley
BRADLEY COUNTY) County Greeting:

    You are hereby commanded to take
the Boddy of William D. Dillion instantly if to be found
in your County and safely keep so that you have him before
the Judge of our Circuit Court now sitting for Bradley County at the Court House in Cleveland then and thare to answer
the charge of the State exhibited against him by presentment
for Retailing spireteous liqurs and have you then and thare
this writ Witness Henry Price, Clerk of our said Court at
office in Cleveland, the 2nd September, A. D. 1841.

Henry Price, Clerk
By James Lauderdale, D c

Capias --

The State
  vs   )   Ishued 2nd September, 1841.
William D. Dillion)

Tipling -

The State   )
  vs   )   Came the Attorney General who prose-
Wm. D. Dillon   )   cutes for the State and the defendant
                       being charged in the Bill of Indibtment
                       for plea says he is guilty in manner
and form as charged.

It is therefore considered by the Court that he the
defendant for this his offence be fined in the sum of twenty dollars besides costs and that he remain in Custody untill the fine cost be paid or security given   (P-368)
thare for and thare upon comes Robert Mathis and undertook
with the Defendant that he the defendant would pay and satisfy the fine and costs aforesaid or that he the said Robert Mathis, would do it for him upon which it is considered
by the Court that the Court Recover of he the defendant and
the said Robert Mathis the fine and costs aforesaid and
that execution Issue therefore.

Bond   --

Know all men by these Presents we, Eli Cleveland and
Spencer Jarnagin are jointly and severly held and firmly
bound unto Samuel Parks and Enoch Woods in the penal sum
of two hundred and fifty dollars to be void on condishions
that the said Eli Cleveland will with effect prosecute a
suit by action of ejectment which he this day commenced
against the said Parks and Woods in the Circuit Court for
Bradley County or in Case of failure of such prosecution
pay and satisfy all costs and damages as may be awarded
against him by our said Court

Witness our hands and seals this 20th day of January
1840.

Eli Cleveland
By his attorney, S. Jarnagin
(Spencer Jarnagin)

State of Tennessee,

To the Sheriff of Bradley County, Greeting: You
are hereby commanded to summons Samuel Parks and Enoch
Woods, If to be found in your County to appear before our
Circuit Court to be held for the County   (P-369)   of
Bradley at the Court House in Cleveland on the 4th Monday
of April next to answer John Den ---- of Eli Cleveland of
a plea of tresspass wharefore with force and armes they
broke and entered the ---- of the said plaintiffs and
Injured him to his damage five hundred dollars here in fail
not and have you then and thare this writ, Witness, Henry
Price, Clerk of our said Court at office in Cleveland the
forth Monday of December, 1839, and of American Independence
the ----.

Henry Price,
Clerk.

Indorsement --

Summons --

John Den, Lissee of   )
   Eli Cleveland   )
      vs   )   Isude 20th January, 1840.
Samuel Parks &   )
Enoch Woods   )   Came to hand 25th March, 1840.

Summond Enoch Woods, the 27th
March 1840, and delivered a copy of the Declaration to him
at the same time, and summoned Samuel Parks the 1st of April
1840 Delivered a Copy of the Decleration at the same time.
James Lauderdale, Sheriff,

Jarnagin & Bradford, Attorneys.

STATE OF TENNESSEE   )   Circuit Court
)
BRADLEY COUNTY   )   April Term, 1840.

John Den by attorneys complains of Richard Fen summonsed
by the Sheriff &c. for that where at on the 1st day of January 1840, E. C. Cleveland at Mouse Creek in the County

aforesaid demised and to farm let a tract of land situated
and being in the County aforesaid to the said John Den
and being the North West quarter of section twenty two
Township first range first West of the Basis line Ocoee
District, Beginning on the North East corner   (P-370)
of said quarter containing one hundred and sixty acres
with the appertainances to have and to hold the same to
the said John Den, and his assigns from the said first
day of January, 1840, for and during and until the full
and term of twenty years from thence next ensueing and
fully to be complete and ended; by virtue of which said --
the said John Den, Entered into the tenements a hed became
and was possesed thare of for the said term of twenty years
to him granted and the said John --- being thereof possesed
the said Richard Fen, on the 3rd day of January in the year
last aforesaid with force and armes &c, entered into the
said tenements with the appertanences in which the said
John Den force this farm and other wrongs to the said John
Den, then and thare did against the said Peace and dignity
of the State and to the damage of the Plaintiff, John Den,
five hundred dollars.

                    Cannon & Jarnagan
                    Attorneys for Plaintiff

Messrs Samuel Parks & Enoch Woods,

     I am Informed that you are in posession of or claims
title to the premises in the declaration mentioned or to
some part thare of and I being send as casual ejetor only
and having no claim or title to the same do advise you to
appear before the Judge of the Circuit Court at a Court
to be held at the Court House in the Town of Cleveland
on Monday of April, 1840, and thare and thare by a rule
of said Court cause your selves to be made Defendants or
you will be turned out of posession.

     30th July, 1840.

                    Your Obt Servt,

                    Richard Fen.
(P-371)
     Indorsement on Declaration

John Den, Lasse of   )
Eli Cleveland   )
     vs   )   Issued 20th January, 1840
Samuel Parks &   )
Enoch Woods   )   Came to hand the 25th March, 1840.
                              Executed by Delivering a copy of

the within Declaration to Enoch Woods, the 27th March, 1840 & Delivered a copy of this Declaration to Samuel Parks, the 1st April, 1840.

James Lauderdale, Sheriff.

John Den, Lasse of   )
Eli Cleaveland   )
   vs   )   Ejectment
Richard Fen   )
  with Notice to   )   And the said Samuel Parks and
  Samuel Parks &   )   Enoch Woods the tenements in
  Enoch Woods   )   possession comes into open Court
                                       and confesses Leas entry ouster
                                       and thare upon being persuaded
to defend in the place of the Casual Ejector agrees that
upon the trial that they will rely and there upon the said
defendants by attorney comes and defends the peace and injury when &c. say they are not guilty of the said trespass
and Ejectment in the plantiffs decleration mentioned laid
to their charge or any part thereof in manner and form as
the said plaintiff hath complained against them and of this
they put themselves upon the County.

Jas. F. Gillispie &
Levi Trewhitt

And the Plaintiff doth the like for Defendants.

Jarnagin & Cannon
Attorneys

Plea

Eli Cleaveland, Lassee   )
   vs   )   Filed 3rd day of the term
Samuel Parks &   )
Enoch Woods   )
(P-372)
   Tuesday 28th, April, 1840

Eli Cleaveland, Lassee   )   On motion of the Plaintiffs
   vs   )   Attorneys and by consent of
Samuel Parks &   )   the parties leave is given
Elijah Woods   )   the plaintiff to amend by
                                      inserting the Christian
name of Elijah Woods.

Eli Cleveland, Lessee   )
   vs   )   The plaintiff by his attorney
Samuel Parks &   )   appears and also Came Samuel
Enoch Woods   )

Parks and Enoch Woods the Tenements in possession who on
application admited as defendants in the --- and stead of
the Casual Ejector upon this agruing to enter into the
Common rule to admit leave Entry and ouster plead not guilty
and upon the trial rely upon the title Entry.

Monday August, 23rd, 1841.

Eli Cleveland, Lessee ⎞
vs ⎬ Ejectment
Samuel Parks ⎠

This day came the parties
by their attorneys and thare
upon the plaintiffs attorney suggested the death of the defendant and on his motion & by consent of the parties cause
is Revied against Susan Parks, Widow of the said Samuel
Parks, Widow of the said Samuel Ruth Price, James C. Price
& wife Almeros Price, Thomas Langdon and his wife, James
Langdon, George W. Parks, Thomas J. Parks, William Parks,
Polly Ann Parks, Robert Parks, Richard Parks, and ---- and
Samuel Hunter Parks, (P-373) C. Morgan Parks, John
Parks heirs of Samuel Parks deceased and thare upon the
said Thomas & Richard Parks, Calvin Morgan Parks, William
Parks, Polly A. Parks, Robert Parks, John Parks and Samuel
Hunter Parks who are minors under twenty one years of age
by their testamenary Guardian George W. Parks & William
W. Cowan, consented to said revival and thare upon came
the following Jury to Viz:

Samuel Howard, John Burk, John Davis, Joseph McAndrew
James Grisham, John A. Dearmond, Baker Armstrong, Isaac
Smith, Edward Edwards, James Shadle, Joseph Seabourn, San-
uel B. Cathy, Robert Mathis, who having been duly summond
elected tried and sworn the truth to speak upon their oath
do say that the defendants ancesters and testatories was
Jointly of the trespass to Ejectment in the plaintiffs decleration mentioned in manner and form as the Plaintiff
in his declaration hath alledged & by reason thare of as-
seses the Plaintiffs damage to one cent & is tharefore considered by the Court that the Plantiff recover of the defendant his term yet unexpired in his decleration mentioned
together with his damage & costs in this behalf Expended
for which an execution may Issue and the Plaintiff by Attorney stays the Isuance of a writ of possesion untill the
further order of this Court & thare upon the Plantiffs by
his attorney confessed a Judgement to the defendant for one
half of the cost in this behalf exspanded .
(P-374)
It is therefore considered by the Court that the defendant recover of the Plaintiff a judgement for one half
of the cost in this behalf exspended for which an Execution

may Issue &c.

Bond

Know all men by these Presents that John Wever and
Spencer Jarnagin are jointly and severly held and firmly
bound unto Wm. M. Biggs and James Thompson, in the penal
sum of two hundred and fifty dollars to be void on condition the said John Weaver will with effect prosecute
a suit of action of ejectment which on this day commenced
against the said William M. Biggs, and James Thompson,
Hamilton Bigs in the Circuit Court for Bradley County or
in case of failure of such prosecution pay and satisfy all
costs and damages as may be awarded against him by our said
Court Witness our hands and seals this 31st day of January
1839.

John Weaver   (Seal)

By S. Jarnagin Attorney
(Spencer Jarnagin)

State of Tennessee,

To the Sheriff of Bradley County, Greeting: You
are hereby commanded to summons William M. Biggs and James
Thompson and Hamilton Biggs if to be found in your County
to appear before our Circuit Court to be helden for the
County of Bradley at the Court House in Cleveland on the
4th Monday of April next to answer John Den, Lessee,
(P-375)   of John Weaver of a plea of Trespess with force
and armes where upon they broke and entered the claths of
the said plaintiff to his damage five hundred dollars here
in fail not and have you then there this writ

Witness Henry Price, Clerk of our said Court at office
in Cleveland the fourth Monday, December, 1838.

Henry Price, Clerk.

Summons --

John Den, Lessee of
   John Weaver   )
      vs   )
William M. Biggs   )   Issued 31st January
James Thompson & Hamilton Biggs   )   1839.
)

Came to hand the first day of February, 1839. Executed by summoning Wm. Biggs and Hamilton Biggs the 12th February, 1839, and delivering to each of them at the same time a copy of the Declaration.

James Lauderdale, Sheriff

Executed by summoning James Thompson the 8th day of April 1839, and delivering to him at the same time a copy of the Declaration.

John F. Oneal,
Depty Sheriff

Jarnagin & Bradford, Attorneys

State of Tennessee

Bradley County Circuit Court

John Den, Lassee Atterney

Complains of Richard Fen, who has ben summond by the Sheriff of a plea of Tresspass with force and armes wherefore he Broke and entered the Clase of the said plantiff and injured him to his damage five hundred dollars F - this heretofore on the twenty second day of January in the year of our Lord one Thousand Eight hundred and Thirty nine. In the County and State aforesaid a certain John Weaver did demise grant and to form let unto the said John Den, a certain tract tenement or parcel of land containing Eighty Seven Acres lying and being in the County and State aforesaid being the North east frastional quarter of section thirty four in the first fractional township North in range second east of the Pasis line in the Ocoee District in the County and State aforesaid for the term of ten years thence next insueing to be fully completed and ended By virtue of which said demise so made aforesaid and ended By virtue of which said demise so made as aforesaid by the said John Weaver he the said John Den entered into and took the posesion of --- so demised to him as aforesaid and was thare of peaceabley possesed in his own right and afterwards on the 23rd day of January in the year of our Lord one thousand Eight hundred and thirty nine in the County and State aforesaid the said Richard Fen with force and armes entered upon him the said John Den and ejected him from his farm as aforesaid so demissed to him as aforesaid and ejected him therefore this term tharein not being then made or yet expired and other wrongs and injuries then and there did to the said John Den against

the peace and dignity of the State and to the damage of
the said John Den five hundred dollars whare fore he sews
and has pledged a prosecution &c.

Jarnagin & Bradford
Attorneys for Plantiff

(P-377)
> Messers William Biggs and James Thompson
> and Hamilton Biggs

Gentlemen:

I am informed that you are in possession of
or claim title to the whole or some part of the
land in the foregoing Decleration in Ejectment
and I, being sued as casual Ejector and having no
bill there to, do advise you to appear before the
honorable the Circuit Court for Bradley County at
a Court to be held for said County on the fourth
Monday of April next at the Court house in Cleveland, and then and there by a rule of said have
your selves made defendants in any room and stead,
otherwise, I shall suffer on Judgment by defendant to be entered against me and you will be turned
out of possession January 31st, 1839.

Your friend

Richard Fen.

Decleration

Indorsment

John Den, Lessee of
   John Weaver
vs
Richard Fen, with
   Notice to Wm.M. Biggs &
   James Thompson to Wm. Biggs
   to Hamilton Biggs
	Issued 31st January
	1839
	
	Came to hand the 1st
	day of February, 1839
	delivered a copy of
	the within Declera-

tion to James Thompson and also to Hamilton Biggs this the
12th day of February, 1839.

James Lauderdale, Sheriff
For Bradley County

And James Thompson the 8th day of April, 1839.

James Oneal, Depty,
Sheriff

John Den, Lassee   Plea
John Weaver   )
   vs   )   And the defendants by their attor-
James M. Biggs   )   neys came into Court and by special
James Thompson   )   rule of the Court confesses lease
Hamilton Biggs   )   entry and ouster and agree on tryal
                          to rely upon the Titles only and
                          tharefore the said defendants for
plea say the plantiffs his action aforesaid against them
ought not to have and maintained because they say they are
not guilty of the Tresspass and Ejectment in manner and
form as the Plantiff in his declaration hath thareof Complained against them and of this they put themselves upon
the County.

Trewhitt & Campbell, Attorneys
For Defendants

And the Plantiff also
Jarnagin & Bradford, Attorneys
For Plantiffs

Plea --

John Den, Lessee for   )
John Weaver   )
   vs   )   Filed April 24th, 1839
William M. Biggs &   )
James Thompson   )

Wednesday 24th, April, 1839.

John Weaver, Lessee   )   The defendants in possession
William M. Biggs &   )   came into Court and agree to
James Thompson   )   enter into common rule to
Hamilton Biggs   )   admit Lease entry and ouster
                             plead not guilty and upon
                             the Trial rely upon the title
only.

Tuesday 24th December, 1839.

John Weaver, Lassee   )
   vs   )   The parties appear and by con-
Hamilton Thompson   )   sent and with assent of the
James Thompson   )   Court this cause is continued

until next Term.

Tuesday 29th, December, 1840.

John Weaver, Lassee)
vs)
Hamilton Biggs &)
James Thompson)

The parties by their attorneys appear and by consent is continued untill the next term.

(P-379)   Tuesday 31st August, 1841.

John Weaver, Lassee)
vs)
Marshall Hamilton Biggs)
William M. Biggs)
James Thompson)

Came the parties by their attorneys and thare upon to try the Issue Joined between the parties.

Came a Jury to wit:
Samuel Howard, John Burk, John Davis, Joseph McAndrew, James Grisham, John A. Dearmond, Isaac Smith, Edward Edwards, James Shadle, Joseph Seabourn, and John P. Angley who were elected tried and sworn well and truly to try the Issue Joined in this cause and are respected from rendering their verdict untill tomorrow and by leave assent are suffered to sepperate.

Wednesday 1st, September, 1841.

John Weaver, Lassee)
vs)
Marshal H. Biggs)
William M. Biggs)
James Thompson)

Came the parties by their Attorney and there upon Came the same Jury who was on yesterday elected tried and sworn well and truly to try the Issue Joined between the parties and resumed the consideration of this cause and the Jurors upon their oath aforesaid say that the defendants are not guilty of the trespass and ejectment in the Plantiffs declaration mentioned it is tharefore considered by the Court that the defendants recover of the Plantiff their cost about their defence in this behalf expended for which execution may Issue.

John Weaver, Lasse)
vs)
Marshall H. Biggs)
James Thompson)
William M. Biggs)

On petition of Spencer Jarnagin Esqr. Attorney for   (P-380) Plantiff a rule is granted him to show Cause why a new Tryal shall be had in this cause.

John Weaver, Leas.   )
        vs   )   Came the Parties by their attorney
Wm. Biggs &   )   and the rule to show cause why a
Attorney   )   new Tryal shall be had comes on
)   and after argument of conult it is
                            considered by the Circuit Court
that the rule is discharged.

        Warrant

STATE OF TENNESSEE   )   To any lawful officer of said
)   County William R. Roberts hav-
BRADLEY COUNTY   )   ing given information to me on
)   oath that George W. Humphries
                            on Sundry times December, 1840
in the County of Bradley did unlawfully make or have in
his possession Counterfeit Money to the --- of thirteen
dollars in the resemblence of spanish Mill dollars, I thare
fore command you in the name of the State to take the body
of the said George W. Humphreys and bring him forthwith before me or some other Justice of the Peace for said County
to answer the said charge and delt with as the law directs

        given under my hand and seal this 14th of December 1840.

                        John McPherson
                        Justice of the Peace
                        for Bradley Co.

The State   )
        vs   )   Endorsement
George W. Humphreys   )
                            Came to hand the same day Issued
                            and on the same day arrested the
body of George W. Humphries this the 14th December, 1840.

                        A. A. Clingan,
                        Sheriff

(P-381)
    The Warrant being read and heard, The defendant plead
not guilty but the Evidence being heard found guilty of
the charge By me and that the is a Constable and given
under my hand and seal

    This the 15th day of December, 1840.

                        John McPherson
                        Justice of the Peace.

Bill of Indictment

STATE OF TENNESSEE	)	Circuit Court
	)	December Term, Eighteen hundred
BRADLEY COUNTY	)	and forty.

The grand Jurors in behalf of the State of Tennessee
elected empanneled sworned and charged to enquire for the
body of the County of Bradley aforesaid their oaths present that a Certain George W. Hunphreys, late of said
County labourer on the tenth day of November in the year
of our Lord One thousand Eight hundred and forty with
force and armes in the County of Bradley aforesaid and
within the Jurisdiction of this Honorable Court felaneaus-
ly and fraudulently did make proper use and assist and he
conseadeed in making proparing and useing a Certain Machine and Instrument intendid for the forging Counterfeiting aduterating a certain silver coin called a spanish Mill
Dollar which said silver coin when genuine is Current Coine
by law and useage in the State of Tennessee and the said
Jurors aforesaid upon their oath aforesaid do futher present that the said George W. Humphreys on the said tenth
day of November in the year of our Lord one thousand Eight
hundred and forty with force and armes in   (P-382)   the
County of Bradley aforesaid felonously and fraudulently
did keep in his possession and consealed and assisted in
consealing a certain Machine and Instrument and intended
for the purpose of forgeing Counterfeiting and adultera-
ting ancertain silver coin called a spanish Mill Dollar
which said silver coin is when genuine is current coin by
law usage in the State of Tennessee, and the Jurors aforesaid do futher present that the said George W. Humphreys
on the tenth day of November, Eighteen hundred and forty
with force and armes in the County of Bradley aforesaid
feloniously and fraudulently did make and begin to make
proper and complete a certain base on adulterated coin
called a Spanish Milled dollar which said silver coin when
genuine is Current Coin by law and used in the State of
Tennessee with intent to impose the same upon Community as
good genuine and Current silver coin of the State of Tennessee and the Jurors aforesaid do futher present that the said
George W. Humphreys on the tenth day of November Eighteen
hundred and forty with force and armes in the County of
Bradley aforesaid felounously and fraudulantly did keep in
possession and consealed and assist and be concerned in consealing a certain Base and adulterated coin made imatation
---- silver called a Spanish dollar coin which said silver
coin when genuine is current coin   (P-383)   by law and
usage in the State of Tennessee, with intent to impose the
same upon community as good genuine and current silver coin

in the State of Tennessee, he the said George W. Humphreys
then and there well knowing the said base and adulterated
coin so kept in possession and consealed as aforesaid to
be such and the said Jurors aforesaid upon their oath aforesaid upon their oath aforesaid do futher present that the
said George W. Humphreys on the tenth day of November Eighteen
hundred and forty, with force and armes in the County of
Bradley aforesaid feloniously and fraudulently did make and
prepare and begin to make and prepare and assist and be concerned in making and prepareing a certain peice of base and
adulterated metal intended by him to be converted into the
Counterfeit resemblance of a Certain silver coin called a
Spanish Milled dollar which said silver coin when genuine
is by law and usage Current in the State of Tennessee.

And the Jurors aforesaid do futher present that the
said George W. Humphreys on the tenth day of November Eighteen hundred and forty with force and armes in the County
of Bradley aforesaid feloneously and fradulently did keep
in his possession and consealing certain peace of Base and
adulterated metal by him intended to be converted into the
Counterfeit resemblance of a Certain silver Coin called a
Spanish Milled dollar which said silver coin when genuine
is by law and usage current in the State of Tennessee with
intent to impose the said Counterfeit resemblance of the
said Silver coin upon the   (P-384)   Community as good
genuine and current silver coin inthe State of Tennessee
he the said George W. Humphreys then and there well knowing
the said peice of Base and aduterated meal -- was such, contrary to the form of the State in such case made and provided and against the Peace and dignity of the State.

                              Samuel Frazier,
                                 Attorney General for the 3rd
                                 Solicitorial District

        Indorsement --

The State   )
    vs   )   William P. Roberts
George W. Humphreys   )   John McPherson,
                              N. Roberts, Mary Driskel,
                              Andrew Lane, John Lane
Clabourn Mathis, Jacob Glandon, A. Gordin, Thomas Morgan
Alfred Lewis, Witnesses sworn in open Court and sent be-
fore the Grand Jury.

        January 2nd 1841.

                       Henry Price, Clerk.

Writ

State of Tennessee   )
)
Bradley County   )   To the Sheriff or any lawful
                              Constable of said County

       This day came before me Charles Cates, a Justice of
the Peace for said County Gilford Gatlin, and made oath
that he had good reasons to believe and doth believe that
one Isaac Woodall and David Bigham on or about the 15th
day of January last in the County aforesaid with force and
armes did feloniously steal take and carry away certain
gray Gelding the property of the said Gilford Gatlin, of
the value of forty dollars good and lawful money of this
State, these are therefore to command you in the name of
the State to take the bodies of the said Isaac Woodall and
David Bingham and Bring them   (P-385)   before me or
some other Justice of the peace for said County to answer
the primises and futher to be delt with as the law directs
given under my hand and seal this 16th October, 1840.

                               Charles Cate (Seal)
                               Justice of the Peace
                               for Bradley County

Witnesses for the State
       Elizabeth Esman
       Hiram Grimett

                  Witnesses for Defendant

                      George Richardson, James A. Bates
                      Malinda Woodall, Isaac Edwards
                      and John Fitzgerald

                  Witnesses for State,

                      John Eastman & Elizabeth Eastman

Endorsements --

The State   )   Executed by Irresting the Body of
    vs   )   Isaac Woodall and brought for trial
Isaac Woodall   )   before Jesse Poe, Esqr. on the 20th
David Bingham   )   of October, 1840. And Bingham not
Jesse Poe   to be found in my County and all

the within Witnesses is summond

                J. R. Wells, Constable

Bingham Taken --

Executed by Irresting the body of David Bingham and bringing him for trial before Joseph R. Mee, Esqr. on the 22nd day of October, 1840.

                J. R. Wells, Constable

Bill of Indictment

STATE OF TENNESSEE	)	Circuit Court
	)	
BRADLEY COUNTY	)	December Term, Eighteen hundred and forty

The Grand Jurors in behalf of the State of Tennessee elected empannlled sworn and charged to enquire for the body of the County of Bradley aforesaid upon their oath present that a certain Isaac Woodall, late of said County born on the fifteenth day of January in the year of our Lord one Thousand Eight hundred and forty with force and armes in the County of Bradley aforesaid one gray gelding of the value of forty dollars, good and lawful Money of the State of Tennessee and of the United States then and there   (P-386)   being the goods and chattles of one Gilford Gatlin feloneously did steal take and carry a way from and out of the possision of the said Gilford Gatlin Contrary to the form of the State in such cause made and provided and against the peace and dignity of the State.

                Samuel Frazier,
                  Atterney General for the
                  3rd Solicitorial District.

The State	)	
vs	)	Gilford Gatlin
Isaah Woodall	)	John Eastman, Elizabeth
Gilford Gatlin	)	Eastman, Silas M. Wann,
Prosecutor	)	Witnesses for the State

Sworn in open Court and sent before the Grand Jury the 13th January, 1841.

                Henry Price, Clerk.

The State   )
  vs   ) In this cause the defendant who stands
Isaah Woodall) charged by recognezance to appear this
            day to answer of fellony for stealing
            being solemnly called and required
to come into open Court and answer said charge or according to the Tenner sufford of said recognizance not but made
default and Abraham Barnes, Bail for the said defendant
being solomely called and required to come into open Court
and bring with him the body of the Defendant according to
the Tener effect of his said recognezance failed so to do
but make default.

It is therefore considered that the said defendant
hath forfeited to the State of Tennessee two hundred and
fifty dollars according to the Tenor and effect of his
said recognezance unless he shew sufficient cause (P-387)

To the County at the next term and that the said Abraham
Barnes hath also profeited to the State of Tennessee to
the tenor & effect of his said recogneziance unless he
shew sufficient cause to the County at the next term and
that Scirifacious severly Issue accordingly

   Scirefacious --

The State   )
  vs   ) Abraham Barnes, who stands bound
Isaah Woodall) by recognizance for the appearance
            of the defendant at the August Term
            of our said Court and against whom
a Scerefacious Isude directed to the Sheriff of Bradley
County which said Scerifacious is returned made known
to the said Abram - Barnes surrenders the defendant who
is in the Jail of Bradley County in discharge of this
said recognezance.

The State   )
  vs   ) Came the attorney General who prose-
Isaah Woodall) cutes for the State and the defendant
            is Brought to the Barr in Custody
            of the Sheriff also came the Jury
who was also yesterday placed under the care of Alexander
A. Clingan, Sheriff and resumed the consideration of this
cause who say they cannot agree ordered by the Court that
the Sheriff take charge of the Jury aforesaid and that
the Defendant be remained to Jail and thare safely keep
until tomorrow morning.

The State) Came the Attorney General who prosecutes
  vs   ) on the Part of the State and the defendant

being brought to the Bar of the Court and there upon came
the Jury who was on yesterday was respited from rendering
their verdict in this cause.

(P-388)

The State	)	The attorney General reported to
vs	)	the Court the following bill of
Isaah Woodall	)	cost which is ordered to be filled
		and take in the bill of cost A. B.

Aken to 72 diets for Jury at April Term, 1841 $18.00

to 24 lodgings at 12½ cents each $3.00

                                $21.00

       Larceny ---

The State	)	
vs	)	Came the State who presents for the
Isaah Woodall	)	State and the defendant is brought
		to the Bar in custody of the Sheriff
		and thare upon Came a Jury to viz:

    Samuel N. Carr, Andrew J. Parks, John Cowan, Jacob
Brown, Nathaniel Hays, Jeptha Randolph, Lancaster Randolph
John Benton, James Parks, Marshall Borden, William Wood &
Robert S. Brashears all good and lawful citizens of the
County of Bradley who being duly summoned elected tried
and sworn well and truly to try and true deliverance make
between the State of Tennessee and the defendant who are
respected from rendering their verdict and plased under
the charge of the Sheriff until they return into Court at
the meeting thare of on tomorrow Morning to resume the consideration of this cause ordered that the defendant be remaned to Jail.

    Tuesday 26th August, 1841.

The State	)	
vs	)	Came the State by her attorney Gene
Isaah Woodall	)	eral and the defendant is Brought
		to the Bar upon custody of the Sher-
		iff and thare upon came the Jury

that was on yesterday respited from rendering their verdict and placed under the care of the Sheriff who are respited from rendering their verdict and are placed under
the charge of the Sheriff until the meeting of the Court
tomorrow Morning and that the defendant be remanid to the
Jail.   (P-389)

Friday August 27th, 1841.

The State   )
  vs   ) Came the State by her Attorney Gen-
Isaah Woodall) eral and the defendant being brought
            to the Bar of the Court in Custody of
            the Sheriff and the Jury who were on
yesterday respited from rendering their verdict say they
have not argued and they are respited from rendering their
verdict till tomorrow and placed under the care of the Sheriff untill the meeting of the Court tomorrow morning.

    Ordered that the defendant be remanded to the Jail.

The State   )
  vs   ) Came Samuel Frazier Attorney General
Isaah Woodall) for the 3rd Solicitorial District
            who prosecutes for the State and the
            defendant is brought to the Bar of
the Court in custody of the Sheriff and thare upon came
the Jury who was on yesterday who was respited from rendering their verdict and put under the Sheriff and say that
they can not agree and by consent a Miss Trial is entered
in this Cause ordered that the defendant be remanded to
Jail, and thare safely kept until he give secureity in the
sum of one thousand dollars with two good securetys Jointly
in the sum of one thousand dollars or other wise discharged
by due cause of Leave.

    And thereupon came James Poley into open Court and
acknowledges him self indebted to the State of Tennessee
in the sum of two hundred and fifty dollars to be levied of
his goods and chattles Lands and tenements to the use of
the State to be void if he make his personal appearance before the Judge of the Circuit Court at a Court to be held
for Bradley County at the Court house in the Town of Cleveland (P-390) On the first Wednesday after the forth
Monday in August, next, thare and then prosecute and give
evidence on part of the State against the defendant and
not depart the Court without leave.

    Wednesday 31st, August, 1841.

    Larceny Horse Stealing

The State   )
  vs   ) Came the Attorney General who prose-
Isaah Woodall) cutes for the State and by leave of
            the Court enters a Nolle prosequi signed
            in this cause.

It is therefore considered by the Court that the Clerk tax the Legal Cost in this Cause for the Inspection of the Court.

The State)
vs) The State Dr to Thomas T. Davis, Jailer
Isaah Woodall) for Boarding defendant in Jail from
the Twentyeth of October 1840, to the
2nd day of January 1841, Making 75
days at 37½ cents per day $28.82½

To five Turn keys at 50 cts each 2.50

$31.32½

Sworn to in open Court 2nd of September, 1841.

Henry Price, Clerk

Thomas T. Davis.

Friday the 3rd September, 1841.

The State)
vs) On charge of Horse Stealing
Isaah Woodall)
Attorney General $3.00

Henry Price, Clerk chargeing Prisoners & Place 50 & 8 subpoenas at 20 cents each To Recording and fileing on Recognezance at 25 & 2 orders at 25 cents each 50 - Final Judgment 75 cents copy of cost 25 cents 2 continuance at 37½ per each 75 cents Recording ---- after first Judgement $162 per spreading bill of Endorsement on this record 25 cents. $5.87½

A. A. Clingan, Sending 2 Subpoenas .50

J. R. Wells, Suerving 5 subpoenes $1.25

Justice Poe for -- defendant .50
$8.12½

(P-391)
State Witnesses Silas M. Wear

11 days 75 cents per day 80 miles $11.45
John Eastman, 13 day 75 cts per day 9.75
Elizabeth Eastman, 13 day 75 cts per day 9.75
Samuel Cate, 8 day 75 cts per day 6.00
J. R. Wells, 7 day 75 cts per day 22miles 6.00
$42.95

Thomas T. Davis, Jailor for bording the defendant
in Jail from the 20th $7.12
                                                         $50.07

October 1840 until 2nd day of January
    making in all 75 days at 37½ cts per day $28.12

5 Turn Keys at 50 cts each   2.50
                                                         $30.62

Judgment for cost on the said
    Bill of cost   .25¢
                                                         $85.97

     I certify that I have carefuly examined the foregoing
Bill of cost and the same is legally and correctly taxed.

September the 2nd, 1841.

                         Samuel Frazier, Attorney for
                              the 3rd Solicitorial District.

     I have examined the foregoing Bill of cost and certi-
fy the same to be correct and legally taxed.

     given under my hand this 3rd day of September, 1841.

                         Charles F. Keith, Judge.

     It appearing to the satisfaction of the Court that a
Nole Proseque has been entered in this suit it is tharefore considered by the Court that the Clerk make out a
capias of the foregoing Bill of Cost amounting to Eighty
five dollars and Seven cents and that the same be certified
to the Treasurer of the State of Tennessee for payment the
Attorney General returned into Court the following Bill of
Cost which is certifyed and ordered to be spread on the
record which is in the words and figures to wit.

(P-392)   On Charge of Larceny --

The State   )
    vs   )   Henry Price, Clerk
David Bingham   )
                      presed a plea 50 causeing 6 subpoenies
                      12½ cents each 75 cents Renewing and
taking 11 recognizances at 25 cents each $2.75 cts final
Judgement 75 cts Copy of writ 25 cents Spredeing Bill of Indictment on the Record 25 cts & 3 continuences at 37½ cents

each $1.12½ cts recording proseeding $162½ cents Judgment for cost on said Bill of Cost 25 cets.

$9.25

J. K. Wells serving 5 subp. at 25 cts each   1.25

John Hays surving 1 subp. at 25   "   "   .25
Justice Joseph R. Mee for 1indi.deft.   .50
Caust Wells, surveing Warrant
    50 cts. 3 subp. 25 cents each $1.25

State Witnesses J. K. Wells 7 day
    75 cents per day 44 miles   7.00

John Eastman 12 days 75 cents per day   9.00

Elizabeth Eastman, 12 days 75 cents
    per day   9.00

Guilford Galiton, 10 days 75 cents
    per day 64 miles 4 cents per mile   7.50

~~John Eastman, 12 days 75 cents per day~~   ~~9.00~~

Silas M. Wear, 9 day 75 cts per day &
    60 miles at 4 cents per mile   7.17

Thomas T. Davis 2 day 75 cts per day   1.50

Thomas T. Davis, for bording Defendant
    in Jail from the 23rd October, 1840,
    until the second day of January, 1841
    making in all 72 days at 37½ Per day $27.00

Four Turnkeys at 50 cents each   2.00

Attorney Generals Fee   3.00

Joseph R. Mee, 8 day 75 cents per day

42 miles   7.68

    I certify that I have examined the foregoing Bill of cost and the same is legally and correctly taxed.

    September the 2nd, 1841.

                Samuel Frazier, Attorney
                    for the 3rd Solicitorial
                    District

(P-393)   Wednesday 29th, December, 1841.

Larceny ---

The State   )
    vs   )   Came the State by her Attorney Gen-
Isaah Woodall   )   eral and the Defendant to the Bar in
                       Custody of the Sheriff of Bradley
                       County and came a Jury to wit:

    John I. Roland, Sampson H. Prowell, Arthur Orr, James
Campbell, Robert Thornhill, William Wooden, John McNair,
Aron Collins, William Hays, Lewis R. Fain, Andrew Hooper
and Erby Colier, all good and lawful citizens of Bradley
County who being summoned elected tried and sworn will
and truly try and true Deliverance make between the State
of Tennessee and the Defendant who are respited from rendering their Verdict and are placed under the care of the Sheriff untill tomorrow morning ordered that the defendant be
removed to Jail.

The State   )
    vs   )   Came the attorney General who prose-
Isaah Woodall   )   cutes for the State and the Defendant
                       is brought to the Barr in Custody of
                       the Sheriff and there upon came the
same Jury, who was on yesterday respited from rendering
their verdict in this cause and was placed under care of
the Sheriff and resumed the consideration of this cause who
are this day respited from rendering their verdict and are
placed under the care of the Sheriff untill the meeting of
the Court, tomorrow morning ordered that the defendant be
remained to Jail.

    Friday 31st, December, 1841.

The State   )
    vs   )   Came the State by her attorney
Isaah Woodall   )   General and the Defendant is brought
                       to the Bar in Custody of the Sheriff
                       and came the same Jury who has here-
to fore been sworn in this cause and on yesterday placed
under the care of the Sheriff and resumed   (P-394)   the
consideration of this and upon their oath do say that they
cannot agree and are placed under the care of the Sheriff
until morning at the meeting of the Court.

    Ordered that the Defendant be remaned to Jail.

    Saturday 1st January, 1842.

The State   )
    vs   )   Came the attorney General who prose-
Isaah Woodall   )   cutes on behalf of the State and the
                       prisenor is brought to the Bar in

348

Custody of the Sheriff and thare upon came the same Jury
who was on yesterday respited from rendering their verdict
and placed under the care of the Sheriff untill the meeting
of the Court tomorrow morning and resumed the consideration
of this cause who say they cannot agree and by consent of
the parties and with leave of the court a miss trial is entered in this cause and the defendant is ordered to Jail
and thare to be safely kept until he be discharged by due
cause of leave and the order made at the last term of this
Court for the defendant to give security is received.

The State   )
     vs   )   The attorney General reported to Court
Isaah Woodall   )   the plantiffs Bill of cost which was
                            ordered to be recorded and taxed in
                            the bill of cost the State Detter to
Thomas T. Davis for bording 12 Jurors six meals each at
Twenty five cents each per meal making - - - $18.00

and to lodging said Jury three nites at twelve and a half
cents each Juror for each night $4.50

Making in all the sum of $22.50

(P-395)
     Sworn to in open Court this 1st day of
July, 1842.

                    Thomas T. Davis

                    Henry Price, Clerk

     Indictment Larceny ---

The State   )
     vs   )   Came the defendant into open Court
Isaah Woodall   )   and acknowledged himself indebted
                           to the State of Tennessee in the Sum
                           of one thousand dollars to be levied
of his goods and chattles lands and tenement yet to be void
on Condition he make his personal appearance before the
Judge of our next Circuit Court to be held for the County
of Bradley at the Court house in Cleveland on Wednesday
after the 4th Monday of April next & before said Court answer
a charge of the State Exhibited against him by Indictment
for Larceny and not depart the Court with out leave.

The State   )
     vs   )

Isaac Woodall &)
David Bingham   )

State of Tennessee   )   To any lawful officer of said
)   County, Greeting: Silas M. Wann
Bradley County   )   makes oath before me
                           James A. Hain, one of the Jus-
                           tices of the Peace for said
County and saith that some time between the 20th of June
and the 15th of July 1839, he had a Bee gum alias Bee skep
Stolen from his bee bunch in said County and that he has
reasons to suspect and does suspect David Bingham & Isaah
Woodall for feloniously stealing taking and carrying away
these are tharefore in the name of the State to command
you to apprehend and bring the   (P-396)   Bodys of the
aforesaid David Bingham & Isaah Woodall and bring them or
either of them before me to answer the aforesaid complaint
and to be further delt with as the law directs.

        Given under my hand and seal this
          22nd day of October 1840.

                        James A. Hain (Seal)
                            Justice of the Peace

        Executed by Iresting the Body of David Bigham and
Brought before Joseph Mee, Esqr. on the 22nd of October
1840, and Woodall, not arrested because confined in the
Jail of this County.

                        J. R. Wells,
                            Constable.

        Indictment --

STATE OF TENNESSEE   )   Circuit Court
)
BRADLEY COUNTY   )   December Term, Eighteen
                                hundred and forty

The grand Jurors in behalf of the State of Tennessee elected
empanneled sworn and charged to enquire for the body of the
County of Bradley aforesaid upon their oath present that a
Certain David Bigham, late of said County labourer -- on the
fifteenth day of July In the year of our Lord one thousand
Eight hundred and thirty nine with force and armes in the

County of Bradley aforesaid one Bee Stand of the value of
fifty cents good and lawful money of the State of Tennessee
and sworn of Tame bees of the value of one dollar and fifty
cents good and lawful money of the State of Tennessee and
one pint of honey in the comb of the value of Twenty five
cents good and lawful Money of the State of Tennessee The
whole of the value of two dollars and twenty five cents
good and lawful money of the State of Tennessee and of the
United States and them being (P-397)   the goods and
chattles of me Silas M. Wann, feloniously did steal take
and carry away from and out of the possession of the said
Silas M. Wann contrary to the form of the State in such
case made and provided and against the Peace and dignity
of the State.

                    Samuel Frazier, Attorney
                         For the 3rd Solicitorial District.

The State   )
    vs   )   Silas M. Wann
Davis Bigham   )   Prosecutor

    Silas M. Wann, John Eastman, Elizabeth Eastman, Wit-
nesses for the State sworn in open Court and sent before
the Grand Jury, January the 1st, 1841 .

                    Henry Price, Clerk

      Friday 1st January, 1841

The State   )   Indictment --
    vs   )
David Bigham   )   Larceny --

            The attorney General for the 3rd Sol-
icatorial District, Comes to prosecute on behalf of the
State and the Defendant is brought to the Bar of the Court
in Custody of the Sheriff of Bradley County and being arranged and charged on said Bill of Indictment pleads not guilty
to the same and for his Trial puts himself upon the County and
the attorney General doth the like and by consent this cause
is continued till next term as on affidavit of the defendant
and the defendant is remained to Jail thare to be safely kept
untill he find Securities him self in the sum of five hundred
Dollars and his surities each the sum of two hundred and fifty
dollars.

Saturday 2nd, January, 1841

The State   )
     vs   )   The Attorney General comes to prose-
David Bigham   )   cute on behalf of the State and Silas
                          M. Wann   (P-398)   Comes into Court
                   and acknowledges himself Indebted to
the State of Tennessee in the sum of two hundred and fifty
dollars to be levied of his goods chattles lands and tenements but to be void on conditions that he make his personal appearance before the Judge of the Circuit Court at a
Court to be held for the County of Bradley at the Court
house in Cleveland on the 4th Monday of April next and against
the defendant for a Larceny and not depart the Court without
leave.

          Larceny - Stealing a Bee hive.

State   )
     vs   )   The attorney General comes to prose-
David Bigham   )   cute in behalf of the State and the
)   defendant is brought to the Bar of the
                          Court in custody of the Sheriff of
Bradley County and the said David Bigham and his securities
James A. Bates & George W. Price acknowledged them selves
indebted to the State of Tennessee.

     That is to say the defendant David Bigham in the sum
of five hundred dollars and the said James A. Bates and
George W. Price, jointly and severly in the sum of Five
hundred dollars to be levied of their goods chattles lands
and tenements but to be void on conditions that the said
David Bigham make his personal appearance before the Judge
of the Circuit Court at a Court to be held for the County of
Bradley at the Court House in Cleveland on the 4th Monday of
April next on the 3rd day of said term and answer a charge
of the State against him for petit larceny and not depart the
Court with out leave.

          Larceny --

The State   )   Came the Attorney General who prose-
     vs   )   cutes for the State and this cause is
David Bigham   )   Continued until the next term   ((P-399)
                          of this Court as of affidavit of De-
                          fendant and thare upon came David Big-
ham and James A. Bates & George W. Price who acknowledges
themselves indebted to the State of Tennessee as follows to
wit:

     The said David Bigham in the sum of five hundred dol-
lars and the said James A. Bates & George W. Price jointly

in the sum of five hundred dollars to be levied of their
respective goods and chattles lands and tenements but to
be void on conditions the said David Bigham shall make his
personal appearance before the Judge of the Circuit Court
at the Court house in Cleveland on the first Wednesday after
the first Monday in August next, there and then answer a
charge of the State exhibited against him for Larceny and
not depart the Court without leave of the Court.

State	)	James A. Bates one of the Securetys
vs	)	for the defendant appears in open
David Bigham	)	Court and surrendered the defendant in
		discharge of his said recognizance

which was accordingly taken and ordered
into the Custody of the Sheriff and was also taken accordingly.

State	)	
vs	)	Came the State by her Attorney Gen-
David Bigham	)	eral who prosecutes for this solici-
		torial District and the Defendant is
		brought to the Bar in Custody of the

Sheriff and this cause is continued until tomorrow morning
on affidavit of the defendant.

Ordered that the defendant be remaned to Jail.

State	)	
vs	)	Came the Attorney General who prose-
David Bigham	)	cutes on part of the State and by
		leave of the Court enters a Nole pro-
		sequi in this cause.

(P-400)   Larceny --

State	)	
vs	)	Came the attorney General who prose-
David Bigham	)	cutes for the State and the defendant
		being brought to the Bar in Custody of
		the Sheriff and this Cause is contin-

ued till next term of this Court on affidavit of the Attorney General ordered that the defendant be remanded to Jail
and thare safely kept until he gives security in the sum
of Five hundred dollars with two or more securitys Jointly in the sum of five hundred dollars or until he be discharged by due cause of Leave.

State   )
    vs   )   The State Dr. to Thomas T. Davis
David Bigham   )   Jailer of Bradley County for bording
                       the defendant in Jail from the 23rd
                       of October 1840, until the 2nd day of
January, 1841, making in all 72 days at 37½ cents per day
Twenty seven dollars $27.00 to 4 Turn keys at 50 cents each
2.00

      Sworn to in open Court this the 2nd day of
         September, 1841.

              Henry Price, Thomas T. Davis.

The State   )
   vs   )   Si Fa
David Bigham   )
)   This day came the attorney General
                 who prosecutes for the State and the
                 defendant in his own proper person
and the forfeiture here to fore taken in this cause is set
aside and the defendant together with George W. Price, who
confessed Judgment for the cost.

      It is therefore considered by the Court that the State
of Tennessee recover of the defendant and George W. Price
all costs in this behalf for which Execution may Issue.

     A Bond

      Know all men by these presents that we George W. Cate
are jointly and severly   (P-401)   held and firmly bound
unto William Cate in the penal sum of two hundred and fifty dollars to be void on conditions that the said George
W. Cate will with effect prosecute a suite by action of
Tresspass on the case that he this day commenced against
the said William Cate and his wife Sarah Cate in the Circuit Court for Bradley County or in case of failure of such
prosecution pay and satisfy all costs and damages as may
be awarded against him by our said Court.

      Witness our hands and seals this 14th day of Decem-
ber, 1840.

                   G. W. Cate   (Seal)

                   John Mount   (Seal)

Test

Henry P ---   Writ ---

State of Tennessee,

         To the Sheriff of Bradley County, Greeting:

     You are hereby commanded to summons William Cate and Sarah Cate his wife if to be found in your County to appear before our Circuit Court to be holden for the County of Bradley at the Court House in Cleveland on the 4th Monday in December, next, to answer George W. Cate of a plea of Tresspass on the case for defamatory words spoken against his wife to his damage One Thousand dollars.

     Here in fail not and have you then and thare this writ

     Witness Henry Price, Clerk of our said Court at office in Cleveland the 4th Monday of August 1840, and of American Independence the 65th.

         Henry Price, Clerk.

George W. Cate vs William Cate & Sarah Cate	Issude December, the 14th 1840. Executed by summoning William Cate & Sarah Cate on the 17th December 1840.

         A. H. Pitner,
           Depty Sheriff

(P-402)   Tuesday 31st, August, 1840.

George W. Cate vs William Cate & Sarah Cate	Came the parties in their own proper persons and the Plantiff Dismisses his said suit and the Defendant confesses Judgment for the Caust.

     It is therefore considered by the Court of his suit for which Execution may Issue.

To the Honorable Charles F. Keith, Judge of the
3rd Jucial District of Tennessee.

By your petitioner Calvin Lutey a citizen of the County of Bradley respectfully represents to your honor that
a Judgement was rendered against him in favor of one Humphrey Robinson, on the day of — — 1840. By one Samuel
George, Esqr. for ten dollars and costs.

Your petioner prayed an appeal from said Judgement on
the day of the Trial which was granted by said Justice and
your petitioner gave bond and security for the prosecution
of his said appeal according to the requirements and di-
rections of said Justice your petioner further states that
said Justice not in the standing he has ben requested to do
so has wholly failed and refused to return the papers in
said cause to Court as required by act of assembly in such
case made and provided and says he is directed by the plantiff to Isue Execution against your petitioner on Judgement.

And now may it please your Honor to show that injustice
has been done your petitioner he respectfully states that
he contracted with the said Humphry Robinson for about
seventy bushels of corn or more if he chose to take it,
that the day appointed for petitioner to attend by being
unable to obtain a   (P-403)   waggon a few days afterwards he went to the plantiff when he was to receive the
corn with a waggon to haul it away but the corn was so
much damaged that your petitioner would not receive it and
returned home with his waggon empty, Afterwards petitioner
was sued by plantiff for refuseing to take damaged corn
when his contract was for good corn as was well understood
at the time of makeing. And Judgement is unjust and ap-
pressive.

Thare fore your petitioner considered himself injured
and aggreived and prays your honor to order that writs
of Certiorari and supersedias to Issue to remove the proceedings in said cause to the Circuit Court of Bradley
County at its next Term that a new trial may be had and
Justice done your petitioner and that all further proceedings in said cause be in the meantime stayed and super-
ceeded.

This is the first application for said writs.

Sworn to in open Court this 2nd day of January, 1841.

Calvin S. Lutey

Henry Price,
Clerk.

Know all men by these presents that we, Calvin S. Luty, David Luty all of the County and State of Tennessee our heirs executors and adminstrators are held and firmly bound unto Humphrey Robinson his heirs executors adminstrators assignes in the sum of One Hundred and twenty five dollars to be void on conditions that the said Calvin Lutey shall prosecute with effect a writ Certiorari by him this day obtained to remove the proceedings of a suit where in Humphry Robinson is plantiff and Calvin S. Luty is defendant from Samuel George, Esquire, into our Circuit Court for the County of Bradley, or in case of failure thare in perform what ever Judgement   (P-404)   shall be awarded and rendered by said Court in said Cause or in case said certiorari shall be dismissed by said Court for informality or want of sufficient substance or for any other cause pay and satisfy such Judgement as the Court shall award or shall have given against him.

Witness our hands and seals this the 23rd day of April, 1841.

Calvin S. Luty (Seal)

David Luty (Seal

State of Tennessee,

To Samuel George, one of the acting Justices of the peace for the County of Bradley, Greeting: Where as Humphry Robinson complained of and recovered a Judgement against Calvin S. Luty, before you and we for certain reasons being desirous that the record of that suit should be certified to us do hereby command you to enclose all the papers relative to said suit under your hand and seal distinctly and plainly together with this writ and transmit the same to a Court to be held by the Judge of the Circuit Court of law the County of Bradley at the Court house in Cleveland on the 4th Monday in April, 1841, in order that our said Court may do therein want of right and according to law ought to be done.

Witness Henry Price, Clerk of our said Court at office in Cleveland on the 4th Monday of December, A. D. 1840, and of American Independence the 65th.

Henry Price, Clerk
By James Lauderdale

Humphry Robinson   )   I, Samuel George, one of the
        vs   )   acting Justices of the Peace

Calvin Luty   )   in and for Bradley County do here by
                  ----- all the papers now in my posses-
                  sion or office in the above mentioned
                  suit given under my hand and seal.

This the 24th day of April, 1841.

Samuel George,
Justice of the Peace

(P-405)
Bill of Caust Constable Atkinson Howard

Serving Warrant	"	"	"	.50
Summoning Witnesses	"	"	"	.75
Judgement By Samuel George	"	"	"	.25
				$1.50

Humphry Robinson   )
    vs   )   Calvin S. Luty presents his pe-
Calvin Luty   )   tition for writ of Certiorari
                      and supersedas in this cause sworn
                      to in open Court which is granted
ordered that said writs Issue agreeably to the prayer of
the petitioner on his giving bond and securety which is
directed to be taken by the Clerk.

Monday April Term, 1841.

Hunphrey Robinson   )
    vs   )   The plantiff by his attorney
Calvin S. Luty   )   appears on motion a rule is
                      granted him to show cause why
                      the defendants writs of cer-
tiorari and supercedas should be dismissed.

Humphry Robinson   )
    vs   )   Came the parties by their attor-
Calvin S. Luty   )   neys and came on for argument
                      the Rule hereto fore entered
                      in this cause it being fully
understood by the Court It is ordered by the Court that the
rule entered heretofore entered in --- cause be discharged

Humphry Robinson)   Came the parties by their Attorneys
vs)   and by consent this cause is con-
Calvin S. Luty)   tinued, till next Monday.

Humphry Robinson)
vs)   Certiorari
Calvin S. Luty)

   Came the parties in their own
proper persons and the plantiff
dismisses his suit and the defendant confesses Judgement for the   ----

It is thare fore considered by the Court that the
plantiff recover   (P-406)   of the Defendant the cost
of this suit so confessed as aforesaid for which Execution may Issue.

To the Honeable Charles F. Keith, Judge &c.

Your petitioner William Cate, a citizen of Bradley
County Represents to your Honor that some time in the
month of November as your petitioner now recollects he
alterd an adminstration sale of the personal property of
Robert Cate, deceased the said Robert was the Son of your
petitioner and he was anctious to make the said property
bring as much as possible your Petitioner States thare
was a valuable yoke of steers put up to sell at said sale
and your petitioner haveing given said Steers to his Son
Robert in his life time and being well acquainted with
them he knew they were valuable and your petitioner at
said sale bid the sum of Sixty dollars for said Steers
after the said sale was over and your petitioner demanded
the Steers before he would give his note the Widow of Robert Cate refused to give up said Steers saying she had a
Saw mill and could not get along with out them your Petitioner then states that he could get out of paying for
them that he did not want them much as she seemed anxious
to keep them Matilda Cate the Widow and Isaac Day was the
adminstraters of said estate he then went to Isaac Day
and he told your petitioner that I should never pay for
the Steers but requested your petitioner to give his note
for the Sixty dollars   (P-407)   the amount of said
Steers stateing at the same time he only wanted your Petitioners note to settle with the Court and that when
that was done he would return said note to your Petitioner
without his paying any thing the matters so went on from
time to time and Isaac Day still promiseing send his note

to him untill some time in the month of July last an officer came to the house of your petitioner with a warrant and notified your petitioner to attend Trial before
one --- Francisco a Justice of the Peace for Bradley
County upon said Note in the name of Isaac Day & Matilda
Cate for themselves or for the use of John Collins and
Judgement was rendered as your Petitioner was informed
for the sum of Sixty dollars besides Intrust and costs
your Petitioner States that said Judgement is Wholey unjust and ---- your petitioner that he never received any
consideration for said note that the Adminstrators of said
estate refused to let your petitioner have said Stears for
which said note was given and they have kept said Stears
ever since and have worked them two years or thare abouts
untill they are worth but little and they have taken this
advantage to both keep the Stears and get their value your
petitioner would have appealed but was not able to attend
the Trial from bad health untill it was to late to take
an appeal and as the same is wholly unjust he prays your
honor to grant him your least gracious writs of Certiorari supersedeas dirrect to   (Pages 408 & 409 are Blank)
(P-410)   Francisco, a Justice of the Peace for Bradley
to bring in to the first Circuit Court for said County all
the proceeding in said cause and supersedings directed
Charles Price constable to desist from all further proceedings upon the Execution so that Justice may be done in the
prineses this is the first application for writs and he
prays they may be granted.

STATE OF TENNESSEE   )   Personally appeard before Charles
)   F. Keith, Judge &c. William
BRADLEY COUNTY   )   Cate and made oath that the facts
                              set forth in the foregoing pe-
                              tition thare are of his own knowl-
edge are true, and thare from information he believes to be
true.

    Subscribed same before*this 13th day of August, 1840.

              Charles F. Keith &c.

State of Tennessee Gent ---

        To the Clerk of the Circuit Court of Bradley
County in their Judicial Circuit let writs of Certiorari
and supersedeas Issue agreeable to the prayer of the foregoing petition on the Petitioner giving bond and security as
the law directs.

Given under my hand this 31st day of August, 1840.
*me

Charles F. Keith, Judge
of the 3rd Judicial Circuit

        Know all men by these presents that We William Cate,
and William D. Benton of Bradley County and State of Tennessee, our heirs executors and adminstrators are held and
firmly Bound unto Isaac Day & Matilda Cate, Heirs, executors,adminstrators or assigns in the sum of One hundred
and Thirty Dollars to be void on conditions that the said
William Cate shall prosecute with effect a writ of Certiorari by him this day obtained to remove the proceedings
(P-411)   of a suit wherein Isaac Day and Matilda Cate,
Adminstrators are plantiff and William Cate is defendant
before Benjamin Francisco a Justice of the peace into our
Circuit Court for the County of Bradley or in case of failure thare in perform what ever Judgement shall be awarded
and rendered by said Court in said Cause or in case said
Certiorari shall be dismissed by said Court or in formality
or want of sufficient substance or for any other cause
pay and satisfy such Judgement as the Court shall have giv-
en against him.

        Witness our hands and seals this 24th day of September
1840.

                        his
                William X Cate   (Seal)
                        mark

                William D. Benton   (Seal)

James Lauderdale,

State of Tennessee,

                To Chas J. Price, Constable of the County
of Bradley Greeting: You are hereby commanded that from
all other proceedings upon a judgement that Matilda Cate,
Adminstrator and Isaac Day, Adminstrator of Robert Cate,
Deceased for the use of John Collins, lately obtained a
Judgment against William Cate before Benjamin Francisco
one of the Justices of the Peace in and for Bradley County
you desist and all together supercede as the same by our
Writ of certiorari is removed to our Circuit Court of Brad-
ley County and you are hereby commanded to notify the said
Matilda Cate adms. and Isaac Day admr's of Robert Cate,De-
ceased for the use of John Collins to appear before the
Judge of our Circuit Court at a Court to be held for the
County aforesaid at the Court House in Cleveland on the 4th
Monday of December next then and thare to answer William
Cate in the said suit and have you then and thare this writ

        Witness Henry Price, Clerk of our said Court at office

in Cleveland the 4th Monday of August, 1840, and of American Independence, the 64th.

Henry Price, Clerk.

Issude Septr. 25th, 1840, by James Lauderdale.

Isaac Day & Matilda Cate   )
        vs   )
William Cate   )

Executed and returned as the law directs this 25th of December, 1840.

C. J. Price,
Constable

(P-412)
State of Tennessee,

To Benjamin Francisco, one of the Justices of the Peace in and for the County of Bradley, Greeting:

Whare as Isaac Day, Adminstrator and Matilda Cate, Adm'rs of Robert Cate, Deceased, for the use of John Collins, lately complained of and recovered a Judgement against Wm. Cate before you andwwe for certain reasons being desirous that the records of that suit should be certified to us do here by command you to enclose all the papers relative to said suit under your hand and seal distinctly and plainly together with this writ and transmit the same to a Court to be held by the Judge of the Circuit Court of law and equity for the County of Bradley at the Court House in Cleveland on the 4th Monday of December next in order that our said Court may do tharein what of right and according to law ought to be done.

Witness Henry Price, Clerk of our said Court at office in Cleveland, the 4th Monday August, 1840, and of American Independence the 64th.

Henry Price,
Clerk

Isude Sept. 25th, 1840.

By James Lauderdale.

Isaac Day & Matilda Cate,	)	Came Levi Trewhitt
Administrators of Robert Cate	)	Attorney for Plan-
Deceased for the use of	)	tiff and suggests
John Collins	)	the death of John
vs	)	Collins which was
William Cate	)	not denied.

Isaac Day, Adm. & Matilda Cate,	)	The death of John Col-
adm. of Robert Cate, deceased	)	lins haveing here to
for the use of	)	fore been suggested
William Cathey	)	By motion of Levi Trew-
vs	)	hitt, Attorney for
William Cate	)	plantiff this suit is
		revived in the name
		of Isaac Day the Adm.

of John Collins, Deceased.

Isaac Day & Matilda Cate	)	Certiorari
Adm for the use of Isaac	)	
Day, Adm of John Collins	)	This day came on for
Deceased	)	Argument
vs	)	
William Cate	)	The suit here to entered
		in this cause and after
		argument of Council, It

is considered by the Court that the rule be made absolute
and the writs of certiorari and supersedeas be dismissed.

Know all men by these presents that we, Michael Hilter-
Brand, Robert W. Duggan, are jointly and severly held and
firmly bound unto Silas M. Wann & David Melton, in the
Penal sum of two Hundred and fifty dollars, to be void on
condition that the said Michael HilderBrand will with
effect prosecute a suit by action of Tresspass on the case
which he this day commenced against the said Silas M. Wann
& David Melton in the Circuit Court for Bradley County or
in case of failure of such prosecution pay and satisfy all
costs and damages as may be awarded against him By our said
Court.

Witness our hands and seals this 19th day of March, 1840.

Teste --   )   Michael Helterbrand (Seal)
Henry Price   )   Robert W. Duggan (Seal)

State of Tennessee,

        To the Sheriff of Bradley County, Greeting:

        You are hereby commanded to summons Silas M.
Wann and David Melton if to be found in your County to
appear before our Circuit Court to be holden for the County
of Bradley at the Court House in Cleveland on the fourth
Monday of April, next, to answer Michael Helderbrand, assignee of Joseph Cookston of a plea of Tresspass on the
case to his damage one Thousand Dollars.

        Herein fail not have you then and thare this writ.

        Witness Henry Price, Clerk, of our said Court at office
in Cleveland the 4th Monday of December, 1839, and of American Independence the 64th.

                    Henry Price, Clerk

Michael Heldebrand   )
        vs   )   Issude 19th March, 1840.
Silas M. Wann &   )
David Duggan   )   Came to hand the 1st
                             Febuany, 1840.

        Execution by summoning Silas M. Wann and David Melton
the 6th of April, 1840.

                    James Lauderdale
                    Sheriff

STATE OF TENNESSEE   )   Circuit Court
)
BRADLEY COUNTY   )   Court

        April Term, 1840.

        Michael Heldebrand, Assignee of Joseph Cookston, by
his attorney complains of Silas M. Wann, and David Melton
summond to answer &c. of a plea of Tresspass on the case
that whare as the defendants on the 16th day of February
1839, at the County of Bradley, aforesaid Executed and delivered to the said Joseph Cookston, their promisary note

in writing of that date signed with their proper names
and to their Court have now shewed by which the said defendants promised against the 1st day of February, 1839.
the date of said promisory note to pay the said Joseph
Cookston, Six hundred and Sixty five dollars in current
Bank note for value received in consideration that the
said Joseph Cookston had before that time sold and delivered to the said defendants goods wares and merchandize
of great value to wit of the value of Six hundred & Sixty
five dollars as a fore said and at the request of the said
defendants and the said Plantiff in fact says that the
aforesaid sum of Six hundred and sixty five dollars in Current Bank notes on the first day of December next after the
16th day of February 1839, was of great value to wit of the
value of Six hundred and Sixty five dollars   (P-415)
in the Current coin of the United States of America and
afterwards to wit on the 21st day of February 1839, and before the said promissary note fell due the said Joseph
Cookston, assigned and transfered the said promissory note
in writing his own proper signature being thare to subscribed for a valuable consideration to the plantiff herein
and which said assignment is all so to the Court here now
showed and of which said assignment the defendants at the
County aforesaid had notice yet there after requested the
defendants have not yet paid to the plaintiff the said sum
of Six hundred and Sixty five dollars in Current Bank notes
or any part thare of as above mentioned but wholy fail and
refuse so to do to the damage of one thousand dollars and
thare upon he sues pledges &c.

Thos J Campbell
Attorney

And the said defendants Comes and defends the wrong and
injury, When &c. and for plea says the said Plantiff his
action aforesaid ought not to have maintain against them
because they say that they did not assume and undertake
in manner and form as the said plantiff in his declaration
hath alledged and of this they put them selves upon the
County.

Trewhitt,
Attorney

And the Plantiff
   likewise

Campbell,
Attorney for Plantiff

Michael Helderbrand   )
     vs   )   The parties by their
Silas M. Wann & David Melton)   attorneys appeared and

by consent this cause is continued untill the next term.

(P-416)
Monday August, 23rd 1841.

Michael Helderbrand)
   assignee of Joseph Cookston)
     vs) Came the parties by
Silas M. Wann &) their attorneys and
David Melton) thare upon came a
                                  Jury of good and law-
                                  ful men citizens of
Bradley County to wit Jeremiah Dearing, Joseph Carson, George
T. Parker, Thomas Lowery, James Britton, Burk Prady, James E.
Walker, George W. Cate, Joseph L. Swan, Edward George, Isaac
Martin and Henry Bower, who being elected and sworn to will
and truly try the Isue Joined between the parties upon their
oath aforesaid do say the defendants did assume and undertake
in manner and form as the Plaintiff in chargeing hath alledged and assess the Plantiff damage by reason thereof to the
sum of Six hundred and sixty*dollars and thirty cents.

It is therefore considered by the Court that the plantiff recover of the defendants the said sum of Six hundred
and Sixty Eight dollars and thirty cents the damages afforesaid by the Jury afforesaid assessed in maner and form af-
fore said together with all costs in this behalf expended
for which an Execution may Issue.

Warrant   ---

STATE OF TENNESSEE) Summons
)
BRADLEY COUNTY) Edward Williams and William
                          Wiggins, to appear before some
                          Justice of the Peace for said
County to answer Levi Trewhitt and Thomas J. Campbell, for
the use of Euclid Waterhouse in lieu of debt due by note
under seal given under my hand and seal January 1st, 1840.

                                Sampson H. Prowell
                                  Justice of the Peace
                                  for Bradley County

(P-417)
Levi Trewhitt &) Issude January 1st, 1840
Thomas J. Campbell for)
the use of Euclid Waterhouse) Came to hand January 5th
*eight) 1840.

```
        vs              )   Executed by summoning the Defend-
Edward Williams &       )   ant the 17th of January, 1840, and
William Wiggins         )   set Trial on the 18th before Rob-
                            ert H. Pharris, James Brown, Depty
                            Sheriff
```

Judgement --

I, give Judgement in this cause for the plantiff against the defendant for one hundred dollars and cost of said suit this the 18th day of January, 1840.

                        Robert H. Pharris
                        Justice of the Peace

Appeal ---

In this cause

The defendant prayed an appeal to the next term of the Court for Bradley County which is granted. He haveing given Bond and securety as the law directs this 18th day of January, 1840.

Bond ---

```
STATE OF TENNESSEE     )   We bind our selves to Levi Trew-
                       )   hitt, Thomas J. Campbell for the
BRADLEY COUNTY         )   use of Euclid Waterhouse in the
                           Sum of two hundred and twenty
                           dollars if Wiggins or James Cath-
```
ey who has this day April to the next Circuit Court for Bradley County from a Judgement of Robert H. Phariss, a Justice of said County in favor of Euclid Waterhouse, against William Wiggins for one hundred dollars and cost of suit shall prosecute said appeal sufficiently or in case of failure shall comply with and perform the Judgements of said Court.

This the 18th day of January, 1840.

```
Robert Phariss                  )   William Wiggins  (Seal)
    A Justice of the Peace       )   James Cathey     (Seal)


Levi Trewhitt &                 )   The parties by their attorneys
T. J. Campbell &                )   appeared & this cause is con-
Euclid Waterhouse               )   tinued till next term   (P-418)
    vs                          )
William Wiggins                 )
```

Levi Trewhitt &   )
T. J. Campbell for   )   Came the parties by their at-
Euclid Waterhouse   )   torneys and thare upon to try
    vs   )   the Brother of Contriveing
William Wiggins   )

                         Came a Jury to wit:

    John Roberts, Sampson H. Prowell, James A. Hair, John
Kinkanan, Gavin R. Humtoile, Joseph R. Mee, Isaac Huffaker,
James Campbell, Thomas Taylor, Benjamin Francisco, John
Igoe, John Hardwick all good and lawful men citizens of
Bradley County who being summond tried and sworn well and
truly to try the controversy in dispute upon their oath
do say they find for the plantiff assesses his damages to
one hundred and twenty dollars.

    It is therefore considered by the Court that the Plan-
tiff recover of the defendant the sum of one hundred twelve
dollars and all costs, and that Execution Issue to collect
the same.

    Debt ---

Levi Trewhitt &   )
T. J. Campbell for the   )   Came the Parties by their
use of Euclid Watterhouse)   Attorneys and thare upon
)   came on to be argued and
)   determined the Defendants
    vs   )   Rule heretofore entered
William Wiggins   for a new Trial and after
                             argument of Council and
mature deliberation of the Court It is considered by the
Court that said Rule be discharged and a new Trial refused
and on motion of the Plantiff by their attorney   (P-419)
It is further considered by the Court that the plantiff
recover of the Defendants and James Cathey their security
in their appeal Bond the sum of one hundred and twelve*by
the Jury and all costs for which Execution may Issue.

    Warrant ---

STATE OF TENNESSEE   )   To any lawful officer of said
)   County to execute and return
BRADLEY COUNTY   )
                     You are hereby commanded to
*dollars the damage heretofore found

summon William Humberd to appear before me or some other
Justice of the Peace for said County to answer the complaint of Jeremiah Johnson in a plea of debt under fifty
dollars due by note of hand

Given under my hand and seal

This 30th day of March, 1841.

James Mitchell,
Justice of the Peace

J. Johnson   )
    vs   )   Executed for trial before Esquire
Wm. Humberd   )   Howard on the 9th day of April, 1841.

James Donohoo, Depty Sheriff

Judgement   ---

Jeremiah Johnson   )
    vs   )   I give Judgement in this cause
William Humbered   )   for the defendant against the
                           Plantiff for Ten dollars 47 cents
                           the excess of Defendants claim
presented as a set off over that of Plantiff together with
that of the cost for which execution may Issue

This April the 9th, 1841.

Samuel Howard,
Justice of the Peace

From which Judgement Jeremiah Johnston demands an
appeal to the next Term of the Circuit Court, which is
granted him he haveing given Bond and security according to law.

April 12th, 1841

Samuel Howard,
Justice of the Peace

(P-420)
    We Bind our selves to William Humbered in the sum of
twenty one dollars to be void if Jeremiah Johnston who has
this day appealed to the next term of the Circuit Court
for Bradley County from a Judgement of Samuel Howard, a
Justice of the Peace of said County, in favor of William
Humberd against him for ten dollars 47 cents shall prosecute

said appeal sucessfully or in case of failure shall comply with and perform the Judgement of the Court

This April the 12th, 1841.

Jeremiah Johnston

Joseph E. Johnston

Arbitration ----

STATE OF TENNESSEE   )
)
BRADLEY COUNTY   )   Where as Jeremiah Johnston and
                                        William Humbered have refused
                                        to us as arbitrators all mat-
ters in dispute between them in relative to a suit now
in the Circuit Court accounts the occupiing and the clear-
ing up land to determine the same and we haveing suit at
the Court house in Bradley County on the Thirtieth day of
October, 1841, and having heard all the matters alledged
and approved by them and after fully considering and under-
standing the whole matters do determine and award that
William Humbered shall have fourty one dollars for Clear-
ing and Cleaning up the amount of land, that the said William Humbered cultivated and thare accounts be equally
adjusted and that Jeremiah Johnston pay all costs accruing on said suit

Given under our hands and seals

This 30th day of October, 1841.

S. Prowell,

Edman Ramsey

Wm. B. Dearin

James Tucker &

Nicholas Hays.

(P-421)
Jeremiah Johnston   )
     vs   )   Came the parties by their
William Humbered   )   Attorneys and also in Proper
                                   person & by consent only ---

and the   is warned and the plantiff argus Judgement may
be entered against him for Eleven dollars and fifty cents.

It is tharefore considered by the Court that the defendant recover of the Plantiff the sum of Eleven dollars
and fifty cents and all costs and that he have Execution
may Issue.

―――――――――――
―――――――――

Bond ---

Know all men by these presents that we, McClung, Wallace & Co. & Thomas C. Lyon are Jointly and severely held
and firmly bound unto F. W. Earnest, George E. Mountcastle
& one Wm. J. Johnston in the penal sum of two hundred and
fifty dollars to be void on condition that the said Earnest
Mountcastle and Johnston in the Circuit Court for Bradley
County, otherwise to pay and satisfy all costs that may be
awarded for failure.

Witness our hands and seals

This 5th day of August, 1840.

McClung, Wallace & Co.
By Thomas C. Lyon.

State of Tennessee,

To the Sheriff of Bradley County, Greeting: You are
hereby commanded to summons Felix W. Earnest, as the Sheriff of McMinn County, has been commanded to summons George
E. Mountcastle and William J. Johnston To appear before the
Judge of the Circuit Court to be held for the County of
Bradley at the Court house in Cleveland, on the 4th Monday
of August next to answer Mathew McClung, Campbell Wallace
& Hugh L. McClung, Merchants trading in pardnership under
the name of McClung, Wallace & Co. of a plea that they render unto them the sum of One hundred   (P-422)   and forty
nine dollars which they owe to them and unjustly detain from
them to their damage One hundred dollars here in fail not
and have you them and thare this summons

Witness Henry Price, Clerk of our said Court at office
in Cleveland the 4th Monday in April, 1840.

Henry Price, Clerk.

McClung, Wallace & Co.   )
          vs   )   Issude August 6th, 1840.
Felix W. Earnest   )
                               Came to hand August 7th and
                               Summond Felix W. Earnest
the same day.

                    A. H. Pitner
                      Sheriff.

        State of Tennessee,

            To the Sheriff of McMinn County Greeting:

    You are hereby commanded to summons George E. Mount-
castle & William J. Johnston as the sheriff of Bradley
County has been commanded to summons Felix W. Earnest
to appear before the Judge of the Circuit Court to be
held for the County of Bradley at the Court House in
Cleveland on the 4th Monday of August, next, to answer
Mathew McClung, Campbell, Wallace and Hugh L. McClung, Merchants trading in pardnership under the name of McClung,
Wallace & Co. of a plea that they tender unto them the sum
of One hundred dollars,

    Here in fail not and have you then and thare this sum-
mons.

    Witness Henry Price, Clerk of our said Court at office
in Cleveland.

    The 4th Monday of August, 1840.

                Henry Price, Clerk.

    I certify that this is a counter part of an original
Summons Isshude from my office.

                Henry Price, Clerk.

    Came to hand August 10th, 1840. Summoned George W.
Mountcastle, August 11th, 1840. Came to hand the 17th
August, 1840.
                S. Beavers, Sheriff.

    Summons William J. Johnston, August the 18th, 1840.

                C. L. King,
                  Depty Sheriff.

(P-423)

STATE OF TENNESSEE	)	Circuit Court
	)	
BRADLEY COUNTY	)	December Term, 1840.

Mathew McClung, Campbell, Wallace and Hugh L. McClung, Merchants trading in pardnership under the name McClung, Wallace & Co. By Attorney, complain of Felix W. Earnest, George E. Mountcastle and William J. Johnston of a plea that they tender unto them the sum of one hundred and forty nine --- which they owe to them and from them unjustly detain.

For that were as heretofore to wit on the 24th day of February 1840, at to wit in Bradley County aforesaid the said F. W. Earnest by the style of F. W. Earnest, made and delivered his certain writen obligation signed and sealed when he promised one day after date for value received to pay to G. E. Mountcastle, meaning the said George E. Mountcastle the sum of one hundred and forty nine dollars and the said G. E. Mountcastle afterwards at to wit in the County aforesaid to wit on the day of --- 1840, by his indorsement on the Back of said Writing obligatory ordered and directed the same to be paid to the said William J. Johnston afterwards to wit on the --- 1840, at to wit in the said County endorsed the same by the name of John Johnston and thare in ordered directed the same to McClung, Wallace & Co.

The plaintiff here in which said writing now here to the Court shown never the less The said defendants nor either of them although often requested have not yet paid the said sum above mentioned and demanded or any part thare of but to pay the same have hither to wholly failed and refused and do still refuse to the damage of the plantiffs ---- dollars Where upon they sue and C.

Thomas C. Lyon, Attorney
for Plantiff.

(P-424)

And the said Defendant by their Attorneys Come and defend the rong and injury when and soforth and say that the said declaration and the matters thare in contained in manner and form as the same are a leave stated and set forth are not sufficient in law for the said Plantiffs to have or maintain thare aforesaid action thareof against them the said defendants and that the said defendants are not Bound by law to answer the same and this they are ready to veryfy wharefore for want of sufficient declaration in this behalf they the said Defendants pray a Judgement and that the said Plantiffs may be bound for having not mantained thare aforesaid action against them &c.

Rawls, Attorney for
Defendants

Amended Declaration ---

STATE OF TENNESSEE) Circuit Court
)
BRADLEY COUNTY) August Term, 1841

McClung, Campbell, Wallace & Hugh L. McClung, Merchants
Trading in Pardnership Trading under the name of McClung,
Wallace & Co. By Attorney complain of Felix W. Earnest, (G
George E. Mountcastle & Wm. J. Johnston, who have been
summoned by the Sheriff of a Plea that they render unto
them the sum of One hundred and forty nine dollars which
they owe to them and from unjustly detained. For that
whareas heretofore to wit on the 24th day of February,1840.
At to wit in Bradley County aforesaid the said Defendant
Felix W. Earnest by the name and style of Felix W. Earnest
(P-425) made his certain writing obligatory signed with
his name as aforesaid and sealed with his seal wherein he
Bound himself one day after date for value Received to pay
to the said Mountcastle by the name of G. E. Mountcastle,
one hundred and forty nine dollars and then and thare delivered the same to said Mountcastle and the said Mountcastle aforesaid endorsed his name thare on by the style
of G. E. Mountcastle and then and there by ordered and appointed the contents thare of to be paid to the said Defendant Wm. J. Johnston for value Received and then and thare
delivered the same and the said Wm. J. Johnston to whom the
said writing so made payable afterwards to wit on the ---
& year last aforesaid in the County aforesaid for value Received indorsed his name thare on and then and thare by the
Style of Wm. J. Johnston ordered and appointed the contents
thereof to be paid to the & which is now herewith the said
endorsement shown to the Court said plantiffs by the name
of McClung, Wallace & Co. and afterwards to wit on the ---
day of February, 1840, when said writing became due & payable according to its tenor and effect the same was duly
---- to the same defendant Felix W. Earnest and payment
thereof demanded according to its tenor and the said Defendant, Earnest, then and thare failed and refused to pay
the same or any part thareof of all which the said Defendants had due notice wherefore and by force of the stature
in such case provided on action has occurd to the said
Plantiffs to have and demand of said Defendants the said
sum in said writing specified to geather with all legal
(P*426) Intrust and damages never the less the said Defendants although often requested have not paid the said
sum of One hundred and forty nine dollars or any part
thereof, but to pay the same have heretofore wholly failed

and refused and do still refuse to the damage of the Plantiffs One hundred dollars and there fore they sue &c.

T. C. Lyon, Attorney for Plantiff

And the said Defendants by their Attorney Came and defend the wrong and injury where and when and say that the said plantiffs ought not to have and mantain their aforesaid action thereof against them because they say that they will &c. truly Paid the debt in the Plantiffs decleration mentioned by before the say out of the original writ in this cause and of this they put their selves on the County.

Rawles, Atty for Defendant

And the Plantiff also
    Lyons, Atty.

McClung, Wallace & Co.)	Came Thomas C. Lyon, Esqr.
vs)	Attorney for Plantiff, and
George E. Mountcastle)	by leave of the Court en-
Daniel Kenner,)	ters a Nolle Prosequi in
Wm. Johnson &)	this cause as to William
Wm. Britton)	Johnston and Daniel Keener

McClung, Wallace & Co.)	Came the Plantiffs by their
vs)	Attorney Spencer Jarnagin,
George E. Mountcastle)	Esqr. and by leave of the
Daniel Keener)	Court enters a Nolle Prose-
Felix W. Earnest)	qui as to George E. Mount-
Gustavis Barrum &)	Castle (P-427) Dan-
Wm. J. Johnston)	iel Kenner & Wm. J. Johnston
	also leave is granted him to
	amend his writ and Declara-

tion by striking out George T. Barrum and inserting Gustavis T. Barum and time is given defendant to plead so as not to delay trial.

McClung, Wallace & Co.)	Came the parties by their
vs)	Attorneys and thare upon
George E. Mountcastle)	came a Jury to wit:
Wm. J. Johnston &)	
Felix W. Earnest)	John Roberts, Sampson H.
	Prowell, James A. Nair,
	John Kincannon, George R.

Hambrite, Joseph R. Mee, Isaac Huffaker, James Campbell, Thomas Taylor, Benjamin Francisco, John Igoe, John Hardwick all good and lawful men, Citizens of Bradley County who be-

ing summond elected and tried and sworn well and truly to
try the Issue Joined between the parties upon their oath
do say that the defendants hath paid the debt in the plantiffs decleration except the sum of One hundred and fifty
dollars and asses the damage to twelve dollars & ninety
nine cents.

It is therefore considered by the Court that the plantiff recover of the defendant the Sum of One hundred and
fifteen dollars debt and Twelve dollars and ninety nine
cents the damage so assessed as aforesaid and the costs of
suit and that he have his Execution.

Pages 428 - 429 - 430 are blank.

THE END

BRADLEY COUNTY

CIRCUIT COURT MINUTE BOOK B
1838-1841

NEW INDEX

NOTE: Page numbers in this index refer to those of the
original volume from which this copy was made. These numbers are carried throughout the copy within parenthesis.

Caney, John B., 91
Cannon & Jarnagin, 370
Cans, Fredrick A., 25
Carmichail, John B., 355,
*   357
Carr, Andrew, 262, 263, 264,
265
Carr, James, 343, 344
Carr, John, 360, 361
Carr, Samuel N., 388
Carr, William, 29
Carson, Joseph, 416
Carter, Hamilton, 109
Carter, John, 19, 95, 96, 97,
98, 99, 100, 113, 173
Carter, Levi, 81, 97
Carter, Malone, 266
*Carmichail, William, 355,
357
Carter, Robert, 13
Carter, Samuel, 266
Carter, Scion, 13
Cate, Charles, 27, 63, 64,
78, 120, 168, 179, 250,
310, 384, 385
Cate, George W., 19, 140, 173,
233, 400, 401, 402, 416
Cate, Hubbart (Hubberd), 315,
316, 317, 318, 322, 323,
324, 326, 327
Cate, John B., 78, 168, 179,
250
Cate, John I., 120
Cate, Matilda, 406, 407, 410,
*   411, 412
Cate, Samuel, 391
Cate, Sarah, 401, 402
Cate, William, 401, 402, 406,
410, 411, 412
Cathey, James, 417, 419
Cathey, S. B., 367
Cathey, Samuel B., 373
Cathey, William, 412
Chambers, J. M., 146, 148,
150, 157, 159, 161, 192,
195, 198, 201, 209
Chambers, John, 102, 141,
143, 237
Champon, William, 105
Cherokee Nation, 3
Childress, Anna, 49
Childress, Lemuel, 31, 32, 33,
34, 36, 38, 39, 41, 43,
*Cate, Robert, 406, 411, 412

44, 46, 48, 51, 53, 55
Childers (Childress), William,
30, 31, 32, 33, 34, 35,
36, 37, 38, 39, 40, 41,
42, 43, 44, 45, 46, 47,
48, 49, 50, 51, 52, 53,
54, 55, 56, 57, 61, 62,
63, 199, 200
Clark, Attorney, 93, 94
Clark, Daniel, 106, 132
Clark, David, 135
Clark, William, 118
Cleveland (Cleaveland), Eli,
368, 369, 371, 372
Cline, John, 274, 346
Cline, John L., 275, 276,
277, 278
Clingan, A. A., 10, 27,
114, 164, 348, 361,
380, 390
Clingan, Alexander A., 10,
57, 77, 96, 119, 253,
279, 346, 387
Cockram, John, 265, 266
Coe, Vernon, 113
Coffee, Joel, 293
Coffee, John T., 314
Coffel, Phillip, 347, 348
Coffman, Andrew, 96
Coker, William, 88, 207
Coleman, Absolom, 29, 69,
76, 153, 187, 191, 208,
230, 303, 337, 340
Colier, Erby, 393
Collins, Aron, 393
Collins, John, 301, 407,
411, 412
Colville, George, 333
Conner, Alfred, 257, 258,
259, 260
Cookston, Joseph, 413, 414,
415, 416
Coon, John, 299
Cooper, E. E., 78
Cooper, Edward, 279
Cooper, Elbert, 168
Cooper, Elbert E., 105, 120,
*   179, 250
Copeland, Alfred, 206, 207,
208
Copeland, John, 118, 207,
208
Couch, Sylvanas, 11, 12
*Copeland, A., 208

Elderage, Thos., 335
Elliott, John, 26
Ellison, Robert H., 19, 34,
    140, 233, 240, 242,243
Ervin, John, 113, 132
Esman, John, 287

Fain, Lewis R., 393
Farmer, James, 109
Farmer, Robert A., 19, 88,
    140, 173, 224, 233
Felts, William, 352, 353
Fen, Richard, 369, 370, 371,
    375, 376, 377
Fergerson (Fergison), Moses,
    259, 264
Fergerson, William, 287
Finley, James, 109
Fisher, Emoly, 124
Fisher, Noah, 34, 135, 140,
    233
Fitzgerald, John, 101, 118,
    185, 187, 188, 189, 190,
    193, 234, 235, 385
Fletcher, J. A., 102, 141,
    143, 145, 148, 150, 157,
    159, 161, 192, 195, 198,
    209, 237
Fletcher, James A., 21, 58,
    133, 212, 244, 247, 290,
    291
Ford, Berry, 247
Ford, Mordecai, 221
Forester, Andrew, 791
Forester, Justice, 65
Forester, William, 63, 64,
    67, 81, 114, 115, 118,
    119, 240, 241, 242, 243
Foreman, Samuel, 288
Forsyth, William, 172, 173
Foster, A. B., 79
Foster, Andrew B., 80, 183
Foster, Thomas, 79
Fouts, Soloman, 29, 69
Fox, Andrew, 239, 240
Francisco, Benjamin, 259,
    264, 407, 411, 412, 418,
    427
Frazier, Samuel, 25, 95, 109,
    113, 123, 127, 153, 164,
    166, 169, 170, 181, 183,
    185, 188, 204, 206, 217,

221, 234, 252, 255,257,
266, 279, 291, 294,296,
315, 317, 318, 320,322,
328, 341, 362, 364,365,
384, 386, 389, 391,392,
397
Freeman, E. H., 214
French, William, 92
French, William B., 92, 93,
    94
Fulks, John, 277, 301, 303,
    310, 320, 324, 337,340,

Gasaway, Henry, 294, 295
Gather, Hamilton H. 147,148
Gather, Hamilton H. B., 149
Gather, I. B., 148, 149
Gatlin, Guilford (Gilford),
    102, 141, 143, 145, 148,
    150, 157, 159, 161, 192,
    195, 198, 201, 209, 236,
    384, 386, 392
George, Edward, 416
George, Samuel, 347, 348,
    402, 403, 404, 405
Giddion, Samuel, 153
Gifford, John M., 102,141,
    142, 143, 145, 147,
    148, 149, 150, 157,
    201, 236
Gillespie, Charles K., 61,
    101, 102, 103, 121
Gillespie, J. F., 5, 149,
    264
Gillespie, Jas. F., 371
Gillespie, John F., 28, 80,
    119, 120, 121, 122, 123,
    149, 158
Gillian, William, 104, 105,
    106, 107, 108
Gilliland, William, 287
Glandon, Jacob, 384
Glandon, Isaac, 29, 69,
    118, 134, 135, 137,
    138, 139, 140, 285
Glass, John G., 162, 163,
    210, 301, 302, 303,
    304, 334, 335, 336,
    337
Glass, Lewis A., 197, 198,
    199, 200
Goodner, John, 92, 94, 277,
    301, 310

Goodwin, Lucion, 259
Gordin, A., 384
Grant, Abagail (Mrs.), 81,
    84
Grant, John, 81, 84
Grant, William, 21, 24, 26,
    133, 182, 183, 203, 204,
    207, 212, 216, 220, 221,
    226, 244, 247, 255, 256,
    257, 259, 266
Green, John, 287
Gregg, Abraham, 296
Griggsly, John, 116
Grimes, John, 266
Grimett, Alexander P., 322
Grimett, Herman, 293
Grimett (Grimmett), Hiram,
    107, 116, 129, 385
Grimett, Preston, 328, 329
Grisham, James, 367, 373,
    379
Grogan, W., 38, 40, 43, 45,
    47, 49, 50, 52, 54
Grogan, William, 31, 33, 35,
    62
Guinn, Alman, 266, 285
Guinn, Joshua, 91, 94, 293

Haggard, James, 91, 94, 101,
    118, 191, 208, 230, 252,
    324
Hagler, A. W., 33
Hagler, Abraham, 317
Hagler, Abraham H., 291, 316,
*   322, 324, 328, 329, 333,
Hain, James A., 395, 396
Hair, James A., 418
Hair, John, 265
Hair, John D., 262, 263
Hambright, Benjamin, 338,
    339, 340
Hambright, G. R., 166, 167
Hambright, George, 165,
Hambright, George R., 165,
    167, 427
Hammond, William, 17, 165,
    166, 338, 339, 340
Hannah, Hugh, 167
Hannah, John, 88, 324
Hannah, Thomas, 167
Hardwick, Charles, 88, 91
*Hagler, Abraham W., 319,
    320, 321

Hardwick, Charles F., 88,
    89, 90
Hardwick, John, 13, 14, 88,
    89, 90, 91, 269, 270,
    271, 324, 418, 427
Harland, David, 88, 89, 90,
    91
Harland, James, 163, 164,
    165
Harle, Balden, 252
Harris, Sims, 343, 344
Hawkins, Benjamin, 118,
    132, 172, 259, 264
Hawkins, James, 63, 224
Haydon, Thomas, 132
Hays (Hayse), John, 69,
    108, 109, 187, 206,
    392
Hays (Hayse), Nathaniel,
    214, 216, 388
Hays, Nicholas, 420
Hays, N. W., 81
Hays, William, 393
Haynes, George M., 63, 88,
    101
Heights, John, 235
Helderbrand, David, 88
Helderbrand (Helterbrand),
    Michael, 253, 413, 414,
    415, 416
Henerys, William, 250
Henry, James M., 333, 341
Henry, W. M., 78
Henry, William, 179
Henry, Wm., 168, 120
Hess, John, 106
Hicks, C. W., 158
Hicks, Carrington, 156, 157,
    158
Hicks (Hix), Joseph B., 316,
    317, 319, 326
Hodges, John, 105
Holmes, David, 287
Hood, Robert, 29, 63, 69,
    76, 113, 191, 208, 230,
    333
Hook, John A., 72, 75
Hooper, Andrew, 393
Horne, Hannah, 206
Horne (Horn), Riley, 206,
    207
Howard, Samuel, 95, 311*313,
    361, 362, 363, 367, 373,
    379, 419, 420   *312

Huffaker, Isaac, 64, 66, 132,
191, 208, 230, 310, 418,
427
Hughes, John, 29, 124, 125,
189, 193
Humberd, Wm., 419
Humbered, William, 419, 420,
421
Humphries, George W., 380,
381, 382, 383, 384
Humtoile, Gavin R., 418
Hutcherson (Hutchison), Elias,
21, 133, 244, 247

Igobright, Thomas, 244, 246
Igou (Igoe), John, 105, 114,
303, 310, 324, 333, 337,
418, 427
Igou (Igoe), Joseph L., 19,
140, 233
Irvin, John, 152, 196, 197

Jameson, Benjamin C., 241
Jarnagin, Attorney, 170
Jarnagin & Bradford, 5, 61,
90, 91, 177, 264, 276,
309, 310, 333, 337, 369,
375, 376, 378
Jarnagin & Cannon, 371
Jarnagin, S. 88, 92, 368,
374
Jarnagin, Spencer, 238, 276,
368, 374, 379, 426
Jenkins (Jinkens), Jameson,
316, 317, 319
Johnson(Johnston), Jeremiah,
419, 420, 421
Johnson, Veny, 279
Johnson, William, 170, 171
Johnston, Elam, 183
Johnston, John, 423
Johnston, Joseph E., 420
Johnston, Josiah, 277, 301,
303, 310, 324, 337,
340
Johnston, Thomas, 355
Johnston, William, 426
Johnston, William J., 421,
422, 423, 424, 425, 426,
427

Jones, John, 153, 154
Jones, Nathan, 252
Jones, Thomas, 153, 155

Kance, F. A., 151, 195,
196
Kance, Frederick A., 150,
151, 152, 194, 195,
196, 197, 244
Kance, R. A., 247
Kants (Cants), F. A., 151
Keith, Alexander H., 103
Keith, Charles F., 242, 266,
269, 351, 365, 391, 402,
406, 410
Kelly, F. D., 176
Kelly, Francis D., 175
Kelly, William, 287
Kelly, William D., 179, 250
Kelly, Wm., 168
Kelly, Wm. D., 78, 120
Kemp, William, 324
Kennedy, Allen, 4
Kennedy, John, 94
Kennedy, John C., 12, 13, 14,
15, 173, 227, 228, 269,
270, 271
Kennedy, John W., 19, 91,101,
108, 109, 140, 171, 173,
224, 233, 264, 277, 301
Kenner, Daniel, 426, 427
Kenesaha (Indian), 295, 296
Kerr, William, 69, 76, 228,
230
Kerr, William, Jr., 228,229
Kerr, William M., 105
Keys, A. D., 6
Keys, Alexander D. 3
Kincannon, John, 96, 224,
259, 264, 293, 418,427
King, C. L., 422

Ladd, Boles, 132
Land, Joseph, 340
Langdon, Thomas, 372
Lane, Andrew, 384
Lane, James F., 262, 263,
265
Lane, John, 384
Lane, John B., 96

Lane, Middleton, 333
Lane (Lain), Samuel, 34, 63,
    110, 111, 224, 330, 331,
    333, 334
Lang, James, 245
Langdon, James, 372
Langdon, Thomas, 372
Langly, Francis, 207
Larrison, John F., 19, 118,
    140, 173, 187, 224, 233,
    285
Larrison, William I., 63, 64
Lauderdale, James, 9, 17, 79,
    92, 110, 120, 121, 134,
    162, 166, 167, 169, 172,
    174, 175, 176, 180, 185,
    198, 199, 207, 216, 226,
    228, 231, 232, 235, 236,
    237, 238, 261, 263, 271,
    274, 285, 287, 289, 292,
    299, 302, 305, 313, 335,
    338, 345, 346, 367, 369,
    371, 375, 377, 404, 411,
    412, 414,
Lavender, William, R., 362,
    364
Lawson, James, 294
Lawson, Reynolds, 245, 246,
    248, 249
Lawson, Russell, 29, 69, 244,
    245, 246, 247, 248, 249,
    294
Lawson, William, 128
Lea, James A., 211, 212
Leuty, David, 182, 183
Lewis, Alfred, 384
Liddle, William L., 142, 143,
    144
Lilard, Abraham, 266, 279,
    291, 294, 295, 342
Long, Alexander, Sr., 316,
    319, 320, 321
Long, Alexander D., Sr., 317
Long, James, 133, 212, 226
Lowery, Barcla H., 343, 344
Lowery, Basely H., 324
Lowery, Thomas, 416
Lowery(Lowry), William, 200,
    201, 202, 203
Lutey (Luty), Calvin S., 402,
    403, 404, 405
Luty, David, 403, 404

Lyon, Thomas C., 421, 423,
    425, 426

Mahaffy (Mahaffee), John,
    7, 8, 9, 10
Mapels, Buonepart, 287
Maroney, George W., 235
Martin, Isaac, 416
Martin, Zacheriah, 353, 354
Massey, James, 118, 187, 285,
    343, 344
Maston, John B., 18
Mathews (Mathis), Clabourn,
    384
Mathews (Mathis), George,
    126, 127, 128, 129, 130,
    220, 221, 222, 223, 224
Mathews(Mathis), Harlan, 126,
    127, 128, 129, 130, 135,
    136, 220, 221, 222, 223,
    224
Mathews (Mathis), James, 126,
    127, 130, 131, 132
Mathews (Mathis), John M.,
    34, 78, 120, 129, 130,
    131, 135, 168, 179, 223,
    225, 250
Mathews (Mathis), Robert,
    366, 367, 368, 373
Maxwell, David, 156
Mayfield, Jesse, 16, 17, 18,
    19, 170, 171
Mays, Elijah, 106
Mays, Julia Ann, 104, 105,
    106, 107
McAndrew, Joseph, 310, 367,
    373, 379
McCallie, Thomas, 69, 70,
    72, 73, 74, 75, 76,
    77, 143, 345, 346
McCallister, James, 193
McCarty, Benjamin, 21, 133,
    212, 226, 244, 247
McCarty, John L., 1, 2, 3,
    4, 5, 6
McCarty, Thomas, 102, 141,
    145, 148, 150, 157,
    159, 161, 192, 195,
    198, 209
McCarty, William, 341, 343
McClanahan, John, 23, 24

McClatchey, Hamilton, 105
McClung & French & Co., 349
McClung, Hugh L, 92, 93, 94,
    421, 422, 423, 424
McClung, Mathew, 421, 422,
    423
McClung, Wallace & Co., 421,
    422, 423, 424, 425, 426,
    427
McFall, Richard, 96
McGhee, John, 96, 293
McGurgen, James, 311, 312, 313,
    313, 314
McJunkin, Samuel, 228, 229,
    230, 231, 232, 233, 266,
    268, 269, 270, 271, 272
McKamy, William, 151, 195,
    196
McKinley, Peter, 91, 94
McKissick, Abraham, 34, 343,
    344
McKissick, John, 287
McMillan, Joseph W., 102
McMillan, William, 113
McMinn County, 195, 239, 240,
    421
McMinn, John, 69, 76, 113, 122,
    132, 191, 208
McMinn, Thomas, 303, 337
McNair, John, 29, 102, 141,
    143, 145, 148, 150, 157,
    159, 161, 192, 195, 198,
    201, 209, 237, 393
McNutt, Thomas, 163, 164
McPherson, John, 380, 381,
    384
Mee, Jesse, 77, 346
Mee, John, 135, 224, 277,
    301, 303, 310, 337
Mee, Joseph, 20, 212, 244,
    247, 396
Mee, J. R., 133, 349, 350,
    352, 353
Mee, Joseph R., 77, 226, 304,
    337, 349, 351, 354, 392,
    418, 427
Mee, William, 34
Melton, David, 413, 414, 415,
    416
Merrit(Merritt), Samuel, 91,
    94, 264
Missouri, 272

Mitchell, James, 355, 419
Mitchell, Joseph, 355, 356,
    357
Moore County, 272
Moore(More), Jesse C., 299,
    300, 301
Moroon, Samuel, 340
Morgan, Crosslin & Johnson,
    357
Morgan, Thomas, 384
Mount, John, 401
Mountcastle, George E., 421,
    422, 423, 424, 425, 426,
    427,
Mullay, John C., 144, 145,
    146, 147, 159, 160
Murfey, Alexander, 287
Murphy(Murphey), John, 205,
    230, 259
Murrey (Murry, Maury), Ben-
    jamin, 31, 37, 43, 52,
    54, 102, 141, 143, 146,
    148, 150, 157, 159,
    161, 192, 195, 198,
    201, 209, 237
Murrell, George M., 202
Murrell, Onslone G., 5

Nair, James A., 427
Nash, Peter W., 102, 141,
    143, 145, 150, 157,
    159, 161, 192, 195,
    198, 201, 209, 237,
    253, 310
Newman, R. M., 144
Night, William, 96

Oconner, Daniel, 311, 312,
    313, 314
Oneal, James, 377
Oneal, John, 96, 294
Oneal, John F., 375
Oneal (Oneil), John S., 11
    258
Orr, Arthur, 393
Orsburn, Shearwood (Sherwood)
    274, 275, 276, 277,
    278
Orsburn, Thomas, 277, 278

Price, Josiah S., 80, 81, 82,
    84, 85, 86, 87, 88, 132,
    224
Price, Lewis, 21, 212
Price, Ruth, 372
Prowell, S. H., 56
Prowell, Sampson H., 62, 78,
    120, 168, 179, 250, 393,
    416, 418, 420, 427
Pursley, Alexander, 63

Ragen, David, 13, 207
Rains, Hiram, 68
Rains, John, 63, 64, 65, 66,
    67, 68, 69, 113, 114,
    115, 116, 117, 118, 119
Ramsey, Edman, 420
Randolph, Jeptha, 259, 293,
    343, 344, 388
Randolph, Lancaster, 293, 388,
Raper, John, 259
Raper, William, 175, 176
Rawls (Rawles), Attorney, 424,
    426
Reed, George, 101, 125, 131,
    135, 221
Reed, George W., 126, 127,
    262
Reed, J. T., 147, 160, 202
Reed, James T., 146, 160, 202
Reed, Jemima, 123, 124, 125
Reed, John, 135
Reuble, John G., 340
Rice, Elijah C., 1, 2, 3, 4,
    6
Rice, John, 1
Richards (Ritchards), Henry,
    277, 303, 310, 337
Richardson, George, 385
Richardson, Henry, 301
Riddle, James, 204, 260, 261,
    262
Rinkle, Jacob, 358, 359
Robbs, Jacob, 25, 26
Roberts, John H. Sr., 293
Roberts, John, 418, 427
Roberts, N., 384
Roberts, William P., 384
Roberts, William R., 380
Robinson, Humphry (Humphries)
    402, 403, 404, 405

Rogers, A. T., 81, 86
Rogers, William, 105
Roland, John I., 393
Romines, Right, 230, 231,
    232, 233
Rose, Rutherford, 25, 208,
    255
Rose, Wincen, 255
Rose, Winsten C., 20, 21
Ross, John, 330, 331, 333,
    334
Ross, John K, 333
Rucker, Willford, 358, 359
Russell, Andrew, 80, 82, 83,
    85, 86, 87, 88
Russell, I. B., 110
Russell, J. B., 330
Russell, Jacob, 217
Russell, Jacob B., 217
Ruth, Jacob, 343, 344

Sally, George M., 259
Sallee, George W., 34
Samples, Samuel, 88, 187,
    230
Samples, William, 216, 217
Saterfield, Elizabeth, 47,
    49
Saterfield, Hester, 33
Satterfield, William, 35
Scott, Stephen, 109
Scott, Steven, 231
Seabourn, Joseph, 21, 133,
    212, 226, 244, 247,
    310, 347, 367, 373,
    379
Seabourn, K. C., 347
Seabourn, Kinsey C., 236
Sears, William, 7, 8, 9
Selvedge, G. W., 272, 292
Selvedge, George W., 183,
    184, 220, 360
Shaddle (Shadle), James,
    102, 137, 138, 141, 143,
    145, 148, 150, 157, 159,
    161, 192, 195, 198, 201,
    209, 236, 367, 373, 379
Shaw, William M., 274
Sheppard, Lewis, 16, 17, 18,
    19
Shields, Arnett, 12, 13, 14, 15
    187, 224

195, 198, 201, 209, 236
Thornburry, William, 264
Thornhill, Robert, 393
Thornhill, William, 264, 293
Towns, John, 29, 30, 32, 35,
    37, 40, 69, 76, 113, 132,
    191, 208, 230
Traynor, J. D., 313
Traynor, John D., 78, 98, 99,
    100, 164, 168, 266, 268,
    269, 270, 271, 272, 274,
    312
Trewhitt, Campbell & Vandyke,
    72
Trewhitt, & Campbell, 378
Trewhitt, Attorney, 18, 61,
    72, 73, 74, 75, 178, 229,
    230, 231, 233, 276, 303,
    332, 333, 335, 336, 337,
    340, 415, 416
Trewhitt, Levi, 16, 82, 85,
    86, 91, 94, 121, 123,
    228, 272, 274, 277, 302,
    338, 371, 412, 417, 418
Triplett, William, 101, 304,
    305, 310, 311, 343, 344
Tucker, James, 420
Tucker, John, 304, 305, 310,
    311, 333
Turk, Hiram K., 7, 159, 161,
    168, 178, 179, 180, 181,
    182, 195, 209
Turner, H., 324
Turner, William, 141

Ulan, S. M., 185

Vandyke, T. N., 6
Vandyke, T. Vernon, 3
Van, Menerva, 45, 47, 49
Vann, Jesse, 35
Vernon, William, 143, 145,
    148, 150, 157, 159, 161,
    192, 195, 198, 201, 209

Walker, James E., 416
Walker, John, 1, 2, 3, 4, 5,
    6, 190
Wallace, Campbell, 92, 93,

94, 421, 422, 423, 424
Wallace, French & Co.,
    92, 93
Wallis, William (Will), 23,
    24
Wann(Wan), Silas M., 130,
    327, 386, 395, 397,
    413, 414, 415, 416
Wasaha (Indian), 295, 296,
    297, 298, 299
Waterhouse, Euclid, 416,
    417, 418
Wear, Silas M., 391, 392
Weatherly, Robert, 187
Weatherly, William, 63
Weaver, James, 118
Weaver (Wever), John, 374,
    375, 376, 377, 378, 379,
    380
Webb, Alexander, 118, 203,
    204, 205, 240, 242,
    243
Webb, James, 63, 113, 205
Webb, John W., 140, 141,
    142
Welbourn, John, 281
Wells, J. K., 395
Wells, J. R., 348, 349, 350,
    351, 353, 353, 354, 385,
    390, 391, 396
Westfield, David, 42, 51, 54
Westmoreland (Wesmoreland),
    George, 24, 152, 196,
    197, 285
Westmoreland, William, 96
White, A. G., 164
White, David R., 154
White, Eden, 154
White, W. H., 90
White, Isaac, 153, 154,
    155, 156
White, James M., 262, 263,
    265
White, William, 155
Wies, David, 293
Wiggins, William, 416, 417,
    418
Wilburn, John, 22, 23, 24,
    283, 284
Williams, Edward, 290, 291,
    292, 293, 416, 417
Williams, Frederick S., 101,
    118

THE END

www.ingramcontent.com/pod-product-compliance
Lightning Source LLC
Chambersburg PA
CBHW080243030426
42334CB00023BA/2682